Political Science Research Methods

Ninth Edition

In memory of our friend and colleague, H. T. Reynolds

Sara Miller McCune founded SAGE Publishing in 1965 to support the dissemination of usable knowledge and educate a global community. SAGE publishes more than 1000 journals and over 800 new books each year, spanning a wide range of subject areas. Our growing selection of library products includes archives, data, case studies and video. SAGE remains majority owned by our founder and after her lifetime will become owned by a charitable trust that secures the company's continued independence.

Los Angeles | London | New Delhi | Singapore | Washington DC | Melbourne

Political Science Research Methods

Ninth Edition

Janet Buttolph Johnson

University of Delaware

H. T. Reynolds

University of Delaware

Jason D. Mycoff

University of Delaware

FOR INFORMATION:

CQ Press

An imprint of SAGE Publications, Inc.

2455 Teller Road

Thousand Oaks, California 91320

E-mail: order@sagepub.com

SAGE Publications Ltd.

1 Oliver's Yard

55 City Road

London EC1Y 1SP

United Kingdom

SAGE Publications India Pvt. Ltd.

B 1/I 1 Mohan Cooperative Industrial Area

Mathura Road, New Delhi 110 044

India

SAGE Publications Asia-Pacific Pte. Ltd.

18 Cross Street #10-10/11/12

China Square Central

Singapore 048423

Acquisitions Editor: Scott Greenan

Content Development Editors: Elise Frasier, Scott Harris

Editorial Assistant: Sam Rosenberg

Production Editor: Bennie Clark Allen

Copy Editor: Melinda Masson

Typesetter: C&M Digitals (P) Ltd.

Proofreader: Susan Schon

Indexer: Jeanne Busemeyer

Cover Designer: Janet Kiesel

Marketing Manager: Jennifer Jones

Printed in Canada

Library of Congress Cataloging-in-Publication Data

Names: Johnson, Janet Buttolph, 1950- author.

Title: Political science research methods / Janet Buttolph Johnson, University of Delaware, H.T. Reynolds, University of Delaware, Jason D. Mycoff, University of Delaware.

Description: Ninth Edition. | Thousand Oaks, California : CQ Press, an imprint of SAGE Publications, Inc., [2019] | Previous edition: 2016. | Includes bibliographical references and index.

Identifiers: LCCN 2019006738 | ISBN 9781544331430 (Paperback. : alk. paper)

Subjects: LCSH: Political science—Research—Methodology.

Classification: LCC JA71 .J55 2019 | DDC 320.072/1—dc23 LC record available at https://lccn.loc.gov/2019006738

19 20 21 22 23 10 9 8 7 6 5 4 3 2 1

BRIEF CONTENTS

DETAILED CONTENTS

TABLES, FIGURES, AND FEATURES

TABLES

FIGURES

HELPFUL HINTS

HOW IT'S DONE

PREFACE

A political science student may ask, "My interest is government and politics; why do I have to study research design, question wording, document analysis, and statistics?" Our goal in *Political Science Research Methods* is to address this question by demonstrating that with a modicum of effort applied toward studying these topics, undergraduates can analyze many seemingly complicated political issues and controversies in ways that go far beyond accounts in the popular press and the political arena.

Political Science Research Methods, now in its ninth edition, continues to hold true to the three primary objectives that have guided us since the book's inception. Our first objective is to illustrate important aspects of the research process and to demonstrate that political scientists can produce worthwhile knowledge about significant political phenomena using the methods we describe in this book. To show this as vividly as possible, we begin again with several case studies of political science research drawn from different areas of the discipline that address key issues and controversies in the study of politics. We made an effort in this edition to include a wide variety of examples from the main subfields of political science using different study designs and methods of data collection. We continue to make changes to fulfill our other two objectives: (1) to give readers the tools necessary to conduct their own empirical research projects and evaluate others' research, and (2) to help students with limited mathematical backgrounds understand the statistical calculations that are part of social science research. Though we are increasingly concentrating on what various procedures can (and cannot) tell us about the real world, we've tried to include examples of procedures and their associated calculations most likely to be used by students. We still provide separate computational details from the narrative by placing many equations in "How It's Done" boxes. The book makes an effort to encourage students to understand and think about the practical and theoretical implications of statistical results. We hope that by meeting these goals, this book will continue to satisfy the needs of our undergraduate and graduate students as they embark on their studies in the field.

STRUCTURE AND ORGANIZATION OF THE BOOK

In this ninth edition, we have responded to feedback that called for increased coverage of qualitative research and a reduction in length. We continued to refine our focus on what instructors say matters most. We carefully streamlined each chapter to deliver greater clarity of concepts and added new learning objectives to encourage close reading of main takeaways. In addition, the colorful interior visually highlights the content's accessibility.

Because research methods may overwhelm some students at first, we have gone to some length (in the first chapter, especially, but also throughout the book) to stress that research methods topics can be relevant to the understanding of current events. This book is organized to show that research starts with ideas and then follows a series of logical steps. Chapter 1 introduces the case studies that are integrated into our discussion of the research process in the subsequent chapters. We chose these cases, which form the backbone of the book, to demonstrate a wide range of research topics within the discipline of political science: American politics, international relations, comparative politics, and public policy. We refer to these cases throughout the book to demonstrate the issues, choices, decisions, and obstacles that political scientists typically confront while doing research. We want to show what takes place behind the scenes in the production of research, and the best way to do this is to refer to actual articles. The advantage to this approach, which we feel has been borne out by the book's success over the years, is that it helps students relate substance to methods. For this edition, we updated and extended the example of research into the gender gap in politics, which is especially useful as it demonstrates the use of quantitative content analysis as a data collection method. We retained the example on the causes of income inequality and redistribution in Organisation for Economic Co-operation and Development (OECD) countries. We have replaced the other research examples with three new ones, two of which correct earlier omission of case study and qualitative empirical research in political science. The first of these is an investigation into the cause of the difference in tax compliance between northern and southern Italy. We chose this research as an example of qualitative case study research and historical institutionalism. The second new example investigating the cause of different government responses to public protests in three newly consolidated democracies demonstrates the comparative method and the considerations that go into selecting cases for comparison. The third new example is a quantitative analysis of the impact of international election observers on Armenian elections using a natural experimental design. Chapter 2 examines the definition of scientific research and the development of empirical political science. We discuss the role of theory in the research process and review some of the debates in modern and contemporary political science. We have added a section on data access and research transparency underscoring the responsibility of researchers to substantiate their claims. We have also modified a table to reflect that qualitative research can indeed be empirical. In response to adopter input, chapter 3 still focuses on the task of helping students to identify and refine appropriate research topics. For instructors who plan to have their students conduct independent research projects, it makes sense to introduce this topic early in the discussion of the research process. This chapter also contains an extended discussion of how to conduct and write a literature review. Examples of literature searches now use Google Scholar to reflect its common use by students. Chapter 4 addresses the building blocks of social scientific research: hypotheses, core concepts, variables, and measurement. It combines material that was previously covered in chapters 4 and 5. We have eliminated the rather lengthy discussion of scales and their construction. Chapter 5 has been overhauled substantially and now covers sampling. As a result, it is considerably shorter and focuses on the essentials of sampling beginning with a discussion of sampling before moving on to sampling methods. This chapter includes a new section on sample size and margin of error that replaces the more technical discussion of standard error equations that are now first introduced in subsequent statistical chapters. There is a "Helpful Hints" box that reviews symbols in support of a simplified, standardized approach used across all of the statistics chapters.

Chapter 6 has been rewritten to focus on the logic of demonstrating causation. It focuses solely on the classic experimental design, leaving the discussion of other research designs to later chapters. This allows students to grasp an essential aspect of empirical political science research: the identification of causes of political phenomena. Chapters 7 and 8 discuss qualitative research designs and data collection methods, respectively. Chapter 7 is entirely new and focuses on case study designs. It begins with a discussion of the comparative method and the logic of comparative research designs. It then addresses the growing use of case studies to explore causal mechanisms through process tracing research designs and illustrates the practice with an example. Chapter 8 introduces the main sources of data for political science research: observation, documents, and interviews. As in past editions, the advantages and disadvantages of each approach are reviewed, albeit more succinctly. The ethical requirements for research involving human subjects are reviewed. The remainder of the chapter focuses on data collection in qualitative research using examples. The practice of interviewing is given substantial coverage. Challenges associated with presenting qualitative data while adhering to data accessibility and research transparency (DA-RT) and human subjects requirements are discussed.

Chapters 9 and 10 parallel the previous two chapters by focusing on quantitative research designs and data collection methods. Chapter 9 presents more experimental designs, natural experiments, and field experiments. Quasi-experiments and commonly used observational research designs (cross-sectional and longitudinal designs) are also discussed. Chapter 10 discusses sources of data for quantitative studies: statistical data compiled by others, quantitative content analysis, and survey research. It includes updated and web-based sources of aggregate statistics and survey questions and data.

Chapters 11 through 14 focus on data analysis and how we interpret data and present them to others. Chapter 11 has been revised to simplify the presentation of descriptive statistics. One small data set—for ease of calculation—is used to demonstrate calculations, and the use of technical terms is consistent and kept to a minimum. There is a greater emphasis on interpretation of the statistics. Chapter 12, on statistical inference and hypothesis testing, has been streamlined to focus on the normal distribution and how to calculate z and t scores, how to use their associated tables, and their interpretation. It covers testing of statistical hypotheses and includes examples of significance tests for means and proportions as well as calculating confidence intervals. Our goal is to make the logic of the tests more comprehensible. The material included in chapters 13 and 14 has been substantially rearranged and streamlined compared to the eighth edition. In chapter 13, we investigate relationships involving categorical data, both bivariate and multivariate. Construction and interpretation of contingency tables are explained. Measures of association are presented including calculations for some to demonstrate the logic behind them and to help their interpretation. The chapter concludes with an explanation of analysis of variance (ANOVA) and the F test. Chapter 14 covers regression, both ordinary least squares regression (bivariate and multivariate) and logistic regression, an increasingly important statistical tool in social research. In all of this, we attempted to be as rigorous as possible without overwhelming readers with theoretical fine points or computational details. The content is still accessible to anyone with a basic understanding of high school algebra. Our goal, as always, is to provide an intuitive understanding of these sometimes intimidating topics without distorting the concepts or misleading our readers.

Finally, in chapter 15, we present a new research report, using a published journal article that investigates the impact of the March for Science on the public's attitudes toward science and scientists to illustrate the research process. As in the past, this article is annotated, although we have changed the format so that students can see more clearly where in the article the authors address key aspects of the research process. We strongly suggest that instructors who assign a research paper have their students consult the example in this chapter and use it to pattern their own writing.

In addition to the "How It's Done" feature, the "Helpful Hints" boxes continue to give students practical tips. Each chapter contains suggested reading lists and lists of terms introduced. A glossary at the end of the book, with more than 250 definitions, lists important terms and provides a convenient study guide.

ONLINE RESOURCES FOR STUDENTS AND INSTRUCTORS

The edge every student needs
SAGE edge™ **for CQ Press**
http://edge.sagepub.com/johnson9e

SAGE edge offers a robust online environment featuring an impressive array of tools and resources for review, study, and further exploration, keeping both instructors and students on the cutting edge of teaching and learning. SAGE edge content is open access and available on demand. Learning and teaching have never been easier!

SAGE edge for Students provides a personalized approach to help students accomplish their coursework goals in an easy-to-use learning environment.

- Mobile-friendly **eFlashcards** strengthen understanding of key concepts.
- Mobile-friendly practice **quizzes** encourage self-guided assessment and practice.
- **Chapter summaries** reinforce the most important material.
- Carefully selected **web resources** enhance exploration of key topics.
- **Data sets** and files are available for *Working with Political Science Research Methods*, fifth edition.

SAGE coursepacks for instructors makes it easy to import our quality content into your school's learning management system (LMS)*. Intuitive and simple to use, it allows you to

Say NO to:
- required access codes
- learning a new system

Say YES to:
- using only the content you want and need
- high-quality assessment and multimedia exercises

*For use in: Blackboard, Canvas, Brightspace by Desire2Learn (D2L), and Moodle

Don't use an LMS platform? No problem, you can still access many of the online resources for your text via SAGE edge.

<u>**SAGE coursepacks includes:**</u>

- Our content delivered **directly into your LMS**

- **Intuitive, simple format** that makes it easy to integrate the material into your course with minimal effort

- **Assessment tools** that foster review, practice, and critical thinking, and offer a more complete way to measure student engagement, including:

  - **Chapter quizzes** that identify opportunities for improvement and ensure mastery of key learning objectives

  - **Test banks** built on Bloom's Taxonomy that provide a diverse range of test items with ExamView test generation

  - **Activity and quiz options** that allow you to choose only the assignments and tests you want

  - **Instructions** on how to use and integrate the comprehensive assessments and resources provided

- Editable, chapter-specific **PowerPoint® slides** that offer flexibility when creating multimedia lectures so you don't have to start from scratch but you can customize to your exact needs

- **Sample course syllabi** with suggested models for structuring your course that give you options to customize your course in a way that is perfect for you

- **Instructor manual** for each chapter, including a chapter overview, learning objectives, lecture outline, discussion questions, and written assignments and projects, to support your teaching

- **All tables and figures** from the textbook

- **Solutions manual and data sets** that accompany the exercises in *Working with Political Science Research Methods,* Fifth Edition

ACCOMPANYING WORKBOOK

In addition to updating all of the website materials, Jason D. Mycoff has substantially revised the accompanying workbook, *Working with Political Science Research Methods,* fifth edition, to align with the new organization of the ninth edition, and provided many new exercises while retaining the ones we feel worked well in the previous edition. Based on user feedback, Mycoff looked for opportunities to add more problems for practicing statistical calculations, more variation in subfield coverage, and new data sets. The new edition also includes the student version of SPSS so students can work with their own copy in courses that use SPSS. Each workbook chapter briefly reviews key concepts covered by the corresponding chapter in the text. Students and instructors will find data sets and other documents and materials used in the workbook exercises at http://edge.sagepub .com/johnson9e. The data sets, available on a variety of platforms, may also be used for additional exercises and test items developed by instructors. Instructors may want to add on to the data sets or have their students do so as part of a research project. A solutions manual for adopters of the workbook is also available online at http://edge.sagepub.com/johnson9e.

In closing, we would like to make a comment on statistical software. Instructors remain divided over the extent to which computers should be part of an introductory research course and what particular programs to require. While the student version of SPSS is included with the workbook, neither the workbook exercises nor the textbook problems are written specifically for SPSS. We encourage instructors and students alike to explore the many online statistical resources such as Survey Documentation Analysis (SDA), Inter-university Consortium for Political and Social Research (ICPSR), American FactFinder, Rice Virtual Lab in Statistics, and VassarStats in addition to software like SPSS, Stata, and SAS for their analytical needs.

ACKNOWLEDGMENTS

We would like to thank our careful reviewers who helped us shape this new edition:

Anna Brigevich, North Carolina Central University

Natasha V. Christie, University of North Florida

Moser Deegan, Muhlenberg College

Ewa Golebiowska, Wayne State University

Ronald J. McGauvran, University of North Texas

Carl L. Palmer, Illinois State University

Amanda M. Rosen, Webster University

Each of these reviewers has helped make the ninth edition stronger than ever, and we are grateful for their assistance.

We would like to thank several people who have contributed to this edition: Melinda Masson, our copy editor; Bennie Clark Allen, our production editor; and David Felts, assistant managing editor of production. We are especially thankful for the continued support and patience of acquisitions editor Scott Greenan, senior content development editor Scott Harris, editorial assistant Lauren Younker, and marketing manager Jennifer Jones at CQ Press. We would also like to thank Elise Frasier for her developmental editing work. A book with as many bells and whistles as this one needs many sets of eyes to watch over it. We are glad to have had so many good ones.

Finally, Jan and Jason wish to thank H. T. Reynolds for his many contributions to the previous eight editions of the text.

Janet Buttolph Johnson
H. T. Reynolds
Jason D. Mycoff

ABOUT THE AUTHORS

Janet Buttolph Johnson is associate professor emerita of political science and international relations at the University of Delaware, where she specializes in public policy, state and local politics, and environmental policy and politics.

H. T. Reynolds is professor emeritus of political science at the University of Delaware. He is author of *Governing America*, with David Vogler; *Analysis of Nominal Data*, second edition; and several articles on methodology.

Jason D. Mycoff is associate professor of political science and international relations at the University of Delaware. His research is on American political institutions, in particular the U.S. Congress, congressional committees, and parties.

1 INTRODUCTION

Political scientists are interested in learning about and understanding a variety of important political phenomena.

Some of us are interested in the political differences among countries and wonder why women make up a larger percentage of legislators in some countries than in others, or we may wonder what conditions lead to stable and secure political regimes without civil unrest, rebellion, or government repression.

Another area of interest is the relationships and interactions between nations and how some nations exercise power over others.

Other political scientists are more interested in the relationship between the populace and public officials in democratic countries and, in particular, whether or not public opinion influences the policy decisions of public officials.

Still others are concerned with how particular political institutions function. Does Congress serve the interests of well-financed groups rather than of the general populace? Do judicial decisions depend upon the personal values of individual judges, the group dynamics of judicial groups, or the relative power of the litigants? To what extent can American presidents influence the actions of federal agencies? Does the use of nonprofit service organizations to deliver public services change government control of and accountability for those services?

These are just a very few examples of the types of questions political scientists investigate through their research.

This book is an introduction to **empirical research**—a methodology that requires scholars to clearly state hypotheses or propositions that can be evaluated with actual, "objective" observation of political phenomena. Students should learn about how political

CHAPTER OBJECTIVES

1.1 Describe how political scientists use empirical research methods to investigate important questions about politics and government.

1.2 Understand why researchers use a variety of data collection methods in their empirical study of political phenomena.

1.3 Understand why some research findings are summarized quantitatively using statistics while others are summarized qualitatively using categorical assessments.

scientists conduct empirical research for three major reasons. First, citizens in contemporary American society are often called upon to evaluate statements and arguments about political phenomena and the validity of information used to support those statements and arguments. Debates about the wisdom of the death penalty, for example, frequently (but not always) hinge on whether or not it is an effective deterrent to crime, and debates about term limits for elected officials involve whether or not such limits increase the competitiveness of elections and the responsiveness of elected officials to the electorate. How do we know if these claims are true? What does the research on these topics tell us? Similarly, evaluating current developments in the regulation of financial markets can be informed by research on what influences the behavior of regulatory agencies and their staff. In these and many other cases, thoughtful and concerned citizens find that they must evaluate the accuracy and adequacy of the theories and research of political (and other social) scientists.

A second reason is that an understanding of empirical research concepts is integrally related to students' assimilation and evaluation of knowledge in their coursework. An important result of understanding the scientific research process is that a student may begin to think more independently about concepts and theories presented in courses and readings. For example, a student might say, "That may be true under the given conditions, but I believe it won't remain true under the following conditions." Or, "If this theory is correct, I would expect to observe the following." Or, "Before I will accept that interpretation, I'd like to have this additional information." Students who can specify what information is needed and what relationships among phenomena must be observed in support of an idea are more likely to develop a deeper understanding of the subjects they study.

A third, and related, reason for learning about political science research methods is that students often need to conduct research of their own, whether for a term paper in an introductory course on American government, a research project in an upper-level seminar, a senior thesis, or a series of assignments in a course devoted to learning empirical research methods. Familiarity with empirical research methods is generally a prerequisite to making this a profitable endeavor.

The prospect of learning empirical research methods is often intimidating to students. Sometimes, students dislike this type of inquiry because it involves numbers and statistics. To understand empirical research well, one must have a basic knowledge of statistics and how to use statistics in analyzing data and reporting research findings. But not all empirical research involves the collection of numerical data requiring statistical analysis. It may involve listening to and interpreting what people say or reading and classifying documents such as treaties or constitutions. The empirical research process we describe here is first and foremost a way of thinking and a prescription for disciplined reasoning. Statistics will be introduced only after an understanding of the thought process involved in empirical research is established, and then in a way that should be understandable to any student familiar with basic algebra. On a final note, understanding the research process involves an appreciation of the ethical obligations of conducting research, including transparency and integrity in the collection and reporting of data, and avoiding harm to humans in the course of research from choice of research topic to publication of findings. We will be discussing the ethical dimensions of conducting research at appropriate points throughout the chapters.

The plan for this book is as follows:

Chapter 2 discusses what we mean by the scientific study of political phenomena. We also review the historical development of political science as a discipline and introduce alternative perspectives on what is the most appropriate approach to the study of political phenomena; not all political scientists agree that politics can be studied scientifically or that the results of such efforts have been as useful or inclusive of important political phenomena as critics wish.

In chapter 3, we address an aspect of the research process that often poses a significant challenge to students: finding an interesting and appropriate research topic and developing a clearly stated research question. Therefore, in this edition, we show how to explore "the literature" and find out what political scientists and others have written about political phenomena in order to sharpen the focus of a research topic, a discussion that came later in previous editions. Chapter 3 focuses on investigating relationships among concepts and developing explanations for political phenomena. It also includes an example and discussion of how to write the literature review section of a research paper.

Chapter 4 builds on the discussion in chapter 3 by adding the "building blocks" of scientific research: defining complex concepts, formulating hypotheses, identifying independent and dependent variables, and specifying units of analysis. This chapter also addresses the challenge of developing valid and reliable measures of political phenomena. It also discusses how our choices about how we measure variables affect the statistics we may use later to analyze the data we collect. The concept of level of measurement is introduced.

Chapter 5 covers the logic and basic statistical features of sampling. Various types of samples, including probability and nonprobability samples, are described. Much of our information about political phenomena is based on samples, so an understanding of the strengths and limitations of sampling is important.

Chapter 6 introduces the challenge of demonstrating causation in empirical research. The classic experimental research design is presented and explained as a basis for evaluating the ability of other research designs to support causal claims.

Chapter 7 is the first of two chapters devoted to qualitative research methods. This chapter stresses the contribution that qualitative research makes to the understanding of political phenomena including establishing causation. Qualitative research designs, the logic of comparative case study designs, and process tracing are discussed.

Chapter 8 provides a general introduction to the main sources of data used by political scientists, discusses their advantages and disadvantages, and reviews the obligation of researchers to adhere to ethical requirements where human subjects are involved. The remainder of the chapter is devoted to a discussion of observation, interviewing, and document use as sources of data in qualitative research. Particular attention is paid to demonstrating validity and reliability of data used in qualitative studies especially as it relates to professional guidelines for data accessibility and research transparency (DA-RT) guidelines.

Chapters 9 and 10 parallel the chapters on qualitative research. Chapter 9 discusses quantitative research designs: experimental designs, field experiments, quasi-experimental designs, and nonexperimental designs, comparing them to the classic experimental design with respect to demonstrating causation. Chapter 10 introduces the major data collection methods used in quantitative analyses: surveys or polling, content analysis, and the running record. It reviews various types of polls and their strengths and weaknesses, as well as the design of survey instruments. The basics of quantitative content analysis are explained. The chapter addresses issues arising with the use of statistical and other records and concludes with some guidelines for data management.

Chapter 11 offers an extensive discussion of descriptive statistics and the analysis of single variables. We present a variety of graphical options useful in displaying data, as visual representations of data are often an extremely effective way to present information. Tips on recognizing and avoiding misleading uses of graphical displays are an essential part of this chapter.

Chapter 12 is devoted to the concepts of statistical inference, hypothesis testing, and calculating estimates of population parameters. This chapter builds on the foundation established in the earlier chapter on sampling.

Chapter 13 then moves on to the analysis of categorical data analysis—the investigation of the relationship between variables when the independent variable is measured at the nominal or ordinal level. Contingency table analysis with and without a control variable is covered as is analysis of variance (ANOVA). Measures of association are presented.

Chapter 14 is the final statistics chapter. Here we explore regression techniques used in the quest for explanation and demonstrating causality. These involve multivariate analysis, as the explanation of a political phenomenon rarely is based on simply one other factor or variable.

As in previous editions, we conclude with an annotated example of an actual, peer-reviewed research article. Chapter 15 contains a new example that allows students to see the discussion and application of many of the concepts and statistical procedures covered in earlier chapters.

Researchers conduct empirical studies for two primary reasons. One reason is to accumulate knowledge that will apply to a particular problem in need of a solution or to a condition in need of improvement. Studies of neighborhood beautification efforts and their effect on crime rates, the impact of raising the minimum wage on the number of minimum wage jobs, or the effectiveness of alternative approaches to get residents to reduce their water consumption during droughts are some examples. Such research is often referred to as **applied research** because it has a fairly direct, immediate application to a real-world situation.

Researchers also conduct empirical research to satisfy their intellectual curiosity about a subject, regardless of whether the research will lead to changes in government policy or private behavior. Many political scientists, for example, study the decision-making processes of voters, not because they are interested in giving practical advice to political candidates but because they want to know if elections give the populace influence over the behavior of elected public officials. Such research is sometimes referred to as **pure, theoretical, or recreational research** to indicate that it is not concerned primarily with practical applications.[1]

Political scientists ordinarily report the results of their research in books or articles published in political science research journals (see chapter 3 for a discussion of how to find articles in these journals). Research reported in academic journals typically contains data and information from which to draw conclusions. It also undergoes peer review, a process by which other scholars evaluate the soundness of the research before it is published. Political science research questions and analyses also may appear in newspapers and magazines, which have a wider audience. Such popularly presented investigations may use empirical political science methods and techniques as well.

In the remainder of this chapter, we describe several political science research projects that were designed to produce knowledge about significant political phenomena. We will refer to these (and other) examples throughout this book to illustrate many aspects of the research process. These examples illustrate a variety of research topics and methods of investigation. They also show how decisions about aspects of the research process affect the conclusions that may be drawn about the phenomena under study. And they represent attempts by political scientists to acquire knowledge by building on the research of others to arrive at increasingly complete explanations of political behavior and processes.

RESEARCH ON INCOME INEQUALITY

In 1936, Harold Lasswell published *Politics: Who Gets What, When, How*.[2] Ever since, political scientists have liked this title because it succinctly states an important truth: politics is about winning and losing. No political system, not even a perfectly democratic one, can always be all things to all people. Inevitably, policies favor some and disadvantage others. So important is this observation that one of political science's main tasks is to discover precisely which individuals and groups benefit the most from political struggle and why.

A major controversy in the early years of the twenty-first century has been the apparent growth of economic inequality in the United States. Although there is disagreement among social scientists about the extent of the problem, many now believe that large disparities in income and well-being threaten not just the economy but democracy as well. At times, the rhetoric can become feverish:

The 99.99 percent is lagging far behind. The divide between the haves and have-nots is getting worse really, really fast. . . . If we don't do something to fix the glaring inequities in this economy, the pitchforks are going to come for us. No society can sustain this kind of rising inequality. In fact, there is no example in human history where wealth accumulated like this and the pitchforks didn't eventually come out. You show me a highly unequal society, and I will show you a police state. Or an uprising. There are no counterexamples. None. It's not if, it's when.[3]

Other commentators, however, are not as concerned:

If one looks at after-tax income, the increase in income inequality over time is greatly reduced. If one goes further and factors in the government's attempts to redistribute income, income inequality is not increasing in the U.S. at all. This after-tax, after-transfer income essentially is a measure of how much stuff you can consume (either by buying it or because somebody gave you free stuff). And, as demonstrated by Gary Burtless of The Brookings Institution (a center-left think tank), income inequality measured this way has actually decreased in the U.S. over the decade from 2000–2010.[4]

Inequality has concerned political scientists for decades. Democracy, after all, assumes political equality, and if people have widely varying levels of income, are they (can they be) politically equal? Before reaching definitive conclusions, however, one needs to study systematically and objectively the level, the causes, and the effects of disparities in income and wealth.

In a 2005 study, Lane Kenworthy and Jonas Pontusson analyzed trends in the distribution of gross market income—the distribution of income before taxes and government transfers—for affluent Organisation for Economic Co-operation and Development (OECD) countries using data from the Luxembourg Income Study.[5] Kenworthy and Pontusson were interested in whether inequality in market income had increased and to what extent government policies had responded to changes in market income inequality. In particular, they were interested in testing the median-voter model developed by Allan H. Meltzer and Scott F. Richard.[6]

According to the median-voter model, support for government redistributive spending depends on the distance between the income of the median voter and the average market income of all voters. The greater the average market income in comparison to the median income, the greater the income inequality and, thus, the greater the demand from voters for government spending to reduce this gap. Countries with the greatest market inequalities should have more such government spending.

One way to test the median-voter model is to see whether changes in redistribution are related to changes in market inequality. One would expect that larger changes in market inequality would cause larger changes in redistribution if governments were responsive to the median voter. Kenworthy and Pontusson found this to be the case, although the United States, Germany, and the United Kingdom did not fit the pattern very well. In further analyses in which they looked at country-by-country responsiveness to market inequality over several decades, they found that most OECD countries are responsive to market income inequalities, although to varying degrees, and that the United States is the least responsive.

Perhaps, Kenworthy and Pontusson suggested, government responsiveness to market inequality is related to voter turnout. If one assumes that lower-income voters are less likely to turn out to vote than are higher-income voters, then one would expect that the lower the turnout, the less likely governments would be pressured to respond to income inequality. The median-voter model still would apply, but in countries with low voter turnout, the median voter would be less likely to represent lower-income households. Kenworthy and Pontusson used regression analysis and a scatterplot (you will learn about these in chapter 14), shown in figure 1-1, to show that the higher the voter turnout, the more responsive a country is to market income inequality. The results provide a possible explanation for why the United States is less responsive to changes in market inequality than are other nations: the United States has the lowest turnout rate among the nations included in the analysis.

In 2010, an entire issue of the journal *Politics & Society* was devoted to the topic of income inequality. In the lead article, "Winner-Take-All Politics: Public Policy, Political Organization, and the Precipitous Rise of Top Incomes in the United States," Jacob S. Hacker and Paul Pierson took issue with much of the previous research on the causes of income inequality in the United States.[7] First, they dismissed economic accounts that attribute growth in inequality to "apolitical processes of economic change" for failing to explain differences among nations, as illustrated in figure 1-2. This figure shows that the top 1 percent's share of national income is the highest in the United States (16 percent) and that it increased the most, almost doubling, between the 1970s and 2000. Second, they attacked previous political analyses on three counts: for downplaying "the extreme concentration of income gains at the top of the income ladder" (figure 1-3 shows the gain in the top 1 percent's share of national pretax income from 1960 to 2007), for missing the important role of government policy in creating what they called a "winner-take-all" pattern, and for focusing on the median-voter model and electoral politics instead of important changes in the political organization of economic interests. They argued that the median-voter model and the extreme skew in income don't add up. Even accounting for lower turnout among lower-income voters, the difference between the income of the median voter and the incomes at the very top is too big to argue that politicians are responding to the economic interests of the median voter.

Their explanation for the "precipitous rise" in top incomes in the United States rejects the median-voter model. Instead, they argue that policies governing corporate structure and pay, the functioning of financial markets, and the framework of industrial relations have had much to do with changes in pretax income (so-called market income).

This brief review of some of the research on income inequality illustrates that political science research is relevant to important issues in American politics and shows how political scientists use theory, comparison, and historical analysis in their investigations. One can be certain that additional research will be conducted to measure the impact of the 2017 changes in federal tax law on income distribution in the United States.

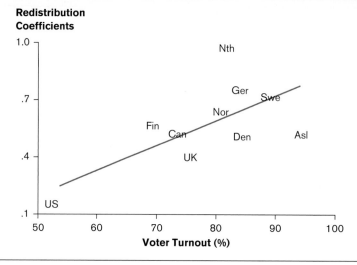

FIGURE 1-1 ■ **Redistribution Coefficients by Average Voter Turnout**

Source: Reprinted from Lane Kenworthy and Jonas Pontusson, "Rising Inequality and the Politics of Redistribution in Affluent Countries," *Perspectives on Politics* 3, no. 3 (2005): 462. © 2005 American Political Science Association, published by Cambridge University Press.

Note: Asl = Australia; Can = Canada; Den = Denmark; Fin = Finland; Ger = Germany; Nth = The Netherlands; Swe = Sweden; UK = United Kingdom; US = United States. Presidential elections for the United States; general parliamentary elections for the other countries. Redistribution data are for working-age households only.

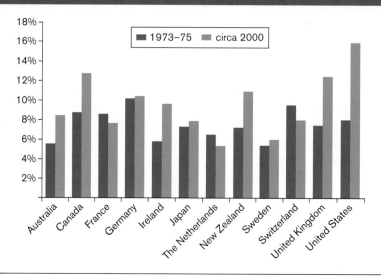

FIGURE 1-2 ■ **The Top 1 Percent's Share of National Income, Mid-1970s versus Circa 2000**

Source: Andrew Leigh, "How Closely Do Top Incomes Track Other Measures of Inequality?" *Economic Journal* 117, no. 524 (2007): 619–33, https://doi.org/10.1111/j.1468-0297.2007.02099.x, cited in Jacob S. Hacker and Paul Pierson, "Winner-Take-All Politics: Public Policy, Political Organization, and the Precipitous Rise of Top Incomes in the United States," *Politics & Society* 38, no. 2 (2010): fig. 2, p. 160. Copyright © 2010 SAGE Publications. Reprinted by Permission of SAGE Publications.

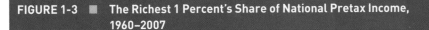

FIGURE 1-3 ■ The Richest 1 Percent's Share of National Pretax Income, 1960–2007

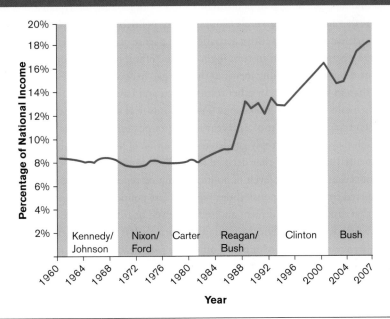

Sources: Thomas Piketty and Emmanuel Saez, "Income Inequality in the United States, 1913–1998," *Quarterly Journal of Economics* 118, no. 1 (2003): 1–39; updated tables and figures for Piketty and Saez available at http://elsa.berkeley.edu/~saez/TabFig2007.xls, as cited in Jacob S. Hacker and Paul Pierson, "Winner-Take-All Politics: Public Policy, Political Organization, and the Precipitous Rise of Top Incomes in the United States," *Politics & Society* 38, no. 2 (2010): fig. 1, p. 156. Copyright © 2010 SAGE Publications. Reprinted by Permission of SAGE Publications.

Note: Excluding capital gains.

POLITICS AND THE GENDER GAP

Much has been written about underrepresentation of women in public office. Based on data from 193 countries, women made up on average only 24.1 percent of legislators in the lower house of parliament in 2018.[8] Rwanda had the highest percentage, with 61.3 percent. The United States ranked 75th: in the 115th U.S. Congress, there were 110 women, or 20.5 percent of the membership.[9] In the 116th Congress (2019–2021), women make up 23.7 percent of the members: 23.4 percent of the House of Representatives and 25 percent of the Senate.[10] At the state level in 2019, the average of female state legislators is 28.7 percent, up from 25.4 percent in 2018, but the picture is quite varied, with Nevada at the top, with 50.8 percent, and Mississippi at the bottom, with 13.8 percent.[11] What accounts for this gender gap? Is it because women make up a small proportion of the professions that are typical recruiting grounds for candidates? Are women less interested in politics and running for office, and if so, why? Do family considerations weigh more heavily on women, making the demands of public office too difficult to contemplate?

Research by Richard L. Fox and Jennifer L. Lawless addresses these questions. In a national random sample of nearly four thousand high school and college students, they found "a dramatic gender gap in political ambition."[12] In looking for explanations for this gender gap, they found that parental encouragement, politicized educational and peer experiences, participation in competitive activities, and a sense of self-confidence are associated with a young person's interest in running for public office, but that young women report fewer of these factors than young men and that the gap between men and women in college is greater than in high school. In other research, Fox and Lawless study the political ambitions of men and women in professions (lawyers, business leaders, educators, and political activists) typically thought of as recruitment grounds for candidates for public office. Even though they found a "deeply gendered distribution of household labor and child care among potential candidates," they deemed that differences in family roles and responsibilities did not account for lower levels of political ambition reported by women. Even women unencumbered by family responsibilities reported less political ambition than men. They conclude that candidate recruitment and self-perceived qualifications are the best explanations for the gender gap in political ambition. Women are less likely than men to report that they have been recruited to run for public office by a party leader, elected official, or political activist, or to consider themselves qualified to run for public office even after controlling for differences in family structures, roles, and responsibilities.[13]

What happens when women are elected to political office? What is the effect of the presence of women in legislative bodies? Does it result in substantive as well as symbolic representation (the perception that women can and should govern)? Is a "critical mass" necessary before such representation effects occur? Is the number of women in a legislative body the critical factor, or might the rules governing deliberation in the legislature also be important? This latter factor is one investigated by Tali Mendelberg, Christopher F. Karpowitz, and J. Baxter Oliphant.[14] They note that research has not shown a clear, positive effect of descriptive representation (number or proportion of women) for women's substantive or symbolic representation. They propose that "the way in which participants interact while speaking may enhance or undermine women's status in deliberation, and that numbers affect this interaction, but in combination with rules." In particular, they note that previous research on the "authoritative use of speech acts" indicates that men are more likely to speak first and talk longer, receive positive feedback on their input, interrupt others in a negative manner, and fail to yield when interrupted. Women tend to speak less and not in the beginning of deliberations, receive little or no positive feedback on their ideas, be interrupted in a negative manner, and yield when interrupted.

Mendelberg, Karpowitz, and Oliphant investigate whether these patterns are affected by a group's decision rule: by majority or by consensus or unanimity. They hypothesize that under a unanimous rule, women will receive more respect in deliberations and the expectation of deference by women during discussions will be overridden, *but* only when women are in the minority, not when they predominate (based on previous research). To test their hypothesis, they set up 94 five-member discussion groups composed of between 0 and 5 women, and randomly assigned each group to unanimous or majority rule. Each group was given the identical decision task except for the decision rule. The researchers recorded and

FIGURE 1-4 ■ Negative Proportion of Negative and Positive Interruptions Received by Women from Men by Group Decision Rule

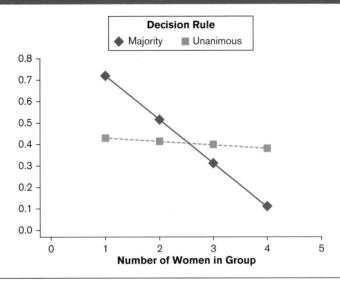

Source: Tali Mendelberg, Christopher F. Karpowitz, and J. Baxter Oliphant, "Gender Inequality in Deliberation: Unpacking the Black Box of Interaction," *Perspectives on Politics* 12, no. 1 (2014): fig. 1, p. 24.

transcribed each individual's speech. They counted the number of times each person spoke and coded the number and tone (positive, neutral, or negative) of interruptions, the gender of the speaker, and the gender of the person interrupting.

Figure 1-4 shows just some of the results. Graphical representation of data is an efficient and effective way of presenting research findings, and learning how to interpret such graphs is an important, albeit at times challenging, aspect of reading research articles. This figure shows the negative proportion of negative and positive interruptions (neutral interruptions are not included in this analysis) received by women from men by group decision rule and number of women in the group. The proportion of negative interruptions is measured on the vertical axis, the number of women in the group is measured along the horizontal axis, and each line represents the type of decision rule. In majority-rule groups, the composition of the group has a clear effect on the proportion of negative comments, ranging from over 70 percent when there is only one woman in the group to less than 20 percent when there are four women. Under unanimous rule, the tone of interruptions women receive from men is positive (less than half of the interruptions are negative), and the number of women in a group has no effect on the proportion of negative interruptions. Compared to majority rule, the unanimous rule helps women when they are in the minority; when women are in the minority in majority-rule groups, the tone of interruptions they receive from men is negative. But when women are in the majority in majority-rule groups (and their votes are necessary to win), the tone of men's interruptions becomes positive. In this decision-making context, women's status is important, and they are afforded more respect.

Another way of looking at the gender gap in deliberation is to compare men and women with respect to the relative frequency with which they receive positive interruptions. Relative frequencies, a data analysis technique described at length in chapter 11, are a common method of summarizing data. To make the graph in Figure 1-5, for every mixed-gender group the researchers take the proportion of a person's speaking turns that received a positive interruption and calculate the group's average for women divided by its average for men. Next, they separate the groups by decision rule and average the results for groups in which women are in the minority and for groups in which they are in the majority. One can see in figure 1-5 that women receive less than half of the proportion of positive interruptions (the horizontal red line represents equal proportions) when they are in the minority in majority-rule groups. In other decision-making contexts, women receive about the same or even higher proportions of positive interruptions compared to men.

This research by Mendelberg, Karpowitz, and Oliphant makes an important contribution to understanding links between demographic representation and substantive and symbolic representation of women, as well as to the broader question of under what circumstances participation in group deliberations by low-status individuals leads to their voices being heard.

We include one last example of gender politics research. It investigates whether and when Hillary Clinton chose to "talk like a man" throughout her political career. This

FIGURE 1-5 ■ Ratio of Women's to Men's Positively Interrupted Speaking Turns, Mixed Groups (Raw)

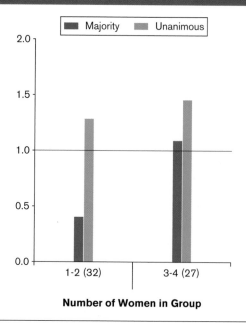

Source: Tali Mendelberg, Christopher F. Karpowitz, and J. Baxter Oliphant, "Gender Inequality in Deliberation: Unpacking the Black Box of Interaction," *Perspectives on Politics* 12, no. 1 (2014): fig. 1, p. 24.

research by Jennifer J. Jones has several noteworthy features from the perspective of research methods.[15] One, it is an example of content analysis—the quantitative analysis of written and spoken language, pictures, and other aspects of human communication, which we will discuss in greater depth in chapter 10. Two, it illustrates the importance of measurement and how researchers add to our understanding of political phenomena by using novel measurement schemes (in this case, measuring "talking like a man"). And, three, it raises questions about the scope of research: What are the implications of choosing to focus on a single case, one woman? On one hand, by analyzing Clinton's speech, Jones has selected a very important case as Clinton has been a highly visible political figure for several decades and she has served in multiple political capacities or roles. And, not inconsequential for the researcher, transcripts of Clinton's speech (interviews and debates) were readily available. On the other hand, research focusing on a single, atypical case may limit the extent to which we can expect other women with different political careers to exhibit the same patterns as Clinton. Or, stated in more formal research terms, are the research results *generalizable*?

Jones reviews previous research that notes that women in leadership positions face competing expectations: women are expected to possess certain character and behavior traits (warm, sympathetic, and friendly), yet the traits voters typically associate with leadership (strong, determined, and authoritative) are considered masculine rather than feminine traits.[16] Thus, Jones argues that women in politics have to be concerned about their self-presentation. In particular, she argues that when women in policy-making contexts interact with their male colleagues, they adopt masculine styles of communication in order to be effective and exercise power because such contexts are governed by male norms.

In order to test this hypothesis, Jones needs to define what is meant by masculine and feminine linguistic style. Drawing upon research that found reliable and consistent gender differences in linguistic style and incorporating some aspects of previously used coding schemes for measuring gendered communication, Jones creates two indices of linguistic style, one for feminine style and one for masculine style. Each index consists of six linguistic markers as shown in table 1-1. Her indices include "function words" (articles, prepositions, pronouns, and auxiliary verbs), which "shape and connect the content of our thoughts into meaningful forms of communication."[17] She argues that "[b]y analyzing function words, which are often discarded or ignored in coding schemes, my approach picks up on less overt, more implicit expressions of gender than is typical of many studies in the politics and gender literature."[18] Furthermore, function words can be consistently measured—a pronoun is a pronoun, a preposition is a preposition, and an article is an article.

Jones analyzes 567 interview and debate transcripts from 1992 to 2013 for linguistic markers using Linguistic Inquiry and Word Count (LIWC), a text analysis program. Jones does not include speeches or other formal addresses on the grounds they do not reflect a person's natural language. For each transcript, she calculated a feminine to masculine ratio by taking the sum of feminine linguistic markers and dividing by the sum of masculine linguistic markers. The ratio of feminine to masculine styles over time is shown in Figure 1-6. The ratio of feminine to masculine styles is consistently positive although there is a general downward trend with significant variations.

TABLE 1-1   ■   Differences in Linguistic Style between Men and Women

Feminine		Masculine	
Linguistic Marker	**Examples**	**Linguistic Marker**	**Examples**
Pronouns, especially first-person singular	*anyone, she, this, yours, I, me, myself*	First-person plural pronouns	*let's, our, ourselves, us, we, we're*
Verbs and auxiliary verbs	*listening, need, went, am, been, will*	Articles	*a, an, the*
Social references	*children, citizen, email, said, talking, who*	Prepositions	*above, for, in, to, under, without*
Emotion words	*brave, cried, disagree, evil, relief, safe*	Anger words	*annoyed, cruel, disgust, hate, kill*
Cognitive mechanisms	*because, believe, know, result, think, thus*	Big words (> 6 letters)	*American, industrial, reconciliation*
Tentative words	*chance, guess, maybe*	Swear words	*bastard, bitch, shit*

Source: Jennifer J. Jones, "Talk 'like a Man': The Linguistic Styles of Hillary Clinton, 1992–2013," *Perspectives on Politics* 14, no. 3 (2016): table 1, p. 631.

FIGURE 1-6   ■   Ratio of Feminine to Masculine Styles over Time

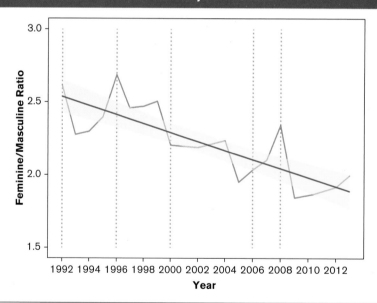

Source: Jennifer J. Jones, "Talk 'like a Man': The Linguistic Styles of Hillary Clinton, 1992–2013," *Perspectives on Politics* 14, no. 3 (2016): fig. 1, p. 632.

Note: Figure 1-6 gives a yearly time-series plot ratio of feminine to masculine linguistic markers. The dotted lines represent election years in which Clinton actively campaigned for herself (2000, 2006, 2008) or Bill (1992, 1996). The light gray line represents a smoothed generalized linear estimate (with shaded confidence intervals) from the ratio modeled in table 2 (see original article for table).

Jones argues that changes in the ratio are consistent with what one might expect: when Hillary Clinton was campaigning for her husband in 1992 and 1996, she used a higher ratio of feminine to masculine markers, which would be consistent with her "expected role as a supportive wife and first lady."[19] The abrupt decline in the ratio by 1993 coincides with Clinton's leading role on the administration's health reform task force where "she was charged with communicating details of the policy and persuading industry and interest group leaders, lawmakers, and the public to support it."[20] Once her role on the task force ended in 1995 and she was no longer charged with pushing the president's agenda, her language returned to a more feminine style. Clinton's style changed abruptly once again when she ran for the U.S. Senate in 2000, which Jones points out is "consistent with the expectation that female candidates adopt a masculine self-presentation to look 'tough enough' for the job."[21] Clinton's linguistic style was most masculine when she served in the Senate and as secretary of state during which time, Jones argues, her "self-presentation was constrained by the masculine norms of behavior and interaction within these institutions."[22]

While we don't show the results here, Jones's data allow her to analyze Clinton's linguistic style during her campaign for the Democratic presidential nomination as she struggled to present both a masculine (leadership capability) and feminine (likable) side. In addition, Jones examines how individual markers change as Clinton's style changes. Jones's research examines the linguistic style of only one politically ambitious woman, albeit a notable and important one, but it suggests a promising direction for future work into the ways in which male and female politicians communicate over time and in different political contexts.

THE CASE OF ITALIAN (NON) TAX COMPLIANCE

John D'Attoma's examination of the tax compliance in Italy and explanation of why tax compliance is higher in northern regions compared to southern regions is an example of research using historical institutional analysis.[23] That is, he focuses on the institutional context in which politics is conducted to explain political outcomes. His research demonstrates at least two important aspects of the research process: (1) different research approaches may lead to different conclusions; and (2) there may be important ethical dimensions to research conclusions if, for example, they imply that some populations are morally deficient. According to D'Attoma, tax compliance is known to be low in Italy and lower in the south than in the north as shown in figure 1-7.

D'Attoma's explanation of why this is the case differs from previous explanations, which focused on cultural factors and personal morals. Researchers employing what is known as the "social capital" approach concluded that southern Italians have less civic virtue (defined as "high civic awareness and a shared consensus regarding the legitimacy of political institutions and public policy, together with political competence and trust") and lower levels of social capital (defined as "features of social life, such as networks and trust").[24] Lower tax compliance, as well as lower levels of economic development and government performance in southern regions, has been blamed on the "faulty character" and presence of "amoral familism" among their inhabitants. Societies characterized by amoral familism are tied together by "bonding" social capital and emphasize family relations to the exclusion of all

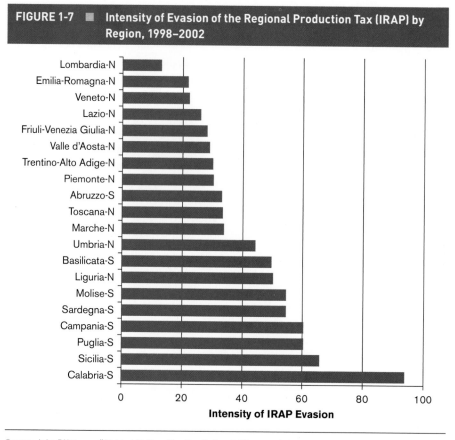

FIGURE 1-7 ■ **Intensity of Evasion of the Regional Production Tax (IRAP) by Region, 1998–2002**

Source: John D'Attoma, "Divided Nation: The North-South Cleavage in Italian Tax Compliance," *Polity* 49, no. 1 (January 2017): fig. 1, p. 79.

others. In "bonding" societies, ethical behavior is confined to the immediate family and closest friends. Because taxes can be perceived as hurting the family by imposing a cost in order to benefit people outside the familial unit, compliance is low. In contrast, in societies characterized by "bridging" social capital, individuals are drawn together regardless of socioeconomic status, race, or ethnic background: tax compliance is higher because taxes are perceived as going toward common benefits.[25]

D'Attoma notes there is ample evidence that, in general, individuals are more likely to pay taxes if they believe the government is spending their tax money honestly and efficiently and if there is a perception that their tax burden and the quality of services received in return are well matched.[26] Tax compliance in Italy fits this pattern. Italy's tax burden (the ratio of tax revenue to gross domestic product) is one of the highest in the European Union, and it consistently ranks near the bottom of the European Quality of Government index[27] compared to other European nations, with the south ranking lower than the north.

Figure 1-8 shows the relationship between percentage of irregular work (used as a measure of tax avoidance) and quality of government ratings for regions in Italy. Northern

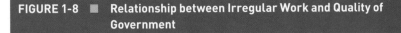

FIGURE 1-8 ■ Relationship between Irregular Work and Quality of Government

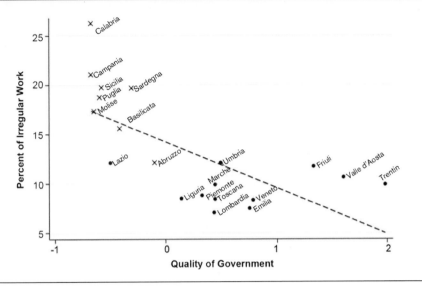

Source: John D'Attoma, "Divided Nation: The North-South Cleavage in Italian Tax Compliance," *Polity* 49, no. 1 (January 2017): fig. 2a, p. 75.

regions generally rank lower than southern regions on percentage of irregular work and higher in quality of government. The question is, what is at the root of this difference?

Critics, including D'Attoma, of the social capital approach argue that researchers have overlooked evidence of substantial social capital in the south. Therefore, lack of social capital in the south can't be a valid explanation for differences between the north and south. Furthermore, D'Attoma argues, isn't it possible that public institutions and the elites that govern them cause or foster civic attitudes? D'Attoma contends that the moralist argument fails to take into account historical differences between the north and the south in institutions (both the government and the Catholic Church), political competition, and impact of public policies.

To provide evidence in support of his contention that historical institutional context is a more valid explanation of variation in tax compliance in Italy, D'Attoma examines the Italian political landscape dating from the unification of Italy in the nineteenth century to the fall of the First Republic in 1992. Among the features of this landscape are

- After unification, the politically dominant north demanded disproportionate tax revenues from the south, which were used to fund public works projects largely benefiting the north.

- The Catholic Church largely disintegrated in the south as the state sold off church lands to the wealthy landed elite such that Catholic associations were nonexistent, while in the north a Catholic workers' movement emerged to challenge the socialist labor movement. This enhanced political competition.

- During the Fascist period, industrial policies concentrated economic development in the north, exacerbating economic differences.

- After the fall of Fascism and the end of World War II, the rise of political parties and active political competition in the north contrasted with a political monopoly by the Christian Democrats in the south. The result was a large difference in the pattern of distributing government spending and benefits—in the north through public institutions and in the south through the distribution of individualized benefits based on personal and private connections so that a perception that there was a link between paying taxes and the provision of government benefits did not develop.

Thus, D'Attoma argues, there is ample evidence to support an alternative explanation for differences in attitudes and political behavior, including tax compliance, between northern and southern Italians. Historical differences in government and church institutions and political environments as well as tax burdens and distribution of government services explain differences between the north and south tax behavior today. Thus, according to D'Attoma, historical institutional analysis gets to the real root or cause of these differences.

PROTESTS AND REPRESSION IN NEW DEMOCRACIES

Our final example of recent research by political scientists examines why elected governments respond to protests, in particular, backlash protests, the way they do. Backlash protests refer to the expansion of protests after governments respond to initial protests with violence, albeit with less-lethal tools of repression. Governments are then confronted with a choice between expanding the use of tools of repression to include more violent, perhaps lethal methods and exercising restraint and finding alternative means to resolve a political crisis. What do they choose to do, and why? It is an example of comparative research—here the researchers (S. Erdem Aytaç, Luis Schiumerini, and Susan Stokes) select three cases of countries that responded differently to backlash protests.[28] Turkey, Brazil, and Ukraine each faced national uprisings in 2013, which began similarly: "modest-sized groups of protesters pressing for policy (but not regime) change were attacked by police; the attacks were widely publicized, in large part through the social media; and major national uprisings ensued."[29] Authorities in Turkey responded by increasing the level of repression resulting in deaths and injuries, whereas authorities in Brazil and Ukraine instructed their police to back off and offered concessions to the protesters.

By studying these cases in depth using public opinion polls and surveys of demonstrators and interviews with elites such as police officials, Aytaç, Schiumerini, and Stokes are able to compare and contrast the factors related to rival explanations such as differences in degree of political centralization, democratic consolidation, civilian control over the police, governments' ideologies, costliness of protesters' demands, the social class composition of demonstrators, their network structures, or the extent to which authorities expect they will be held to account for high levels of repression. It is this last factor that the authors found to be critical:

> [W]e argue that the decision of an elected government often boils down to its assessment of the degree to which it will be held accountable for high levels of repression. Secure governments, ones that maintain a stable electoral support base that maps closely onto an overlapping social cleavage, are relatively free to inflict harm at high levels. By contrast, less secure governments, those with volatile electoral support, are more sensitive to electoral sanctioning and have incentives to refrain from repression.[30]

Their assessment of the factors for the three countries is shown in table 1-2. Tables such as these are a common method of summarizing information and make it easier to compare and contrast cases on critical dimensions identified by researchers.

Aytaç, Schiumerini, and Stokes conclude that the key relevant feature distinguishing Turkey from Brazil and Ukraine was the security of the government's hold on office. Party affinities in Turkey coincide with socioreligious cleavages in Turkish society, and supporters of the ruling party were not prevalent among the protesters. It could be anticipated by authorities that harsh treatment of protesters would not erode support of the ruling party among its popular base.

TABLE 1-2 ■ Extrication Strategies: Where the Cases Fall on Favored and Rival Explanations					
	Security of Office	Centralization	Democratic Consolidation	Control over the Police	Extrication Strategy
Turkey	High	High	Low	High	Repression
Brazil	Low	Low	High	High	Restraint
Ukraine	Low	High	Low	Medium	Restraint
	Ideology of Government	Nature of Threat	Social Class of Protesters	Extrication Strategy	
Turkey	Conservative	Low	High	Repression	
Brazil	Leftist	Medium	High	Restraint	
Ukraine	Conservative	High	High	Restraint	

Source: S. Erdem Aytaç, Luis Schiumerini, and Susan Stokes, "Protests and Repression in New Democracies," *Perspectives on Politics* 15, no. 1 (2017): table 4, pp. 74–75.

THE OBSERVER EFFECT IN INTERNATIONAL POLITICS: EVIDENCE FROM A NATURAL EXPERIMENT

Political scientists often confront a thorny issue when conducting their research: How do they prove causation? We will have much to say about this issue in later chapters, but for the moment, let's consider that political scientists often have very little control over factors (frequently referred to as treatment factors) they think are important in explaining political outcomes: they must wait for these factors to occur or change in the real world. Furthermore, observable variation in outcomes of interest typically takes place in complex environments, which may include many other factors besides the one researchers are interested in, that could affect or cause outcomes. Our mental picture of a political scientist is not one of a person in a lab coat conducting a tightly controlled experiment. Nonetheless, there are times when variation in a causal factor occurs naturally in a relatively controlled setting. These so-called natural experiments allow researchers to be more confident in their claims that differences in outcomes are due to differences in occurrences in the causal factor.

Such is the case in our last example of political science research. Susan Hyde took advantage of a natural experiment to investigate whether the presence of international election monitors leads to cleaner elections.[31] As Hyde explains:

> Until 1962, there had been no recorded cases in international election observation in sovereign states. By 2004 upwards of 80 percent of elections held in nonconsolidated democracies were monitored, and any leader of a developing country wishing to hold a legitimate election was expected to invite international election observers. Although the record of election observation demonstrates that observers grew willing to condemn fraudulent elections over the course of the 1990s, it remains unknown whether international monitors can actually bring about cleaner elections, as proponents of election monitoring assert.[32]

Numerous types of electoral manipulation have been reported by international observers: military intimidation of voters, ballot-box stuffing, improper attempts to influence voters inside the voting booth, vote-buying schemes, intentional inflation of the vote tallies, jailing of opposition voters, failure to distribute ballots to opposition strongholds, and manipulation of voter-registration lists.[33] Hyde's research is limited to manipulations that occur in and around the polling station on Election Day. Hyde takes advantage of a natural experimental situation that occurred in the 2003 presidential elections in Armenia in which international observers were assigned to polling stations on Election Day using a method that resembled random assignment. Because the majority of election fraud in the election could be expected to benefit the incumbent, if the presence of international observers caused a reduction in Election Day fraud, the share of the vote received by the incumbent should be lower at the polling stations that were visited by observers compared to those polling stations that were not visited.

In addition to the method by which observers were assigned to polling stations and that assignments were not preannounced, Hyde's research benefited from two other factors. One was that widespread and centrally orchestrated fraud occurred on Election Day, and the other was that polling-station-level election results were made public. There were two rounds in the Armenian presidential election, which permitted numerous comparisons among polling stations as reported in table 1-3.

Table 1-3 reports the results of comparing the average incumbent vote share for polling stations under different observation conditions. The third column of the table presents the difference in the vote share between the two polling station conditions. In the first comparison, the difference was 5.9 percent, and as expected, the average incumbent vote share was greater among polling stations that were not observed in round 1 of the election compared to those that were observed. The results of an appropriate *t* test are also reported. *T* tests are a statistical procedure used to test how risky (risk in terms of making a wrong conclusion) it is to conclude that the difference between the two groups is due to the difference in the treatment condition. The risk is reported as a probability represented by *P*. The closer *P* is to zero, the lower the risk and the more confident you can be in concluding that the observed difference is due to the experimental treatment. You will learn how to conduct *t* tests in a later chapter.

TABLE 1-3 ■ **Difference of Means Tests Comparing "Treatment" and "Control" Groups**				
	Average Incumbent Vote Share among Polling Stations That Were . . .	**vs.**	**Average Incumbent Vote Share among Polling Stations That Were . . .**	**Difference**
1.	Not observed in R1	vs.	Observed in R1	5.9%
	54.2%		48.3%	$t(1762) = 5.92$
	(R1 vote share)		(R1 vote share)	$P > \|t\| = 0.00$
2.	Not observed in R2	vs.	Observed in R2	2.0%
	69.3%		67.3%	$t(1761) = 2.47$
	(R2 vote share)		(R2 vote share)	$P > \|t\| = 0.014$
3.	Never observed	vs.	Observed in both R1 and R2	4.5%
	70.7%		66.2%	$t(1116) = 4.48$
	(R2 vote share)		(R2 vote share)	$P > \|t\| = 0.00$
4.	Never observed	vs.	Observed in both R1 and R2	5.8%
	62.8%		57%	$t(1116) = 5.36$
	(Average of R1 and R2 vote share)		(Average of R1 and R2 vote share)	$P > \|t\| = 0.00$
5.	Never observed	vs.	Observed in one or both rounds	4.6%
	62.7%		58.1%	$t(1761) = 5.65$
	(Average of R1 and R2 vote share)		(Average of R1 and R2 vote share)	$P > \|t\| = 0.00$
6.	Never observed	vs.	Observed only in R1	4.4%
	70.7%		66.3%	$t(1138) = 4.40$
	(R2 vote share)		(R2 vote share)	$P > \|t\| = 0.00$

(Continued)

TABLE 1-3 ■ (Continued)

	Average Incumbent Vote Share among Polling Stations That Were . . .	vs.	Average Incumbent Vote Share among Polling Stations That Were . . .	Difference
7.	Never observed 70.7% (R2 vote share)	vs.	Observed only in R2 68.7% (R2 vote share)	2.0% $t(1013) = 1.73$ $P > \lvert t \rvert = 0.084$
8.	Observed only in R2 68.7% (R2 vote share)	vs.	Observed in both R1 and R2 66.2% (R2 vote share)	2.5% $t(621) = 1.93$ $P > \lvert t \rvert = 0.054$
9.	Observed in both R1 and R2 66.3% (R2 vote share)	vs.	Observed only in R1 66.2% (R2 vote share)	.11% $t(746) = 0.094$ $P > \lvert t \rvert = 0.93$
10.	Observed only in R1 68.7% (R2 vote share)	vs.	Observed only in R2 66.3% (R2 vote share)	2.4% $t(643) = 1.83$ $P > \lvert t \rvert = 0.067$

• Reported results reflect two-sample t tests with equal variances.

Source: Susan Hyde, "The Observer Effect in International Politics: Evidence from a Natural Experiment," *World Politics* 60, no. 1 (2007): table 1, p. 53.

CONCLUSION

Political scientists are continually adding to and revising our understanding of politics and government. As the several examples in this chapter illustrate, empirical research in political science is useful for satisfying intellectual curiosity and for evaluating real-world political conditions. New ways of designing investigations, the availability of new types of data, and new statistical techniques contribute to the ever-changing body of political science knowledge. Conducting empirical research is not a simple process, however. The information a researcher chooses to use, the method that he or she follows to investigate a research question, and the statistics used to report research findings may affect the conclusions drawn. For instance, some of these examples used sample surveys to measure important phenomena such as public opinion on a variety of public policy issues. Yet surveys are not always an accurate reflection of people's beliefs and attitudes. In addition, how a researcher measures the phenomena of interest can affect the conclusions reached. Finally, some researchers conducted experiments in which they were able to control the application of the experimental or test factor, whereas others compared naturally occurring cases in which the factors of interest varied.

Sometimes, researchers are unable to measure political phenomena themselves and have to rely on information collected by others, particularly government agencies. Can we always find readily available data to investigate a topic? If not, do we choose a different topic or collect our own data? How do we collect data firsthand? When we are trying to measure cause and effect in the real world of politics, rather than in a carefully controlled laboratory setting, how can we be sure that we have identified all the factors that could affect the phenomena we are trying to explain? Finally, do research findings based on the study of particular people, agencies, courts, communities, or countries have general applications to all people, agencies, courts, communities, or countries? To develop answers to these questions, we need to understand the process of scientific research, the subject of this book.

TERMS INTRODUCED

Applied research. Research designed to produce knowledge useful in altering a real-world condition or situation.   5

Empirical research. Research based on actual, "objective" observation of phenomena.   1

Pure, theoretical, or recreational research. Research designed to satisfy one's intellectual curiosity about some phenomenon.   5

NOTES

1. *Recreational research* is a term used by W. Phillips Shively in *The Craft of Political Research*, 2nd ed. (Englewood Cliffs, NJ: Prentice-Hall, 1980), chap. 1.

2. Harold Lasswell, *Politics: Who Gets What, When, How* (New York: Whittlesey House, 1936). A more recent statement of the idea is found in Benjamin I. Page, *Who Gets What from Government* (Berkeley: University of California Press, 1983).

3. Nick Hanauer, "The Pitchforks Are Coming . . . for Us Plutocrats," *Politico*, July/August 2014. Accessed December 28, 2014. Available at http://www .politico.com/magazine/story/2014/06/the-pitch forks-are-coming-for-us-plutocrats-108014.html# .VKMNwsk08uc.

4. Jeffrey Dorfman, "Dispelling Myths about Income Inequality," *Forbes*, May 8, 2014. Accessed December 27, 2014. Available at http://www .forbes.com/sites/jeffreydorfman/2014/05/08/ dispelling-myths-about-income-inequality/.

5. Lane Kenworthy and Jonas Pontusson, "Rising Inequality and the Politics of Redistribution in Affluent Countries," *Perspectives on Politics* 3, no. 3 (2005): 449–71. Accessed February 11, 2019. Available at https://doi.org/10.1017/S1537592705050292.

6. Allan H. Meltzer and Scott F. Richard, "A Rational Theory of the Size of Government," *Journal of Political Economy* 89, no. 5 (1981): 914–27.

7. Jacob S. Hacker and Paul Pierson, "Winner-Take-All Politics: Public Policy, Political Organization, and the Precipitous Rise of Top Incomes in the United States," *Politics & Society* 38, no. 2 (2010): 152–204. Accessed February 20, 2019. Available at http://pas.sagepub .com/content/38/2/152.full.pdf.

8. Women in National Parliaments. Information is based on 193 countries as of December 1, 2018. Some country information is from years prior to 2018. Accessed February 11, 2019. Available at http://archive.ipu .org/wmn-e/world.htm.

9. Center for American Women and Politics, "History of Women in the U.S. Congress." Accessed February 11, 2019. Available at http://www.cawp.rutgers.edu/ history-women-us-congress.

10. Center for American Women and Politics, "Women in the U.S. Congress 2019." Accessed February 11, 2019. Available at http://www.cawp.rutgers.edu/ women-us-congress-2019

11. Center for American Women and Politics, "Women in State Legislatures 2019." Accessed February 11, 2019. Available at http://www.cawp.rutgers.edu/ women-state-legislature-2019.

12. Richard L. Fox and Jennifer L. Lawless, "Uncovering the Origins of the Gender Gap in Political Ambition," *American Political Science Review* 108, no. 3 (2014): 499–519.

13. Richard L. Fox and Jennifer L. Lawless, "Reconciling Family Roles with Political Ambition: The New Normal for Women in Twenty-First Century U.S. Politics," *The Journal of Politics* 76, no. 2 (2014): 398–414.

14. Tali Mendelberg, Christopher F. Karpowitz, and J. Baxter Oliphant, "Gender Inequality in Deliberation: Unpacking the Black Box of Interaction," *Perspectives on Politics* 12, no. 1 (2014): 18–44.

15. Jennifer J. Jones, "Talk 'like a Man': The Linguistic Styles of Hillary Clinton, 1992–2013," *Perspectives on Politics* 14, no. 3 (2016): 625–42.

16. Ibid., 627.

17. Ibid., 630.

18. Ibid., 631.

19. Ibid., 632.

20. Ibid., 633.

21. Ibid.

22. Ibid., 635.

23. John D'Attoma, "Divided Nation: The North-South Cleavage in Italian Tax Compliance," *Polity* 49, no. 1 (January 2017): 66–99.

24. Ibid., 71.

25. Ibid., 71–72.

26. Ibid., 73–75.

27. The European Quality of Government index is based on nationally representative public opinion surveys conducted in 251 European regions about perceptions of local education, health, and law enforcement institutions. Participants are asked to rate each of the three institutions on quality, impartiality, and corruption. The index was developed by researchers at the University of Gothenburg in Sweden. See Ibid.

28. S. Erdem Aytaç, Luis Schiumerini, and Susan Stokes, "Protests and Repression in New Democracies," *Perspectives on Politics* 15, no. 1 (2017): 62–82.

29. Ibid., 63.

30. Ibid., 64.

31. Susan Hyde, "The Observer Effect in International Politics: Evidence from a Natural Experiment," *World Politics* 60, no. 1 (2007): 37–63.

32. Ibid., 38.

33. Ibid., 42.

STUDENT STUDY SITE

for CQ Press

Give your students the SAGE edge!

SAGE edge offers a robust online environment featuring an impressive array of free tools and resources for review, study, and further exploration, keeping both instructors and students on the cutting edge of teaching and learning. Learn more at **edge.sagepub.com/johnson9e.**

2 THE EMPIRICAL APPROACH TO POLITICAL SCIENCE

Political scientists Jeffrey Winters and Benjamin Page wonder if the United States, despite being a nominal democracy, is not in fact governed by an oligarchy, a relatively small number of very wealthy individuals and families.[1] Their work leads them to conclude:

> We believe it is now appropriate to . . . think about the possibility of *extreme* political inequality, involving great political influence by a very small number of wealthy individuals. We argue that it is useful to think about the US political system in terms of oligarchy.[2]

What are we to make of a (perhaps startling) claim such as this? How do we know it's true? Should we accept it?

As the title of our book and this chapter suggest, we have confidence in a statement like Winters and Page's *if* they arrive at their (tentative) conclusion through empiricism. This term is perhaps best explained by reference to an old joke.

Three baseball umpires are discussing their philosophy of calling balls and strikes. The first umpire says, "I call 'em as I see 'em." The next one replies, "That's nothing. I call 'em as they *are*." Finally, the third chimes in, "Oh yeah! Well, they ain't *nothing* until I call 'em."

We put aside Umpires 1 and 3 until later in the chapter. For now, let's concentrate on the second one. We call him a strict or strong empiricist. He believes there are in fact things like balls and strikes, and he can always tell the difference by merely looking at the pitches as they are thrown. He believes no interpretation is necessary; the facts (the pitches) speak for themselves, and the umpire simply reports on where the ball travels, nothing more, nothing less. Importantly, this umpire believes that his observations are accurate and objective. The teams, players, managers, and fans have no bearing, he believes, on his judgments.[3]

An empiricist, in other words, uses impartial observation to judge the tenability of arguments. A political science "umpire" demands that data and measurements support whatever point is being made. Statements can be believed and accepted to the extent that they are derived from empirical or observational evidence. If, on the other hand, their "truthfulness" depends on belief, authority, or faith instead of "hard data," they are set aside for philosophers and others to evaluate.

CHAPTER OBJECTIVES

2.1 Identify eight characteristics of empiricism.

2.2 Discuss the importance of theory in empiricism.

2.3 Explain the five steps in the empirical research process.

2.4 Describe practical obstacles that challenge the empirical approach.

2.5 Summarize competing perspectives.

Empiricism is an ideal. Most who adopt this methodology would admit that personal judgment plays a part in their research—they are perhaps closer to the first umpire, who calls the game as he "sees it." But so important is empiricism that we need to take a detour to clarify why many political scientists prefer this methodology to other ways of obtaining knowledge. Although not everyone agrees, it does seem to have a "privileged" place in the discipline, and we need to explore its philosophical basis. This leads us to a discussion of the scientific method.[4]

Although empiricism does have a dominant place in contemporary political science, we stress that it has its share of critics, and we certainly don't maintain that it is the only or even the best way to study politics. There is plenty of room, we believe, for different research stances. Proponents of alternatives work under many different labels, so we simply classify them as *nonempiricists*.[5] Furthermore, there are substantial debates among empiricists over appropriate methods and approaches, particularly over the advantages of quantitative versus qualitative analysis.[6] We'll have more to say about this in chapters 7 and 9.

ELEMENTS OF EMPIRICISM

What, then, distinguishes the empirical or scientific approach? In our daily lives, we "know" things in many different ways. We know, for example, that water boils at 212 degrees Fahrenheit and that a virus causes Ebola. We also may know that democracy is "better" than dictatorship. In some cases, we know something because we believe what we read in the newspaper or heard on the radio or what a trusted authority told us. In other cases, we know things based on personal experience or because they appear to be consistent with common sense.

Modern political science, though, relies heavily on one kind of knowledge: knowledge obtained through objective observation, experimentation, and logical reasoning.[7] This way of knowing differs greatly from information derived from myth, intuition, faith, common sense, sacred texts, and the like. It has certain characteristics that these other types of knowledge do not completely share. The ultimate goal of scientific research, which is not always attained, is to use its results to construct theories that explain political phenomena.[8]

Scientific knowledge exhibits several characteristics. Most important, scientific knowledge depends on **verification**. That is, our acceptance or rejection of a statement regarding something "known" must be influenced by observation.[9] Thus, if we say that people in the upper classes have more political power than members of the lower strata, we must be able to provide tangible evidence to support this statement.

A contention cannot be accepted simply because someone said so or our instinct tells us so. It must be supported by evidence. The empirical nature of scientific knowledge distinguishes it from mystical knowledge. In the latter case, only "true believers" are able to observe the phenomena that support their beliefs, and observations that would disprove their beliefs are impossible to specify. Knowledge derived from superstition and prejudice is usually not subjected to accepted methods of empirical verification, either. Superstitious or prejudiced persons are likely to note only phenomena that reinforce their beliefs, while ignoring or dismissing those that do not. Thus, their knowledge is based on selective and biased experience and observation.

On the flip side, some philosophers of science insist that a key characteristic of scientific claims is **falsifiability**, meaning the statements or hypotheses can in principle be rejected in the face of contravening empirical evidence. A claim not refutable by any conceivable observation or experiment is nonscientific. In this sense, the findings of science are usually considered tentative, because they are "champions" only so long as competing ideas do not upend them. Indeed, the philosopher Karl Popper argued that scientists should think solely in terms of invalidating or falsifying theories, not proving them.[10]

In view of the importance of verification and falsification, researchers must always remain open to alterations and improvements of their research. To say that scientific knowledge is *provisional* does not mean that the evidence accumulated to date can be ignored or is worthless. It does mean, however, that future research could significantly alter what we currently believe. In a word, scientific knowledge is *tentative*, and because of this property, empirical research is thought to be self-corrective.

Scientific knowledge is supposedly "value-free." Empiricism addresses what is, what might be in the future, and why. It does not typically address whether or not the existence of something is good or bad, although it may be useful in making these types of determinations. Political scientists use the words *normative* and *nonnormative* to express the distinction. Knowledge that is evaluative, value-laden, and concerned with prescribing what ought to be is known as **normative knowledge**. Knowledge that is concerned not with evaluation or prescription but with factual or objective determinations is known as **nonnormative knowledge**. Most scientists would agree that science is (or should attempt to be) a nonnormative enterprise.

This is not to say that empirical research operates in a valueless vacuum. A researcher's values and interests, which are indeed subjective, affect the selection of research topics, periods, populations, and the like. A criminologist, for example, may feel that crime is a serious problem and that long prison sentences deter would-be criminals. He or she may therefore advocate stiff mandatory sentences as a way to reduce crime. But the researcher should test that proposition in such a way that personal values and predilections do not bias the results of the study. And it is the responsibility of other social scientists to evaluate whether or not the research meets the criteria of empirical verification. Scientific principles and methods of observation thus help both researchers and those who must evaluate and use their findings. Note, however, that within the discipline of political science, as well as in other disciplines, the relationship between values and scientific research is frequently debated. We have more to say about this subject later in the chapter.

An additional characteristic of scientific knowledge helps to identify and weed out prejudices (inadvertent or otherwise) that may creep into research activities.[11] Scientific knowledge must be **transmissible**—that is, the methods used in making scientific discoveries must be made *transparent* so that others can analyze and replicate findings. The transmissibility of scientific knowledge suggests "science is a social activity in that it takes several scientists, analyzing and criticizing each other, to produce more reliable knowledge."[12] To accept results, people must know what data were collected and how they were analyzed.

A clear description of research procedures allows this independent evaluation. It also permits other scientists in some cases to collect or obtain access to the same data and test the original propositions themselves. If researchers use the same procedures but do not replicate the original results, something is amiss, and the reasons for the discrepancy must be found. Until then, both sets of results are suspect.

In an effort to improve the transparency in political science research, in 2012 the American Political Science Association adopted a set of data accessibility and research transparency (commonly referred to as DA-RT) principles as part of its *Guide to Professional Ethics*.[13] The guidelines declared that "[r]esearchers have an ethical obligation to facilitate the evaluation of their evidence-based knowledge claims . . . so that their work can be tested or replicated." Researchers are expected to meet this obligation in three aspects:

1. Data access: Researchers making evidence-based knowledge claims should reference the data they used to make those claims. If these are data they themselves generated or collected, researchers should provide access to those data or explain why they cannot.

2. Production transparency: Researchers providing access to data they themselves generated or collected should offer a full account of the procedures used to collect or generate the data.

3. Analytic transparency: Researchers making evidence-based knowledge claims should provide a full account of how they draw their analytic conclusions from the data (i.e., clearly explicate the links connecting data to conclusions).

Adherence to and implementation of these principles is not without controversy and debate among political scientists.[14] In later chapters in which we address data collection and analysis, we will discuss how these principles can be met. In some cases, this may pose substantial challenges and raise other research ethics issues.

HELPFUL HINTS
TYPES OF ASSERTIONS

It is sometimes tricky to tell an empirical statement from a normative one. The key is to infer the author's intention: Is he or she asserting that something is simply the way it is, no matter what anyone's preference may be? Or is the person stating a preference or desire? Sometimes normative arguments contain auxiliary verbs, such as *should* or *ought*, which express an obligation or a desire.

Empirical arguments, by contrast, often use variations of *to be* or direct verbs to convey the idea that "this is the way it really is in the world." Naturally, people occasionally believe that their values are matters of fact, but scientists must be careful to keep the types of claims separate. Finally, people often state opinions (beliefs) as if they were a matter of fact in rhetorical sentences, as in "No tax hike ever created a job." Without verification, this is not an empirical statement.

When reading research reports or (even more important) when following political discussions in the media, on the internet, or on the campaign trail, try to keep in mind that statements that seem to be of the same type can be surprisingly different:

- **Empirical:** A verifiable assertion of "what is"

- **Normative:** An assertion of "what should be"

- **Rhetorical:** A statement to the effect that "my belief is a fact"

This idea of transmissibility leads to another characteristic of empirical knowledge: it is **cumulative**, in that both substantive findings and research techniques are built upon those of prior studies. As Isaac Newton famously observed of his own accomplishments, "I have stood on the shoulders of giants." He meant that the attainment of his revolutionary insights depended in part on the knowledge other scientists had generated in the previous decades and centuries. The process of constantly testing and refining prior research produces an accumulated body of knowledge. (You'll see examples of this fact in chapter 3, which explains literature reviews.)

Another important characteristic of scientific knowledge is that it is **general**, or applicable to many rather than just a few cases. Advocates of the scientific method argue that knowledge that describes, explains, and predicts many phenomena or a set of similar occurrences is more valuable than knowledge that addresses a single phenomenon or case.[15] For example, the knowledge that states with easier voter registration systems have higher election turnout rates than do states with more difficult systems is preferable to the knowledge that Minnesota has a higher turnout rate than does Alabama, for example. Knowing that party affiliation strongly influences many voters' choices among candidates is more useful to someone seeking to understand elections than is the simple fact that John Doe, a Democrat, voted for a Democratic candidate for Congress in 2018. The empirical approach thus strives for empirical generalizations, statements that describe relationships between particular sets of facts.[16] For example, the assertion that positive campaigns lead to higher voter turnout than do those that are characterized by mudslinging and name-calling is intended to summarize a relationship that holds in different places and at different times. Furthermore, many political scientists would assert that insofar as it is possible, it is important to quantify the relationships—for example, by how much do more difficult voter registration systems depress voter turnout, or how many fatalities might be avoided on average by states adopting stringent vehicle safety inspection programs? Another characteristic of scientific knowledge is that it is **explanatory**; that is, it provides a systematic, empirically verified understanding of why a phenomenon occurs. In scientific discourse, the term *explanation* has various meanings, but when we say that knowledge is explanatory, we are saying that a conclusion can be derived (logically) from a set of general propositions and specific initial conditions. The general propositions assert that when things of type X occur, they will be followed by things of type Y. An initial condition might specify that X has in fact occurred. The observation of Y is then explained by the conjunction of the condition and the proposition. The goal of explanation is, sometimes, to account for a particular event—the emergence of terrorism, for example—but more often it is to explain general classes of phenomena such as wars or revolutions or voting behavior.

Explanation, then, answers "why" and "how" questions. The questions may be specific (e.g., "Why did a particular event take place at a particular time?") or more general (e.g., "Why do upper-class people vote more regularly than, say, blue-collar workers?"). Observing and describing facts are, of course, important. But most political scientists want more than mere facts. They are usually interested in identifying the factors that account for or explain human behavior. Studies of turnout are valuable because they do more than simply describe particular election results; they offer an explanation of political behavior in general.

An especially important kind of explanation for science is that which asserts *causality* between two events or trends. A causal relationship means that in some sense, the emergence or presence of one condition or event will always (or with high probability) bring about another. Causation implies more than that one thing is connected to or associated with another. Instead, it means one *necessarily* follows the other. Chapter 1 touched on the issue of why economic inequality appears to be increasing in the United States. Some political scientists, for instance, believe that "de-unionization" (the weakening of organized labor) has led to (caused) an increase in inequality in the United States. But is there, in fact, a causal connection, or is the relationship merely fortuitous? Statements asserting cause and effect are generally considered more informative and perhaps more useful than ones simply stating that an unexplained connection exists. But they are difficult to establish. The issue of how to design a research strategy in which an investigator is intending to demonstrate causality is discussed in chapter 6.

Explanatory knowledge is also important because, by offering systematic, reasoned anticipation of future events, it can be predictive. Note that prediction based on explanation is not the same as forecasting or soothsaying or astrology, which does not rest on empirically verified explanations. An explanation gives scientific reasons or justifications for why a certain outcome is to be expected. In fact, many scientists consider the ultimate test of an explanation to be its usefulness in prediction. Prediction is an extremely valuable type of knowledge, since it may be used to avoid undesirable and costly events and to achieve desired outcomes. Of course, whether or not a prediction is "beneficial" is a normative question. Consider, for example, a government that uses scientific research to predict the outbreak of popular unrest but uses the knowledge not to alleviate the underlying conditions but to suppress the discontented with force.

In political science, explanations rarely account for all the variation observed in attributes or behavior. So exactly how accurate, then, do scientific explanations have to be? Do they have to account for or predict phenomena 100 percent of the time? Most political scientists, like scientists in other disciplines, accept probabilistic explanation, in which it is not necessary to explain or predict a phenomenon with 100 percent accuracy.

Scientists also recognize another characteristic of scientific knowledge: **parsimony**, or simplicity. Suppose, for instance, two researchers have developed explanations for why some people trust and follow authoritarian leaders. The first account mentions only the immediate personal, social, and economic situation of the individuals, whereas the second account accepts these factors but adds deep-seated psychological states stemming from traumatic childhood experiences. And imagine that both provide equally compelling accounts and predictions of behavior. Yet, since the first relies on fewer explanatory factors than does the second, it will generally be the preferred explanation, all other things being equal. This is the principle of Ockham's razor, which might be summed up as "keep explanations as simple as possible."

THE IMPORTANCE OF THEORY

Theory plays an important role in research. The accumulation of observed relationships sometimes leads to the creation of a **theory**—that is, a body of statements that systematize knowledge of and explain relationships between phenomena. The process of reasoning going from specific observations to a general explanation or theory is known as **induction**. Two crucial aspects of empirical theory are that (1) it leads to specific, testable predictions, and (2) the more observations there are to support these predictions, the more the theory is confirmed. You will notice that many, if not most, published examples of empirical research are theory-driven; that is, the predictions or propositions about the relationships under investigation are based on what a theory or theories would lead us to expect. The process of **deduction** entails reasoning from a general theory to a specific expectation.

An Example: Proximity Theory of Voting

To clarify some of these matters, let us take a quick look at an example. The "proximity theory of electoral choice" provides a concise explanation for why voters choose parties and candidates.[17] Superficially, the theory may seem simplistic. Its simplicity can be deceiving, however, for it rests on many years of multidisciplinary research[18] and involves considerable sophisticated thinking.[19] But essentially the theory boils down to the assertion that people support parties and candidates who are "closest" to them on policy issues. Furthermore, this theory would predict that candidates will try to position themselves so that they are closer to more voters than are their opponents.

Take a particularly simple case. Suppose we consider the immigration debate. Positions on this issue might be arrayed along a single continuum running from, say, "All undocumented immigrants should have a path to citizenship" to "All undocumented immigrants should be deported" (see figure 2-1). Proximity theorists believe that both voters and candidates (or parties) can be placed or located on this scale and, consequently, that the distances or proximities between them (voters and candidates) can be compared. The theory's prediction is straightforward: an individual votes for the candidate to whom he or she lies closest on the continuum.[20]

To expand a bit, theorists in this camp argue that (1) analysts using proper measurement techniques can position both issues and candidates on scales that show how "close" they are to each other and to other objects, and (2) voters vote for candidates who are closest (most proximate) to themselves on such scales. People choose nearby candidates out of their desire to maximize utility, or the value that results from one choice over another. Knowing this fact, candidates adjust their behavior to maximize the votes they receive. Adjusting behavior

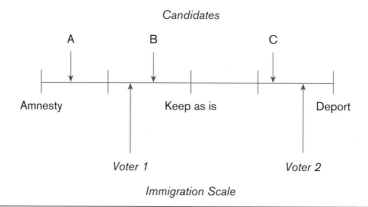

FIGURE 2-1 ■ Proximities on Immigration Issues

Proximities on Immigration Issues

means not only taking or moving to positions as close as possible to those of the average or typical voter (the so-called median voter) but also, if and when necessary, obscuring one's true position (that is, following a strategy of ambiguity).[21] Figure 2-1, for instance, shows that Voter 1's position is closest to Candidate B's; therefore, Voter 1 would presumably vote for that person. Similarly, Voter 2 would prefer Candidate C. Note also that Candidate A could attract Voter 1's support by moving closer to the middle, perhaps by campaigning on an "amnesty-only-for-children-of-illegal-immigrants" platform.

The proximity theory has many of the characteristics of an empirical theory. Note that it does not take a stance for or against one side or the other in the immigration debate. Rather, it explains why things happen as they do, and it offers specific and testable predictions. It is also an implicitly causal theory in that it hypothesizes that the desire to maximize utility "causes" voters to vote for specific candidates. It is general since it claims to apply to any election in any place at any time. As such, it provides a much more sweeping explanation of voting than a theory that uses time- and place-bounded terms such as "the 2014 guber-natorial election in Pennsylvania." In addition, it provides a parsimonious or relatively simple account of candidate choice. It does not invoke additional explanatory factors such as psychological or mental states, social class membership, current economic conditions, or even partisanship to describe the voting act. Most important, although the proximity theory rests on considerable formal (and abstract) economic and decision-making reasoning, it puts itself on the line by making specific empirical predictions, which can be checked by asking voters (1) their positions on immigration and (2) how they voted.

As a theory, it incorporates or uses numerous primitive or undefined terms such as *issue*, *candidate*, and *utility*. These words and concepts may have well-accepted dictionary meanings, but the theory itself takes their common understanding for granted. When a theory is challenged, part of the dispute might involve slightly divergent interpretations of these terms. At the same time, the theory makes explicit various other assumptions. It assumes, among other things, that a researcher can place individuals on issue dimensions, that people occupy these positions for reasonably long time periods, that voters are rational in that they maximize utility, and that candidates have objective positions on these issues.[22] Moreover, by assumption, certain possibilities are not considered. The theory does not delve into the question of whether or not a person holds a "correct" position on the scale, given his or her objective interests. Finally, to test the proximity or spatial idea, researchers assume that one can assign individuals meaningful spatial positions by asking certain kinds of questions on surveys or polls.[23] This may be a perfectly reasonable assumption (we touch on that matter in chapter 10), but it is an assumption nevertheless. Still, spatial modelers, as those who use proximity theory are called, go to great lengths to define and explain key concepts. How *distance* is defined is a serious matter because different definitions can lead to different substantive conclusions.[24]

The Explanatory Range of Theories

Theories are sometimes described by their explanatory range, or the breadth of the phenomena they purport to explain. Usually, one does not have a theory of "why Donald Trump won the election in 2016." (It is, of course, possible to find several theories that account for this particular outcome. But note that the 2016 election results are an instance, or "token," of the kind of event with which these theories deal.) Instead, a good theory of electoral outcomes presumably pertains not only to a specific presidential contest but also to other presidential elections or other types of elections in other times and places.

In the social sciences, so-called narrow-gauge or middle-range theories pertain to limited classes of events or behaviors, such as a theory of voting behavior or a theory about the role of revolution in political development.[25] Thus, a theory of voting may explain voter turnout by proposing factors that affect people's perceptions of the costs and benefits of voting: socioeconomic class, degree of partisanship, the ease of registration and voting laws, choices among candidates, availability of election news in the media, and so forth.[26] Global or broad-range theories, by contrast, claim to describe and account for an entire body of human behavior. A theory of federalism might explain why subnational governments do not adopt redistributive programs (those that redistribute wealth from wealthier residents to poorer ones) as much as one might expect based on need.[27] A really general theory, for example, might attempt to account for increases or decreases in economic inequality in any society at any time.[28] In short, theories play a prominent role in natural and social sciences because they provide general accounts of phenomena.[29] Other things being equal, the broader the range of the things to be explained, the more valuable the theory.

A BRIEF OVERVIEW OF THE EMPIRICAL RESEARCH PROCESS

So what exactly is the empirical or scientific research process? In reality, no scientist in the field or laboratory adheres to a prescribed set of steps like someone following a script. Scientists rely not just on formal procedures but also on intuition, imagination, and even luck at times. Nevertheless, we may conceptualize what they do by identifying the underlying logic of their activities. Here is an idealization of a scientific research program.

Development of an Idea to Investigate or a Problem to Solve

A scientist gets topics from any number of sources, including literature about a subject, a general observation, an intuition (or hunch), the existence of conflicts or anomalies in reported research findings, and the implications of an established theory. For example, a report on income inequality may indicate that it varies considerably from country to country or that it is increasing. A logical response would be to ask why. As another instance, consider newspaper accounts that suggest that evangelical Christians tend to support conservative candidates because of "moral values." Several research questions are raised by these accounts: Do evangelicals base their choices of candidates on their proximity to candidates' positions on moral issues while other voters base their choices on other types of issues such as economic issues? Is turnout among evangelicals higher in elections where there are distinct differences between candidates on moral issues than in elections where the differences are small?

Hypothesis Formation

After selecting a topic, an investigator tries to translate the idea or problem into a series of specific hypotheses. As we see in chapter 4, hypotheses are tentative statements that, if confirmed, show how and why one thing is related to another or why a condition comes into existence. These statements have to be worded unambiguously and in a way that their specific claims can be evaluated by commonly accepted procedures. After all, one of the requirements of science is for others to be able to independently corroborate a discovery. If assertions are not completely transparent, how can someone else verify them? In the preceding example, we might hypothesize that evangelical Christians are more likely than others to base their vote on candidates' positions on moral issues.

"Data" Collection

This is where the rubber meets the road: the essence of science comes in the empirical testing of hypotheses through the collection and analysis of data. Consider the case of religion and voting just mentioned. We need to define clearly the concepts of *moral values* and *evangelical Christian*. We might, for instance, tentatively identify evangelicals as people who adhere to certain Christian denominations and moral values as attitudes toward abortion and same-sex marriage. A researcher could write a series of questions to be administered in a survey or a poll to elicit this information. Only when concepts are defined and decisions made about how to measure them can data collection and analysis begin.

Interpretation and Decision

At some point, the investigator has to determine whether or not the observed results are consistent with the hypotheses. Though simple in principle, judging how well data support scientific hypotheses is usually not an easy matter. Suppose, for example, we find that 75 percent of evangelical Christians opposed same-sex marriage and 90 percent of these individuals voted for a House candidate in 2014 who opposed same-sex marriage. So far, so good. But suppose, in addition, that 70 percent of nonevangelicals also opposed same-sex marriage and that more than 90 percent of these people also voted for House candidates opposed to same-sex marriage in the same election. It appears that attitudes might be affecting voting, but the data do not necessarily establish a connection between religious preference and whether or not votes are based on moral issues. Weighing quantitative or statistical evidence requires expertise, practice, and knowledge of the subject matter, plus good judgment (and this skill is often difficult to teach). Still, chapters in this book are devoted to showing ways to make valid inferences about tenability of empirical hypotheses.

Modification and Extension

Depending on the outcome of the test, one can tentatively accept, abandon, or modify the hypothesis. If the results are favorable, it might be possible to derive new predictions to investigate. If, however, the data do not or only very weakly support the hypothesis, it will be necessary to modify or discard it. Let us stress here that negative results—that is, those that do not support a particular hypothesis—can still be both interesting and beneficial.[30] As we suggested earlier, some scholars, such as Popper, believe that science advances by disproving claims, not by accepting them. Consequently, a valuable contribution to science can come from disconfirming widely held beliefs, and the only way to do that is to replicate or reinvestigate the research upon which the beliefs rest. The key is not so much the result of a hypothesis test but how substantively important the hypothesis is to begin with.

REACTIONS TO THE EMPIRICAL APPROACH: PRACTICAL OBJECTIONS

Empirical research problems arise because many important concepts are abstract or have many meanings or are value-laden. Chapter 1 showed that a concept such as "talking like a man" needs to be defined carefully and clearly, and that finding an adequate definition of "economic inequality" can be difficult. Should we be looking at individuals or households? Should we use annual income—calculated before taxes, after taxes, or after adding to individual or household income publicly supplied in-kind benefits such as health care or job retraining? Or should we try to measure net wealth (assets minus debts)? The following chapters take up some of these questions.

Furthermore, political scientists must face the fact that human behavior is complex, perhaps even more complex than the subject matter of other sciences (genes, subatomic particles, insects, and so on). Complexity has been a significant obstacle to the discovery of general theories that accurately explain and predict almost every kind of behavior. After all, developing a theory with broad applicability requires the identification and specification of innumerable variables and the linkages among them. Consequently, when a broad theory is proposed, it can be attacked on the grounds that it is too simple or that too many exceptions to it exist. Certainly, to date no empirically verified generalizations in political science match the simplicity and explanatory power of Einstein's famous equation $E = mc^2$.[31]

There are still other obstacles. The data needed to test explanations and theories may be extremely hard to obtain. Indeed, often the potentially most informative data are totally unavailable. People with the needed information, for example, may not want to release it for political or personal reasons. Pollsters, for instance, find refusal to answer certain questions, such as those designed to measure attitudes toward ethnic groups, to be a major problem in gauging public opinion. Similarly, some experiments require manipulation of people. But since humans are the subjects, the researchers must contend with ethical considerations that might preclude them from obtaining all the information they want. Asking certain questions can interfere with privacy rights, and exposing subjects to certain stimuli might put the participants at physical or emotional risk. Tempting someone to commit a crime, to take an obvious case, might tell a social scientist a lot about adherence to the law but would be unacceptable nevertheless.

Self-Reflection and Individuality

Like any other organisms, humans are aware of their surroundings. They have the additional ability to empathize with others and frequently attempt to read others' minds. As John Medearis put it, "human beings—individually, but especially jointly—are self-interpreting and reflective, capable of assigning meanings to their actions and revising these meanings recursively."[32] Observations of this sort led many social scientists and philosophers to question whether or not the scientific method can be applied to the study of something as intrinsically language based as politics. This doubt appears later in the chapter, when we discuss interpretation versus explanation. In the meantime, let us point to a practical problem. Since humans are self-reflective and empathetic creatures, they often anticipate a researcher's goals and adjust their actions accordingly (e.g., "The investigator seems to favor immigration reform, so I will too").

When it comes to studying political behavior such as voting or decision making, another difficulty arises. Many experiments in science assume that the entities under investigation are for all intents and purposes identical and, hence, can be interchanged without fear of compromising the conclusion. An iron ion (Fe^+) from one source is as good as another from somewhere else (no matter where in the universe) when it comes to studying iron's reaction with oxygen. But can the same be said of humans? Consider a political scientist who wants to investigate the effects of negative campaign advertising on attitudes. Suppose Jane and Mary are subjects in a study. We cannot assume that they will react to the experimental stimuli exactly the same way, even though they are the same age, gender, political persuasion, and so forth.

Social scientists have to get around this problem by using groups or samples of individuals and then examining the *average* effect of the stimulus. Any generalization that results has the form: given subjects with characteristics A, B, . . . , X (the stimulus) *on average* affects Y (the response) by *approximately N* units. In other words, sometimes the basic units under the scientist's microscope can be considered pure, even if they are complex molecules, but not so in political science. The objects political scientists study are multifaceted and conscious beings with volition of their own who often change opinions and behaviors; thus, statements about them must necessarily be tentative, general, and time bound.

Finally, there is the inescapable subjectivity of politics. We provide an example that bedevils research into the studies of power. Most political scientists would agree that, if an oligarchy exists in the United States, it should at a minimum make or heavily influence key policy decisions. The problem is, how does one objectively identify "key" policies? Should the choice be left to the judgment of the researcher or knowledgeable/informed experts? Or are there concrete indicators or measures of importance? Suppose we want to classify decision A as "important." On what grounds do we make the assignment? The number of people A affects? Its cost? The number of times it is mentioned in the press? Its length in legal codes? The number of times it is litigated? Any or all of these might be useful. But for a variety of reasons, none of these may capture the significance (or lack of significance) of a decision. Importance often comes from how people interpret or understand policy A, and understanding of this sort, many assert, lies beyond the scope of empirical sciences.[33]

All of these claims about the difficulty of studying political behavior scientifically may have merit. Yet they can be overstated. Consider, for example, that scientists studying natural phenomena encounter many of the same problems. Physicists cannot directly observe elementary particles such as quarks. Nor can astronomers and geologists carry out experiments on most of the phenomena of greatest interest to them. Indeed, they cannot even visit many of the places they study most intensively, like other planets or the center of the Earth. And what can be more complex than biological organisms and their components, which consist of thousands of compounds and chemical interactions? Stated quite simply, it is in no way clear that severe practical problems distinguish political science from any of the other sciences.

Is Political Science Trivial or Irrelevant?

The empirical approach in political science, with its advent in earnest in the 1960s, seemed to bring with it all the accoutrements of rigorous natural sciences: equations and mathematical models, statistical analysis, instrumentation and quantification, computers and electronic databases, esoteric concepts (e.g., "multidimensional issue spaces"). Yet practically from the moment the empirical or scientific perspective arrived on the scene, doubters and skeptics appeared. In the late 1960s and later in 2000, well-publicized "revolts" against hard-core empiricism took place. Among other complaints, critics pointed to the trivial nature of some of the "scientific" findings and applications. Common sense would have told us the same thing, they argued. Of course, as we explained earlier, there is a difference between intuition or common sense and scientific knowledge. To build a solid base for further research and accumulation of scientific knowledge in politics, commonsense knowledge must be verified empirically and, as is frequently the case, discarded when wrong. Still, "scientism" left many political scientists dismayed.

A more serious criticism of the scientific study of politics is that it leads to a failure to focus enough scholarly research attention on important social issues and problems. Some critics contend that, in the effort to be scientific and precise, political science overlooks the moral and policy issues that make the discipline relevant to the real world. Studies rarely address the implications of research findings for important public policy choices or political reform. In other words, the quest for a scientific knowledge of politics has led to a focus on topics that are quantifiable and relatively easy to verify empirically but that are not related to significant, practical, and relevant societal concerns.[34] A related criticism is that researchers are using increasingly sophisticated statistical methods to investigate politics. Understanding these methods, and hence being able to discuss results, is beyond the reach of many political scientists, not to mention students and the general public. This has deleterious effects on the level of discourse about what is known about important political and social issues.[35] These considerations take us back to our umpires. Can researchers really emulate Umpire 2 (the strict empiricist) who claims to "call 'em as they *are*"? Many think not. Political scientists, having been exposed to decades of philosophizing about limitations and problems of the "scientific method," probably now admit to being like Umpire 1 and call balls and strikes as they *see* them. This doesn't mean their research is totally subjective or a matter of opinion; but it is, they realize, so contingent on time, place, language, and culture that finding scientific laws and truths of politics is problematic. Instead of calling them hard-nosed empiricists, we might better call today's political scientists modest or constrained empiricists.

COMPETING POINTS OF VIEW

As widely accepted and useful as science has become in modern times, serious philosophers and social scientists have challenged these premises. We cannot explain all of their objections here, but the essence of their argument is that certain aspects of human life are simply not amenable to systematic and objective analysis. More important, an uncritical faith in realism, objectivity, and material causality is unwarranted. We concentrate on two points:

1. Human actions cannot be explained scientifically but must be *interpreted* from the point of view of the actors. Meaning and understanding are the proper goals.

2. Social scientists have to realize that the world, far from having an independent existence that they observe directly, is partly *constructed* by observers themselves.

To oversimplify, we shall say these two viewpoints constitute "nonempiricism."

HELPFUL HINTS
ASSUMPTIONS OF EMPIRICAL RESEARCH

- An empiricist ("I-call-'em-as-they-are" umpire) makes assumptions about methodology.

- *Realism*: There is a real world that exists independently of observers. (It's there even if we aren't there to see it.)

- *Materialism*: Only concrete and observable (if only indirectly) entities have causal efficacy.

- *Denial of supernatural causes*: Explanations of phenomena based on mysterious, unknowable, unobservable, "hidden" forces are unacceptable.

- *Regularity*: Natural phenomena (human behavior and institutions) exhibit regularities and patterns that can be revealed by reason and observation.

- *Verification and falsification*: Statements about the world must be verified or falsified by

experience or data. (Don't take anything on faith alone.)

- *Irrelevance of preferences*: To the maximum extent, one's values and biases should not affect the decision to reject or accept an empirical claim.

- *Theory and causal explanation*: The goal of science is to create general, verified explanatory theories (even laws).

Interpretation

Some people question the empirical strategy because the subject matter, human institutions and activities, differs from the behavior of material objects such as atoms or stars, and these differences raise all sorts of complexities. One indicator of the inapplicability is that progress in developing and testing contingent causal laws has been agonizingly slow.[36] Moreover, both the methods and the content of the discipline have not come close to the exactitude and elegant sophistication of sciences such as biology or physics, and, consequently, nowhere can we find empirical generalizations with the level of precision and confirmation enjoyed by, say, the theories of relativity and evolution.

Skeptics argue that there are good reasons for this outcome. Since politics inescapably involves **actions**—that is, behavior that is done for reasons—and not mere physical movement, analyzing it brings up challenges not encountered in the natural sciences. Opponents of the empirical approach claim that scientific methods do not explain nearly as much about behavior as their practitioners think. The problem is that to understand human behavior, one must try to see the world the way individuals do. And doing so requires empathy, or the ability to identify and in some sense experience the subjective moods or feelings or thoughts of those being studied. Instead of acting as outside, objective observers, we need to "see" how individuals themselves view their actions. Only by reaching this level of understanding can we hope to answer "why" questions such as "Why did John still vote in the last election even though he was bombarded by countless attack ads on television, the internet, radio . . . everywhere he turned?" The answers require the interpretation of behavior, not its scientific explanation in terms of general laws. In short, **interpretation** means decoding verbal and physical actions, which is a much different task than proposing and testing hypotheses.

Given this way of looking at the research task, some social scientists advocated stressing the interpretation or empathetic understanding of actions and institutions. One of the earliest and best-known proponents of this methodology was Clifford Geertz, an anthropologist, who felt that "man is an animal suspended in webs of significance he himself has spun. I take culture to be those webs, and the analysis of it to be therefore not an experimental science in search of law but an interpretive one in search of meaning."[37] As a simple example of the difference between empirical and interpretative approaches, take journalist James O'Toole's analysis of a close Pennsylvania U.S. Senate election in 2010: "it's now a pretty close race, according to the polls and the body language of the campaigns."[38] Here he relies on both an empirical tool (polling) and intuition (the "body language of the campaigns"). Those who closely follow electoral politics would perhaps agree that a minimum of interpretation and subjective analysis is always helpful.

Another way of looking at interpretation is to consider the concept of **social facts**. What exactly are things like political parties, elections, laws, and administrative regulations? In what sense are they real? They do not have the same kind of material existence as atoms, bacteria, and mountains, but have an entirely subjective existence *only* in the minds of people living in a particular culture. One philosopher remarks that "minds create institutions. There would be no money or marriage or private property without human minds to create these institutions."[39] How, then, should they be studied? The sociologist Émile Durkheim told his students to take them seriously: "the first and most basic rule [of social inquiry] is *to consider social facts as things.*"[40] And many political scientists almost instinctively adhere to that principle. Nonetheless, the notion that much of what is studied is socially constructed raises some thorny epistemological issues.

Constructionism and Critical Theory

Most political scientists take reality pretty much as a given. That is, they posit that the objects they study—elections, wars, constitutions, government agencies—have an existence independent of observers and can be studied more or less objectively. But an alternative perspective, called the social construction of reality or **constructionism**,[41] casts doubt on this uncritical, perhaps blasé attitude. According to constructionism, humans do not simply discover knowledge of the real world through neutral processes, such as experimentation or unbiased observation; rather, they *create* the reality they analyze. This position is perhaps another way of saying, "Facts do not speak for themselves but are always interpreted or constructed by humans in specific historical times and settings." This stance may be likened to Umpire 3, who you may recall says the phenomena under investigation "ain't *nothing* until I call 'em" as though the very act of umpiring creates its own reality.

One version of this position admits that entities (for example, molecules, planets) exist separately from anyone's thoughts about them, but it also insists that much of what people take for granted as being "real" or "true" of the world is built from learning and interaction with others and does not have an existence apart from human thought.[42] Consider the term *Democratic Party.* Instead of having an independent, material existence like an electron or a strand of DNA, a political party exists only because citizens behave as if it exists. This means that two individuals who come from different social, historical, and cultural backgrounds may not comprehend and respond to the term in the same way. What is important in studying, say, individuals' responses to Democratic candidates is fathoming their personal beliefs and attitudes about the party.

Constructionist thinking now plays a strong role in international relations theory, where a concept such as *anarchy* is not considered a "given and immutable" cause of the behavior of states (for example, their desire for security through power politics). Rather, concepts like this one have to be understood in terms of what actors (individuals, states) make of them.[43]

The constructionist viewpoint, which comes in innumerable varieties, challenges the idea of an objective epistemology, or theory of knowledge. Such ideas, however, are of a deeply methodological nature and raise deep philosophical issues that go well beyond the task of describing the empirical methods used in the discipline.[44] We thus acknowledge that the scientific study of politics is controversial but nevertheless maintain that the procedures we describe in the chapters that follow are widely accepted and can in many circumstances lead to valuable understandings of political processes and behaviors. Moreover, they have greatly shaped the research agenda and teaching of the discipline, as can be seen by looking at the evolution of the field in the twentieth century.

The emergence and domination of the empirical perspective have also brought about renewed interest in normative philosophical questions of "what ought to be" rather than "what is."[45] Part of the discipline has become receptive to variations of **critical theory**, or the belief that a proper goal of social science is to critique and improve society (by making it more just and humane) rather than merely understand or explain what is going on. Critical theorists feel, in other words, that simply analyzing a polity as it is amounts to a tacit endorsement of its institutions and the distribution of power. Contrary to the idea that science should be value-free, critical theorists argue that proposing and working for reforms are legitimate activities for the social sciences. They therefore analyze institutions, practices, ideologies, and beliefs not only for their surface characteristics but also for their "hidden meanings" and implications for behavior.

Take, for example, the statement "I'm just not interested in politics."[46] An empirical political scientist might take this simply as a cut-and-dried case of apathy. He or she might then look for variables (e.g., age, gender, ethnicity) associated with "not interested" responses on questionnaires. A critical theorist, by contrast, might ask, "Does this person really have *no* interest in current events? After all, isn't everyone affected by most political outcomes, like decisions about taxes, war and peace, and the environment, and thus in fact *have* an interest in politics? So perhaps we have a case of, say, 'false consciousness,' and it is crucial to uncover the reasons for lack of awareness of one's 'real' stake in politics. Is the indifference a matter of choice, or does it stem from the (adverse) effects of the educational system, the mass media, modern campaigning, or some other source?"

Here is another case. An important challenge to research in political science (as well as in other social science disciplines, such as sociology) has come from feminist scholars. Among the criticisms raised is that "the nature of political action and the scope of political research have been defined in ways that, in particular, exclude *women as women* [emphasis added] from politics."[47] Accordingly, "what a feminist political science must do is develop a new vocabulary of politics so that it can express the specific and different ways in which women have wielded power, been in authority, practiced citizenship, and understood freedom."[48] Even short of arguing that political science concepts and theories have been developed from a male-only perspective, it is all too easy to point to examples of gender bias in political science research. Examples of such bias include failing to focus on policy issues of importance to women, assuming that findings apply to everyone when the population studied was predominantly male, and using biased wording in survey questions.[49]

A related complaint is that political science in the past ignored the needs, interests, and views of the poor, the lower class, and the powerless and served mainly to reinforce the belief that existing institutions were as good as they could be. Those who agree with this complaint are called "critical theorists." Concerns about the proper scope and direction of political science have not abated, although nearly all researchers and teachers accept the need to balance the scientific approach with consideration of practical problems and moral issues.[50]

Let's wrap up our discussion so far before returning to the all-important question: What difference does all this philosophizing make? Table 2-1 lists some of the key differences between what we have been calling the empirical and nonempirical schools.

TABLE 2-1   ■   Methodological Perspectives in Political Science

	Nonempirical	Empirical
Goals	To understand behavior To interpret actions	Causal explanations and predictions of individual and institutional behaviors General theory and laws Information of practical use "Value-free" knowledge
Assumptions	Social facts (at least) are "constructed." Institutions are social creations. Objective observation is not generally possible because our very senses are affected by culturally defined and imposed prior beliefs. Totally value-free research is impossible.	Realism (appearance and reality are the same). Independent, objective observation is possible. Behavior and, implicitly, institutions exhibit regularities. Claims about the real world must be verified. Attitudes (values, biases, beliefs) must not affect observation and analysis. There are no causeless effects.
Basic tool kit	Qualitative	Primarily quantitative
Methods	Qualitative analysis (e.g., ethnography, content and document analysis, study of discourse) Case studies and comparisons	Field studies and observation, content and document analysis Case studies and comparisons Experiments and field experiments Mathematical models Surveys Statistical analysis of data Simulations

	Nonempirical	Empirical
Objections	Observation is impressionistic, subjective, and nonsystematic. Knowledge is "nontransmissible." Findings are tainted by the investigator's values and biases.	Takes "politics out of political science." Concentration on formalism, quantitative measurement, and mathematical analysis leads to trivial and practically meaningless results.
Alleged biases	Conclusions are affected by political and social ideologies.	Inherently favors the status quo and existing power structures.

Source: This table is based partly on tables in Colin Hay, *Political Analysis: A Critical Introduction* (New York: Palgrave, 2002), chap. 1.

CONCLUSION

In this chapter, we described the characteristics of scientific knowledge and the scientific method. We presented reasons why political scientists are attempting to become more scientific in their research and discussed some of the difficulties associated with empirical political science. We also touched on questions about the value of the scientific approach to the study of politics. Despite these difficulties and uncertainties, the empirical approach is widely embraced, and students of politics need to be familiar with it. In chapter 3, we begin to examine how to develop a strategy for investigating a general topic or question about some political phenomenon scientifically.

TERMS INTRODUCED

Actions. Human behavior done for a reason.   39

Constructionism. An approach to knowledge that asserts humans actually construct—through their social interactions and cultural and historical practices—many of the facts they take for granted as having an independent, objective, or material reality.   40

Critical theory. The philosophical stance that disciplines such as political science should assess society critically and seek to improve it, not merely study it objectively.   41

Cumulative. Characteristic of scientific knowledge; new substantive findings and research techniques are built upon those of previous studies.   29

Deduction. The process of reasoning from general theory to making predictions about events or behavior in specific situations.   31

Empiricism. Relying on observation to verify propositions.   25

Explanatory. Characteristic of scientific knowledge; signifying that a conclusion can be derived from a set of general propositions and specific initial considerations; providing a systematic, empirically verified understanding of why a phenomenon occurs as it does.   29

Falsifiability. A property of a statement or hypothesis such that it can (in principle, at least) be rejected in the face of contravening evidence.   27

General. A characteristic of scientific knowledge is that it be applicable to many rather than just a few cases.   29

Induction. The process of reasoning from specific observations to theories about behaviors or events in general.   31

Interpretation. Philosophical approach to the study of human behavior that claims that one must understand the way individuals see their world in order to truly understand their behavior or actions; philosophical objection to the empirical approach to political science.   39

Nonnormative knowledge. Knowledge concerned not with evaluation or prescription but with factual or objective determinations.   27

Normative knowledge. Knowledge that is evaluative, value-laden, and concerned with prescribing what ought to be.   27

Parsimony. The principle that among explanations or theories with equal degrees of confirmation, the simplest—the one based on the fewest assumptions and explanatory factors—is to be preferred; sometimes known as Ockham's razor.   30

Social facts. Values and institutions that have a subjective existence in the minds of people living in a particular culture.   40

Theory. A statement or series of related statements that organize, explain, and predict phenomena.   31

Transmissible. Characteristic of scientific knowledge; indicates that the methods used in making scientific discoveries are made explicit so that others can analyze and replicate findings.   27

Verification. The process of confirming or establishing a statement with evidence.   26

SUGGESTED READINGS

Box-Steffensmeier, Janet, Henry Brady, and David Collier. *The Oxford Handbook of Political Methodology.* New York: Oxford University Press, 2008.

Brady, Henry E., and David Collier, eds. *Rethinking Social Inquiry: Diverse Tools, Shared Standards.* Lanham, MD: Rowman and Littlefield, 2004.

Elster, Jon. *Nuts and Bolts for the Social Sciences.* Cambridge, UK: Cambridge University Press, 1990.

Hay, Colin. *Political Analysis: A Critical Introduction.* New York: Palgrave, 2002.

Hindmoor, Andrew. *Rational Choice.* New York: Palgrave Macmillan, 2006.

King, Gary, Robert O. Keohane, and Sidney Verba. *Designing Social Inquiry: Scientific Inference in Qualitative Research.* Princeton, NJ: Princeton University Press, 1994.

Kuhn, Thomas. *The Structure of Scientific Revolutions.* 2nd ed. Chicago: University of Chicago Press, 1971.

Nielsen, Joyce McCarl, ed. *Feminist Research Methods: Exemplary Readings in the Social Sciences.* Boulder, CO: Westview, 1990.

Rosenberg, Alexander. *The Philosophy of Social Science.* 3rd ed. Boulder, CO: Westview, 2007.

Silver, Brian L. "I Believe." In *The Ascent of Science*, 11–28. New York: Oxford University Press, 1998.

NOTES

1. Jeffrey A. Winters and Benjamin I. Page, "Oligarchy in the United States?," *Perspective on Politics* 7 (December 2009): 731–51.

2. Ibid., 744 (emphasis in original). Also see Jeffrey A. Winters, *Oligarch* (New York: Cambridge University Press, 2014).

3. During his Senate confirmation hearing, Chief Justice John Roberts came close to capturing the essence of the empirical viewpoint when he told the committee, "Judges and justices are servants of the law, not the other way around. Judges are like umpires. Umpires don't make the rules; they apply them." He added, "My job is to call balls and strikes and not to pitch or bat." CNN.com, September 12, 2005. Accessed June 3, 2015. Available at http://www.cnn.com/2005/POLITICS/09/12/roberts.statement. In other words, judges "see" the law and the facts of a case as they are. Judiciary Committee chair Joe Biden, however, challenged Justice Roberts on his umpire analogy: "So, as much as I respect your metaphor, it's very apt, because you get to determine the strike zone. . . . Your strike zone . . . may be very different than another judge's view." *Washington Post*, "Transcript: Day Two of the Roberts Confirmation Hearings," September 13, 2005. Accessed January 10, 2015. Available at http://www.washingtonpost.com/wp-dyn/content/article/2005/09/13/AR2005091300979.html. In other words, the senator believes judges may act like Umpire 3, who in a sense "constructs" reality in his own way.

4. It might be more accurate to use the words "scientific method*s*," since to define what is and what is not science is a notoriously tricky task, and not everyone agrees on an exact definition.

5. Those who follow the philosophy of social science, or epistemology, know that naming the sides in these methodological debates is virtually impossible. Someone we might label a *nonempiricist* might very well foreswear the tag. We are just attempting to sort out tendencies.

6. See James Mahoney, "After KKV: The New Methodology of Qualitative Research," *World Politics* 62, no. 1 (January 2010): 120–47; Henry E. Brady and David Collier, *Rethinking Social Inquiry: Diverse Tools, Shared Standards*, 2nd ed. (Lanham, MD: Rowman and Littlefield, 2010).

7. Careful readers will note that we are combining all sorts of activities under one label. Specialists in one method or another often call themselves different things to emphasize the kind of research they do. For instance, those who rely on deductive reasoning and do not spend much time observing the world often

refer to themselves as "formal modelers" or "rational choice theorists."

8. Whether or not political science or any social science can find causal laws is very much a contentious issue in philosophy. See, for instance, Alexander Rosenberg, *The Philosophy of Social Science*, 3rd ed. (Boulder, CO: Westview, 2007).

9. Ibid., 107.

10. The most ardent proponent of the idea that science really amounts to an effort to falsify (not prove) hypotheses and theories is Karl Popper. See, for example, *The Logic of Scientific Discovery* (New York: Basic Books, 1959).

11. Alan C. Isaak, *Scope and Methods of Political Science*, 4th ed. (Homewood, IL: Dorsey, 1985), 30.

12. Ibid., 31.

13. APSA Committee on Professional Ethics, Rights and Freedoms, *A Guide to Professional Ethics in Political Science*, 2nd ed., rev. (Washington, DC: American Political Science Association, 2012). Accessed February 11, 2019. Available at https://www.apsanet.org/portals/54/Files/Publications/APSAEthicsGuide2012.pdf.

14. For example, see Jeffrey C. Isaac, "For a More *Public* Political Science," *Perspectives on Politics* 13, no. 2 (2015): 269–83; Kristen Renwick Monroe, "The Rush to Transparency: DA-RT and the Potential Dangers for Qualitative Research," *Perspectives on Politics* 16, no. 1 (2018): 141–48. The January 2014 (vol. 47, no. 1) issue of *PS: Political Science & Politics* contains a symposium on openness in political science.

15. It may be tempting to think that historians are interested in describing and explaining only unique, one-time events, such as the outbreak of a particular war. This is not the case, however. Many historians search for generalizations that account for several specific events. Some even claim to have discovered the "laws of history."

16. Isaak, *Scope and Methods*, 103.

17. Many varieties of this theory exist, but they share the components presented here.

18. Anthony Downs, an economist, provided one of the first explications of the theory in *An Economic Theory of Democracy* (New York: Harper & Row, 1957). His ideas in turn flowed from earlier economic analyses. See, for example, Harold Hotelling, "Stability in

Competition," *Economic Journal* 39, no. 153 (1929): 41–57. Accessed February 11, 2019. Available at https://www.jstor.org/stable/2224214.

19. See James Enelow and Melvin Hinch, *The Spatial Theory of Voting: An Introduction* (New York: Cambridge University Press, 1984).

20. This expectation assumes that immigration is important to the voter—that there is not some other issue that is more important that may cause the voter to prefer another candidate.

21. Kenneth Shepsle, "The Strategy of Ambiguity: Uncertainty and Electoral Competition," *American Political Science Review* 66, no. 2 (1972): 555–68.

22. As an example, see Anders Westholm, "Distance versus Direction: The Illusory Defeat of the Proximity Theory of Electoral Choice," *American Political Science Review* 91, no. 4 (1997): 870.

23. Here is an example: "Please look at . . . the booklet. Some people believe that we should spend much less money for defense. Suppose these people are at one end of a scale, at point 1. Others feel that defense spending should be greatly increased. Suppose these people are at the other end, at point 7. And, of course, some other people have opinions somewhere in between, at points 2, 3, 4, 5 or 6 . . . Where would you place YOURSELF on this scale, or haven't you thought much about it?" See variable v3142 in the 2004 American National Election Study. Accessed February 11, 2019. Available at the Survey Documentation and Analysis, University of California–Berkeley, website: http://sda.berkeley.edu/D3/NES2004public/Doc/nes0.htm.

24. The conceptualization of distance and other matters related to the proximity theory are debated in Westholm, "Distance versus Direction," 865–73; and Stuart Elaine Macdonald, George Rabinowitz, and Ola Listhaug, "On Attempting to Rehabilitate the Proximity Model: Sometimes the Patient Just Can't Be Helped," *Journal of Politics* 60, no. 3 (1998): 653–90.

25. A good example is Theda Skocpol, *States and Social Revolutions: A Comparative Analysis of France, Russia, and China* (New York: Cambridge University Press, 1979).

26. See Raymond E. Wolfinger and Steven J. Rosenstone, *Who Votes?* (New Haven, CT: Yale University Press, 1980).

27. See Paul E. Peterson, *The Price of Federalism* (Washington, DC: Brookings Institution Press, 1995).

28. A good example is Thomas Picketty, *Capitalism in the Twenty-First Century* (Boston: Belknap/Harvard, 2014).

29. Isaak, *Scope and Methods*, 167.

30. An often-remarked-on characteristic of scholarly journals is that they tend to report mostly positive findings. An article that shows "X is related to Y" may be more likely to be accepted for publication than one that asserts "X is *not* related to Y." Whether or not a "negative result" makes a significant contribution to knowledge depends on the importance of the original claim. Suppose that a team of psychologists found that "love and marriage" really do *not* "go together." That would be worth publishing.

31. For further discussion of complete and partial explanations, see Isaak, *Scope and Methods*, 143.

32. John Medearis, "Review of *Perestroika! The Raucous Rebellion in Political Science* by Kristen Renwick Monroe," *Perspectives on Politics* 4, no. 3 (2006): 577.

33. For an effort to objectively measure policy importance, see David Mayhew, *Divided We Govern: Party Control, Lawmaking, and Investigations, 1946–2002*, 2nd ed. (New Haven, CT: Yale University Press, 2005).

34. See Charles A. McCoy and John Playford, eds., *Apolitical Politics: A Critique of Behavioralism* (New York: Thomas Y. Crowell, 1967).

35. See Isaak, "For a More *Public* Political Science."

36. See Alexander Rosenberg, *The Philosophy of Social Science*, 3rd ed. (Boulder, CO: Westview, 2007).

37. Clifford Geertz, *The Interpretation of Cultures* (New York: Basic Books, 1973), 5; see also following discussion, pp. 6–7.

38. "Federal Spending Front and Center in Pa., Wash. Senate Races," *PBS NewsHour*, October 26, 2010. Accessed February 11, 2019. Available at https://www.pbs.org/newshour/show/federal-spending-front-and-center-in-pa-wash-senate-races.

39. Colin McGinn, "Is Just Thinking Enough?," review of *Making the Social World: The Structure of Human Civilization*, by John R. Searle, *New York Review of Books*, November 11, 2010. Accessed February 11, 2019. Available at http://www.nybooks.com/articles/archives/2010/nov/11/just-thinking-enough/.

40. Émile Durkheim, *The Rules of Sociological Method and Selected Texts on Sociology and Method*, ed. Steven Lukes (New York: Free Press, 1982), 60 (emphasis in original).

41. The term *constructionism* encompasses an enormous variety of philosophical perspectives, the description of which goes far beyond the purposes of this book. The seminal work that brought the ideas into sociology and from there into political science is Peter L. Berger and Thomas Luckmann, *The Social Construction of Reality* (New York: Doubleday, 1966). An excellent but challenging analysis of constructionism is Ian Hacking, *The Social Construction of What?* (Cambridge, MA: Harvard University Press, 1999). Equally important, members of this school have widely varying opinions about the place of empiricism in social research. Many constructivists feel their position is perfectly consistent with the scientific study of politics; others do not.

42. See John R. Searle, *The Construction of Social Reality* (New York: Free Press, 1995).

43. Alexander Wendt, "Anarchy Is What States Make of It," *International Organization* 46, no. 2 (1992): 391–425.

44. For an excellent collection of articles about the pros and cons of studying human behavior scientifically, see Michael Martin and Lee C. Anderson, eds., *Readings in the Philosophy of Social Science* (Cambridge, MA: MIT Press, 1996).

45. Isaak, *Scope and Methods*, 45.

46. This example is based on an article by Isaac D. Balbus, "The Concept of Interest in Pluralist and Marxian Analysis," *Politics & Society* 1, no. 2 (1971): 151–77.

47. Kathleen B. Jones and Anna G. Jonasdottir, "Introduction: Gender as an Analytic Category in Political Science," in *The Political Interests of Gender*, ed. Kathleen B. Jones and Anna G. Jonasdottir (Beverly Hills, CA: Sage, 1988), 2.

48. Kathleen B. Jones, "Towards the Revision of Politics," in *The Political Interests of Gender*, ed. Kathleen B. Jones and Anna G. Jonasdottir (Beverly Hills, CA: Sage, 1988), 25.

49. Margrit Eichler, *Nonsexist Research Methods: A Practical Guide* (Boston: Allen and Unwin, 1987).

50. See the articles comprising "Political Science and Political Philosophy: A Symposium," *PS: Political Science and Politics* 33, no. 2 (2000): 189–97.

STUDENT STUDY SITE

for CQ Press

Give your students the SAGE edge!

SAGE edge offers a robust online environment featuring an impressive array of free tools and resources for review, study, and further exploration, keeping both instructors and students on the cutting edge of teaching and learning. Learn more at **edge.sagepub.com/johnson9e.**

3

BEGINNING THE RESEARCH PROCESS

Identifying a Research Topic,
Developing Research Questions,
and Reviewing the Literature

Many students find choosing an appropriate research topic to be a challenging part of the research process. In this chapter, therefore, we discuss general attributes of promising research topics, suggest some methods for discovering interesting topics and research questions, and provide guidelines for conducting a systematic review of the literature on a topic and tips on writing a literature review—an important component of all academic articles and research reports.

CHAPTER OBJECTIVES

3.1 Explain the purpose of specifying a research question.

3.2 Identify different sources of ideas for research topics.

3.3 Summarize the reasons why conducting a literature review is helpful.

3.4 Describe the steps in collecting sources for a literature review.

3.5 Discuss how to approach writing a literature review.

3.6 Relate the basic organizational structure of a literature review.

SPECIFYING THE RESEARCH QUESTION

One of the most important purposes of research is to answer questions about political phenomena. The research projects summarized in chapter 1, for example, attempt to answer questions about some important political attitudes or behaviors: Why is wealth distributed more equally among the population in some countries than in others? Why is there a gender gap in legislatures? Why is tax compliance higher in some regions than in others? Why do elected governments react to protests in different ways? In each case, the researchers identified a political phenomenon that interested them and tried to answer questions about that phenomenon.

The phenomena investigated by political scientists are diverse and are limited only by whether they are significant (that is, would advance our understanding of politics and government), observable, and political. Political scientists attempt to answer questions about the political behavior of individuals (voters, citizens, elected or appointed government officials), groups (interest groups, labor unions), institutions (legislatures, bureaucracies, courts, the United Nations), and political jurisdictions (cities, states, nations).

Most students, when confronting a research project for the first time, do not have a well-formulated research question as their starting point. Some will start by saying, "I'm interested in X," where X may be the International Criminal Court, media coverage of a policy issue, public attitudes about an elected official, or some other political phenomenon. Others may not have any specific interest or topic in mind at all. Thus, the first major task in a research effort often is to find a topic and to translate a general interest in a topic into a manageable research question or series of questions or propositions. Framing an engaging and appropriate research question will get a research project off to a good start by defining, and limiting, the scope of the investigation and determining what information has to be collected to answer the question. A poorly specified question inevitably leads to wasted time and energy.

Any of the following questions would probably lead to a politically significant and informative research project:

- Why is voter turnout for local elections higher in some cities than in others?

- Why does the amount spent per pupil by school districts vary (within a state or among states)?

- Do small nations sign more multilateral treaties than large nations?

- Why did some members of Congress vote for the Tax Cuts and Jobs Act of 2017 whereas others opposed it?

- Why do some nations have cap-and-trade programs for carbon dioxide emissions while others do not?

- Why do leaders in parliamentary systems call for snap elections?

A research project will get off on the wrong foot if the question that shapes it fails to address a political phenomenon, is unduly concerned with discrete facts, or is focused on reaching normative conclusions. A political science research project should, of course, focus on a political topic or, at the very least, a political perspective on a broader social issue.

Research questions, if they dwell on discrete or narrow factual issues, may limit the significance of a research project. Although important, facts alone are not enough to yield scientific explanations. What is missing is a **relationship**—that is, the association, dependence, or covariance of the values of one variable with the values of another. Researchers are generally interested in how to advance and test generalizations relating one concept to another. The following research questions are examples of those that will be fundamentally limited in scope. Most if not all of these questions could be answered by quickly consulting public records and reported in a sentence or two:

- How many trade disputes have been referred to the World Trade Organization (WTO) for resolution in the past five years?

- How many political parties are led by a woman?

- How much money was spent on national defense in each African country?

Factual information, however, may lead a researcher to ask "why" questions. For example, someone might notice that the number of trade disputes referred to the WTO has varied from year to year. What explains this fluctuation? When collecting data on the number of disputes, the researcher might notice that the complaints originate in many different countries. It would be interesting, then, to find out how the disputes are resolved. Is there any pattern to their resolution in regard to which countries benefit or the principles and arguments underlying the decisions? Why?

Sometimes, important research contributions come from descriptive or factual research because the factual information being sought is difficult to obtain or, as we discuss in chapter 4, disagreement exists over which information or facts should be used to measure a concept. In this situation, a research effort will entail showing how different ways of measuring a concept have important consequences for establishing the facts. For example, how income inequality should be measured is certainly an important aspect of research on that topic.

Questions calling for normative conclusions are also inconsistent with the research methods discussed in this book. (Refer to chapter 2 for the distinction between normative and empirical statements.) For example, "Should countries that have not signed the Treaty on the Prohibition of Nuclear Weapons sign the treaty?" is an important question, and suitable for the attention of political scientists (indeed, for any citizen), but it is not an empirical research question—the kind of research on which we focus in this book. As written, this question requires a normative response, seeking an indication of what is good or of what should be done. Although scientific knowledge may be helpful in answering questions like these, it cannot provide the answers without regard for an individual's personal values or preferences. Ultimately, the answer to this question involves personal preference, values, and judgment.

Normative questions, however, may lead you to develop an empirical research question. Continuing with the nuclear weapon treaty example, one might instead ask, "Why have many countries that do not possess nuclear weapons signed the treaty while others have not?" This revised question could be answered empirically by researching signatories and nonsignatories, developing a list of common factors in each group as part of a theory, collecting data to analyze, and making conclusions.

SOURCES OF IDEAS FOR RESEARCH TOPICS

Potential research topics about politics come from many sources. These sources may be classified as personal, nonscholarly, or scholarly. Personal sources include your own life experiences and political activities, those of your family and friends, and class readings, lectures, and discussions.

You can also look to nonscholarly sources for research topics, including print, broadcast, and internet sources. Becoming aware of current or recent issues in public affairs will help you develop interesting research topics. You can start by reading a daily newspaper or issues of popular magazines that deal with government policies and politics. The website accompanying this book (http://edge.sagepub.com/johnson9e) offers many possibilities and lists of other websites. The best print sources include national newspapers and magazines featuring in-depth political coverage. First, consider reading major urban daily newspapers like the *New York Times* and the *Financial Times*. Daily newspapers provide the most up-to-date printed political news and discussions. In addition to daily news sources, look at weekly magazines like *Foreign Affairs*, the *Economist*, and the *New Yorker*. Most of these weeklies have a decidedly partisan leaning (either conservative or liberal, Republican or Democrat), but—and this is a key point—they contain serious discussions of domestic and foreign government and politics and are wonderful sources of ideas and claims to investigate.[1] In addition to news articles in magazines and newspapers, an underappreciated source of potential research topics within these printed sources is the editorial and letters-to-the-editor pages. Although these pieces express opinions, you might consider how you could test the claim empirically.

Broadcast news sources can also inspire topical research projects. The best radio and television programs for this purpose are those that include long segments dedicated to political news, discussion, and debate. Radio programs with a civic or political focus featuring a variety of topics include National Public Radio's *Morning Edition* and *All Things Considered*. Television shows such as NBC's *Meet the Press*, CBS's *Face the Nation*, and *Fox News Sunday* and investigative journalism programs like CBS's *60 Minutes* tend to feature long interviews with political actors. Numerous highly partisan or ideological political talk shows do not hesitate to make assertions about political matters that can be put to the empirical test.

Internet sources can include the print and broadcast sources discussed above, found through the publications' and broadcasts' sites on the web. In addition to offering the same content that is printed or broadcast, many print and broadcast sources feature exclusive internet material. Other internet sources include government, university, or organization websites; websites created by individuals; and political blogs. Consider for example, the U.S. Department of Health and Human Services opioid epidemic resource page: www.hhs.gov/opioids/about-the-epidemic/. Here you will find a host of government reports, infographics, maps, and data that might inspire many interesting research questions. Blogs like *Daily Kos* and *Instapundit* have become fixtures in the national political debate, raising topics or uncovering evidence that the traditional news media have not. Blogs, much like talk radio and magazines, often feature political discussion and debate from a particular ideological or partisan perspective.

Although personal and nonscholarly sources are good places to find potential research topics, surveying the scholarly literature will help you identify a topic relevant to the political science discipline. The scholarly literature includes books and articles written by political scientists, other academics, or political practitioners. Such literature establishes which topics and questions are important to political scientists. Simply perusing the list of article titles of several issues of a journal can lead to ideas for a topic. Consider browsing through political science journals published by national associations like the *American Journal of Political Science* or the *American Political Science Review* that publish articles in all of the major subfields of political science, subfield-specific journals like *Comparative Politics* or *International*

HELPFUL HINTS
HOW TO COME UP WITH A RESEARCH TOPIC

- Where possible, collect data for more than one time (e.g., year, election) or for more than one case (e.g., city, state, nation, primary election). Do any patterns emerge? What might explain these patterns?

- Is it difficult to find information to answer a question? Why? Could you make a meaningful contribution by collecting appropriate data?

- Do you think that the ways in which other researchers have measured the phenomena or concepts that interest you are adequate? Are there any validity or reliability problems with the measures? (Measurement validity and reliability are discussed in chapter 4.)

- Find an assertion or statement in the popular press or a conclusion in a research article that you believe to be incorrect. Look for empirical evidence so that you can assess the statement or examine the evidence used by the author to see if any mistakes were made that could have affected the conclusion.

- Find two studies that reach conflicting conclusions. Try to explain or reconcile the conflict. Test conflicting explanations by applying them to different cases or data.

- Take a theory or general explanation for certain political behaviors and apply it to a new situation.

Organization that specialize in publishing comparative and international relations articles, or journals that focus on methods and statistics like *Political Analysis.* There are hundreds of political science journals to choose from.

Still another source of ideas for research papers is a textbook used in substantive courses. These works can be particularly valuable for pointing out controversies within a field. For example, as the discussion of Italian tax compliance in chapter 1 of this textbook illustrated, political scientists disagree about what underlies the discrepancy in tax compliance in southern and northern Italy. You might think about designing a case study of a small number of Italian cities to examine how social capital and institutions in the city influence tax compliance.

To guide you further in finding topics and searching for appropriate sources, this book's companion website lists additional professional journals as well as indexes and bibliographies, data banks, guides to political resources, and the like. A reference librarian will undoubtedly be able to provide additional information and guidance on particular library sources available.

So far, we have talked about using a variety of sources, including the scholarly literature, to help you identify a research topic of interest to you in a general sense. We have not yet indicated how you might search the literature (both scholarly and nonscholarly) once you have at least a general interest in a topic. Before we show you how to conduct a search of the literature, however, we want to talk about why every serious research project conducts what is called a **literature review** and why scholarly articles and books contain a section or a chapter in which the literature related to the topic is discussed.

WHY CONDUCT A LITERATURE REVIEW?

It would be virtually impossible to write something new on "international terrorism" or even "the causes of terrorism in the Middle East" without first knowing a great deal about the subject. Good research, therefore, involves reviewing previous work on the topic to motivate and sharpen a research question. Among the many reasons for doing so are (1) to see what has and has not been investigated, (2) to develop general explanations for observed variations in a behavior or a phenomenon, (3) to identify potential relationships between concepts and to identify researchable hypotheses, (4) to learn how others have defined and measured key concepts, (5) to identify data sources that other researchers have used, (6) to develop alternative research designs, and (7) to discover how a research project is related to the work of others. Let us examine some of these reasons more closely.

Often, someone new to empirical research will start out by expressing only a general interest in a topic, such as terrorism or the effects of campaign advertising or public opinion and international relations, but the specific research question has yet to be formulated (for example, "What kinds of people become terrorists?" or "Do negative televised campaign advertisements sway voters?" or "Does the public support isolationism or international-ism?"). A review of previous research can help you sharpen a topic by identifying research questions that others have asked.

Alternatively, you may start with an overly specific research question such as "Do mar-ried people have different views on abortion policy than those who are single?" Reading the literature related to public opinion on abortion likely will reveal that your specific research question is one of many aimed at answering the more general research question: What are the characteristics or attributes of people who oppose abortion, and do they differ from those of supporters? This latter research question constitutes a topic, whereas the former is likely to be too narrow to sustain a research paper.

After reading the published work in an area, you may decide that previous reports do not adequately answer the question. Thus, you may design a research project to answer an old question in a new way. An investigation may replicate a study to confirm or challenge a hypothesis or expand our understanding of a concept. Replication is one of the cornerstones of scientific work. By testing the same hypothesis in different ways or confirming the results from previous research using the same data and methods, we increase our confidence in results. Replication can therefore help build consensus or identify topics that require further work.

At other times, research may begin with a hypothesis or with a desire to develop an explanation for a relationship that has already been observed. Here, a literature review may reveal reports of similar observations made by others and may also help you develop general explanations for the relationship by identifying theories that explain the phenomenon of interest. Your research will be more valuable if you can provide a general explanation of the observed or hypothesized relationship rather than simply a report of the empirical verifica-tion of a relationship.

In addition to seeking theories that support the plausibility and increase the significance of a hypothesis, you should be alert for competing or alternative hypotheses. You may start

HELPFUL HINTS
DIFFERENTIATING SCHOLARLY FROM NONSCHOLARLY LITERATURE

You can differentiate scholarly from nonscholarly works by looking for a few characteristics. Most important, professional articles and books published in political science or other disciplines will often go through a peer-review process. The most common peer-review standard is that a journal or book editor sends an article or book manuscript submitted for publication to one or more scholars with expertise in the topical area of the article. The review is performed in a blind fashion; that is, the reviewers are not told the author's name to ensure that reviewers assess only the quality of the work. The editor relies on the peer reviewers' comments to suggest revisions of the work and assess whether or not the work makes a sufficient contribution to the literature to deserve publication. The peer-review process helps ensure that the work published in scholarly journals and books is of the best possible quality and of the most value to the discipline. It also assures the reader that, although there still may be mistakes or invalid or unreliable claims, the article or book has been vetted by one or more experts on the topic.

Alternatively, some scholarly journals and books are reviewed only by the editorial staff. Although this method provides a check on the quality of the work, it is usually not as rigorous as a blind peer review. The type of review a journal or book publisher uses will typically be explained in the journal or on the journal or publisher's website.

In addition to a peer-review process, some other indicators can differentiate scholarly from nonscholarly work. Scholarly articles and books are usually written by academics, journalists, political actors, or other political practitioners, so looking for a description of the authors is the place to start. Scholarly books are published by both university presses and commercial presses. If you are still unsure about whether or not a particular work is scholarly, consult with a reference librarian or your instructor.

with a hypothesis specifying a simple relationship between two variables. Since it is uncommon for one political phenomenon to be related to or caused by just one other factor or variable, it is important to look for other possible causes or correlates of the dependent variable. Data collection should include measurement of these other relevant variables so that, in subsequent data analysis, you may rule out competing explanations or at least indicate more clearly the nature of the relationship between the variables in the original hypothesis.

COLLECTING SOURCES FOR A LITERATURE REVIEW

After selecting a research topic using the sources described above, you must begin collecting sources for use in writing a literature review. Although personal and nonscholarly sources can be quite helpful in selecting a research topic, and a literature review can encompass virtually anything published on your topic, we strongly encourage you to become familiar with the scholarly literature. Relying on scholarly rather than nonscholarly sources will improve the quality of a literature review. In addition, as a practical concern, many instructors may not accept or give much credit for citations from nonscholarly sources unless their content constitutes part of your topic. After all, a literature review is supposed to establish the knowledge about a topic that has been attained and communicated according to professional or scientific principles.

Students commonly ask, "How many sources must I find to write my literature review?" The answer, unfortunately, is not straightforward. How many books and articles to include in a literature review depends on the purpose and scope of the project, as well as available resources. If your project is focused largely on reporting the work of others, you will probably need to include more sources than if your project is focused mostly on your own analysis. Furthermore, a more complex topic, or a topic with a larger literature, may require a more in-depth literature review than will a more straightforward topic or one with a smaller literature. Finally, consider how much time and effort you are willing to dedicate to collecting sources. Although we cannot provide a simple answer to the question of how many sources are necessary, we can explain how available time and effort could be best directed and used most efficiently.

Identifying the Relevant Scholarly Literature

It would be impossible for anyone to identify, let alone read or write about, every book or article with relevance to any particular research project. With that caveat in mind, you can think of the first step in collecting sources—identifying the relevant literature—as limiting the search to only those books and articles with the most direct relevance to the research topic of interest. You can begin to narrow the field of potential sources in many ways. The first step is to search comprehensive **electronic databases**, such as Google Scholar, or other databases that include links to full-text articles, such as JSTOR. These databases allow you to quickly locate a large number of articles and possibly books and published conference proceedings related to your topic.

HELPFUL HINTS
PYRAMID CITATIONS

Each time you find what appears to be a useful source, look at its list of notes and references. One article, for example, may cite two more potentially useful papers. Each of these, in turn, may point to two or more additional ones, and so on. Even if you start with a small list, you can quickly assemble a huge list of sources. Moreover, you increase your chances of covering all the relevant literature.

Google Scholar is a universally available **search engine** that can serve as a starting point for building a literature review because you can

- search for peer-reviewed scholarly articles using a simple keyword search,

- search for articles and books written by a particular author, and

- search for all of the articles and books that have cited an article you know to be of interest and for articles that subsequently cited those articles.

Two quick examples highlight the value of these searches. First, suppose you are interested in understanding the gender gap in legislatures.

1. By typing the phrase *legislature gender gap* into the Google Scholar search field, limiting the custom date range on the left side of the search page to work published in 2017, we found 6,400 results (see figure 3-1). This is far too many to read through.

2. You might consider further refining your search by clicking on the three parallel lines in the upper left corner of the search page and choosing advanced search (see figure 3-2). Advanced search allows you to easily search for "all of the words" entered in a search field, "with the exact phrase" entered in a search field, "with at least one of the words" entered in a search field, "without the words" entered in a search field, and "where my words occur" anywhere in the article or only in the title, along with search fields for author and publisher names and date ranges. These advanced search tools allow the researcher to narrow in on the most relevant research. For example, searching for "legislature" and "voting" in the "all of these words" search field and "gender gap" and "constituent" in the "with this exact phrase" search field, and specifying "return articles dated between 2017–2017," yields 214 results. This is still a lot, but after reading through article abstracts in this larger topic, you might narrow the search further with more **search terms**. For example, say that, after reading a few abstracts and articles, you found you were interested in Latinas. Adding "Latina" to the "all of these words" search field reduces the return to 29 articles (see figure 3-3).

3. You may find that not all of the articles are actually relevant to your topic, but if you find one article that is of direct relevance, you can use it to find more like it using the approach we describe next.

A second way to use Google Scholar is to begin with a single article instead of searching for topics.

1. Suppose that at the beginning of your search, you decided to look for an article discussed in chapter 1 of this book, "Reconciling Family Roles with Political Ambition: The New Normal for Women in Twenty-First Century U.S. Politics." You can find this article by searching for the article's title in the Google Scholar search field (see figure 3-4).

2. Clicking on the article title will provide a wealth of information about the article including the abstract and information about the publishing journal, *The Journal of Politics*, as well as links to the full text of the article.

3. As we write this chapter, 19 other published works cite this article. Clicking on the "Cited by 19" link will take you to links to the 19 works including books and articles. Work that cites this article will be related in some way that might be useful to your own work and may be worth including in the literature review.

4. Clicking on one of the authors, JL Lawless, will take you to the many articles authored by Lawless. You will find that much of her published work is on related

topics and may be useful in your own work. Each of the 20 listed publications has been cited by other work. Some have been cited hundreds of times.

5. In a matter of a couple of minutes, you have now found hundreds of articles and books that could be useful in researching your own project on the gender gap in legislatures. Learning to use a search engine that focuses on scholarly work will pay off as you will be using your time more effectively and efficiently.

The larger lesson from this example is that once you find a relevant article, you can sharpen the direction of your search for relevant literature by examining the literature review and works cited in that article. Since the article is directly relevant to the research topic of interest, the sources used in the article will likely be related as well. It is also quite likely that sources citing the relevant article are related to your topic. By building a list of sources in this fashion, you can save a great deal of time and effort as well as collect sources with a greater certainty that you will not overlook important work.

Remember, however, that even though both of the above example strategies will help you find relevant articles quickly, articles without much relevance may also come up in a search. Two articles that share a common search term do not necessarily have much related content. Nor does one article's citing another necessarily mean that the two articles investigate the same topic. Therefore, you should be prepared to review the lists of sources you identify and cull those that are not relevant to your topic.

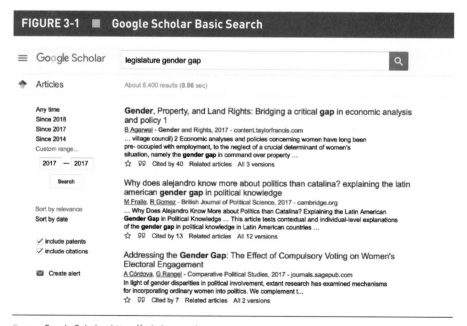

FIGURE 3-1 ■ Google Scholar Basic Search

Source: Google Scholar, https://scholar.google.com.

FIGURE 3-2 ■   Google Scholar Advanced Search

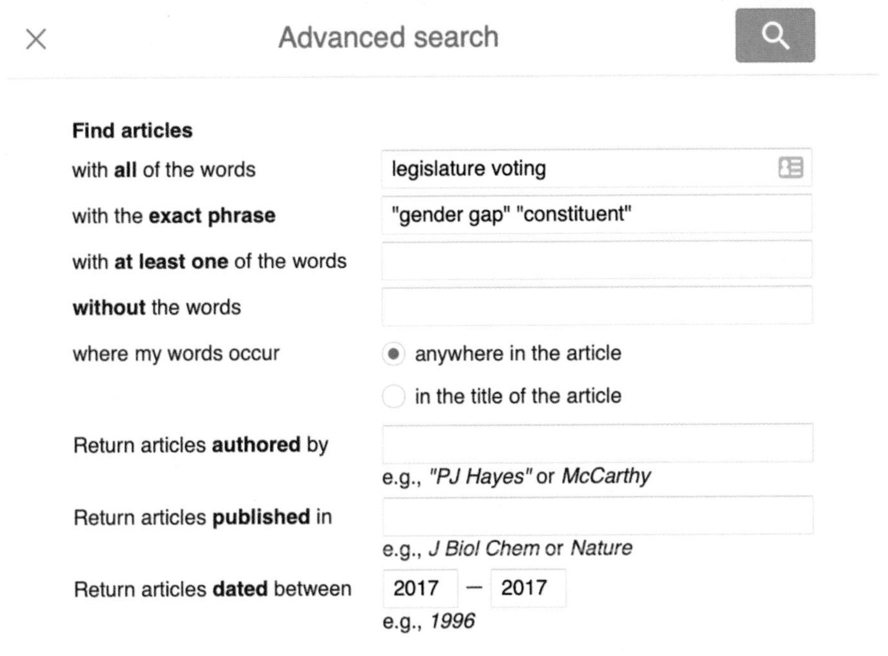

✕	Advanced search 🔍

Find articles

with **all** of the words	legislature voting
with the **exact phrase**	"gender gap" "constituent"
with **at least one** of the words	
without the words	
where my words occur	● anywhere in the article
	○ in the title of the article
Return articles **authored** by	
	e.g., *"PJ Hayes"* or *McCarthy*
Return articles **published** in	
	e.g., *J Biol Chem* or *Nature*
Return articles **dated** between	2017 — 2017
	e.g., *1996*

Source: Google Scholar, https://scholar.google.com.

HELPFUL HINTS
FINDING A TERM ON A PAGE

Most internet browsers have a "hot key" combination that allows you to search for a particular word or phrase on a displayed web page. With Google, for example, use Control-F (or Command-F if you're using a Mac platform). Take advantage of this shortcut when viewing a massive document that has small text or lots of content.

Managing Citations

Google Scholar includes another extremely valuable feature: the ability to electronically store citation information. Clicking on the "star" will allow you to save an article you have found. Likewise, clicking on the "quotation mark" will produce a pop-up box with citation information in multiple formats including popular options like Modern Language Association (MLA), American Psychological Association (APA), and Chicago, which you can copy and paste into your list of references. You can also click on one of the links at the

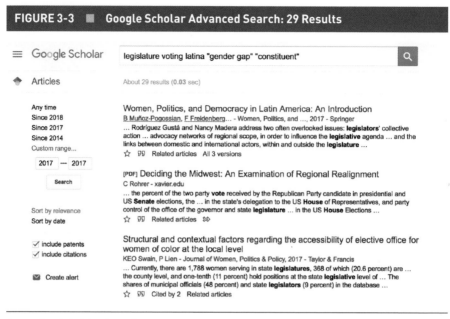

FIGURE 3-3 ■ Google Scholar Advanced Search: 29 Results

Source: Google Scholar, https://scholar.google.com.

FIGURE 3-4 ■ Google Scholar: Title Search

Source: Google Scholar, https://scholar.google.com.

bottom of the pop-up box to save the reference to a reference management program such as BibTeX, EndNote, RefMan, or RefWorks.

Identifying Useful Popular Sources

As most students use the internet on a regular basis, you may be familiar with using it to search for articles and other sources of information on topics of interest. But the wealth of information available on the internet is at once a blessing and a curse. Search engines such as Google may be a good place to start if you are trying to see what sources are available on a topic and you are not looking for a specific reference. These search engines can be quite indiscriminate in what they return, however, and leave the user with pages of unsuitable results. A Google search using the phrase "legislature gender gap" *returned over one million results*. That is the typical result for such open-ended searches. But you can use the same advanced search modifiers as previously explained for Google Scholar in an advanced Google search using the www.google.com/advanced_search link. Using the advanced search function will allow you to more quickly narrow your search and find the most relevant nonscholarly documents.

A Discerning Eye

Intentionally publishing misleading, exaggerated, or even false news stories has been common practice for centuries. Sensationalized stories like the *New York Sun*'s 1835 "great moon hoax" in which the newspaper claimed that an alien civilization was living on the moon appear with some regularity.[2] While the moon hoax was an example of satire mistaken for reality, other examples throughout history have shown that what some call "fake news" has had serious consequences including inciting violence and war.[3] This problem is only exacerbated in the internet era. Over the last couple of years, the validity of news stories and the reliability of news sources have become an important part of public conversation.

The study of research methods can help you identify reliable news sources and spot misleading or false content. We pay special attention in this chapter to identifying sources by investigating authors and publishers to find reliable work and using sources appropriately. Remember our earlier discussion of how you might use scholarly and nonscholarly work for different purposes in a research paper due to the different purposes of the sources. In other chapters, we pay special attention to the difference between empirical and normative work, making claims supported by data, carefully defining terms and concepts, making careful observations, and making data and results public. These tenets of the scientific method can help you in judging the trustworthiness of news sources. While scholarly work is susceptible to fraudulent claims, the double-blind peer-review process helps prevent the spread of misleading or exaggerated claims. Sources written by, edited by, or housed at colleges and universities are more likely to be trustworthy. These sources, however, are less likely to provide current news.

When it comes to nonscholarly, popular news sources, it is important to ask several questions. The International Federation of Library Associations and Institutions, for example, suggests that students consider eight points when consuming news.

1. Consider the source: Learn about the publisher, including its mission and purpose.

2. Check the author: What is the author's background? Is the author credible?

3. Check the date: Understanding a news story requires understanding when the story was produced.

4. Check your biases: One of the easiest ways to fall for false reporting is if the story confirms your own biases.

5. Read beyond the headline: Headlines often do not capture the nuance contained in the full story.

6. Supporting sources: What evidence is included in the story? Is the evidence believable and from a credible source?

7. Is it a joke? Do not confuse satire for news.

8. Ask the experts: Consult with your instructor or a librarian about questionable material.[4]

In addition to these tips, you should seek out additional resources from your campus library. Most college and university libraries have made an effort in recent years to promote good practices in discerning reliable from unreliable news sources and provide resources. You might also consult the American Library Association, which provides a number of useful resources.[5]

Most students rely on internet sources for news, and it is important to cite these sources properly, partly because so much variation exists in the quality of these sources but also, and even more importantly, because academic standards dictate that proper citations be provided for any work consulted. In this way, authors are fully credited for their data and ideas, and readers can check the accuracy of the information and the quality of a literature review.

At a minimum, the citation should include the author or creator of the page and the title of the article, as well as the complete internet address at which the article was found. If the information you retrieve from a website is likely to have changed since you accessed it, as in the case of a crowdsourced encyclopedia article or a page that continuously posts up-to-date data, then you would add the date you accessed the site, perhaps in parentheses after the URL. Following is a generic format for citing a web page in a bibliography:

Author [last name–first name or full organization name]. (Date of publication, if available). *Web Page Title*. Full web address.

For example:

Stroupe, Kenneth S., Jr., & Larry J. Sabato. (2004). *Politics: The Missing Link of Responsible Civic Education* (CIRCLE working paper 18). http://www.civicyouth .org/PopUps/WorkingPapers/WP18Stroupe.pdf.

Citation style will depend on the standards set by your instructor, but include at least enough detail to let a reader retrieve the page and verify information. We have included a number of guides for citing references and conducting and writing literature reviews in the "Suggested Readings" section at the end of this chapter.

Reading the Literature

Once you have identified references for possible inclusion in a literature review, the next step is to figure out how the references fit together in a way that (1) explains the base of knowledge, or what we know about a topic from previous work, with respect to the research question, and (2) establishes how the current project is going to build on that knowledge. The best way to understand the base of knowledge is to read the work that answers the central research questions and understand how each contributes to a comprehensive understanding of the important research questions. To read an entire literature would take far too much time, so it is wise to rely on shortcuts whenever available.

First, following the suggestions in the preceding section, take care in selecting references. Once references are identified and collected, you can rely on the abstract on the first page of most articles and the preface at the beginning of most books to serve as a short description of the whole work and the conclusions contained therein. A good abstract will include a great deal of important information about the contents of an article, including the research question, the theory and hypotheses, the data and methods used to test the hypotheses, and the results and conclusions. Most article abstracts are only two hundred to three hundred words long, so they offer an easy way to assess quickly whether an article is worth reading further. A good preface will include the same kind of information, but a book's length makes this summary much more cursory or general. A preface will also include more attention to organization of the chapters. Reading book reviews in scholarly journals is another way to learn quickly the value of a book to a given project. For most books, you can find a review that will relay the book's theoretical importance or help you understand how it fits in the context of the existing literature and what it adds to the base of knowledge—in addition to assessing the quality of the research.

Use of abstracts, prefaces, and book reviews will help narrow a list of references. This smaller list can then be culled for those references that are essential to motivating the current research project and those that add depth, range, or a unique perspective to the literature review. In addition, the first few pages of political science articles contain most of the description of the key components of the research project—the research question, theory and hypotheses, and data and methods—and include a literature review. The conclusion or discussion of findings will summarize the results and explain how they add to the base of knowledge. Students with limited time for reading articles should read the first few pages and the conclusion and then, if more information is needed, proceed to the rest of the article. Finally, although many political science articles include complex methods and tables, the text describing the results usually includes a more jargon-free description of the results that does not require an advanced understanding of statistics. The same time-saving tips can be applied to books by concentrating on a book's introduction and conclusion as well as selected relevant chapters, which you can identify in the table of contents.

Nonscholarly references like magazine or newspaper articles, or website content, generally are much shorter than references from the scholarly literature and require fewer shortcuts. These sources can typically be read quickly, and in most cases do not provide an abstract.

WRITING A LITERATURE REVIEW

After you have identified the relevant literature and started reading the literature, it is time to begin crafting the literature review. In this section, we explain how you can integrate a collection of related materials into an effective literature review. Essential to this process is limiting the discussion of materials to the most relevant previous work and focusing the literature review on concepts and ideas rather than individual books, articles, or authors. This is important because organizing the literature review in this way will make it easier to establish the base of knowledge and demonstrate how the current research project can extend or add to that knowledge—with a new perspective, new data, or a different method—by resolving conflicting results in the literature or by replicating, and thereby validating, previous research. When thinking about a literature review as motivating a research project in one of these ways, you will see that the literature review is an integral part of a research project and requires a great deal of attention to establish the direction of the project.

The key to organizing and writing an effective literature review is to focus on concepts, ideas, and methods shared across the literature. Many students are used to writing about multiple references with a focus on the individual references, discussing each collected reference in turn. For example, imagine that you have collected ten articles for a literature review. You might decide that the easiest way to organize a review that incorporates all ten articles would be to take the first article, perhaps selected because it was the most relevant, and summarize the most important parts of the article: the research question, theory, hypotheses, data, methods, and results. After summarizing the first article, you then move on to the second article and write a similar summary in the next paragraph, then the third, and so on, until all ten articles have been summarized. We call this approach to a literature review the "boxcar method" because such a review links the independent discussions of each article much like a series of boxcars on a train.

Although this may be the easiest method for including multiple references in a literature review, it is ineffective. It does not explain how the ten articles fit together to establish the base of knowledge to which the current project will add; nor does it establish how the current project will add to that knowledge. By tacking together independent discussions of articles, you will find it difficult to discuss common themes across references, conflicting results or conclusions, or questions left unanswered in the literature.

A more effective way to write a literature review is to focus on the concepts, ideas, and methods in the relevant literature. Think of a literature review as an essay about what has been written on your topic. You are most likely already familiar with doing this if you have written a research paper that did not include your own data analysis. In this case, however, your essay is going to focus on themes and concepts related to your research and your analysis of data. For example, imagine that you have the same ten articles from the previous example, but instead of discussing each independently, you begin by identifying the common themes across all ten articles. The first step might be to group the articles according to their research questions. It is likely that all ten articles address a similar broad topic but do not share exactly the same research questions. You can begin to establish the base of knowledge by identifying, for example, three common research questions among the ten articles (four articles answering question 1, three articles answering question 2, and three articles answering question 3). These three research questions represent the three areas of study the previous literature has undertaken in building our understanding of the broader topical area. Beginning the literature review with a discussion of these three research questions, and citing the articles that use each, will be an effective start to defining the base of knowledge.

Next, you might regroup the articles based on the data or research designs used. Perhaps three of the articles used experiments, and seven of the articles used case studies. Researchers commonly discuss in their literature reviews the different research designs used in the literature because, as explained in chapter 6, different approaches have advantages and disadvantages and will be better or worse for making certain kinds of conclusions.

In addition to differences in research design, each of the three experiments and seven case studies also likely used different data. Some of the case studies may have relied on personal interviews; others may have used participant-observation methods. Likewise, some of the experiments may have collected data from college students, and others may have collected data from the general population. Differences in the method of collecting the data or the populations from which the data were collected might lead to different conclusions.

As a final example, you might sort the ten references by the results or conclusions. It is unlikely that all ten articles came to the same conclusion. In fact, the results of at least one of the ten articles likely contradict the results of the others. Identifying commonalities and contradictions in the literature review allows a researcher to identify ideas that have been established through replication as accepted widely in the literature and areas of disagreement that are ripe for further clarification and explanation. Conflicting results can provide a wonderful motivating factor for new research and establish for the reader the importance and relevance of the current research project.

Compared to the boxcar method, the latter example describes a much more sophisticated literature review because it integrates previous research along conceptual and methodological lines and provides a more effective organization for the researcher to explain the base of knowledge and how the current project fits into that literature. As we noted earlier, the boxcar method may be attractive because it seems easier, but the integrated literature review will better inform the current research project and the reader—and, practically speaking, will earn a better grade for students.

A literature review is not all that different from a conventional research paper in which you write an essay about what is known about a topic. In both cases, the discussion needs to be organized around key themes, and it is your task as the reviewer to choose the important themes on which to focus. A literature review for an empirical research paper tends to focus more on methodological aspects of previous studies in addition to the substantive content of previous research.

ANATOMY OF A LITERATURE REVIEW

To demonstrate further how you might write a highly effective literature review, we include in figure 3-5 a literature review from an article discussed in chapter 1: "Talk 'like a Man': The Linguistic Styles of Hillary Clinton, 1992–2013" by Jennifer J. Jones. We will focus on Jones's use of the literature to introduce her topic as scientifically relevant, build on previous work to develop her theory, highlight disagreements in the literature, and select a proper analytical method.

Note first that this is a scholarly article from a highly respected political science journal, *Perspectives on Politics*. The article is written following the style and citation guidelines for *Perspectives on Politics. Perspectives on Politics* uses endnotes so you will find notes at the end of the article along with a References section that reports the full citation for all cited material. Other journals use different citation styles, but in all cases the author must provide citations acknowledging others' work and a full citation within the article. You should do the same, or your literature review will fail to give credit where credit is due and leave you open to charges of plagiarism.

The first thing to notice in Jones's article is that citations to previous work integrate references by focusing on concepts and ideas rather than discussing every individual article or book separately. You will find that notes often refer to multiple authors, rather than discussing each.

Scientific Relevance

Figure 3-5 includes text from the second page of the article, page 626, in the section titled "Gender and Self-Presentation in Politics." Jones cites two articles in endnote 10

FIGURE 3-5   ■   Anatomy of a Literature Review: Scientific Relevance

Gender and Self-Presentation in Politics

The relationship between gender and democracy is well grounded in broader theories of substantive, descriptive, and symbolic representation.[10] Over the past two decades, a number of studies have examined whether and to what extent women legislators represent women's substantive concerns. In general, this research suggests that when women are involved in the decision-making process there are substantive differences in the issues discussed on the agenda as well as in the policy outcomes that result.[11] Despite this, however, women's substantive interests cannot be advanced simply by increasing the "sheer numbers" of women in public office.[12] Representation and the advancement of women in society takes place in non-political contexts too—on the boards of multinational companies, in news media, blockbuster films, social movements, and more. The realm of electoral politics is one—albeit crucial—arena where women's substantive representation occurs, but it is mutually dependent on women's representation in other areas of civil society. Still, the disproportionate number of women in public office and positions of leadership has implications beyond representation. It has consequences for the salience of gender in politics, the types of individuals who run for public office, as well as the behaviors and decisions that women express in these roles.

Source: Jones, Jennifer J. 2016. "Talk 'like a Man': The Linguistic Styles of Hillary Clinton, 1992–2013." *Perspectives on Politics* 14(3):625–42.

that establish that "[t]he relationship between gender and democracy is well grounded in broader theories of substantive, descriptive, and symbolic representation." This represents one of the primary purposes of a literature review, establishing that the article has scientific relevance as others have worked on the topic. The remainder of this paragraph further elaborates on the research that has been done over the previous two decades and the important relationship that has been established between the number of women in politics, representation, the policy agenda, policy outcomes, the salience of gender in politics, and more.

Building a Theory

The sections "Gender Identity and Performance," "Perceptions of Gender and Political Leadership in Electoral Contexts," "Masculine Norms of Interaction in Institutional Settings," and "Do Women Have to Talk like Men to Be Considered Viable Leaders?" represent different components of Jones's theoretical perspective. Within each section, she builds her theory focusing on previous work that contributes to her ideas. For example, figure 3-6

FIGURE 3-6 ■ Anatomy of a Literature Review: Building a Theory

Gender Identity and Performance

Drawing from social identity theory[13] and self-categorization theory,[14] much research has been dedicated to understanding how social identities are manifest in a given context and how they influence perceptions of political actors and events. A well-established body of research in political psychology demonstrates that social identities including gender, race, religion, and partisanship fuel group-based attachments, and consequently shape perceptions, attitudes, and judgments of the political world.[15] However, the availability or salience of a particular social identity largely depends on the context or situation. In the context of an election, for example, partisanship is a highly salient identity that influences the way partisan voters perceive and evaluate candidates. Gender identities are ubiquitous yet they intersect with race, ethnicity, class status, and more in the larger scheme of identity politics. For this reason, important research has begun to address the broader dynamics of intersectionality.[16] Still, the salience of gender is key to understanding the explicit and implicit assumptions made about who a female politician is and how she should behave. When women are a minority within a group such as in the U.S. Senate and House of Representatives, their identity as women is more salient. Accordingly, as women reach positions of higher power and authority, their gender is increasingly salient. A female chief executive or commander-in-chief defies normal expectations, which heightens the salience of her gender and thereby increases the likelihood that attitudes toward gender will affect how she is perceived and evaluated by others. This is also true for members of other minority groups who have long been marginalized in politics. Attitudes toward race, for example, factor significantly into public evaluations of Barack Obama.[17] The salience of one's identity is thus consequential.

Gender is also a performative act and is made more or less salient based on one's performance. As Judith Butler explains, "we act and walk and speak and talk in ways that consolidate an impression of being a man or being a woman."[18] Accordingly, gender is a set of actions learned through cultural socialization, narratives, language, and other performative acts, which conform to or reject societal expectations of gender.[19] For a female politician, this performance factors into her strategic self-presentation. It is tied to the societal expectations and electoral constraints she perceives as well as the institutional norms of behavior that shape interaction and impact her ability to achieve her goals. In terms of their gendered self-presentation, then, female politicians have two primary audiences—their public constituencies (who they represent) and their (primarily male) colleagues in government with whom they must cooperate to be successful in setting forth their policy agendas and priorities. Therefore, it is important to consider how perceptions of gender and leadership as well as institutional norms of behavior affect the strategic self-presentation of women in politics.

Source: Jones, Jennifer J. 2016. "Talk 'like a Man': The Linguistic Styles of Hillary Clinton, 1992–2013." *Perspectives on Politics* 14(3):625-42.

features the "Gender Identity and Performance" section on page 626. Jones begins by pointing to both identity theory and self-categorization theory, with endnotes citing relevant theoretical work in social psychology. It is important to note here that a political science research project need not only cite other political science work, but can cite relevant work across disciplinary lines.

Disagreement in the Literature

Another purpose of a literature review is to consider disagreements in the literature. It is not uncommon to find work with contradictory results when using different methods or even the same method. Furthermore, different scholars often explain the same political phenomenon with different theories. Jones explains such a disagreement on page 628 (see figure 3-7). In this section of her article, Jones reports that "there is no unified consensus on the mechanisms that determine how a candidate's gender will influence perceptions among the electorate." Endnotes 28 and 29 cite work that support the notion that female politicians "may attempt to present themselves in a way that minimizes the salience of their gender" through communication strategies. The next endnotes identify literature that

---

FIGURE 3-7 ■ Anatomy of a Literature Review: Disagreement in the Literature

Still, there is no unified consensus on the mechanisms that determine how a candidate's gender will influence perceptions among the electorate. Female politicians (especially experienced politicians such as Clinton) who aspire toward public office and leadership positions are undoubtedly aware of these competing expectations and recognize the need to navigate double binds. Therefore, they may attempt to present themselves in a way that minimizes the salience of their gender. This idea is supported in prior work on the communication strategies of women running for public office. In debates and candidate ads, female candidates are more likely to identify with stereotypically masculine character traits than their male opponents.[28] Female candidates who emphasize masculine traits are also more likely to win their races.[29] However, there is also evidence that female candidates are more successful when they can capitalize on gender stereotypes favorable toward women and women's issues.[30] Several studies find voters attribute ideology and partisanship based on a politician's gender, viewing men as more conservative and women as more liberal.[31] Other studies find that voters stereotypically associate female candidates with traditional gender traits and abilities and believe they are more competent when dealing with issues related to social welfare, but less competent on issues of crime, defense, and the economy, in which men are assumed to be more competent.[32] In contrast, in a recent study by Deborah Brooks, survey respondents rated male and female candidates similarly on traits such as competence, empathy, and the ability to handle an international crisis.[33] In the same study, inexperienced female candidates were rated as stronger, more honest, and more compassionate than inexperienced male candidates.[34] Although the implications of these studies are mixed, they nevertheless indicate that gender factors significantly into public perceptions of politicians and candidates for office and is thus an important consideration for women's self-presentation. The work by Brooks, among others, reflects a growing trend toward data-driven approaches to the double bind that, in time, may paint a clearer picture of the obstacles female politicians face. Therefore, in addition to looking toward voters (and self-report measures) to understand how gendered power dynamics manifest in the self-presentation of women in politics, it is also important to consider the institutional, procedural, and implicit pressures that shape interactions within the political arena.

Source: Jones, Jennifer J. 2016. "Talk 'like a Man': The Linguistic Styles of Hillary Clinton, 1992–2013." *Perspectives on Politics* *14(3):625–42.*

provides support for the opposite—that "female candidates are more successful when they can capitalize on gender stereotypes favorable toward women and women's issues." Discussing a disagreement in the literature not only relays to the reader an important controversy, but also identifies one way in which Jones's work will have value to the discipline, by adding further evidence to our understanding of how female public officials and candidates for office navigate political communication. Jones's article makes a clear contribution when she conceptualizes "feminine" and "masculine" styles. This discussion focuses on the three different cited works, but rather than discuss each in turn, a style we recommend against, Jones discusses the ideas.

Data and Methods

You should also notice that Jones's literature review is not only useful for locating her research question in the literature and building her theory. Jones cites other work throughout the paper for many purposes. On page 632, in the Methods and Data section, Jones cites previous work in endnote 84 to defend her categorization of masculine and feminine language (see figure 3-8). The cited authors used a similar approach in published work. By citing this work, Jones is explaining that other scholars accept this method as valid. There are, of course, many other ways that a literature review can be of value in a research project. When working on a term paper, a senior thesis, or another project, it will be useful to consider this example and others to get the most out of your own literature review.

FIGURE 3-8 ■ Anatomy of a Literature Review: Methods and Data

Methods and Data

I investigate Clinton's linguistic style using an original corpus[80] of 567 interview and debate transcripts from 1992–2013. All interview transcripts with Hillary Clinton available on the Clinton Presidential Library's website were included in this analysis and constitute the majority of data analyzed from 1992–1999.[81] All interview transcripts (including newspaper, magazine, broadcast, and cable TV) and debate transcripts featuring Clinton between 1992–2013 available through archived databases and on the Department of State's website were also included.[82] This corpus thus represents a comprehensive collection of interview and debate transcripts featuring Clinton between 1992–2013. I then analyzed the feminine and masculine linguistic markers within these texts using Linguistic Inquiry and Word Count (LIWC), a text analysis program.[83] LIWC has been used to examine the linguistic patterns of political texts in a number of studies. One, for example, found that candidates running for president and vice president in 2004 used high rates of articles, prepositions, positive emotions, and big words,[84] markers that are more consistent with a masculine linguistic style. Another study found a low rate of pronouns, social, swear, and emotion words and a high rate of articles and big words in congressional speeches regardless of gender, indicating that a formal, masculine linguistic style is indeed pervasive in the chambers of the U.S. Congress.[85] Finally, for each transcript I calculated a feminine to masculine ratio by taking the sum of feminine linguistic markers and dividing by the sum of masculine linguistic markers described earlier in table 1.[86]

Source: Jones, Jennifer J. 2016. "Talk 'like a Man': The Linguistic Styles of Hillary Clinton, 1992–2013." *Perspectives on Politics* 14(3):625-42.

CONCLUSION

No matter what the original purpose of your literature review may have been, it should be thorough. In your research report, you should discuss the sources that provide explanations for the phenomenon you are studying and that support the plausibility of your hypotheses. You should also discuss how your research relates to other research and use the existing literature to document the significance of your research. You can look to the example in the previous section or to an example of a literature review contained in the research report in chapter 15. Another way to learn about the process is to read a few articles in any of the political science journals that we listed earlier in this chapter and take some time to study the literature reviews carefully, looking for effective styles that would suit your own project.

TERMS INTRODUCED

Electronic databases. A collection of information (of any type) stored on an electromagnetic medium that can be accessed and examined by certain computer programs.   56

Literature review. A systematic examination and interpretation of the literature for the purpose of informing further work on a topic.   53

Relationship. The association, dependence, or covariance of the values of one variable with the values of another.   50

Search engine. A computer program that visits web pages on the internet and looks for those containing particular directories or words.   56

Search term. A word or phrase entered into a computer program (a search engine) that looks through web pages on the internet for those that contain the word or phrase.   57

SUGGESTED READINGS

Fink, Arlene. *Conducting Research Literature Reviews: From the Internet to Paper.* 4th ed. Thousand Oaks, CA: Sage, 2014.

Galvan, Jose L. *Writing Literature Reviews: A Guide for Students of the Social and Behavioral Sciences.* 5th ed. Glendale, CA: Pyrczak, 2013.

Williams, Kristen. *Research and Writing Guide for Political Science.* New York: Oxford University Press, 2014.

NOTES

1. The *Political Science Research Methods* CD contains several text documents that illustrate this point and allow the reader to extract empirical and testable claims from verbal arguments.

2. Sarah Zielinski, "The Great Moon Hoax Was Simply a Sign of Its Time," *Smithsonian*, July 2, 2015. Accessed March 22, 2018. Available at https://www.smithsonianmag.com/smithsonian-institution/great-moon-hoax-was-simply-sign-its-time.

3. Jacob Soll, "The Long and Brutal History of Fake News," *Politico*, December 18, 2016. Accessed March 22, 2018. Available at https://www.politico.com/magazine/

story/2016/12/fake-news-history-long-violent-214535.

4. International Federation of Library Associations and Institutions, "How to Spot Fake News." Accessed March 22, 2018. Available at http://www.prattlibrary.org/uploadedFiles/www/locations/central/information_services/how-to_guides/How-to-Spot-Fake-News.pdf.

5. ALA Public Programs Office, "Fake News: A Library Resource Roundup," *Programming Librarian*, February 23, 2017. Accessed March 22, 2018. Available at http://www.programminglibrarian.org/articles/fake-news-library-round.

STUDENT STUDY SITE

for CQ Press

Give your students the SAGE edge!

SAGE edge offers a robust online environment featuring an impressive array of free tools and resources for review, study, and further exploration, keeping both instructors and students on the cutting edge of teaching and learning. Learn more at **edge.sagepub.com/johnson9e.**

4

THE BUILDING BLOCKS OF SOCIAL SCIENTIFIC RESEARCH

Hypotheses, Concepts, Variables, and Measurement

In chapters 1 and 2, we discussed what it means to acquire scientific knowledge and presented examples of political science research intended to produce this type of knowledge. In chapter 3, we discussed how to search for a topic and begin to pose an appropriate research question. In this chapter, we focus on taking the next steps beyond specifying the research question. These steps require us to (1) propose a suitable explanation for the phenomena under study by identifying independent and dependent variables as well as possible antecedent and intervening variables, (2) formulate testable hypotheses, (3) define the concepts identified in the hypotheses, and (4) specify how the concepts will be measured as accurately as possible. Although we discuss these steps as if they occur in sequence, the actual order may vary. All the steps must be taken eventually, however, before a research project can be completed successfully. The sooner the issues and decisions involved in each of the steps are addressed, the sooner the other portions of the research project can be completed.

PROPOSING EXPLANATIONS

Once a researcher has developed a suitable research question or topic, the next step is to propose an explanation for the phenomenon the researcher is interested in understanding. Proposing an explanation involves identifying other phenomena that we think will help us account for the object of our research and then specifying how and why these two (or more) phenomena are related. Or, alternatively, we may identify a political phenomenon and want to know whether or not it has any impact on other political phenomena. Developing an explanation involves thinking about relationships between concepts. Your literature review should give you plenty of ideas about relationships between concepts.

In the examples referred to in chapter 1, the researchers proposed explanations for the political phenomena they were studying. Lane Kenworthy and Jonas Pontusson investigated whether increases in inequality of market incomes led to increases in government spending for redistributive programs.[1] John D'Attoma wanted to explain why tax compliance in southern Italy was lower than in the northern region of the country.[2] Susan Hyde investigated whether the presence of international observers reduced election fraud.[3] S. Erdem Aytaç, Luis Schiumerini, and Susan Stokes suspected that the security of a government's hold on office and its expectation that harsh measures taken against protesters would not affect its base of support is a key factor in explaining a government's reaction to escalating protests.[4] Jennifer J. Jones investigated whether the different political positions that Hillary Clinton held affected the way she spoke.[5]

Variables

To help clarify relationships between phenomena, political scientists refer to phenomena as variables and identify several types. A phenomenon that we think will help us explain political characteristics or behavior is called an **independent variable**. Independent variables are thought to influence, affect, or cause some other phenomenon. A **dependent variable** is thought to be caused, to depend upon, or to be a function of an independent variable. Thus, if a researcher has hypothesized that acquiring more formal education will lead to increased income later on (in other words, that income may be explained by education), then years of formal education would be the independent variable, and income would be the dependent variable. In our examples above, the dependent variables are government spending for redistributive programs, tax compliance, the amount or presence of election fraud, type of government response to escalating protests, and speaking style, and the independent variables are inequality of market incomes, electoral security, government performance, presence of international observers, and political role.

As the word *variable* connotes, we expect the value of the concepts we identify as variables to vary or change. A concept that does not change in value is called a **constant** and cannot be used to investigate a relationship. Unfortunately, sometimes a concept is expected to vary and thus be suitable for inclusion in a research project, only for a researcher to discover later that the concept does not vary in the context in which it is being used. For example, a student working on a survey to be distributed to her classmates wanted to see if students having served in the military or having a family member in the military had different attitudes toward the war in Iraq than did students without military service connections. She discovered that none of the students had any military service connections: having no military service connections was a constant. As a result, she had to think of other factors that might account for differences in student attitudes toward the war in Iraq.

Proposed explanations for political phenomena are often more complicated than the simple identification of one independent variable that is thought to explain variation in a dependent variable. More than one phenomenon is usually needed to account adequately for most political behavior. For example, suppose a researcher proposes the following relationship between state efforts to regulate pollution and the severity of potential harm from pollution: the higher the threat of pollution (independent variable), the greater the effort to regulate pollution (dependent variable). The insightful researcher would realize the possibility that another phenomenon, such as the wealth of a state, might also affect a state's regulatory effort. As another example, remember from chapter 1 that Kenworthy and Pontusson thought that larger changes in market inequality would cause larger changes in redistribution but that changes in redistribution would also be affected by turnout rates in national elections.[6] In later chapters, we will discuss how one measures the impact of independent variables, individually and in combination, on a dependent variable. Sometimes, in addition to proposing that independent variables are related to the dependent variable, researchers propose relationships between the independent variables. In particular, we might want to determine which independent variables occur before other independent variables and indicate which ones have a more direct, as opposed to indirect, effect on the phenomenon we are trying to explain (the dependent variable). A variable that occurs prior to all other variables and that may affect other independent variables is called an **antecedent variable**. A variable that occurs closer in time to the dependent variable and is itself affected by other independent variables is called an **intervening variable**. Consider these examples.

Suppose a researcher hypothesizes that a person who favored national health insurance was more likely to have voted for Barack Obama in 2008 than was a person who did not favor such extensive coverage. In this case, the attitude toward national health insurance would be the independent variable, and the presidential vote the dependent variable. The researcher might wonder what causes the attitude toward national health insurance and might propose that those people who have inadequate medical insurance are more apt to favor national health insurance. This new variable (adequacy of a person's present medical insurance) would then be an antecedent variable, since it comes before and affects (we think) the independent variable. Thinking about antecedent variables pushes our explanatory scheme further back in time and, we hope, will lead to a more complete understanding of a particular phenomenon (in this case, presidential voting). Notice how the independent variable in the original hypothesis (attitude toward national health insurance) becomes the dependent variable in the hypothesis involving the antecedent variable (adequacy of health insurance). Also notice that in this example, adequacy of health insurance is thought to exert an indirect effect on the dependent variable (presidential voting) via its impact on attitudes toward national health insurance.

Now consider a second example. Suppose a researcher hypothesizes that voters' years of formal education affect their propensity to vote. In this case, education would be the independent variable, and voter turnout the dependent variable. If the researcher then begins to consider what about education has this effect, he or she has begun to identify the intervening variables between education and turnout. For example, the researcher might hypothesize that formal education creates or causes a sense of civic duty, which in turn encourages voter turnout, or that formal education causes an ability to understand the different issue positions of the candidates, which in turn causes voter turnout. Intervening variables come between an independent variable and a dependent variable and help explain the process by which one influences the other.

An **arrow diagram** is a handy device for presenting and keeping track of explanations. The arrow diagram specifies the phenomena of interest; indicates which variables are independent, alternative, antecedent, intervening, and dependent; and shows which variables are thought to affect which other ones. In figure 4-1, we present arrow diagrams for the two voting examples we just considered.

In both diagrams, the dependent variable is placed at the end of the time line, with the independent, alternative, intervening, and antecedent variables placed in their appropriate locations to indicate which ones come earlier and which come later. Arrows indicate that one variable is thought to explain or be related to another; the direction of the arrow indicates which variable is independent and which is dependent in that proposed relationship.

Arrow diagrams are especially useful for complex explanatory schemes involving numerous independent, alternative, antecedent, and intervening variables. Figure 4-2 shows two examples of arrow diagrams that have been proposed and tested by political scientists. Both diagrams are thought to explain presidential voting behavior. In the first diagram, the ultimate dependent variable, Vote, is thought to be explained by Candidate Evaluations and Party Identification. The Candidate Evaluations variable, in turn, is explained by the Issue Losses, Party Identification, and Perceived Candidate Personalities variables. These, in turn, are explained by other concepts in the diagram. The variables at the top of the diagram tend to be antecedent variables (the subscript $t - 1$ denotes that these variables precede variables with subscript t, where t indicates time); the ones in the center tend to be intervening variables. Nine independent variables of one sort or another figure in the explanation of the vote.

The second diagram also has Vote as the ultimate dependent variable, which is explained directly by only one independent variable, Comparative Candidate Evaluations. The latter variable, in turn, is dependent upon six independent variables: Personal Qualities Evaluations, Comparative Policy Distances, Current Party Attachment, Region, Religion, and Partisan Voting History. In this diagram, sixteen variables figure, either indirectly or directly, in the explanation of the Vote variable, with the antecedent variables located around the perimeter of the diagram and the intervening variables closer to the center. Both of these diagrams clearly represent complicated and extensive attempts to explain a dependent variable.

Note that arrow diagrams show hypothesized causal relationships. A one-headed arrow connecting two variables is a shorthand way of expressing the proposition "X directly causes Y." If arrows do not directly link two variables, the variables may be associated or correlated, but the relationship is indirect, not causal. As we discuss in greater depth in chapter 6, when we assert X causes Y, we are in effect making three claims. One is that X and Y covary—a change in one variable is associated with a change in the other. Also, we are claiming that a change in the independent variable (X) *precedes* the change in the dependent variable (Y). Finally, we are stating that the covariation between X and Y is not simply a coincidence or spurious—that is, due to change in some other variable—but is direct.

We have discussed the first two steps in the research process—asking a question and then proposing an explanation by suggesting how concepts or variables are related to one another—as occurring in this order, but quite often this is not the case. Researchers might start out with a theory and make deductions based on it. In other words, they start with an explanation and look for an appropriate research question that the theory might answer. Theory is an important aspect of explanation, for in order to be able to argue effectively that something causes something else, we need to be able to supply a reason or, to use words from the natural sciences, to identify the *mechanism* behind the relationship. This is the role of theory. For example, the theory of the median voter supplies a reason for changes in government policies.

FORMULATING HYPOTHESES

A **hypothesis** is an explicit statement that indicates how a researcher thinks phenomena of interest (variables) are related. It proposes a relationship that subsequently will be tested with empirical observations of the variables. A hypothesis is a guess (but of an educated nature) that indicates how an independent variable is thought to affect, influence, or alter a dependent variable. Since hypotheses are proposed relationships, they may turn out to be incorrect and not supported by the empirical evidence.

Characteristics of Good Hypotheses

It is important to start a research project with a clearly stated hypothesis because it provides the foundation for subsequent decisions and steps in the research process. A poorly formulated hypothesis often indicates confusion about the relationship to be tested or can lead

FIGURE 4-1 ■ Arrow Diagram of Adequacy of Medical Insurance and Voter Turnout Examples

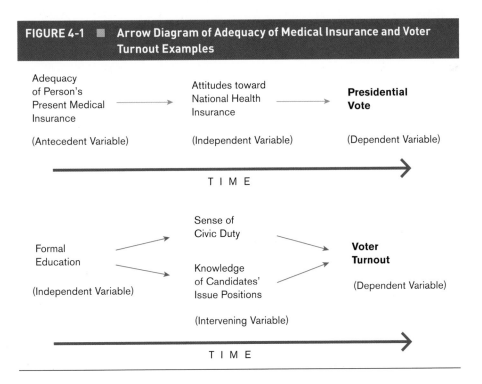

FIGURE 4-2 ■ **Two Causal Models of Vote Choice**

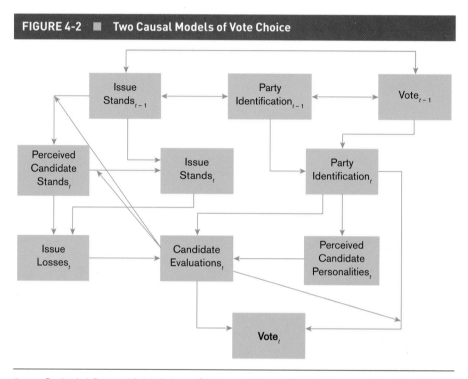

Source: Benjamin I. Page and Calvin C. Jones, "Reciprocal Effects of Policy Preferences, Party Loyalties and the Vote," *American Political Science Review* 73 (December 1979): 1083. Copyright © 1979 American Political Science Association. Reprinted with permission of Cambridge University Press.

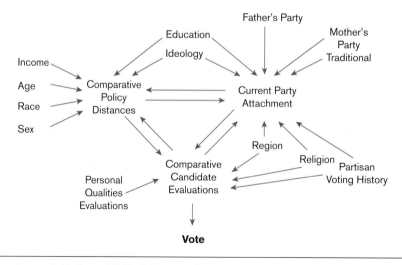

Source: Gregory B. Markus and Philip E. Converse, "A Dynamic Simultaneous Equation Model of Electoral Choice," *American Political Science Review* 73 (December 1979): 1059. Copyright © 1979 American Political Science Association. Reprinted with permission of Cambridge University Press.

to mistakes that will limit the value or the meaning of any findings. Many students find it challenging to write a hypothesis that precisely states the relationship to be tested: it takes practice to write consistently well-worded hypotheses. A good hypothesis has six characteristics: it is (1) an empirical statement, (2) stated as a generality, (3) plausible, (4) specific, (5) stated in a manner that corresponds to the way in which the researcher intends to test it, and (6) testable.

Empirical Statement

Hypotheses should be empirical, rather than normative, statements. Consider someone who is interested in democracy. If the researcher hypothesizes that "Democracy is the best form of government," he or she has formulated a normative, nonempirical statement that cannot be tested. The statement communicates the preference of the researcher; it does not explain a phenomenon. Instead, this researcher ought to be able to state how the central concept—in this case, democracy—is related to other concepts (such as literacy, size of population, geographical isolation, economic development, citizen satisfaction with government, or well-being of the population). Therefore, to produce an acceptable hypothesis, the researcher ought to make an educated guess about the relationship between democracy and another of these concepts; for example, "Democracy is more likely to be found in countries with high literacy than in countries with low literacy." This hypothesis now proposes a relationship between two phenomena that can be observed empirically. Or one might think that democracy is preferable to other systems because it produces higher standards of living. We cannot prove that one thing is preferable to another, but we could certainly compare countries on numerous measures of well-being, such as health status. The hypothesis might then be "Compared with people living under dictatorships, citizens of democracies have higher life expectancies." Whether the hypothesis is confirmed empirically is not necessarily related to whether the researcher thinks the phenomenon (in this case, democracy) is good or bad.

To be sure, empirical knowledge can be relevant for normative inquiry. Often, people reach normative conclusions based on their evaluation of empirical relationships. Someone might reason, for example, that negative campaign ads cause voters to become disgusted with politics and not vote in elections; one might further reason that because low turnout is bad, negative campaign ads are bad as well. The first part of the assertion is an empirical statement, which could be investigated using the techniques developed in this book, whereas the next two (low turnout and negative ads being bad) are normative statements.

Generality

A second characteristic of a good hypothesis is generality. Wherever possible, it should propose a relationship pertaining to many occurrences of a phenomenon rather than just to one occurrence. Knowledge about the causes of a particular occurrence of a phenomenon is worthwhile knowledge and can be helpful in formulating more general guesses about the relationships between concepts, but by starting with a general hypothesis, we are signaling that we are attempting to expand the scope of our knowledge beyond individual cases. Stating hypotheses in the plural form, rather than the singular, makes it clear that testing the hypothesis will involve more than one case.

The four hypotheses in the left column below are too narrow, whereas the four hypotheses in the right column are more general and more acceptable as research propositions:

Senator X voted for a bill because it is the president's bill and they both are Democrats.	Senators are more likely to vote for bills sponsored by the president if they belong to the same political party as the president.
The United States is a democracy because its population is affluent.	Countries with high levels of affluence are more likely to be democracies than countries with low levels of affluence.
The United States has a high murder rate because so many people own guns.	Countries with more guns per capita will experience more murders per capita than countries with fewer guns.
Joe is a liberal because his mother is one too.	People tend to adopt political viewpoints similar to those of their parents.

Note that in each of the hypotheses on the right, the concepts being related in the hypothesis become clearer, as does the general nature of the relationship. So, for example, senators' support or opposition to bills sponsored by a president is thought to be influenced by whether or not they belong to the same party as the president. This hypothesis would apply to both Democratic and Republican senators.

Plausibility

A third characteristic of a good hypothesis is that it is plausible. There should be some logical reason for thinking that it might be confirmed. Of course, since a hypothesis is a guess about a relationship, whether it will be confirmed cannot be known for certain. Any number of hypotheses could be thought of and tested, but many fewer are plausible ones. For example, if a researcher hypothesized that "People who eat dry cereal for breakfast are more likely to be liberal than are people who eat eggs," we would question his or her logic even though the form of the hypothesis is perfectly acceptable. It is difficult to imagine why this hypothesis would be confirmed.

A researcher should therefore be able to justify why the relationship in each hypothesis is plausible and could be supported. The need to formulate plausible hypotheses is one of the reasons why researchers conduct a literature review early in their research projects. Literature reviews can acquaint researchers with both general theories and specific hypotheses that have been advanced by others. There are no hard-and-fast rules to ensure plausibility, however. After all, people used to think that "Germs cause diseases" was an implausible hypothesis and that "Dirt may be turned into gold" was a plausible one.

Specificity

The fourth characteristic of a good hypothesis is that it is specific. The researcher should not simply state that variables are associated; rather, he or she should indicate the direction of the expected relationship between two or more variables. Following are examples of **directional hypotheses** that specify the nature of the relationship between concepts:

- Median family income is higher in urban counties than in rural counties.
- States that are characterized by a "moralistic" political culture will have higher levels of voter turnout than will states with an "individualistic" or "traditionalistic" political culture.

The first hypothesis indicates which relative values of median family income are related to which type or category of county. Similarly, the second hypothesis predicts a particular relationship between specific types of political culture (the independent variable) and voter turnout (the dependent variable).

The direction of the relationship between concepts is referred to as a **positive relationship** if the concepts are predicted to increase in size together or decrease in size together; that is, as X increases, so does Y, and as X decreases, so does Y. The following are examples of hypotheses that predict positive relationships:

- The more education a person has, the higher his or her income.
- As the percentage of a country's population that is literate increases, the country's political process becomes more democratic.
- The older people become, the more likely they are to be conservative.
- People who read a daily newspaper are more informed about current events than are people who do not read a daily newspaper.
- States with lower per capita incomes spend less money per pupil on education than states with higher per capita incomes.

If, however, the researcher thinks that as one concept increases in size or amount, another one will decrease in size or amount, then a **negative relationship** is suggested, as in the following examples:

- Older people are less tolerant of social protest than are younger people.
- The more income a person has, the less concerned about mass transit the person will be.
- More affluent countries have less property crime than do poorer countries.

In addition, the concepts used in a hypothesis should be defined well enough so their meaning is not ambiguous. For example, a hypothesis that suggests "There is a relationship between personality and political attitudes" is far too ambiguous. What is meant by personality? Which political attitudes? A more specific reformulation of this hypothesis might be "The more self-esteem a person has, the less likely the person is to be an isolationist." Now personality has been narrowed to self-esteem, and the political attitude has been defined as isolationism—both more precise concepts. Eventually, even these two terms must be given more precise definitions when it comes to measuring them. (We return to the topic of defining concepts and begin to address the challenge of measuring concepts later in this chapter.) As the concepts become more clearly defined, the researcher is better able to specify the direction of the hypothesized relationship.

Following are four examples of ambiguous hypotheses that have been made more specific:

How a person votes for president depends on the information he or she is exposed to.	The more information favoring Candidate X a person is exposed to during a political campaign, the more likely that person is to vote for Candidate X.
A country's geographical location matters for the type of political system it develops.	The more borders a country shares with other countries, the more likely that country is to have a nondemocratic political process.
A person's capabilities affect his or her political attitudes.	The more intelligent a person is, the more likely he or she is to support civil liberties.
Guns do not cause crime.	People who own guns are less likely to be the victims of crimes than are persons who do not own guns.

Correspondence to the Way in Which the Researcher Intends to Test the Hypothesis

A fifth characteristic of a good hypothesis is that it is stated in a manner that corresponds to the way in which the researcher intends to test it—that is, it should be "consistent with the data."[7] For example, although the hypothesis "Higher levels of literacy are associated with higher levels of democracy" states how the concepts are related, it does not indicate how the researcher plans to test the hypothesis. In contrast, the hypothesis "As the percentage of a country's population that is literate increases, the country's political process becomes more democratic" suggests that the researcher is proposing to use a time-series design by measuring the literacy rate and the amount of democracy for a country or countries at several different times to see if increases in democracy are associated with increases in literacy (that is, if changes in one concept lead to changes in another).

If, however, the researcher plans to test the hypothesis by measuring the literacy rates and levels of democracy for many countries at one point in time to see if those with higher literacy rates also have higher levels of democracy, it would be better to rephrase the hypothesis as "Countries with higher literacy rates tend to be more democratic than countries with lower literacy rates." This way of phrasing the hypothesis reflects that the researcher is planning to use what is known as a cross-sectional research design to compare the levels of democracy in countries with different literacy rates. This differs from comparing a country's level of democracy at more than one point in time to see if it changes in concert with changes in literacy.

Testability

Finally, a good hypothesis is testable. It must be possible and feasible to obtain data that will allow one to test the hypothesis. Hypotheses for which either confirming or disconfirming evidence is impossible to gather are not subject to testing, and hence are unusable for empirical purposes.

Consider this example of a promising yet difficult-to-test hypothesis: "The more a child is supportive of political authorities, the less likely that child will be to engage in political dissent as an adult." This hypothesis is general, plausible, fairly specific, and empirical, but in its current form it cannot be tested because, to our knowledge, no data exist to verify the proposition. The hypothesis requires data that measure a set of attitudes for individuals when they are children and a set of behaviors when they are adults. Consequently, a frustrating practical barrier prevents the testing of an otherwise acceptable hypothesis. Students in one-semester college courses on research methods often run up against practical constraints. A semester is not usually long enough to collect and analyze data, and some data may be too expensive to acquire. In fact, many interesting hypotheses go untested simply because even professional researchers do not have the resources to collect the data necessary to test them.

Hypotheses stated in tautological form are also untestable. A **tautology** is a statement linking two concepts that mean essentially the same thing; for example, "The less support there is for a country's political institutions, the more tenuous the stability of that country's political system." This hypothesis would be difficult to disconfirm because the two concepts—support for political institutions and stability of a political system—are so similar. To conduct a fair test, one would have to measure independently—in different ways—the support for the political institutions and the stability of the political system.

In their study of government maltreatment of citizens, Steven C. Poe and C. Neal Tate defined human rights abuses as coercive activities (such as murder, torture, forced disappearance, and imprisonment of persons for their political views) designed to induce compliance with a ruling regime.[8] Other researchers have included lack of democratic processes and poor economic conditions in their definitions of human rights abuses, but Poe and Tate did not include these concepts because they wanted to use democratic rights and economic conditions as independent variables explaining variation in human rights abuses by governments.

Many hypotheses, then, are not formulated in a way that permits an informative test of them with empirical research. Readers of empirical research in political science, as well as researchers themselves, should take care that research hypotheses are empirical, general, plausible, specific, consistent with the data, and testable. Hypotheses that do not share these characteristics are likely to cause difficulty for the researcher and reader alike and make a minimal contribution to scientific knowledge.

Specifying Units of Analysis

In addition to proposing a relationship between two or more variables, a hypothesis also specifies, or strongly implies, the types or levels of political actor or entity to which the hypothesis is thought to apply. This entity is called the **unit of analysis** of the hypothesis, and it also must be selected thoughtfully. A clearly established unit of analysis structures and helps to organize the collection of data to measure variables of interest.

As noted in chapter 2, political scientists are interested in understanding the behavior or properties of all sorts of political actors (individuals, groups, states, government agencies, organizations, regions, nations) and events (elections, wars, conflicts). The particular type of actor whose political behavior is named in a hypothesis is the unit of analysis for the research project. In a legislative behavior study, for example, the individual members of the House of Representatives might be the units of analysis in the following hypothesis:

- Members of the House who belong to the same party as the president are more likely to vote for legislation desired by the president than are members who belong to a different party.

In the following hypothesis, a city is the unit of analysis, since attributes of cities are being explored:

- Northeastern cities are more likely to have mayors, while western cities have city managers.

Civil wars are the units of analysis in this hypothesis:

- Civil wars that are halted by negotiated peace agreements are less likely to re-erupt than are those that cease due to the military superiority of one of the parties to the conflict.

Elections are the unit of analysis in this example:

- Elections in which the contestants spend the same amount of money tend to be decided by closer margins of victory than elections in which one candidate spends a lot more than the other candidate(s).

Finally, consider this proposition:

- The more affluent a country is, the more likely it is to have democratic political institutions.

Here the unit of analysis is the country. It is the measurement of national characteristics—affluence (the independent variable) and democratic political institutions (the dependent variable)—that is relevant to testing this hypothesis. In sum, the research hypothesis indicates the researcher's unit of analysis and the behavior or attributes that must be measured for that unit.

Cross-Level Analysis: Ecological Inference and Ecological Fallacy

Sometimes researchers conduct what is called **cross-level analysis**. In this type of analysis, researchers use data collected for one unit of analysis to make inferences about another unit of analysis. Christopher H. Achen and W. Phillips Shively pointed out that "for reasons of cost or availability, theories and descriptions referring to one level of aggregation are frequently testable only with data from another level."[9] A discrepancy between the unit of analysis specified in a hypothesis and the entities whose behavior is empirically observed can cause problems, however.

A frequent goal of cross-level analysis is to make an **ecological inference**—that is, to use aggregate data to study the behavior of individuals.[10] Data of many kinds are collected for school districts, voting districts, counties, states, nations, or other aggregates in order to make inferences about individuals. The relationships between schools' average test scores and the percentage of children receiving subsidized lunches, national poverty and child mortality rates, air pollution indexes and the incidence of disease in cities, and the severity of state criminal penalties and crime rates are examples of relationships explored using aggregate data. The underlying hypotheses of such studies are that children who receive subsidized lunches score lower on standardized tests, poor children are more likely to die of childhood diseases, individuals' health problems are due to their exposure to air pollutants, and harsh penalties deter individuals from committing crimes. Yet, if a relationship is found between group indicators or characteristics, it does not necessarily mean that a relationship exists between the characteristics for individuals in the group. The use of information that shows a relationship for groups to infer that the same relationship exists for individuals when in fact there is no such relationship at the individual level is called an **ecological fallacy**.

Let's take a look at an example to see how an ecological fallacy might be committed as a result of failing to be clear about the unit of analysis. Suppose a researcher wants to test the hypothesis

"Democrats are more likely to support a sales tax increase than are Republicans." Individuals are the unit of analysis in this hypothesis. If the researcher selects an election in which a sales tax increase was at issue and obtains the voting returns as well as data on the proportions of Democrats and Republicans in each election precinct, the data are aggregate data, not data on individual voters. If it is found that sales tax increases received more votes in precincts with a higher proportion of Democrats than in precincts with a higher proportion of Republicans, the researcher might take this as evidence in support of the hypothesis. There is a fundamental problem with this conclusion, however. Unless a district is 100 percent Democratic or 100 percent Republican, the researcher cannot necessarily draw such a conclusion about the behavior of individuals from the behavior of election districts. It could be that support for a sales tax increase in a district with a high proportion of Democratic voters was very high among non-Democrats and that most of the support for a sales tax increase in the Republican-dominated districts came from Republicans, not Democrats. If this is in fact what happened, we would have a case of an ecological fallacy: what was true at the aggregate level was not true at the individual level.

Use of aggregate data to examine hypotheses that pertain to individuals may be unavoidable in some situations because individual-level data are lacking. Achen and Shively pointed out that before the development of survey research, aggregate data generally were the only data available and were used routinely by political scientists.[11] Several statistical methods have been developed to try to adjust inferences from aggregate-level data, although a discussion of these is beyond the scope of this book.[12]

Another mistake researchers sometimes make is to mix different units of analysis in the same hypothesis. "The more education a person has, the more democratic his or her country is" doesn't make much sense because it mixes the individual and country as units of analysis. However, though "The smaller a government agency, the happier its workers" concerns an attribute of an agency and an attribute of individuals, it does so in a way that makes sense. The size of the agency in which individuals work may be an important aspect of the context or environment in which the individual phenomenon occurs and may influence the individual attribute. In this case, the unit of analysis is clearly the individual, but a phenomenon that is experienced by many cases is used to explain the behavior of individuals, some of whom may well be identically situated.

In short, a researcher must be careful about the unit of analysis specified in a hypothesis and its correspondence with the unit measured. In general, a researcher should not mix units of analysis within a hypothesis.

DEFINING CONCEPTS

In our daily life, we use labels or *concepts* to name and describe features of our environment. For example, we describe some snakes as poisonous and others as nonpoisonous, some politicians as liberal and others as conservative, some friends as shy and others as extroverted. These attributes, or concepts, are useful to us because they help us observe and understand aspects of our environment, and they help us communicate with others.

Concepts also contribute to the identification and delineation of the scientific disciplines within which research is conducted. In fact, to a large extent, a discipline maintains its identity because different researchers within it share a concern for the same concepts. Physics, for example, is concerned with the concepts of gravity and mass (among others); sociology, with social class and social mobility; psychology, with personality and deviance. By contrast, political science is concerned with concepts such as democracy, power, representation, justice, and equality. The boundaries of disciplines are not well defined or rigid, however. Political scientists, developmental psychologists, sociologists, and anthropologists all share an interest in how new members of a society are socialized into the norms and beliefs of that society, for example. Nonetheless, because a particular discipline has some minimal level of shared consensus concerning its significant concepts, researchers can usually communicate more readily with other researchers in the same discipline than with researchers in other disciplines.

Some concepts—such as *car*, *chair*, and *vote*—are fairly precise because there is considerable agreement about their meaning. Others are more abstract and lend themselves to differing definitions—for example, *liberalism*, *crime*, *democracy*, *equal opportunity*, *human rights*, *social mobility*, and *alienation*. A similar concept is *orange*. Although there is considerable agreement about it (orange is not usually confused with purple), the agreement is less than total (whether a particular object is yellow, orange, or red is not always clear).

Many interesting concepts that political scientists deal with are abstract and lack a completely precise, shared meaning. This hinders communication concerning research and creates uncertainty regarding the measurement of a phenomenon. Consequently, a researcher must explain what is meant by the concept so that those reading and evaluating the research can decide if the meaning accords with their own understanding of the term. Although some concepts that political scientists use—such as *amount of formal education*, *presidential vote*, and *amount of foreign trade*—are not particularly abstract, other concepts—such as *election fraud*, *talking like a man*, and *income inequality*—are far more abstract and need more careful consideration and definition.

Researchers get help defining concepts by reviewing and borrowing (possibly with modification) definitions developed by others in the field. For example, a researcher interested in the political attitudes and behavior of the American public would find the following definitions of key concepts in the existing literature:

- *Political participation:* "Those activities by private citizens that are more or less directly aimed at influencing the selection of government personnel and/or the actions they take"[13]

- *Political violence:* "All collective attacks within a political community against the political regime, its actors—including competing political groups as well as incumbents—or its policies"[14]

- *Political efficacy:* "The feeling that individual political action does have, or can have, an impact upon the political processes—that it is worthwhile to perform one's civic duties"[15]

- *Belief system:* "A configuration of ideas and attitudes in which the elements are bound together by some form of constraint or functional interdependence"[16]

Each of these concepts is somewhat vague and lacks complete shared agreement about its meaning. Furthermore, it is possible to raise questions about each of these concept definitions. Notice, for example, that the definition of *political participation* excludes the possibility that government employees (presumably "nonprivate" citizens) engage in political activities and that the definition of *political efficacy* excludes the impact of collective political action on political processes. Consequently, we may find these and other concept definitions inadequate and revise them to capture more accurately what we mean by the terms.

Clear definitions of concepts are important if we are to develop specific hypotheses and avoid tautologies. Clear definitions also are important so that the knowledge we acquire from testing our hypotheses is transmissible and empirical. For these reasons, measurement of variables is a critical aspect of the research process and requires significant thought and consideration.

DEVISING MEASUREMENT STRATEGIES

In order to test empirically the accuracy and utility of a scientific explanation for a political phenomenon, we will have to observe or measure the presence of the phenomenon as well as the concepts we are using to understand that phenomenon. If this test is to be adequate, our measurements must be as accurate and precise as possible. The process of measurement is important because it provides the bridge between our proposed explanations often referring to abstract concepts and the empirical world they are supposed to explain. Measures should be free of **measurement bias**, a type of measurement error that results in systematically over- or undermeasuring the value of a concept. For example, a question in a survey might be worded in such a way as to lead respondents to choose a particular response. Despite the best efforts of research to measure concepts accurately and precisely and avoid measurement bias, there is always the possibility that some **random measurement error**—that is, an error in measurement that has no systematic direction or cause—will occur. **Operational definitions** of concepts describe exactly how researchers are going to measure their concepts. How researchers measure or **operationalize** their concepts can have a significant impact on their findings; differences in measurement can lead to totally different conclusions. Developing operational definitions of concepts can be quite challenging, and researchers give a lot of consideration to their choice of operational definitions.

Suppose, for example, that a researcher is interested in the kinds of political systems that different countries have and, in particular, why some countries are more democratic than others. *Democracy* is consequently a key concept that needs definition and measurement. The word contains meaning for most of us; that is, we have some idea of what is democratic and what is not. But once we begin thinking about the concept, we quickly realize that it is not as clear as we originally thought. In fact, a group of researchers wrote in 2011, "Perhaps no other concept is as central to policymakers and scholars. Yet, there is no consensus about how to conceptualize and measure regimes such that meaningful comparisons can be made through time and across countries."[17] To some, a country is democratic if it has "competing political parties, operating in free elections, with some reasonable level of popular participation in the process."[18] To others, a country is democratic only if legal guarantees protect free speech, the press, religion, and the like. To others, a country is democratic if the political leaders make decisions that are acceptable to the populace. And to still others, democracy implies equality of economic opportunity among the citizenry. If a country has all these attributes, it would be called a democracy by any of the criteria, and there would be no problem classifying the country. But if a country possesses only one of these attributes, its classification would be uncertain, since by some definitions it would be democratic but by others it would not. Different definitions require different measurements and may result in different research findings.

Kenworthy and Pontusson's investigation of income inequality in affluent countries also illustrates well the impact on research findings of how a concept is measured.[19] One way to measure income distribution is to look at the earnings of full-time-employed individuals and to compare the incomes of those at the top and the bottom of the earnings distribution. Kenworthy and Pontusson argued that it is more appropriate to compare incomes of households than incomes of individuals. The unemployed are excluded from the calculations of individual earnings inequality, but households include the unemployed. Also, low-income workers disproportionately drop out of the employed labor force. Using working-age household income reflects changes in employment among household members. Kenworthy and Pontusson found that when individual income was used as a basis for measuring inequality, inequality had increased the most in the United States, New Zealand, and the United Kingdom, all liberal market economies. They further found that income inequality had increased significantly more in these countries than in Europe's social market economies and Japan. When household income was used, the data indicated that inequality had increased in all countries with the exception of the Netherlands.

Let us consider another example: imagine that a researcher is interested in why some individuals are more liberal than others. The concept of *liberalism* might be defined as "believing that government ought to pursue policies that provide benefits for the less well-off." The task, then, is to develop an operational definition that can be used to measure whether particular individuals are liberal or not. The following question from the General Social Survey might be used to operationalize the concept:

A. Some people think that the government in Washington ought to reduce the income differences between the rich and the poor, perhaps by raising the taxes of wealthy families or by giving income assistance to the poor. Others think that the government should not concern itself with reducing this income difference between the rich and the poor. Here is a card with a scale from 1 to 7. Think of a score of 1 as meaning that the government ought to reduce the income differences between rich and poor, and a score of 7 as meaning that the government should not concern itself with reducing income differences. What score between 1 and 7 comes closest to the way you feel? (CIRCLE ONE)[20]

An abstract concept, liberalism has now been given an operational definition that can be used to measure the concept for individuals. This definition is also related to the original definition of the concept, and it indicates precisely what observations need to be made. It is not, however, the only operational definition possible. Others might suggest that questions regarding affirmative action, same-sex marriage, school vouchers, the death penalty, welfare benefits, and pornography could be used to measure liberalism.

The important thing is to think carefully about the operational definition you choose. How a concept is operationalized affects how generalizations are made and interpreted. For example, general statements about liberals or conservatives apply to liberals or conservatives only as they have been operationally defined, in this case by this one question regarding government involvement in reducing income differences. As a consumer of research, you should familiarize yourself with the measurement strategies used by researchers so that you are better able to interpret and generalize research results.

To be useful in providing scientific explanations for political behavior, measurements of political phenomena must correspond closely to the original meaning of the researcher's concepts. They must also provide the researcher with enough information to make valuable comparisons and contrasts. Hence, the quality of measurements is judged in regard to both their *accuracy* and their *precision*.

THE ACCURACY OF MEASUREMENTS

There are two primary concerns when it comes to the accuracy of quantitative measures: measurement reliability and measurement validity. In this section, we discuss these two dimensions of measurement accuracy. In later chapters, we will point out particular challenges posed by various data collection methods to researchers' attempts to demonstrate the validity and reliability of their measures.

Reliability

Reliability describes the consistency of results from a procedure or measure in repeated tests or trials. In the context of measurement, a reliable measure is one that produces the same result each time the measure is used. An unreliable measure is one that produces inconsistent results—sometimes higher, sometimes lower.[21] Measures might be unreliable because the physical process of measurement permits errors to occur or because the measurement scheme or measurement instructions are ambiguous and, as a result, persons answering survey questions, for example, may interpret them differently.

The reliability of political science measures can be calculated in many different ways, but all of these calculations rely on the same basic logic—comparing two sets of results to assess how similar the results are. For example, the test–retest method involves applying the same measure to the same observations at two periods in time, then comparing the results. For example, we might ask survey respondents to answer a survey question on support for a political party in the morning, then ask the same respondents the same question in the afternoon—a short enough time interval that support for a party would not change.

The measure is said to be reliable if the results from the morning and afternoon are similar, and unreliable if the results vary dramatically.

Alternatively, if you are worried that the respondents may answer the second iteration differently because they have already seen the same question asked before, you might consider the **alternative-form method**. Alternative-form reliability measures the same concept more than once, but it uses two different measures of the same concept rather than the same measure. For example, a researcher could devise two different questions to measure the concept of support for a party, ask the same respondents questions at two different times using one set of questions the first time and the other set of questions the second time, and compare the results. Or, rather than using two similar measures at two different points in time with the same respondents, the **split-halves method** applies two measures of the same concept at the same time. The results of the two measures are then compared. This method avoids the problem that the concept being measured may change between measures. If individual scores on the two measures of party support are similar, then the measure may be said to be reliable.

Validity

A second concern with the accuracy of a measure is validity. Essentially, a valid measure is one that measures what it is supposed to measure. Unlike reliability, which depends on whether repeated applications of the same or equivalent measures yield the same result, **validity** refers to the degree of correspondence between the measure and the concept it is thought to measure. In other words, using a survey question as an example, is the actual level of an individual's party support reflected in the response to a survey question, or did the question fail to measure the true level of support? Or, even worse, did the question fail to measure party support at all and instead measure support for just one candidate for office?

It is harder to test validity than reliability, as we will see below, but there are ways to evaluate the validity of a measure. The first and most basic test for validity is face validity. **Face validity** may be asserted (not empirically demonstrated) when a measure appears to accurately measure the concept it is supposed to measure. Face validity may only be asserted, rather than empirically demonstrated, because face validity is essentially a matter of judgment. The researcher simply considers the measure and the concept it is supposed to measure and decides whether or not the measure is valid. It should be obvious why face validity is bound to be problematic.

Unfortunately, many alternatives to face validity are not much better. For example, **content validity** involves determining the full domain or meaning of a particular concept and then making sure that all components of the meaning are included in the measure. This is an improvement over face validity because the researcher is carefully considering the full definition of a concept and making sure that the measure incorporates the full definition, but in the end, it is a matter of judgment.

While there are many more tests of validity, we will discuss just one more: different forms of **construct validity**. Construct validity can be understood in two different ways: convergent construct validity and discriminant construct validity. **Convergent construct**

validity is when a measure of a concept is related to a measure of another concept with which the original concept is thought to be associated. In other words, a researcher may specify, on theoretical grounds, that two concepts ought to be related in a positive manner (say, political efficacy with political participation or education with income) or a negative manner (say, democracy with human rights abuses). The researcher then develops a measure of each of the concepts and examines the relationship between them. If the measures are positively or negatively correlated, then one measure has convergent validity for the other measure. In the case that there is no relationship between the measures, then the theoretical relationship is in error, at least one of the measures is not an accurate representation of the concept, or the procedure used to test the relationship is faulty. The absence of a hypothesized relationship does not mean a measure is invalid, but the presence of a relationship gives some assurance of the measure's validity.

Discriminant construct validity involves two measures that theoretically are expected *not* to be related; thus, the correlation between them is expected to be low or weak. If the measures do not correlate with one another, then discriminant construct validity is demonstrated.

In sum, the reliability and validity of the measures used by political scientists are seldom demonstrated to everyone's satisfaction. Most measures of political phenomena are neither completely invalid or valid nor thoroughly unreliable or reliable but, rather, are partly accurate. Therefore, researchers generally present the rationale and evidence available in support of their measures and attempt to persuade their audience that their measures are at least as accurate as alternative measures would be. Nonetheless, a skeptical stance on the part of the reader toward the reliability and validity of political science measures is often warranted.

Note, finally, that reliability and validity are not the same thing. A measure may be reliable without being valid. One may devise a series of questions to measure liberalism, for example, that yields the same result for the same people every time but that misidentifies individuals. A valid measure, however, will also be reliable: if it accurately measures the concept in question, then it will do so consistently across measurements—allowing, of course, for some random measurement error that may occur. It is more important, then, to demonstrate validity than reliability, but reliability is usually more easily and precisely tested.

THE PRECISION OF MEASUREMENTS

In addition to accuracy, **precision** of measurements is important; that is, measurements should contain as much information as possible about the attribute or behavior being measured. The more precise our measures, the more complete and informative can be our test of the relationships between two or more variables. We can measure precision using levels of measurement.

Levels of Measurement

When we consider the precision of our measurements, we refer to the **level of measurement**. The level of measurement indicates the type of information that we think our measurements contain and the mathematical properties that determine the type of comparisons that can be made across a number of observations on the same variable.

There are four different levels of measurement—nominal, ordinal, interval, and ratio—and each level indicates the information and mathematical properties of a variable. As we move from nominal at the bottom of the scale to ratio at the top of the scale, information and mathematical properties increase with each level.

We begin with **nominal-level measure**, the level that has the fewest mathematical properties of the four levels. A nominal-level measure indicates that the values assigned to a variable represent only different categories or classifications for that variable. In such a case, no category is more or less than another category; they are simply different. For example, suppose we measure the predominant language spoken in a country. We would record this variable by writing down a number that represents each language: (1) Arabic, (2) French, (3) Portuguese, and so on. The numbers chosen in this example are meaningless beyond indicating that each language is different from the others. One could choose any number for each language as long as that number was different from the others. As such, nominal variables have scant mathematical properties. Furthermore, there is little information included in this variable. We know the languages are different, but no additional information is included in the variable.

An **ordinal-level measure** has all of the properties of a nominal measure but also assumes observations can be compared in terms of having more or less of a particular attribute. Hence, an ordinal-level measure captures more information about the measured concept and has more mathematical properties than a nominal-level measure. For example, we could create an ordinal measure of formal education completed with the following categories: "eighth grade or less," "some high school," "high school graduate," "some college," and "college degree or more." Here we are concerned not with the exact difference between the categories of education but only with whether one category is more or less than another. When coding this variable, we would assign higher numbers to higher categories of education. The intervals between the numbers have no meaning; all that matters is that the higher numbers represent more of the attribute than do the lower numbers. An ordinal variable measuring partisan affiliation with the categories "strong Republican," "weak Republican," "leaning neither Republican nor Democrat," "weak Democrat," and "strong Democrat" could be assigned codes 1, 2, 3, 4, and 5 or 1, 2, 5, 8, and 9 or any other combination of numbers, as long as they were in ascending or descending order.

Because nominal and ordinal measures rely on categories, it is important to make sure these variables are both exhaustive and exclusive. *Exhaustive* refers to making sure that all possible categories—or answer choices—are accounted for. The simplest solution to make sure a variable is exhaustive is to include an "other" category that can be used for values that are not represented in the identified categories. *Exclusive* refers to making sure that a single value or answer can only fit into one category. Each category should be distinct from the others, with no overlap. Nominal- and ordinal-level measures are referred to as **categorical measures**.

HELPFUL HINTS
DEBATING THE LEVEL OF MEASUREMENT

Suppose we ask individuals three questions designed to measure social trust, and we believe that individuals who answer all three questions a certain way have more social trust than persons who answer two of the questions a certain way, and these individuals have more social trust than individuals who answer one of the questions a certain way. We could assign a score of 3 to the first group, 2 to the second group, 1 to the third group, and 0 to those who did not answer any of the questions in a socially trusting manner. In this case, the higher the number, the more social trust an individual has.

What level of measurement is this variable? It might be considered to be ratio level, if one interprets the variable as simply the number of questions answered indicating social trust. But does a person who has a score of 0 have no social trust? Does a person with a score of 3 have three times as much social trust as a person with a score of 1? Perhaps, then, the variable is an interval-level measure, if one is willing to assume that the difference in social trust between individuals with scores of 2 and 3 is the same as the difference between individuals with scores of 1 and 2. But what if the effect of answering more questions in the affirmative is not simply additive? In other words, perhaps a person who has a score of 3 has a lot more social trust than someone with a score of 2 and this difference is more than the difference between individuals with scores of 1 and 2. In this case, then, the measure would be ordinal level, not interval level.

The next level of measurement, **interval-level measurement**, includes the properties of the nominal level (characteristics are different) and the ordinal level (characteristics can be put in a meaningful order). But unlike the preceding levels of measurement, the intervals between the categories or values assigned to the observations do have meaning. The value of a particular observation is important not just in terms of whether it is larger or smaller than another value (as in ordinal measures) but also in terms of *how much* larger or smaller it is. For example, suppose we record the year in which certain events occurred. If we have three observations—1950, 1962, and 1977—we know that the event in 1950 occurred twelve years before the one in 1962 and twenty-seven years before the one in 1977. A one-unit change (the interval) all along this measurement is identical in meaning: the passage of one year's time.

Another characteristic of an interval level of measurement that distinguishes it from the next level of measurement (ratio) is that an interval-level measure has an arbitrarily assigned zero point that does not represent the absence of the attribute being measured. For example, many time and temperature scales have arbitrary zero points. Thus, the year 0 CE does not indicate the beginning of time—if this were true, there would be no BCE dates. Nor does 0°C indicate the absence of heat; rather, it indicates the temperature at which water freezes. For this reason, with interval-level measurements, we cannot calculate ratios; that is, we cannot say that 60°F is twice as warm as 30°F. So while the interval level of measurement captures more information and mathematical properties than the nominal and ordinal levels, it does not have the full properties of mathematics.

The final level of measurement is a ratio-level measure. This type of measurement involves the full mathematical properties of numbers and contains the most possible information about a measured concept. That is, a ratio-level measure includes the values of the categories, the order of the categories, and the intervals between the categories; it also precisely indicates the relative amounts of the variable that the categories represent because its scale includes a meaningful zero. A common ratio-level measure in political science is income in dollars. Each dollar number is different, the numbers have a meaningful order ($1, $2, $3, etc.), the interval between dollars is the same anywhere on the scale (the difference between $1 and $2 is the same as the difference between $1,000 and $1,001), and the zero is meaningful ($0 of income is the absence of income). Interval- and ratio-level measures often are referred to as *quantitative* data in later chapters.

Identifying the level of measurement of variables is important, because the level of measurement indicates the data analysis techniques that can be used and the conclusions that can be drawn about the relationships between variables. Higher-order methods often require higher levels of measurement, while other methods have been developed for lower levels of measurement. The decision of which level of measurement to use is not always a straightforward one, and uncertainty and disagreement often exist among researchers concerning these decisions. Few phenomena inherently require one particular level of measurement. Often, a phenomenon can be measured with any level of measurement, depending on the particular technique designed by the researcher and the claims the researcher is willing to make about the resulting measure.

Dichotomous variables—that is, variables with only two categories—are special cases as they can be used as nominal-, ordinal-, or even ratio-level variables. For example, we could measure nuclear capability with two categories, where a country that has nuclear capabilities would be coded as a 1 and a country that does not would be coded as a 0. One could interpret this variable as nuclear capability being present or absent in a country, and therefore a 1 represents more of the concept, nuclear capability. Zero and one are different, they can be put in meaningful order, the interval matters, and zero is meaningful, so it meets all of the requirements of a ratio-level variable. Dichotomous variables, therefore, highlight an important aspect of the level of measurement—that the level of measurement is primarily valuable as a label used in thinking about the properties of a variable. Some variables you encounter will be difficult to place in one level or the other, and that is okay. The biggest value of contemplating the level of measurement is that we are challenged to think about the properties of a variable before using the variable in analysis.

Working with Precision: Too Little or Too Much

Researchers usually try to devise as high a level of measurement for their concepts as possible (nominal being the lowest level of measurement and ratio the highest). Aside from the added value of more information and mathematical properties, there are some practical considerations. It is easy to transform ratio-level information (e.g., age in number of years) into ordinal-level information (e.g., age groups). However, the reverse, transforming ordinal into ratio, cannot be done. Similarly, researchers frequently begin an analysis with ordinal and nominal measures with quite a few categories but subsequently collapse or combine the data to create fewer categories. They do this so that they have enough cases in each category for statistical analysis or to make comparisons easier for the reader to follow. For example, one might want to present comparisons simply between Democrats and Republicans rather than presenting data broken down into categories of strong, moderate, and weak for each party.

It may seem contradictory now to point out that extremely precise measures also may create problems. For example, measures with many response possibilities take up space if they are questions on a written questionnaire or require more time to explain if they are included in a telephone survey. Such questions may also confuse or tire survey respondents. A more serious problem is that they may lead to measurement error.

CONCLUSION

In this chapter, we discussed the beginning stages of a scientific research project. A research project must provide—to both the producer and the consumer of social scientific knowledge—the answers to these important questions: What phenomenon is the researcher trying to understand and explain? What explanation has the researcher proposed for the political behavior or attributes in question? What are the meanings of the concepts used in this explanation? What specific hypothesis relating two or more variables will be tested? What is the unit of analysis for the observations? How are the concepts measured? Are these measurements reliable and valid? If these questions are answered adequately, then the research will have a firm foundation.

TERMS INTRODUCED

Alternative-form method. A method of testing measurement reliability. Measures the same concept more than once, but it uses two different measures of the same concept rather than the same measure. These measures are then compared. If they yield similar results, the measures are considered reliable.   91

Antecedent variable. An independent variable that precedes other independent variables in time.   75

Arrow diagram. A pictorial representation of a researcher's explanatory scheme.   76

Categorical measure. A variable measured using categories. A nominal- or ordinal-level measure.   93

Constant. A concept or variable whose values do not vary.   74

Construct validity. Validity demonstrated for a measure by showing that it is related to the measure of another concept.   91

Content validity. Involves determining the full domain or meaning of a particular concept and then making sure that all components of the meaning are included in the measure.   91

Convergent construct validity. When a measure of a concept is related to a measure of another concept with which the original concept is thought to be associated.   91

Cross-level analysis. The use of data at one level of aggregation to make inferences at another level of aggregation.   85

Dependent variable. The phenomenon thought to be influenced, affected, or caused by some other phenomenon.   74

Dichotomous variable. A variable with only two categories—these variables are special cases as they can be used at the nominal, ordinal, or even ratio level.   95

Directional hypothesis. A hypothesis that specifies the expected relationship between two or more variables.   81

Discriminant construct validity. A method of demonstrating measurement validity by comparing two measures that theoretically are expected *not* to be related. If the measures do not correlate with one another, then discriminant construct validity is demonstrated.   92

Ecological fallacy. The fallacy of deducing a false relationship between the attributes or behavior of individuals based on observing that relationship for groups to which the individuals belong.   85

Ecological inference. The process of inferring a relationship between characteristics of individuals based on group or aggregate data.   85

Face validity. When a measure appears to accurately measure the concept it is supposed to measure. Face validity may only be asserted, rather than empirically demonstrated, because face validity is essentially a matter of judgment.   91

Hypothesis. A tentative or provisional or unconfirmed statement that can (in principle) be verified.   77

Independent variable. The phenomenon thought to influence, affect, or cause some other phenomenon.   74

Interval-level measure. Includes the properties of the nominal level (characteristics are different) and the ordinal level (characteristics can be put in a meaningful order). But unlike nominal and ordinal measures, the intervals between the categories or values assigned to the observations *do* have meaning.   94

Intervening variable. A variable coming between an independent variable and a dependent variable in an explanatory scheme.   75

Level of measurement. Refers to the type of information that we think our measurements contain and the mathematical properties they possess. Determines the type of comparisons that can be made across a number of observations on the same variable.   92

Measurement bias. A type of measurement error that results in systematically over- or undermeasuring the value of a concept.   88

Negative relationship. A relationship in which high values of one variable are associated with low values of another variable or in which low values of one variable are associated with high values of another variable.   81

Nominal-level measure. Indicates that the values assigned to a variable represent only different categories or classifications for that variable.   93

Operational definitions. The rules by which a concept is measured and scores assigned.   88

Operationalization. The process of assigning numerals or scores to a variable to represent the values of a concept.   88

Ordinal-level measure. Indicates that the values assigned to a variable can be compared in terms of having more or less of a particular attribute.   93

Positive relationship. A relationship in which the values of one variable increase (or decrease) as the values of another variable increase (or decrease).   81

Precision. The extent to which measurements are complete and informative.   92

Quantitative measure. An interval- or ratio-level measure. A measure with numerical properties.   90

Random measurement error. An error in measurement that has no systematic direction or cause.   88

Ratio-level measure. This type of measurement involves the full mathematical properties of numbers and contains the most possible information about a measured concept.   95

Reliability. The consistency of results from a procedure or measure in repeated tests or trials.   90

Split-halves method. A method of testing reliability by applying two measures of the same concept at the same time. The results of the two measures are then compared.   91

Tautology. A hypothesis in which the independent and dependent variables are identical, making it impossible to disconfirm.   83

Test-retest method. Involves applying the same measure to the same observations at two periods in time, then comparing the results to test for measurement reliability.   90

Unit of analysis. The type of actor (individual, group, institution, nation) specified in a researcher's hypothesis.   84

Validity. Refers to the degree of correspondence between the measure and the concept it is thought to measure.   91

SUGGESTED READINGS

Achen, Christopher H., and W. Phillips Shively. *Cross-Level Inference*. Chicago: University of Chicago Press, 1995.

King, Gary. *A Solution to the Ecological Inference Problem*. Princeton, NJ: Princeton University Press, 1997.

King, Gary, Ori Rosen, and Martin A. Tanner, eds. *Ecological Inference: New Methodological Strategies*. Cambridge, UK: Cambridge University Press, 2004.

Outhwaite, William, and Stephen P. Turner, eds. *The Sage Handbook of Social Science Methodology*. Los Angeles, CA: Sage, 2007.

NOTES

1. Lane Kenworthy and Jonas Pontusson, "Rising Inequality and the Politics of Redistribution in Affluent Countries," *Perspectives on Politics* 3, no. 3 (2005): 449–71. Accessed February 11, 2019. Available at https://doi.org/10.1017/S1537592705050292.

2. John D'Attoma, "Divided Nation: The North-South Cleavage in Italian Tax Compliance," *Polity* 49, no. 1 (January 2017): 66–99.

3. Susan Hyde, "The Observer Effect in International Politics: Evidence from a Natural Experiment," *World Politics* 60, no. 1 (2007): 37–63.

4. S. Erdem Aytaç, Luis Schiumerini, and Susan Stokes, "Protests and Repression in New Democracies," *Perspectives on Politics* 15, no. 1 (2017): 62–82.

5. Jennifer J. Jones, "Talk 'like a Man': The Linguistic Styles of Hillary Clinton, 1992–2013," *Perspectives on Politics* 14, no. 3 (2016): 625–42.

6. Kenworthy and Pontusson, "Rising Inequality and the Politics of Redistribution."

7. This term is used by Susan Ann Kay in *Introduction to the Analysis of Political Data* (Englewood Cliffs, NJ: Prentice Hall, 1991), 6.

8. Steven C. Poe and C. Neal Tate, "Repression of Human Rights to Personal Integrity in the 1980s: A Global Analysis," *American Political Science Review* 88, no. 4 (1994): 853–72.

9. Christopher H. Achen and W. Phillips Shively, *Cross-Level Inference* (Chicago: University of Chicago Press, 1995), 4.

10. Ibid.

11. Ibid., 5–10.

12. For example, see Gary King, *A Solution to the Ecological Inference Problem* (Princeton, NJ: Princeton University Press, 1997); Achen and Shively, *Cross-Level Inference*;

and Barry C. Burden and David C. Kimball, "Measuring Ticket Splitting," in *Why Americans Split Their Tickets: Campaigns, Competition, and Divided Government* (Ann Arbor: University of Michigan Press, 2002), chap. 3.

13. Sidney Verba and Norman H. Nie, *Participation in America: Political Democracy and Social Equality* (New York: Harper and Row, 1972), 2.

14. Ted Robert Gurr, *Why Men Rebel* (Princeton, NJ: Princeton University Press, 1970), 3–4.

15. Angus Campbell, Gerald Gurin, and Warren E. Miller, *The Voter Decides* (Evanston, IL: Row, Peterson, 1954), 187.

16. Philip E. Converse, "The Nature of Belief Systems in Mass Publics," in *Ideology and Discontent*, ed. David E. Apter (New York: Free Press, 1964), 207.

17. Michael Coppedge and John Gerring, "Conceptualizing and Measuring Democracy: A New Approach," *Perspectives on Politics* 9, no. 2 (2011): 247–67.

18. W. Phillips Shively, *The Craft of Political Research* (Englewood Cliffs, NJ: Prentice Hall, 1980), 33.

19. Kenworthy and Pontusson, "Rising Inequality and the Politics of Redistribution."

20. GSS Data Explorer, "Should Govt Reduce Income Differences," question wording for the variable EQWLTH. Accessed February 10, 2019. Available at https://gssdataexplorer.norc.org/variables/243/vshow.

21. Edward G. Carmines and Richard A. Zeller, *Reliability and Validity Assessment*, A Sage University Paper: Quantitative Applications in the Social Sciences no. 07–017 (Beverly Hills, CA: Sage, 1979).

5 SAMPLING

A researcher's decision whether to collect data for a population or for a sample is usually made on practical grounds. If time, money, and other costs were not considerations, it would almost always be better to collect data for a population, because we would then be sure that the observed cases accurately reflected the population characteristics of interest. However, in many if not most instances, it is simply not possible or feasible to study an entire population. Since research is costly and time-consuming, researchers must weigh the advantages and disadvantages of using a population or a sample. The advantages of taking a sample are often savings in time and money. The disadvantage is that information based on a sample is usually less accurate or more subject to error than is information collected from a population.

Consider, for example, Aytaç, Schiumerini, and Stokes's study, "Protests and Repression in New Democracies,"[1] discussed in greater detail in chapter 1. The authors investigated whether the electoral security of governments in new democracies causes governments to scale up or scale down police repression in response to protests. Of course, asking survey questions of every citizen, in every new democracy, would be impractical. So, the authors selected three cases, Brazil, Turkey, and Ukraine, and relied on sampling to collect responses from a small number of people in each country to make conclusions about the opinions of the entire populations in each country. If an investigation of public opinion rests on one hundred or even one thousand observations, can it really say anything about the millions of people who comprise the general public? Can it, in other words, lead to reliable and valid conclusions?

Our task in this chapter is to provide an answer to two general questions. First, exactly what are samples, and what kind of information do they supply? Do they really provide precise measures of a larger population, or do they just offer rough approximations? That is, how much confidence can we place in statements about a population given observations derived from a very few of its members? Second, how are observations chosen from a

CHAPTER OBJECTIVES

5.1 Describe how sampling works.

5.2 Explain what can be learned from a population sample and its limitations.

5.3 Explain why the sampling distribution is key to using inferential statistics.

5.4 Explain how probability samples create a representative sample for use in inference about the population.

5.5 Explore why nonprobability samples can be a satisfactory choice for some projects.

population for a sample? We begin answering these questions with a discussion of inferences based on samples followed by a description of sampling techniques.

THE BASICS OF SAMPLING

The fundamentals are quite simple, at least in theory (see figure 5-1). Suppose we want to assess how well Americans think President Trump is doing his job. At the outset, we need to clarify what we mean by *Americans*. More formally, we need to define or specify an appropriate population. In the figure, the population is defined to be all adult citizens, aged eighteen and older, in the United States in 2018. A **population** is any well-defined set of units of analysis. A population does not necessarily refer to people. A population might be a set of counties, corporations, government agencies, events, magazine articles, or years. What is important is that the population be carefully and fully defined and that it be relevant to the research question. The polygon in figure 5-1 represents the population of adult American citizens. Since there are millions and millions of citizens, the diagram only symbolizes this huge number. In this hypothetical analysis, our claims refer to these people, not to Germans or Mexicans or children or any other group.

HELPFUL HINTS
POPULATION

Do not be confused by the term *population*, which, as the text indicates, means simply all of the cases of interest. We could define a population as the people living in China. But a population could also consist of a set of all of the nongovernmental organizations operating in Brazil. In the first case, the units of analysis are individuals; in the second case, they are organizations.

Since it is impossible to interview everyone, a more practical approach is to select just a "few" members of the population for further investigation. This is where sampling comes in. A **sample** is any subset of units collected in some manner from a population. (In the figure, the sample consists of just ten out of millions of people.) The sample size and *how* its members are chosen determine the quality (that is, the accuracy and reliability) of inferences about the whole population. The important things to clarify are the method of selection and the number of observations to be drawn.

Once a sample has been gathered, features or characteristics of interest can be examined and measured. The attributes of most interest in empirical research are numerical or quantitative indicators such as averages or percentages. These measures—or **sample statistics**, as they are known—are used to approximate the corresponding population parameters, or values. That is the idea behind the red arrow in figure 5-1: we use sample statistics to estimate population parameters (characteristics). It may be intuitively obvious that the sample

FIGURE 5-1 ■ Population and Sample

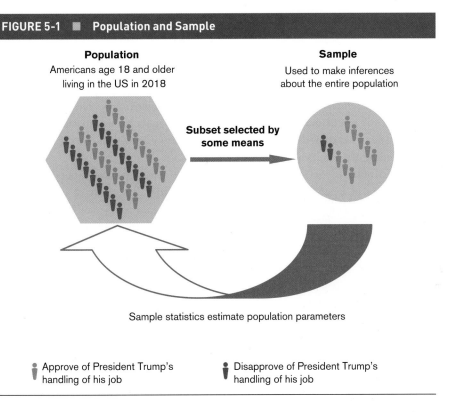

Sample statistics estimate population parameters

👤 Approve of President Trump's handling of his job

👤 Disapprove of President Trump's handling of his job

statistics will not exactly equal the corresponding population values. But, as we demonstrate in this chapter, if we follow suitable procedures, they will be reasonably close.

HOW DO WE USE A SAMPLE TO LEARN ABOUT A POPULATION?

The population parameter of interest in this example is the percentage of American adults who approve of President Trump's handling of his job as president. Samples provide only estimates or approximations of population attributes. Occasionally, these estimates may be right on the money. Most of the time, however, they will differ from the true value of the population parameter. When we report a sample statistic, we always assume there will be a margin of error, or a difference between the reported sample statistics and actual population parameter values. For example, a finding that 53 percent of a random sample approves of the way the president is handling his job does not mean that exactly 53 percent of the public approves. It means merely that *approximately* 53 percent approve. In other words, researchers sacrifice some precision whenever they rely on samples instead of enumerating and measuring the entire population. How much precision is lost (that is, how accurate the estimate is) depends on how the sample has been drawn and its size.

Where does the loss of precision or accuracy come from? The answer is usually chance, or luck of the draw. If you flip a coin ten times, you probably will not get exactly five heads, even though the probability of heads is one-half. Just as with a coin toss, a random sample is not likely to produce a sample statistic that precisely matches the value of a corresponding population parameter. But if we follow proper procedures and certain assumptions have been met (for example, the sample is a simple random sample from a known population), a sample statistic approximates the numerical value of a population parameter. The difficulty is figuring out how far off the estimate is likely to be in any individual case. This is where an understanding of statistics helps.

The goal of **statistical inference** is to make supportable conjectures about the unknown characteristics of a population based on sample statistics. The study of statistics partly involves defining much more precisely what *supportable* means. The key to making inferences from a sample statistic about a population parameter is the sampling distribution.

HELPFUL HINTS
NOTATION

Population parameters are typically denoted by capital Roman or Greek letters. A proportion, such as the proportion of Americans who support President Trump at a particular time, typically is designated P or p. The purpose of sampling is to collect data that provide an accurate inference about a population parameter. An **estimator**, then, is a sample statistic based on sample observations that estimates the numerical value of a population characteristic, or parameter. A specific estimator of a population characteristic or attribute calculated from sample data

is called a sample statistic. Like population parameters, these are typically denoted by symbols or letters. Frequently, we use a hat (^) over a character to denote a sample statistic; in some situations, a lowercase letter is used—for example, a lowercase p for a sample proportion. Sometimes, though, another symbol is used. The population mean (average) is almost always symbolized by μ (the lowercase Greek *mu*). But in this case nearly everyone lets $\bar{Y}$, not $\hat{\mu}$, stand for the sample mean.

Sampling Distribution

Continuing with our presidential approval example, suppose you interview ten *randomly* chosen adult Americans and ask them about President Trump's performance.[2] Suppose further that when asked the question, "Do you approve or disapprove of the way Donald Trump is handling his job as president?"[3] eight of the ten approved and two disapproved. Based on this sample, you could report the sample statistic, .80, or 80 percent approval of President Trump's performance. Finally, suppose for the moment that you possess mystical powers and are able to divine that the true population parameter is exactly .50, or 50 percent. Of course, usually no one knows the population value because at the time of a poll it is unobserved, but we will pretend that we do in order to illustrate the ideas of sampling and inference. Your sample statistic of .80 overestimates the population parameter by quite a bit.

The difference between the sample statistic of .80 and the population parameter of .50 is called the **sampling error**, and arises because only a portion of a population is observed. In this example, you happened to randomly include eight people who approve of the president in your sample of ten. A different sample of ten could just as easily include only two people who approve because the sample size is so small.

What you need is some way to measure the amount of error or uncertainty in the estimate so that you can report the margin of error. That is, you want to be able to say, "Yes, my estimate is probably not equal to the real value, but chances are that it is close." What exactly do words like *chances are* and *close* mean?

To answer those questions, imagine taking another, totally independent sample of ten people residing in the United States. (We will assume that not much time has passed since the first sample, so President Trump's real level of approval in the population is still 50 percent.) This time, the estimate turns out to be .30, or 30 percent.

Repeating the procedure once more, you find that the next estimated proportion of presidential approval is .40, or 40 percent. Finally, you take a fourth independent sample and find that the estimated proportion, .60, is again wide of the mark. So far, two of your estimates have been too high, two too low, and none exactly on target. But notice that the average of the estimates,

$$\frac{\left(.80 + .30 + .40 + .60\right)}{4} = .525,$$

is not far from the real value of .50.

After taking one hundred samples, or one thousand samples, you could plot the percentage of Americans approving of President Trump's handling of his job in a frequency distribution. To do this, you would record the average percent approval from each sample on the *x*-axis and the frequency of observing each approval value on the *y*-axis, as in figure 5-2. As you add more and more marks on the frequency distribution, you will begin to see a bell-shaped distribution appear—the shape of the normal distribution. What would happen, you might wonder, if you repeated the process indefinitely? That is, what would happen if you took an infinite number of independent samples of $n = 10$ and calculated the proportion of presidential approval in each one?[4] (Throughout this discussion, and the entire book, we use *n* to denote the size of a sample.)

A **sampling distribution** is a theoretical frequency distribution of a statistic (like a percentage or a mean) generated from an infinite number of samples drawn from a population. The sampling distribution is normally distributed for every observable variable, no matter the represented concept (at war or not, party ID, race, ideology, level of democracy, etc.). That is a vitally important point because it serves as the basis for inferential statistics. Furthermore, the mean of the sampling distribution equals the population parameter. Because the sampling distribution is a theoretical concept and cannot be observed, one cannot verify this through observation, but you can use many thousands of samples to understand the concept.

Figure 5-2 demonstrates the concept of the sampling distribution. In figure 5-2, we have plotted four frequency distributions for presidential approval. In the upper left, you will see a plot of 100 proportions taken from samples of $n = 10$. Notice that with just 100 sample proportions, the mean of the distribution is .529, and we can begin to see what looks like a bell-shaped normal distribution. Moving to the second distribution in the figure on the lower left, we have plotted the proportions from 1,000 samples of $n = 10$, and the mean is now closer to .500 at .493. The third plot at the top of the right side of figure 5-2 includes proportions from 10,000 samples of $n = 10$ with a mean of .495. The final distribution on the bottom right includes proportions from 100,000 samples of $n = 10$ and has a mean of .500, equal to the population mean. As the number of plotted proportions increases from 100 to 1,000, 10,000, and 100,000 in this illustration, you should note that the mean of each distribution is converging on the population mean as the number of samples increases, and you should be able to more clearly see the bell-shaped normal distribution emerge. If we continued this example to 1,000,000 or 10,000,000 sample proportions, the shape of the normal distribution would become even clearer.

FIGURE 5-2 ■ Sampling Distribution Illustration

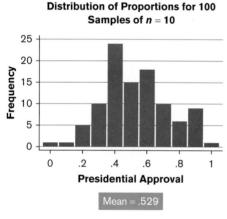

Distribution of Proportions for 100 Samples of $n = 10$

Mean = .529

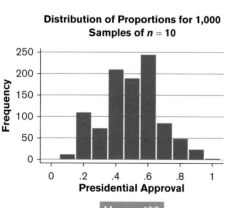

Distribution of Proportions for 1,000 Samples of $n = 10$

Mean = .493

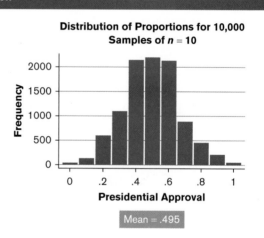

Distribution of Proportions for 10,000 Samples of $n = 10$

Mean = .495

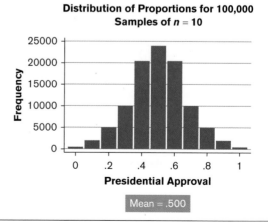

Distribution of Proportions for 100,000 Samples of $n = 10$

Mean = .500

This illustration highlights an important point about samples and the statistics calculated from them. If statistics are calculated for each of many independently and randomly chosen samples, their average or mean will equal the corresponding true, or population, value, no matter the sample size. Statisticians refer to this mean as the **expected value** (*E*) of the estimator. This idea can be stated more succinctly.

In the case of a sample proportion based on a simple random sample, we have

$$E(p) = P,$$

where *p* is the estimated sample proportion, and the equation reads, "The *expected* (or long-run, or average) value of sample proportions equals the population proportion, *P*."

In plain words, although any particular estimate may not equal the parameter value of the population from which the data come, if the sampling procedure were to be repeated an infinite number of times and a sample estimate calculated each time, then the average, or mean, of these results would equal the true value. This fact gives us confidence in the sampling method, though not in any particular sample statistic. Since figure 5-2 includes a maximum of only 100,000 estimates, not an infinite number, it only *illustrates* what can be demonstrated mathematically for sample statistics. As such, our best guess of the value of the population parameter is the value of the sample statistic.

While the value of the sample statistic is the best guess of the value of the population parameter, there is still a chance that the sample statistic could be quite different from the population parameter. Because all variables share the same sampling distribution, we can use the probabilities associated with the normal distribution to estimate how well a sample statistic reflects the population parameter. You will see how this is done in chapter 12 where we elaborate on the normal distribution and the calculation of *z* scores and confidence intervals. For now, we need only understand the intuition that sample estimates will in fact vary from sample to sample, and apply this to a more commonly used concept when discussing samples: the margin of error. When pollsters report the margin of error—say, plus or minus three points—they are informing the reader that while the estimate is, say, .50, a margin of error of three points means that the true value is likely to fall between .47 and .53, but the best guess is .50. The margin of error captures the notion of variability in sampling estimates.

Sample Size and Margin of Error

In our presidential approval example, we used sample sizes of 10 individuals. Your intuition might tell you that a sample of 10 is not large enough for you to trust the results. The problem with small sample sizes, like *n* = 10, is that one could realistically create a sample with no women, or no Republicans, or no senior citizens, and the sample would therefore not be representative of the population. Larger samples are more likely than smaller samples to be representative of the population from which the sample is drawn. In other words, a larger sample of Americans is more likely to include the same characteristics as the population, in the same proportions, than a smaller sample. Larger sample sizes are usually better than smaller sample sizes when it comes to representativeness, but with larger samples come larger costs. Most professional polling organizations use sample sizes of 800 to 1,500 when sampling the adult population of the United States. These sample sizes balance representativeness with cost. As you can see in table 5-1, the margin of error drops precipitously when increasing the sample size at the low end of the scale, but similar changes above $n = 1,250$ make very little difference in the margin of error. It is quite cost prohibitive to sample above $n = 1,500$, and the added sample size would not produce much more certainty. Increasing the sample size from 2,000 to 5,000 only decreases the margin of error from 2.19 to 1.39, a difference of just .80!

SAMPLING METHODS

The chapter to this point has focused on sampling theory and why a sample can be used to make inferences about a population. We now turn our attention to sampling techniques researchers use to create samples from populations. Before proceeding further, we should note that what usually matters most is that samples are obtained according to well-established rules. To understand why, we need to review some terms commonly used in discussions of sampling.[5]

Once we have identified and properly defined our population, all adult Americans in the continuing example, we can turn our attention to creating a complete list of the elements that make up a sampling frame. An **element** (frequently called a unit of analysis) is a single occurrence, realization, or instance of the objects or entities being studied. In

TABLE 5-1 ■ Margin of Error and Sample Size	
n	Calculated Margin of Error
10	30.99%
50	13.86%
100	9.80%
250	6.20%
500	4.38%
1,000	3.10%
1,250	2.77%
1,500	2.53%
2,000	2.19%
5,000	1.39%

Note: Calculated by authors.

our presidential approval example, the elements are individual American adults. Elements might also be individual states, agencies, countries, campaign advertisements, political speeches, wars, organizations, laws, or legislatures, just to name a few. A **sampling frame** is a list from which sampling units are drawn into a sample, and it must be specified clearly. In simple cases, the **sampling unit** is the same as an element. In more complicated sampling designs, it may be a collection of elements.

For reasons that we discuss shortly, a population may be stratified—that is, subdivided or broken up into groups of similar elements—before a sample is drawn. Each **stratum** or layer is a subgroup of a population that shares one or more characteristics. For example, we might divide the population of campaign speeches in the last four presidential elections into four strata, each stratum containing speeches from one of the four elections. The chosen strata are usually characteristics or attributes thought to be related to the dependent variables under study.

Technically speaking, all elements that are part of the population of interest to the research question should be part of the sampling frame as sampling units. If they are not, any data collected may not be representative of the population. The important implication is that as the sample becomes less representative of the population, inferences about the population become less valid. Often, however, sampling frames are incomplete. Consider our presidential approval example. A complete sampling frame would include some hard-to-identify or -locate strata including college students, homeless people, or other transient individuals. People with multiple addresses, or none, can be particularly difficult to include in a sampling frame due to their frequent movement from place to place. The closer the sampling frame is to the population of interest or theoretical population, the better.

Sometimes lists of elements exist that constitute the sampling frame. For example, the Conference of Mayors may have a list of current mayors of cities with fifty thousand residents or more. The existence of a list may be enticing to a researcher, since it removes the need to create one from scratch. But lists may represent an inappropriate sampling frame if they are out of date or incorrect, or if they do not really correspond to the population of interest. Consider, for example, a phone directory as a sampling frame. While the list includes a great many households, it does not include unlisted numbers or cell-phone-only households making the phone directory a problematic sampling frame. Researchers should carefully check their sampling frames for potential omissions or erroneously included elements. Consumers of research should also carefully examine sampling frames to see that they match the populations researchers claim to be studying.

TYPES OF SAMPLES

Researchers make a basic distinction among types of samples according to how the data are collected. We mentioned earlier that political scientists often select a sample, collect information about elements in the sample, and then use those data to make inferences about the population from which the sample was drawn (see figure 5-3). In other words, they make inferences about the whole population from what they know about a smaller group.

Figure 5-3 demonstrates how statistics are used to make inferences about a population from sample data. If a sampling frame is incomplete or inappropriate, **sample bias** will occur. In such cases, the sample will be unrepresentative of the population of interest, and inaccurate conclusions about the population may be drawn. Sample bias may also be caused by a biased selection of elements, even if the sampling frame is a complete and accurate list of the elements in the population.

Because of the concern over sample bias, it is important to distinguish between two basic types of samples: probability and nonprobability samples. A **probability sample** is simply a sample for which each element in the population has a known probability of being included in the sample. This knowledge allows a researcher to calculate how accurately the sample reflects the population from which it is drawn. By contrast, a **nonprobability sample** is one in which each element in the population has an unknown probability of being selected. The probability of selection is required for the use of statistical theory to make inferences. For this reason, probability samples are preferred to nonprobability samples when possible.

In the next several sections, we consider different types of probability samples: simple random samples, systematic random samples, stratified samples (both proportionate and disproportionate), and cluster samples. We then examine nonprobability samples and their uses.

FIGURE 5-3 ■ The Process of Making Inferences from Populations

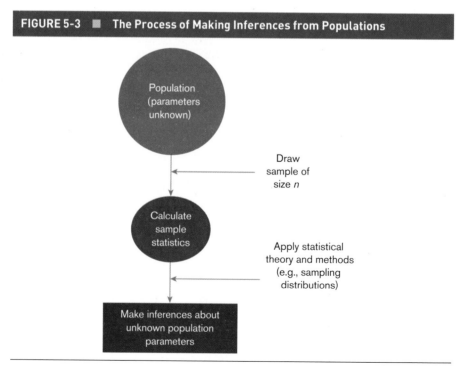

Simple Random Samples

In a **simple random sample**, each element and combination of elements has an equal chance of being selected.[6] The most elementary form of a simple random sample is akin to drawing names from a hat. Imagine that we want to draw a sample of 50 countries from the population of 195 countries in the world. In this procedure, every country name is written on a strip of paper and added to the hat before a select number of paper strips are removed from the hat at random. The selected countries are then included in the sample.

Another procedure for selecting elements at random is by assigning a number to each element in the sampling frame and then using a random number table, which is simply a list of random numbers, generally created using a computer, to select a sample of numbers (see table 5-2). Once a sequential number is assigned, elements can be added to the sample by selecting the numbers at random using the random number table. Continuing with the country example, if we want a sample of 50 from a population of 195 countries, the first step would be to sequentially number each country in the population, 1, 2, 3, and so on, up to 195. We would then generate 50 random numbers between 001 and 195—or enough to draw the required sample size. Each time a number between 001 and 195 appeared, we would select the element in the population with that number. If a number appeared more than once, we would ignore that number after the first time, and simply go on to another number (this is called sampling without replacement). Alternatively, we could include an element more than once if the number appeared at random more than once (this is called sampling with replacement).

Simple random sampling requires a list of the members of the population in the form of a sampling frame (see above). For example, a simple random sample of countries could be chosen from a list of all the countries in the world. One of the most important advantages of a random sample is that because every element in the sampling frame has an equal chance of selection, it is likely, as the sample gets larger and larger, that the sample will share the characteristics of the population (see our discussion of the sampling distribution above). The problem, as we will see, is that obtaining a sampling frame that is the same as the population is not always easy or even possible.

TABLE 5-2 ■ Fifty Random Numbers									
046	033	035	065	086	180	163	015	043	077
109	092	041	187	100	114	052	058	131	107
084	187	172	186	063	163	131	110	070	142
009	180	005	147	112	189	132	155	129	193
089	191	123	018	104	126	153	157	033	058

Note: The fifty random numbers lie between 1 and 195 and were computer-generated.

Systematic Random Samples

Assigning numbers to all elements in a list and then using random numbers to select elements may be a cumbersome procedure. Fortunately, a systematic sample, in which elements are selected from a list at predetermined intervals, provides an alternative method that is sometimes easier to apply. It too requires a list of the target population, but the list is randomized to maintain a random sample. That is, every kth element on the list is selected, where k is the number that will result in the desired number of elements being selected. This number is called the sampling interval, or the "skip" or number of elements between elements that are drawn, and is simply $k = N/n$, where N is the "population" size and n is the desired sample size.

Returning to our example of the 195 countries of the world, we could treat the countries as a list with 195 entries. If we wanted a sample size of $n = 10$, we would divide the total by 10 to get the sampling fraction or interval: $k = 195/10 = 19.5$, and round up to 20. So, starting at a random point, we could take every 20th country until we had a sample of 10. (If we started at 11, we would include the 11th, 31st, and 51st countries, and so on.) Systematic sampling is useful when dealing with a long list of population elements.

Despite its advantages, systematic sampling may result in a biased sample in at least two situations.[7] One occurs if elements on the list have been ranked according to a characteristic. In that situation, the position of the random start will affect the average value of the characteristic for the sample. For example, if students were ranked from the lowest to the highest grade point average, a systematic sample with students 1, 51, and 101 would have a lower GPA than a sample with students 50, 100, and 150. Each sample would yield a GPA that presented a biased picture of the student population.

The second situation leading to bias occurs if the list contains a pattern that corresponds to the sampling interval. Suppose you were conducting a study of the attitudes of children from large families and you were working with a list of the children listed by age in each family. If the families included in the list all had six children and your sampling interval was six (or any multiple of six), then systematic sampling would result in a sample of children who were all in the same position among their siblings. If attitudes varied with birth order, then your findings would be biased. Something like this does not happen often, but should be considered.

Stratified Samples

A stratified sample is a probability sample in which elements are divided into groups, called strata, based on a characteristic, and elements are selected from each stratum in proportion to its representation in the total population. In stratified sampling, sampling units are divided into strata with each unit appearing in only one stratum. Then a simple random sample or systematic sample is taken from each stratum.

A stratified sample can be either proportionate or disproportionate. In proportionate sampling, a researcher uses a stratified sample in which each stratum is represented in proportion to its size in the population—what researchers call a proportionate sample.

For example, let's consider Visser et al.'s study, "Mail Surveys for Election Forecasting? An Evaluation of the *Columbus Dispatch* Poll."[8] In order to analyze how well mail surveys could be used to predict election outcomes, the authors examined mail surveys in Ohio published by the *Columbus Dispatch*. If the *Columbus Dispatch* surveys were collected using a random sample of Ohioans, the results might be biased because voters in different parts of the state voted at different rates. To account for this possibility, and avoid the bias associated with turnout in different parts of the state, the survey administrators divided the state into six different regions: Cincinnati, Cleveland, Columbus, Dayton, Toledo, and southeastern rural Appalachia.[9] Data were then collected from each stratum in proportion to the percentage of the statewide vote to come from each region in the two previous statewide elections. By using stratified sampling, the newspaper was able to ensure that the sample would be representative of the likely statewide vote distribution.

In selecting characteristics on which to stratify a list, you should choose characteristics of particular theoretical importance in your study. The key is creating strata that are meaningful in the context of your project. In this example, maintaining the proportion of voters in each region is of utmost importance because, otherwise, the sample estimate of voting behavior might be biased.

In the example of stratified sampling we have considered so far, we assured ourselves of a more representative sample in which each stratum was represented in proportion to its size in the population. There may be occasions, however, when we wish to take a **disproportionate sample**. In such cases, we would select a stratified sample in which elements sharing a characteristic are underrepresented or overrepresented in our sample.[10]

For example, consider the dilemma the researchers at the Pew Research Center faced when trying to study the U.S. Hispanic population. When Pew collected survey data in March 2016, Hispanics made up 13 percent of the sample, or 291 out of 2,254 respondents. This sample was fairly representative of the 15 percent of Hispanics in the population. While this comprised enough Hispanic respondents to analyze behavior and make conclusions, researchers could make more precise conclusions if there had been more Hispanics in the sample. In order to strengthen their ability to analyze Hispanics in particular, the researchers decided to oversample Hispanics in a June 2016 survey. Oversampling is taking a disproportionate sample of some units in the population. In this case, researchers intentionally included more Hispanics in the sample relative to everyone else in the population. This resulted in a sample with 24 percent Hispanics, or 543 Hispanics out of a total of 2,245 respondents. The researchers chose to make the sample less representative of the population in order to better analyze Hispanics—something that could not be achieved without oversampling Hispanics.[11] The oversampling of Hispanics would, of course, create problems for making conclusions about the whole population because there are more Hispanics in the sample than in the population. Researchers can correct for that issue by weighting the sample (multiplying by the correct proportions of each racial group) to bring the sample back in line with the full population. Weighting has the effect of reducing the impact of oversampled groups and increasing the impact of undersampled groups.

Cluster Samples

Thus far, we have considered examples in which a list of elements in the sampling frame exists. There are, however, situations in which a sample is needed but no list of elements exists and to create one would be prohibitively expensive. A **cluster sample** is a probability sample in which the sampling frame initially consists of clusters of elements. Since only some of the elements are to be selected in a sample, it is unnecessary to secure a list of all elements in the population at the outset.

In cluster sampling, groups or clusters of elements are identified and listed as sampling units. Next, a sample is drawn from this list of sampling units. Then, for the sampled units only, elements are identified and sampled. For example, consider again Aytaç et al.'s study, "Protests and Repression in New Democracies." Five months after the Gezi Park protests, the authors conducted a probability sample of 1,214 adults in Istanbul. The authors intended to interview respondents in a face-to-face manner. In-person interviews are time intensive in terms of both the interview and the travel to interview locations. As such, limiting geographic locations can save resources. For this project, the authors began by randomly selecting 101 neighborhoods from the districts of Istanbul. Next, they randomly selected streets within the neighborhoods. Finally, the authors chose houses on the selected streets at random and then chose the individual in each house to be interviewed at random according to first name.[12]

This is an example of a random sample because the neighborhoods, streets within neighborhoods, houses on streets, and people within houses were each chosen at random. At the same time, the cluster process reduced the geographic spread of the respondents and thereby saved resources. Note that the authors did not need to know the total number of adults in Istanbul ahead of time because, using this method, each household has an equal chance of being selected. The probability that any given adult in a household will be selected is equal to the probability of one's neighborhood being selected times the probability of one's street being selected times the probability of one's household being selected times the probability of the individual being selected. Thus, cluster sampling conforms to the requirements of a probability sample.

Systematic, stratified (both proportionate and disproportionate), and cluster samples are acceptable and often more practical alternatives to the simple random sample. In each case, the probability of a particular element's being selected is known; consequently, the accuracy of the sample can be determined. The type of sample chosen depends on the resources a researcher has available and the availability of an accurate and comprehensive list of the elements in a well-defined target population.

Nonprobability Samples

A nonprobability sample is a sample for which each element in the total population has an unknown probability of being selected. Probability samples are usually preferable to nonprobability samples because they represent a large population fairly accurately and it is possible to calculate how close an estimated characteristic is to the population value. In some situations, however, probability sampling may be too expensive to justify (in exploratory research, for example), or the target population may be too ill defined to permit probability sampling.

HELPFUL HINTS
SAMPLING IN THE REAL WORLD

Later in the book, in chapter 13, we analyze data from the *United States Citizenship, Involvement, Democracy (CID) Survey, 2006*, a nationwide study of political participation. The project employed a multistage sampling design. A reconstruction of the steps taken to identify and interview respondents shows just how complex (and arduous) sampling can be.[13]

1. *Population:* "Eligible respondents were household members, males or females, age 18 years old and older. . . . The sample was designed to specifically represent the adult population residing in occupied residential housing units, and by definition excluded residents of institutions, group quarters, or those residing on military bases."

2. *Sampling frame:* All residential units.

3. *Stratification levels:* The four standard census regions and metropolitan areas.

4. *Clusters:* "Within each primary stratum, all counties, and by extension every census tract, block group and household, were ordered in a strict hierarchical fashion. . . . Within each metropolitan stratum, MSAs [metropolitan statistical areas] and their constituent counties were arrayed by size (i.e., number of households). Within each MSA, the central-city county or counties were listed first, followed by all non-central-city counties. In the four non-metropolitan strata, states and individual counties within each state were arrayed in serpentine order, North-to-South, and East-to-West. Within county, Census Tracts and Block Groups were arrayed in numerical sequence, which naturally groups together households within cities, towns, and other minor civil divisions (MCDs)."

5. *Selecting households:* "Within each sample PSU [primary sampling unit], two block groups (BG) were selected at random, without replacement. . . . All residential housing units within a sample BG were then identified using the U.S. Postal Service Delivery Sequence File (DSF) and one address selected at random. The next fourteen residential addresses were then identified, along with any intervening commercial, vacant, or seasonal units. The result was a designated walking list that was supplied to each interviewer, along with a map showing the exact segment location, streets, addresses, etc. The street/address listing typically captures about 98% of all occupied housing units."

6. *Interviewer instructions:* "Interviewers were given street/address listings with 15 addresses, and were instructed to work the first ten pieces to a maximum of six callbacks. In order to properly manage the release of sample and strive to work all released sample to its maximum attempts, interviewers were asked to check in once they had attained five interviews or worked the first ten pieces to final dispositions or six active attempts, whichever came first. Throughout the field period the field director made daily decisions regarding whether each interviewer should continue working their first ten pieces or be provided more sample to work. Again, the overall goal was to attain a maximum number of attempts with as little sample as possible within a limited field period and an overall goal of approximately 1,000 completed interviews."

It is perhaps clear now why phone and internet surveys are so popular.

For example, college professors often use a **convenience sample**, a nonprobability sample in which the selection of elements is determined by the researcher's convenience, to investigate political behavior using college students. While recruiting students enrolled in a political science class is not representative of the larger population, it is certainly convenient for the professor who can quickly collect data using college students to test ideas.

Researchers also may feel that they can learn more by studying carefully selected and perhaps unusual cases than by studying representative ones. In many cases when nonprobability samples are used, researchers are forgoing the representativeness of random samples because nonprobability samples are the only samples that will allow the researcher to make observations. Consider, for example, a researcher interested in studying undocumented immigrants. There is no comprehensive list of undocumented immigrants, and some go out of their way to remain difficult to find. In this case, a nonprobability sample might be a better choice if it allowed the researcher to complete the project even if the data were not representative. A brief description follows of some of the types of nonprobability samples.

With a **purposive sample**, a researcher exercises considerable discretion over what observations to study, because the goal is typically to study a diverse and usually limited number of observations rather than to analyze a sample representative of a larger target population. Richard F. Fenno Jr.'s *Home Style*, which describes the behavior of eighteen incumbent representatives, is an example of research based on a purposive sample.[14] Likewise, a study of journalists that concentrated on prominent journalists in Washington, D.C., or New York City would be a purposive rather than a representative sample of all journalists. Purposive sampling techniques are discussed in more depth in chapter 7 in regard to case selection.

A **quota sample** is a sample in which elements are sampled in proportion to their representation in the population. In this respect, quota sampling is similar to proportionate stratified sampling. The difference between quota sampling and stratified sampling is that the elements in the quota sample are not chosen in a probabilistic manner. Instead, they are chosen in a purposive or convenient fashion until the appropriate number of each type of element (quota) has been found. Because of the lack of probability sampling of elements, quota samples are usually biased estimates of the target population. Even more important, it is impossible to calculate the accuracy of a quota sample.

For example, consider again Aytaç et al.'s study, "Protests and Repression in New Democracies." The authors sought to measure public opinion about protests in São Paulo, Brazil, in June 2013. One of the surveys the authors used was a representative sample of the São Paulo population conducted by interviewing 805 residents of São Paulo at several locations across the city. Respondents were randomly selected, but the sample was constructed using quotas for both gender and age because it was important to the authors that the sample accurately reflect the gender and age of the population of protesters.

In a **snowball sample**, respondents are used to identify other persons who might qualify for inclusion in the sample.[15] These people are then interviewed and asked to supply appropriate names for further interviewing—and the sample builds like a snowball. This process is continued until enough persons are interviewed to satisfy the researcher's needs. Snowball sampling is particularly useful in studying a relatively select, rare, or difficult-to-locate population such as undocumented workers. Building a sample by talking with workers and asking them for introductions to others may be useful because undocumented populations may try to avoid detection by the authorities and keep a low profile.

CONCLUSION

In this chapter, we discussed what it means to select a sample out of a target population, the various types of samples that political scientists use, and the kinds of information they yield. Samples allow researchers to save time, money, and other costs. However, this benefit is a mixed blessing, for by avoiding these costs, researchers must rely on information that is potentially less accurate than if they had collected data on the entire target population.

The following guidelines may help researchers who are deciding whether or not to rely on a sample as well as students who are evaluating research based on sample data:

- If cost is not a major consideration, and the validity of the measures will not suffer, it is generally better to collect data for the complete target population than for just a sample of that population.

- If cost or validity considerations dictate that a sample be drawn, a probability sample is usually preferable to a nonprobability sample. The accuracy of sample estimates can be determined only for probability samples. If the desire to represent a target population accurately is not a major concern or is impossible to achieve, then a nonprobability sample may be used.

- Probability samples yield estimates of the target population. All samples are subject to sampling error. No sample, no matter how well drawn, can provide an exact measurement of an attribute of, or relationship within, the target population.

Fortunately, statistical theory gives us methods for making systematic inferences about unknown parameters and for objectively measuring the probabilities of making inferential errors. This information allows the researcher and the scientific community to judge the tenability of many empirical claims.

TERMS INTRODUCED

Cluster sample. A probability sample that is used when no list of elements exists. The sampling frame initially consists of clusters of elements.   114

Convenience sample. A nonprobability sample in which the selection of elements is determined by the researcher's convenience.   116

Disproportionate sample. A stratified sample in which elements sharing a characteristic are underrepresented or overrepresented in the sample.   113

Element. A particular case or entity about which information is collected; the unit of analysis.   108

Estimator. A statistic based on sample observations that is used to estimate the numerical value of an unknown population parameter.   104

Expected value. The mean or average value of a sample statistic based on repeated samples from a population.   107

Nonprobability sample. A sample for which each element in the total population has an unknown probability of being selected.   110

Population. All the cases or observations covered by a hypothesis; all the units of analysis to which a hypothesis applies.   102

Population parameter. A characteristic or an attribute in a population (not a sample) that can be quantified.   104

Probability sample. A sample for which each element in the total population has a known probability of being selected.   110

Proportionate sample. A probability sample that draws elements from a stratified population at a rate proportional to the size of the samples.   112

Purposive sample. A nonprobability sample in which a researcher uses discretion in selecting elements for observation.   116

Quota sample. A nonprobability sample in which elements are sampled in proportion to their representation in the population.

Sample. A subset of observations or cases drawn from a specified population.   102

Sample bias. The bias that occurs whenever some elements of a population are systematically excluded from a sample. It is usually due to an incomplete sampling frame or a nonprobability method of selecting elements.   110

Sample statistic. The estimator of a population characteristic or attribute that is calculated from sample data.   102

Sampling distribution. A theoretical (nonobserved) distribution of sample statistics calculated on samples of size N that, if known, permits the calculation of confidence intervals and the test of statistical hypotheses.   105

Sampling error. The difference between a sample estimate and a corresponding population parameter that arises because only a portion of a population is observed.   105

Sampling fraction. The proportion of the population included in a sample.   112

Sampling frame. The population from which a sample is drawn. Ideally, it is the same as the total population of interest to a study.   109

Sampling interval. The number of elements in a sampling frame divided by the desired sample size.   112

Sampling unit. The entity listed in a sampling frame. It may be the same as an element, or it may be a group or cluster of elements.   109

Simple random sample. A probability sample in which each element has an equal chance of being selected.   111

Snowball sample. A nonprobability sample in which potential respondents are identified by respondents already participating in the sample.   116

Statistical inference. The mathematical theory and techniques for making conjectures about the unknown characteristics (parameters) of populations based on samples.   104

Stratified sample. A probability sample in which elements sharing one or more characteristics are grouped and elements are selected from each group in proportion to the group's representation in the total population.   112

Stratum. A subgroup of a population that shares one or more characteristics.   109

Systematic sample. A probability sample in which elements are selected from a list at predetermined intervals.   112

SUGGESTED READINGS

Govindarajulu, Zakkula. *Elements of Sampling Theory and Methods.* Upper Saddle River, NJ: Prentice Hall, 1999.

Kish, Leslie. *Survey Sampling.* New York: Wiley, 1995. (Originally published 1965.) This is the classic treatment of this subject.

Levy, Paul S., and Stanley Lemeshow. *Sampling of Populations: Methods and Applications.* 3rd ed. New York: Wiley, 1999.

Lohr, Sharon L. *Sampling: Design and Analysis.* Pacific Grove, CA: Duxbury Press, 1999.

Rea, Louis M., and Richard A. Parker. *Designing and Conducting Survey Research: A Comprehensive Guide.* 2nd ed. San Francisco: Jossey-Bass, 1997.

Rosnow, Ralph L., and Robert Rosenthal. *Beginning Behavioral Research: A Conceptual Primer.* 3rd ed. Upper Saddle River, NJ: Prentice Hall, 1998.

NOTES

1. S. Erdem Aytaç, Luis Schiumerini, and Susan Stokes, "Protests and Repression in New Democracies," *Perspectives on Politics* 15, no. 1 (2017): table 4, pp. 74–75.

2. Assume that we have a simple random sample, meaning that each member of the sample has been selected randomly and independently of all the others. We assume the same throughout the discussion in this section. See our discussion of probability samples for further elaboration.

3. Pew Research Center, "Declining Confidence in Trump, Lower Job Ratings for Congressional Leaders," November 2, 2017. Accessed February 12, 2019. Available at http://www.people-press .org/2017/11/02/declining-confidence-in-trump-lower-job-ratings-for-congressional-leaders/#views-of-donald-trump.

4. This procedure, called sampling with replacement, is premised on the assumption that, at least theoretically, people will sooner or later be interviewed twice or more. We ignore this nuance, because it does not affect the validity of the conclusions in this case.

5. This discussion of terms used in sampling is drawn primarily from Earl R. Babbie, *Survey Research Methods* (Belmont, CA: Wadsworth, 1973), 79–81.

6. When used to describe a type of sample, *random* does not mean haphazard or casual; rather, it means that every element has a known probability of being selected. Strictly speaking, to ensure an equal chance of selection, *replacement* is required—putting each selected element back on the list before the next element is selected. In *simple* random sampling, however, elements are selected without replacement. This means that on each successive draw, the probability of an element's being selected increases because fewer and fewer elements remain. But for each draw, the probability of being selected is equal among the remaining elements. If the sample size is less than one-fifth the size of the population, the slight deviation from strict random sampling caused by sampling without replacement is acceptable. See Hubert M. Blalock Jr., *Social Statistics*, 2nd ed. (New York: McGraw-Hill, 1972), 513–14.

7. Blalock, *Social Statistics*, 515.

8. Penny S. Visser, Jon A. Krosnick, Jesse Marquette, and Michael Curtin, "Mail Surveys for Election Forecasting? An Evaluation of the *Columbus Dispatch Poll*," *Public Opinion Quarterly* 60 (1996): 181–227.

9. Ibid.

10. There are two reasons to use disproportionate sampling in addition to obtaining enough cases for statistical analysis of subgroups: the high cost of sampling some strata and differences in the heterogeneity of some strata that result in differences in sampling error. A researcher might want to minimize sampling when it is costly or increase sampling from heterogeneous strata while decreasing it from homogeneous strata. See Blalock, *Social Statistics*, 513–14, 518–19.

11. Andrew Mercer, "Oversampling Is Used to Study Small Groups, Nor Bias Poll Results," *Pew Research Center*, October 25, 2016. Accessed February 12, 2019. Available at http://www.pewresearch.org/

fact-tank/2016/10/25/oversampling-is-used-to-study-small-groups-not-bias-poll-results/.

12. Aytaç et al., "Protests and Repression in New Democracies," Supplementary Materials. Accessed February 12, 2019. Available at https://www.cambridge.org/core/journals/perspectives-on-politics/article/div-classtitleprotests-and-repression-in-new-democraciesdiv/E99269D609B4F3DD1231BD36E44C5BF4#fndtn-supplementary-materials.

13. Marc M. Howard, James L. Gibson, and Dietlind Stolle, *United States Citizenship, Involvement,* *Democracy (CID) Survey, 2006* (Ann Arbor, MI: Inter-university Consortium for Political and Social Research, 2007).

14. Richard F. Fenno Jr., *Home Style: House Members in Their Districts* (Boston: Little, Brown, 1978).

15. Snowball sampling is generally considered to be a nonprobability sampling technique, although strategies have been developed to achieve a probability sample with this method. See Kenneth D. Bailey, *Methods of Social Research* (New York: Free Press, 1978), 83.

STUDENT STUDY SITE

for CQ Press

Give your students the SAGE edge!

SAGE edge offers a robust online environment featuring an impressive array of free tools and resources for review, study, and further exploration, keeping both instructors and students on the cutting edge of teaching and learning. Learn more at **edge.sagepub.com/johnson9e.**

6 RESEARCH DESIGN
Establishing Causation

The goal of many political science projects is to investigate relationships between concepts and test explanations for political phenomena. In chapter 4, we focused on the basic building blocks of the research process. These steps are just part of a project's **research design**: a plan that shows how one intends to study an empirical question. It indicates what specific theory or propositions will be tested, what the appropriate "units of analysis" (e.g., people, nations, organizations) are for the tests, what measurements or observations (i.e., data) are needed, how all this information will be collected, and which analytical and statistical procedures will be used to examine the data. All the parts of a research design should work to the same end: drawing sound conclusions supported by observable evidence. In this chapter, we explain the logic behind testing a causal relationship to supply the observable evidence when answering an empirical research question within the context of a research design. A causal assertion goes beyond the claim that one thing is associated with another. It asserts, instead, that one event or entity "leads to," or "produces," or "brings about" something else. Establishing causal connections is the gold standard of modern empirical political science.

We begin with a discussion of causation followed by an illustration of how causal analysis works in the context of a specific research design: the classical randomized experiment. We then move on to an explanation of the organization of the next four chapters that cover qualitative methods and qualitative analysis in chapters 7 and 8 followed by quantitative analysis in chapters 9 and 10. You should note that these chapters are presented in a parallel style with qualitative and quantitative chapters covering the same issues but from different perspectives. The division between qualitative and quantitative work is only one definition. In practice, political scientists routinely switch between qualitative and quantitative analyses for different projects depending on any project's demands. In fact, many projects use mixed methods with both quantitative and qualitative methods and analyses. As such, students

CHAPTER OBJECTIVES

6.1 Distinguish between a causal and spurious relationship.

6.2 Understand the three necessary components in a causal relationship.

6.3 Illustrate how the classical randomized experiment demonstrates how a research design can be used to verify a causal relationship.

6.4 Understand internal and external validity.

6.5 Understand the distinction between qualitative and quantitative research design.

6.6 Understand the difference between effects-of-causes and causes-of-effects approaches to investigating causal relationships.

should take note of how both qualitative and quantitative methods rely on the same scientific principles and employ similar logic in empiricism. After reading this chapter and the following four chapters, you should have a clear idea of how a research design is constructed, how political scientists can test causal relationships in a research design, and how researchers use both qualitative and quantitative methods and how the two can be combined in mixed methods projects.

VERIFYING CAUSAL ASSERTIONS

Causal versus Spurious Relationships

Celebrities from Angelina Jolie, to Oprah Winfrey, to Arnold Schwarzenegger and many others have used their celebrity in politics. Some make statements in the press, some testify before Congress or serve on presidential commissions, some serve as surrogates on the campaign trail, and some run for public office. The question in which we are interested here is how celebrities affect how citizens view political parties. There are many possible answers to this question. Perhaps, because we know that celebrities are commonly hired to endorse commercial products, and these products seem to sell well, we could hypothesize that celebrity endorsement of a political party *causes* more support for the party among voters.

How could we support such an assertion? Suppose we decide to measure celebrity endorsement of a party by whether or not a celebrity made a financial contribution to a party. Just after an election, it might be possible to interview a sample of voters, ask them if they were aware of former professional football player Peyton Manning's financial support of Republican candidates, and then determine their support for the Republican Party. We might even find a relationship or connection between awareness of Manning's financial support of Republicans and support for the Republican Party.

How do we know that awareness of celebrity support is really *causing* party support? Is it possible that a third factor is really responsible for the relationship? Maybe gender

HELPFUL HINTS
CAUSALITY VERSUS CORRELATION

The ability to tell the difference between causation and correlation is an essential skill for political scientists and interested citizens alike. Why? Because so many arguments about policy and politics contain statements that may or may not be legitimately or reasonably interpreted as causal.

In social science research as well as common parlance, a **correlation** is simply a statement that two things are systematically related. But that's the extent of the information carried by a statement of correlation.

A *causal* declaration, by contrast, communicates much more. A change in the state of one thing *brings about* (in full or in part) a change in the state of another. This statement carries with it claims about time order and the elimination of alternative explanations for the observed relationship.

causes both higher awareness of Manning's support for Republicans and support for the Republican Party. This would be a spurious relationship. A spurious relationship arises because two things are both affected by a third factor and thus appear to be related. Once this additional factor has been identified and controlled for, the original relationship weakens or disappears altogether. Figure 6-1 illustrates causal and spurious relationships in this example.[1] How do you interpret these diagrams? The first one (Causal Relationship) shows a "true" causal connection between X (awareness of Manning endorsement) and Y (support for the Republican Party). The arrow indicates causality: X causes Y. If this is the way the world really is, then celebrity endorsements have a direct link to voting behavior. The arrowhead indicates the direction of causality, because in this example X causes Y and not vice versa. In the second diagram (Spurious Relationship), by contrast, X and Y are not directly related; there is no causal arrow between them. Yet an apparent association is produced by the action of a third factor, Z. Hence, the presence of the third factor, Z (gender = male), creates the impression of a causal relationship between X and Y, but this impression is misleading, because once we take into account the third factor—in language we use later, "once we control for Z"—the original relationship weakens or disappears.

Distinguishing real, causal relations from spurious ones is an important part of any scientific research project. To explain the phenomena fully, we must know how and why two things are connected, not simply that they are associated. Thus, one of the major goals in designing research is to come up with a way to make valid causal inferences. Ideally, such a design does three things:

1. *Covariation:* It demonstrates that the alleged cause (call it X) does in fact covary with the supposed effect, Y. Public opinion polls or surveys can relatively easily identify associations. To make a causal inference, however, more is needed.

FIGURE 6-1 ■ Causal and Spurious Relationships

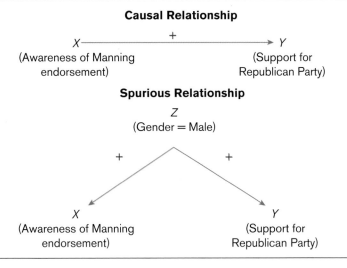

Causal Relationship

X ———————— + ————————→ Y
(Awareness of Manning   (Support for
endorsement)   Republican Party)

Spurious Relationship

Z
(Gender = Male)

+   +

X Y
(Awareness of Manning   (Support for
endorsement)   Republican Party)

2. *Time order:* The research must demonstrate that the cause preceded the effect: X must come before Y in time. After all, can an effect appear before its cause? In many observational settings, it may be difficult, if not impossible, to tell whether X came before or after Y. Still, even if we can be confident of the time order, we have to demonstrate that a third condition holds.

3. *Elimination of possible alternative causes, sometimes termed "confounding factors":* The research must be conducted in such a way that all possible joint causes of X and Y have been eliminated.

In order to find empirical support for a causal relationship between celebrity endorsement and voting behavior, we would need to establish that (1) awareness of Manning's endorsement varies with support for the Republican Party, (2) the voter was aware of Manning's financial support for Republicans before taking a position on the Republican Party, and (3) other possible joint causes of awareness and support have been satisfactorily eliminated.

It might not be going too far to say that causal assertions are the lifeblood of political and policy discourse. Take just about any contentious subject. Its manifest argument may be about "we should" statements. But underlying the argument, we guarantee, you will always find causal assertions (e.g., "We should limit greenhouse gas emissions because they cause an increase in global temperatures"). Since virtually any potential relations of interest could be spurious, how do we discern between direct and indirect linkages among variables? The answer leads to research design, because how we frame problems and plan their solutions greatly affects the confidence we can have in our results. In the next section, we illustrate how researchers can identify causal relationships using a classical randomized **experiment**. This example is intended to demonstrate how a research design, and the choices a researcher makes in designing a research project, can illuminate our understanding of causal relationships. Understanding experimental design is crucial because it provides an especially clear way to see what must be done to validate or confirm or support a causal claim. The lessons learned in this example can be applied in chapters 7 through 10 when we explore qualitative and quantitative research methods and analyses. Also note that while the example here is quantitative, the same logic applies in qualitative designs.

The Classical Randomized Experiment

A **classical randomized experiment** is the ideal starting point for understanding how political scientists can establish a causal relationship.[2] Before getting to an explanation for why the classical randomized experiment is such a valuable teaching tool when it comes to assessing causal assertions, we will discuss the basic components of most classical randomized experiments.

The research question in our earlier example, how celebrities affect how citizens view political parties, is one of the questions Anthony J. Nownes asked in "An Experimental Investigation of the Effects of Celebrity Support for Political Parties in the United States."[3] We will use the Nownes article as an example of the classical randomized experiment and its components.

The classical randomized experiment begins, like many other designs, with sampling. Nownes chose to employ an availability sample of 503 college students at the University of Tennessee. Availability sampling is quite typical when an experiment is in a laboratory setting because it can be difficult to get enough subjects to participate by using other sampling methods discussed in chapter 5. We will return to the consequences of using availability samples in experiments later when discussing external validity.

The most important design component of a classical randomized experiment is the **stimulus**, or **test factor**. A stimulus, or test factor, is a condition applied to participants in an experiment in a way in which the researcher can measure some sort of effect. A stimulus could be reading a news story, watching a debate, listening to a speech, or any number of other examples. The stimulus is the most important component of an experiment because the stimulus is generally hypothesized to affect or not affect the dependent variable and the result answers the research question. Nownes's experiment used paragraphs about two celebrities' financial support for parties as the stimulus, and the stimulus was used to establish causation.

The experimenter creates at least two groups: an **experimental group**, which receives or is exposed to an experimental treatment or stimulus, and a **control group**, so called because its subjects do not undergo the experimental manipulation or receive the experimental treatment or stimulus. An experiment should have one experimental group for every experimental treatment. For example, Nownes employed two experimental groups: one group that was exposed to the Peyton Manning treatment and one group that was exposed to the Jennifer Aniston treatment. Nownes also used a control group that was not exposed to information about Peyton Manning, Jennifer Aniston, or any other celebrity.

Nownes *randomly* assigned subjects to the two experimental groups and the control group. Random assignment to groups is called **randomization**, and it means that membership is a matter of chance, not self-selection. Moreover, random assignment of subjects at the outset ensures that the experimental and control groups are virtually identical in all respects. They will, in other words, contain similar proportions, or averages, of females and males; liberals, moderates, conservatives, and nonpartisans; Republicans and Democrats; voters and nonvoters; and so on. On average, the groups will not differ in any respect.[4] Randomization, as we will see, is what makes experiments such powerful tools for making causal inferences.

Once assigned to groups, the researcher administers a **pretest** that measures responses before the administration of a stimulus. This is an essential step in measuring causation. Subjects in Nownes's experiment completed a questionnaire that included questions about demographics and political views. The questionnaire also included a question about each subject's level of support for the Democratic and Republican Parties. This question is important because it can be used to establish the level of support each subject had for each party before exposure to a stimulus.

Once the pretest is complete, the researcher can administer the stimulus. Nownes administered the treatment as a written cover page. The cover page included two paragraphs for the treatment groups and one paragraph for the control group. The Peyton Manning group's cover page included a short paragraph about Barack Obama and John McCain's love of pets and a second paragraph discussing Peyton Manning's financial contributions to Republican candidates for office. The Jennifer Aniston group's cover page included an identical short paragraph about Barack Obama and John McCain's love of pets and a second paragraph discussing Jennifer Aniston's financial contributions to Democratic candidates for office. The control group's cover page only included the same pet paragraph.

After reading the cover page, the subjects answered the posttest that included the same questions as the pretest. In an experiment, the researcher establishes a dependent variable—the response of interest—that can be measured both before and after the stimulus is given. The measurements are often called pre- and postexperimental measures, and differences in these measures indicate whether or not there has been an experimental effect. An experimental effect, as the term suggests, reflects differences between the two groups' responses to the test factor. *This effect measures the impact of the independent variable on the dependent variable and, consequently, is a main focus of experimental research.* If we were to observe an experimental effect, we would expect to see a difference between the pre- and posttest results for a group exposed to a stimulus. We would not expect to see a difference between the pre- and posttest results for a control group that was not exposed to a stimulus.

The environment of the experiment—that is, the time, location, and other physical aspects—is a critical part of the experimental design. Researchers can maximize their ability to make causal assertions when environmental factors are under the experimenter's direction. Such control means that he or she can control or exclude extraneous factors or influences other than the independent variable that might affect the dependent variable. In Nownes's experiment, both experimental groups and the control group were studied under the same circumstances. Because all groups had the same environmental factors, any differences between the control and experimental subjects cannot be attributed to factors outside of the stimulus. Any differences between measurements of the dependent variable are therefore only attributable to the effect of the stimulus, as the stimulus is the only difference between groups. This is the essential point in this example—if variation is observed between pretest and posttest responses, the only plausible explanation for the variation is *exposure to the stimulus*, because there were no other differences between the different treatment groups and the control group. The subjects answered the same questions, in the same environment, at the same time, and there was not enough time in between the pretest and posttest for any sort of external factor that could change the subjects' answers on the posttest.

The design Nownes employed is representative of the classical randomized experiment. This research design is a valuable teaching tool when thinking about causation and finding evidence to support causal assertions. Remember that we began the chapter considering how we might find support for a causal statement and that causation has three conditions: covariation, time order, and the elimination of possible alternative causes. We are going to focus on just one of Nownes's hypotheses for demonstration purposes: "For respondents who view Peyton Manning positively, evaluations of the Republican Party will become more positive with exposure to information about his financial support for Republicans and the Republican Party."

- *Covariation:* Nownes could establish covariation consistent with the hypothesis if respondents made aware of Peyton Manning's support for Republicans through exposure to the Manning stimulus increased support for the Republican Party. Nownes could measure an increase in support for the Republican Party by comparing the pretest and posttest answers among those in the Manning treatment group or by comparing the answers of those in the Manning experimental group and those in the control group. We would not expect to see any change in the posttest answers among the control group.

- *Time order:* Nownes could establish time order because subjects' opinions of the Republican Party were measured before exposure to the Manning stimulus and after exposure to the Manning stimulus. If there was a difference between the pre- and posttest answers, the difference appeared after exposure to the Manning stimulus.

- *Elimination of possible alternatives:* There are, of course, many different possible explanations for why someone might have exposure to Peyton Manning's political beliefs and support the Republican Party. This experiment eliminated those possible alternatives through randomization of group assignment, the use of a control group, and control over experimental conditions. By randomizing assignment to the two experimental groups and the control group, each group was representative of the larger population of University of Tennessee students. That means that alternative explanations concerning personal characteristics like demographics or ideology could not be responsible for differences between the pre- and posttests within a group, or between the posttests across groups, because the groups were similar to each other and the larger student population. Because there was no variation between the pre- and posttest answers for the control group but the pre- and posttest answers for the experimental groups did vary, we can rule out factors external to the experiment because if such factors were important, Nownes would have observed variation in all of the groups, including the control group. Finally, Nownes controlled all environmental factors during the experiment so that nothing in the environment would change responses on the posttest, and all subjects participated in the exact same environment. All of this is to say that the only remaining explanation for variation was the varying stimulus.

Through covariation, time order, and the elimination of alternative explanations, Nownes established a causal relationship. Other research designs, while employing different techniques, rely on the same logic to establish causal relationships. As we will see in chapters 7 through 10, there are many different qualitative and quantitative research designs, but each can be used to establish causal relationships.

Internal Validity

Statistical theory—and common sense—tells us that properly conducted experiments can lead to valid inferences about causality. In this context, however, *validity* has a particular meaning—namely, that the manipulation of the experimental or independent variable itself, and not some other variable, *did in fact* bring about the observed effect on the dependent variable. Political scientists call this kind of validity "internal validity." **Internal validity** means that the research procedure demonstrated a true cause-and-effect relationship that was not created by spurious factors. Political scientists generally believe that the type of research design we have been discussing—a randomized controlled experiment—has strong internal validity. But it is not foolproof.

Several things can affect a research study's internal validity. As we have argued, the principal strength of experimental research is that the researcher has enough control over the environment to make sure that exposure to the experimental stimulus is the only significant difference between experimental and control groups. Sometimes, however, events other than the experimental stimulus that occur between the pretest and posttest measurements of the dependent variable will affect the dependent variable. Perhaps the students selected to participate in the Nownes experiment took the pretest before the beginning of the semester and the posttest at the end of the semester. Any number of events could occur during that long period in between pre- and posttest, calling internal validity into question.

Another potential confounding influence is *maturation*, or a change in subjects over time that might produce differences between experimental and control groups. For example, subjects may become tired, confused, distracted, or bored during the course of an experiment. These changes may affect their reaction to the test stimulus and introduce an unanticipated effect on posttreatment scores.

Test–subject interaction, the process of measuring the dependent variable prior to the experimental stimulus, may itself affect the posttreatment scores of subjects. For example, simply asking individuals about politics on a pretest may alert them to the purposes of the experiment. And that, in turn, may cause them to behave in unanticipated ways. Continuing with our celebrity example, if the researcher measures the political awareness of the experimental and control groups prior to reading about celebrities' political activity, he or she runs the risk of sensitizing the subjects to certain topics or issues and contributing to a more attentive audience than would otherwise be the case. Consequently, we would not know for sure whether any increase in support for a political party was due to a celebrity's endorsement, the pretest, or a combination of both. Fortunately, some research designs have been developed to separate these various effects.

Selection bias can also lead to problems. Such bias can creep into a study if subjects are picked (intentionally or not) according to some criterion and not randomly. A common selection problem occurs when subjects volunteer to participate in a program. Volunteers may differ significantly from nonvolunteers; for example, volunteers may be more compliant and eager to please, healthier, or more outgoing. Sometimes a person might be picked for participation in an experiment because of an extreme measurement (very high or very low) of the dependent variable. As we stressed, in assigning subjects to experimental and control groups, a researcher hopes that the two groups will be equivalent. If subjects selectively drop out of the study, experimental and control groups that were the same at the start may no longer be equivalent. Thus, **experimental mortality**, or the differential loss of participants from comparison groups, may raise doubts about whether the changes and variation in the dependent variable are due to manipulation of the independent variable.

Another possible problem comes from **demand characteristics**, or aspects of the research situation that cause participants to guess at the investigator's goals and adjust their behavior or opinions accordingly. You may remember from chapter 2 that the human ability to empathize and anticipate others' feelings and intentions (self-reflection) troubles some methodologists, who wonder if this trait does not make behavior inaccessible to scientific inquiry. Most political science experimenters do not think so, but they do realize that test subjects can interact with the experimental personnel and setting in subtle and occasionally unpredictable ways. It has been found that people often want to "help" or contribute to an investigator's goals by acting in ways that will support the main hypotheses.[5] Perhaps something about the experiment on celebrity influence tips off subjects that we, the researchers, expect to find that endorsements affect party support, and perhaps they (even unconsciously) adjust their feelings in order to prove the proposition and hence please us. In this case, it is the desire to satisfy the researchers' objectives that affects support for a party, not the celebrity endorsements themselves. This is not a minor issue. You may have heard about "double-blind studies" in medical research. The goal of this kind of design is to disguise to both patients and attendants who is receiving a real experimental medicine and who is receiving a traditional medicine or placebo, thus reducing the possibility that demand characteristics affect the dependent variable.

In short, a lot of things can go wrong in even the most carefully planned experiment. Nevertheless, experimental research designs are better able to resist threats to internal validity than are other types of research designs. In fact, they provide an ideal against which other research strategies may be compared. Yet even if we devised the most rigorous laboratory experiment possible to test for media effects on political behavior, some readers still might not be convinced that we have found a cause-and-effect relationship that applies to the "real world." What they are concerned about, perhaps without being aware of the term, is externality validity.

External Validity

External validity, the extent to which the results of a study can be generalized across populations, times, and settings, is the touchstone for natural and social scientists alike. Alan S. Gerber and Donald P. Green explained:

> When evaluating the external validity of political experiments, it is common to ask whether the stimulus used in the study resembles the stimuli of interest in the political world, whether the participants resemble the actors who are ordinarily confronted with these stimuli, whether the outcome measures resemble the actual political outcomes of theoretical or practical interest, and whether the context within which actors operate resembles the political context of interest.[6]

In short, the results of a study have "high" external validity if they hold for the world outside of the experimental situation; they have low validity if they only apply to the laboratory.

What sorts of things can compromise one's results? One possibility is that the effects may not be found using a different population. In our example, Nownes found an effect when experimenting with an availability sample of undergraduate students. The results might be valid for students attending the University of Tennessee but not for the public at large. Indeed, the conclusions might not even apply to students at other universities. In general, if a study population is not representative of a larger population, the ability to generalize about the larger population will be limited.

QUALITATIVE AND QUANTITATIVE METHODS AND ANALYSIS: CAUSES-OF-EFFECTS AND EFFECTS-OF-CAUSES APPROACHES

Political scientists use a variety of methods and research designs to study political phenomena. Much of this research aims to explain and identify the causes of political events, activities, and behavior. Gary Goertz and James Mahoney point out that there are two different ways to ask and investigate causal questions. One way, which they label **the causes-of-effects approach**, starts with an outcome (e.g., war, election result, passage of a major piece of legislation) and works backward to the causes. The second way, which they label **the effects-of-causes approach**, starts with a potential cause and works forward to measure its impact on the outcome.[7] They use the example of global warming to demonstrate the difference. If one asks what causes global warming, one is adopting the causes-of-effects approach, whereas if one asks what is the impact of carbon emissions on global temperature, one is adopting the effects-of-causes approach. The methods used by political scientists and other social scientists generally fall into one of two types—qualitative or quantitative—with the types differing "in the extent to which and the ways in which they address causes-of-effects and effects-of-causes questions."[8]

Quantitative methods generally pursue the effects-of-causes approach:

> Quantitative scholars have clearly come down as a group in favor of the effects-of-causes approach as the standard way to do social science. In particular, they have come down in favor of estimating the *average effects* of particular variables within populations or samples. In this tradition scholars view the controlled experiment as the gold standard for research.[9]

As you can see from the earlier discussion in this chapter of the classic randomized experiment, researchers using this design are interested not only in whether the test factor causes a difference in the dependent variables but also (and, generally, more importantly) in the *average size* of the difference. Notice that the classic randomized experiment does not claim to establish that the test factor is the only factor that might cause a change in the dependent variable in the real world. Rather, in this controlled setting, the researcher is able to demonstrate whether or not the test factor had an effect by itself and how large it was. It is possible, even highly likely, that there are other causes that will have an effect on the dependent variable in the real world. In chapter 9, we will discuss quantitative research designs, which allow the researcher to investigate multiple causal factors, but again the emphasis in using these techniques is on the size of the effect of the causal factors singly or in particular combinations, not especially on their overall causal effect.

Qualitative methods, on the other hand, pursue the causes-of-effects approach. In qualitative studies, researchers "are interested in explaining outcomes in individual cases as well as studying the effect of particular causal factors within individual cases."[10] Qualitative studies may be interested in discovering all of the factors that account for a particular outcome, or they may investigate whether a particular factor had an impact on the outcome in a particular case. Qualitative methods are particularly appropriate for investigating any causal mechanisms that may account for observed correlations between variables from quantitative studies.

Another distinction between qualitative and quantitative studies is the number of cases or units of analysis that are included in analyses—whether they are **small N** or **large N studies**. Qualitative studies are small N, whereas quantitative studies can be small N or large N in scope. Quantitative, large N studies were considered preferable to qualitative studies because they could look for relationships that held for large populations and statistics could be used to estimate how confident we could be in accepting the relationships observed in those studies as real or true. Qualitative studies, often referred to as "case studies," were considered to be less scientific because the small number of cases limited the extent to which observations from a case could be generalized to a larger population of cases. Furthermore, it was argued a researcher could choose a case that supported his or her preferred argument. Yet, scholars using qualitative methods argue that the pursuit of causal explanations requires casting a wide investigative net, but doing so for many cases is difficult. Furthermore, it can be said in defense of qualitative methods that they are wholly appropriate when the goal of the research is to explain why relatively rare (and therefore small N), but significant, events occurred. Finally, as we discuss in chapter 7, using a case study to make a causal argument is a rigorous process.

There has been much debate about which method—qualitative or quantitative—best furthers the goal of achieving scientific knowledge in the field of political science, but there is currently a recognition that both approaches have important, albeit different, contributions to make to the empirical study of politics.[11]

In the following four chapters, we embark on a parallel discussion of both qualitative and quantitative research design and data collection. We will discuss research design issues in regard to qualitative methods in chapter 7 and qualitative data collection and analysis in chapter 8. We will then discuss the same issues in regard to quantitative methods in chapter 9 and quantitative analysis in chapter 10.

It is our hope that, through presentation of these chapters in parallel form, you will not only learn a great deal about both qualitative and quantitative methods and analysis, but also see how qualitative and quantitative methods rely on the same scientific principles and use many of the same techniques to test causal relationships. You will also see how researchers can combine qualitative and quantitative methods to take advantage of the strengths and minimize the weaknesses in any single design by engaging in mixed methods.

CONCLUSION

In this chapter, we investigated how political scientists can establish causal relationships by outlining the logic and basic components of the classical randomized experiment. As the Nownes article on celebrities and party support demonstrated, the classical randomized experiment is an excellent starting point for understanding how a research project can be designed and executed to establish causation through covariation, time order, and elimination of alternative explanations. Exposing an experimental group to a stimulus, while not doing so with the control group, allows a researcher to assess differences between pre- and posttest and between experimental group and control group to establish causation. We also explained that different research designs have different levels of internal validity and external validity. In the next four chapters, you will learn a great deal more about research design issues in both qualitative and quantitative methods. You will begin to see the relative advantages and disadvantages of different research designs and why combining both qualitative and quantitative methods in a mixed methods approach is common in political science.

TERMS INTRODUCED

Causes-of-effects approach. An approach to causal questions that starts with an outcome and works backward to the causes. Emphasis is on identifying causes of outcomes.   130

Classical randomized experiment. An experiment with the random assignment of subjects to experimental and control groups with a pretest and posttest for both groups.   124

Control group. A group of subjects that does not receive the experimental treatment or test stimulus.   125

Correlation. A statement that the values or states of one thing systematically vary with the values or states of another; an association between two variables.   122

Demand characteristics. Aspects of the research situation that cause participants to guess the purpose or rationale of the study and adjust their behavior or opinions accordingly.   129

Effects-of-causes approach. An approach to causal questions that starts with a potential cause and works forward to measure its impact on the outcome. Emphasis is on measuring the size of the effect that a cause has on an outcome.   130

Experiment. Research using a research design in which the researcher controls exposure to the test factor or independent variable, the assignment of subjects to groups, and the measurement of responses.   124

Experimental effect. Effect, usually measured numerically, of the experimental variable on the dependent variable.   126

Experimental group. A group of subjects that receives the experimental treatment or test stimulus.   125

Experimental mortality. A differential loss of subjects from experimental and control groups that affects the equivalency of groups; threat to internal validity.   128

External validity. The ability to generalize from one set of research findings to other situations.   129

Internal validity. The ability to show that manipulation or variation of the independent variable actually causes the dependent variable to change.   128

Large *N* studies. Quantitative research designs in which the research examines many cases of a phenomenon.   131

Pretest. Measurement of variables prior to the administration of the experimental treatment or manipulation of the independent variable.   125

Randomization. The random assignment of subjects to experimental and control groups.   125

Research design. A plan specifying how the researcher intends to fulfill the goals of the study; a logical plan for testing hypotheses.   121

Selection bias. Bias due to the assignment of subjects to experimental and control groups according to some criterion and not randomly; threat to internal validity.   128

Small *N* studies. Research designs in which the research examines one or a few cases of a phenomenon in considerable detail.   131

Stimulus or test factor. The independent variable introduced and controlled by an investigator in order to assess its effects on a response or dependent variable.   125

SUGGESTED READINGS

Baele, Stéphane J., and Catarina P. Thomson. "An Experimental Agenda for Securitization Theory." *International Studies Review* 19, no. 4 (December 2017): 646–66. https://doi-org.udel.idm.oclc.org/10.1093/isr/vix014.

Campbell, Donald T., and Julian C. Stanley. *Experimental and Quasi-Experimental Designs for Research.* Chicago: Rand McNally, 1966.

Hakim, Catherine. *Research Design: Strategies and Choices in the Design of Social Research.* Contemporary Social Research Series no. 13. London, UK: Allen and Unwin, 1987.

King, Gary, Robert O. Keohane, and Sidney Verba. *Designing Social Inquiry: Scientific Inference in Qualitative Research.* Princeton, NJ: Princeton University Press, 1994.

NOTES

1. See chapter 13 for a more thorough discussion of spurious relationships.

2. See Donald T. Campbell and Julian C. Stanley, *Experimental and Quasi-Experimental Designs for Research* (Chicago: Rand McNally, 1966), 5–6; and Paul E. Spector, *Research Designs*, A Sage University Paper: Quantitative Applications in the Social Sciences no. 07–023 (Beverly Hills, CA: Sage, 1981), 24–27. Four components of an ideal experiment are identified by Kenneth D. Bailey in *Methods of Social Research* (New York: Free Press, 1978), 191.

3. Anthony J. Nownes, "An Experimental Investigation of the Effects of Celebrity Support for Political Parties in the United States," *American Politics Research* 40, no. 3 (2012): 476–500.

4. If you have trouble following this idea, imagine that you have a large can of marbles, most of which are red but a few of which are blue. Now, draw randomly from the can a single marble and put it in a box. Then draw another marble—again randomly—and put this one in a second box. Repeat this process nineteen more times. At the end, you should have two boxes of twenty marbles each. If you have selected them randomly, there should be approximately the same proportion of red and blue marbles in *each* box. If you started with a can holding 90 percent red marbles and 10 percent blue, for example, each of the two

boxes should hold about eighteen red marbles and two blue ones. These may not be the exact numbers—one, say, might have three blue marbles and the other just one—but these differences will be due solely to chance and will not be statistically significant.

5. Martin T. Orne, "On the Social Psychology of the Psychological Experiment: With Particular Reference to Demand Characteristics and Their Implications," *American Psychologist* 17, no. 11 (1962): 776–83.

6. Alan S. Gerber and Donald P. Green, "Field Experiments and Natural Experiments," in *The Oxford Handbook of Political Methodology*, ed. Janet M.

Box-Steffensmeir, Henry E. Brady, and David Collier (New York: Oxford University Press, 2008), 358.

7. Gary Goertz and James Mahoney, *A Tale of Two Cultures: Qualitative and Quantitative Research in the Social Sciences* (Princeton, NJ: Princeton University Press, 2012), 41.

8. Ibid., 41.

9. Ibid., 41–42.

10. Ibid., 42.

11. See Henry E. Brady and David Collier, eds., *Rethinking Social Inquiry: Diverse Tools, Shared Standards*, 2nd ed. (Lanham, MD: Rowman & Littlefield, 2010).

STUDENT STUDY SITE

SAGE edge for CQ Press

Give your students the SAGE edge!

SAGE edge offers a robust online environment featuring an impressive array of free tools and resources for review, study, and further exploration, keeping both instructors and students on the cutting edge of teaching and learning. Learn more at **edge.sagepub.com/johnson9e.**

7 QUALITATIVE RESEARCH
Case Study Designs

As we pointed out in the previous chapter, a research design is a plan that shows how one intends to study an empirical question. Many factors affect the choice of a design. One is the purpose of the investigation. Whether the research is intended to be exploratory, descriptive, or explanatory will influence its design. The project's feasibility or practicality is another consideration. Some designs may be unethical, while others may be impossible to implement for lack of data or insufficient time and money. Researchers frequently must balance what is possible to accomplish against what would ideally be done to investigate a particular hypothesis. Consequently, many common designs entail unfortunate but necessary compromises, and thus the conclusions that may be drawn from them are more tentative and incomplete than anyone would like.

This chapter explores **case study designs**. These designs involve either a single case or a small number of cases. Recall from chapter 6 that qualitative research is often referred to as small *N* research, whereas quantitative research is referred to as large *N* research. (Note the term *case* is used rather than *unit of analysis*, which is used with large *N* studies.) Research designs associated with quantitative analysis are the subject of chapter 10. The emphasis in both chapters is on understanding how design choices affect the type of empirical claims that can be made,

particularly whether they are causal claims or not. Establishing causal connections is the gold standard of modern empirical political science. But this is no easy task. Thus, this chapter and chapter 9 address the logic behind the search for causation and how to design or plan research to make legitimate causal inferences.

CHAPTER OBJECTIVES

7.1 Explain the importance of case study designs to the study of political phenomena.

7.2 Identify the purposes of case study designs.

7.3 Describe the logic underlying the selection of cases and case comparison.

7.4 Explain the difference between a counterfactual and a mechanistic understanding of causation.

7.5 Describe how process tracing is used to establish causation.

7.6 Understand the limits to generalizing from case studies.

CASE STUDY METHODS

Case study research is an important type of research and, in fact, the only type of research that can be used to answer questions about important, but rare or singular, events. For example, why did the United Nations fail to stop the genocide in Rwanda?[1] Why did democratic consolidation occur in European countries after 1945 where it had not before?[2] And why did rural people support the leftist insurgency in El Salvador at considerable risk to themselves?[3] Two of the research examples introduced in Chapter 1 are case studies. S. Erdem Aytaç, Luis Schiumerini, and Susan Stokes compare the cases of Brazil, Ukraine, and Turkey to investigate why some governments escalate their use of force against citizen protests but others do not.[4] John D'Attoma compares the cases of northern and southern Italy to identify why tax compliance in the two regions differs.[5]

Before we discuss different types and purposes of case study research designs, a brief review of the history of case study research and debate over its contribution to the scientific study of political phenomena will help you to understand current views about the purpose and use of case study research.

Very briefly, the method enjoyed a privileged position in political science research for many years, fell into disfavor, and is now experiencing a newfound appreciation and resurgence. The comparative method (e.g., the systematic comparison of cases) is often traced back to John Stuart Mill's 1843 *A System of Logic* in which he presented several methods of making comparisons including "the method of agreement" and the "method of difference."[6] We will have more to say about the logic of comparisons shortly.

There are several reasons why case studies were the dominant approach to studying politics in the past and why they are still a useful research strategy today. Absent the availability of powerful computing, which has enabled the collection, storage, and analysis of large data sets, researchers were limited to analyzing a single case or comparing a relatively few cases. That is no longer the situation, but there remain significant reasons for engaging in case study research. For example, experimental manipulation of key variables thought to be relevant in explaining past events is not possible, and their manipulation in contemporaneous research is often very difficult or unethical. Thus, researchers must still compare and contrast cases with respect to the presence or absence of causes and outcomes. Furthermore, as pointed out above, some events are relatively rare; therefore, there are not enough observations for statistical analysis. However, case studies were criticized, especially after the advent of large-scale computing, for failing to sufficiently contribute to an accumulation of scientific knowledge about politics and to the development of general theories that were useful in explaining political phenomena. As Alexander L. George and Andrew Bennett state:

> Following the end of World War II, many political scientists were quite favorably disposed toward or even enthusiastic about the prospect of undertaking individual case studies for the development of knowledge and theory. Many case studies were conducted, not only in the field of international relations but also in public administration comparative politics, and American politics. Although individual case studies were often instructive, they did not lend themselves readily to strict comparison or to orderly cumulation. As a result, the initial enthusiasm for case studies gradually faded, and the case study as a strategy for theory development fell into disrepute.[7]

Currently, advocates of case study research contend that case studies have much to contribute to the scientific understanding of politics. While descriptive, relatively atheoretical case studies are recognized as having valid purposes, the emphasis is now on using case studies to test theories and to elucidate causal mechanisms in ways that quantitative methods cannot. As we pointed out in chapter 6, qualitative methods are particularly useful for discovering the *causes of effects*. They differ from quantitative methods in that their purpose is *not* to measure mathematically how variation in a dependent variable is related to variation in an independent variable or variables, or to measure the average value of the dependent variable given specific values of an independent variable for a large number of cases. Rather, case studies may be designed to understand and expose the causal mechanisms that lie behind statistical associations between variables discovered in large N studies. To emphasize the difference between small N and large N studies, case study designs typically refer to causes (C) and outcomes (O) instead of referring to independent and dependent variables.

CASE STUDY TYPES

Case study designs can be categorized according to their purpose or research objective and the logic behind the selection of a case or cases.[8] Here we adopt the typologies put forth by Jack S. Levy.[9]

Purposes of Case Studies

Case studies can be distinguished according to their purpose. Levy suggests a typology with four types: idiographic, hypothesis generating, hypothesis testing, and plausibility probes.

Idiographic case studies aim to describe, explain, or interpret a singular historical episode with no intention of generalizing beyond the case. Idiographic case studies can be further distinguished according to whether they are *inductive or theory-guided*. Inductive case studies lack an explicit theoretical perspective and simply have the purpose of describing all aspects of a case. Another way to think of this type of case study is as a narrative or recounting of events. Theory-guided case studies "are explicitly structured by a well-developed conceptual framework that focuses on some theoretically specified aspects of reality and neglects others."[10] An example of this would be using Anthony Downs's "issue attention cycle" or John W. Kingdon's "three streams" model of policy making to structure a description of the politics of a particular policy.[11] This type of case study is analytical, rather than simply descriptive, yet it does not intend to generate or test hypotheses.

Hypothesis-generating case studies "examine one or more cases for the purpose of developing more general theoretical propositions" that can be tested in future research.[12] For example, researchers might study several cases of conflicts between nations to identify the key factors that seem to have led either to the outbreak of war or to peaceful resolution of the conflict. **Hypothesis-testing case studies** entail testing hypothesized empirical relationships. These types of case studies include investigations of causal mechanisms, an application of case study methods contributing to the resurgence of and respect for case study research. Finally, **plausibility probes** serve several research purposes: "to sharpen a hypothesis or theory, to refine the operationalization or measurement of key variables, or to explore the suitability of a particular case as a vehicle for testing a theory before engaging in a costly and time-consuming research effort."[13]

In idiographic case studies, the researcher typically chooses a case for its historical importance, intrinsic interest, or heuristic value in illustrating a particular analytical framework or theoretical perspective. But, for the latter three types of case studies, the selection of cases is a critical decision in the research process.

The Logic of Case Selection and Case Comparison

Case study research often uses the comparison of cases and logical arguments to make inferences about relationships between causes and outcomes. As stated above, the comparative method is often traced back to the English philosopher John Stuart Mill, who described two comparative strategies. In the **method of difference**, the researcher selects cases in which the outcomes differ, compares the cases looking for the single factor that the cases do not have in common, and concludes that this factor is "the effect, or cause, or a necessary part of the cause, of the phenomenon."[14] The method of difference also applies to situations where the researcher is investigating outcomes that vary in degree (e.g., high, medium, and low levels of an outcome) and identifies a factor that also varies in degree. The method of difference assumes a simple world in which there is a single factor that the cases do not have in common. If there is more than one, which one(s) are causal? Further studies will be needed to settle this question. For this reason, a case study using the method of difference is generally of the hypothesis-generating variety. In the **method of agreement**, the researcher selects cases that share the same outcome and identifies those conditions or causal factors that the cases also have in common. Conditions that the cases do not share are eliminated as possible causal factors.

The information gained from these types of comparisons is limited, however. In the method of agreement, it is possible that some other factor shared by the cases, but not identified by the researcher, accounts for the similarity in outcome. There may be prior or antecedent conditions that account for the shared factor. If the researcher has selected cases in which the antecedent condition is present, further research may involve selecting cases in which it is not. It is also possible that the "causal" factor shared by the cases will be found in another case in which the outcome is not present. In the method of difference, it is possible that the cases differ on some other, unidentified factor. Nevertheless, comparison of cases can lead to the generation of hypotheses and theoretical propositions that can be tested using more cases.

Researchers also rely on logic to improve the strength of their conclusions by selecting a **most likely case** or **least likely case**. A most likely case is one in which theory predicts an outcome is most likely to occur. When the outcome fails to occur, the theory is cast into doubt as it has failed an easy test. The case may suggest important revisions to the theory. An example of a most likely case analysis is the 1973 study by Jeffrey L. Pressman and Aaron Wildavsky in which they examine the implementation of a federal program possessing all of the attributes suggested by theories of implementation to be important for successful implementation, yet the program failed.[15] In a least likely case, a theory faces a difficult test. If, in fact, the theory still appears to explain the outcome, the test provides strong support for the theory. Another selection strategy is to select a **deviant case**. A researcher may choose a case that does not conform to a theory or fit a normal pattern. For example, suppose a researcher looks at the relationship between the average spending per pupil on primary and secondary education and educational outcomes among the states and observes that for the most part as spending increases so do positive educational outcomes, but finds there is a state that achieves very high outcomes while its spending is quite modest in comparison to that of other states. This case would then be carefully examined to identify the reason(s) why it does not fit. Thus, deviant case studies generally contribute to the revision and refinement of theories.

Aytaç et al.'s research on the response of democratic regimes to citizen protests introduced in chapter 1 is an example of a comparative case study using the method of difference.[16] They compare three countries, Brazil, Ukraine, and Turkey, each of which experienced uprisings in 2013. In all three cases, the governments repressed early protests, which led to the mass mobilization of protesters. In two of the countries, Brazil and Ukraine, authorities pulled back the police and made concessions to the protesters. In the third, Turkey, authorities responded by upping the level of repression. The authors then set about systematically comparing the three countries to identify a factor present in Turkey, but absent in Brazil and Ukraine, that might account for Turkey's divergent behavior.

Drawing from previous research into why democracies in general are less repressive, Aytaç et al. suggest that electoral security shapes governments' responses to protest. A key feature of democracy is accountability: In a democracy, authorities can be voted out of office if citizens disapprove of government actions. However, if a government is electorally secure and perceives that there will be no adverse electoral consequences for pursuing a particular action, it will take that action. The researchers present evidence showing that Turkey's regime was much more electorally secure than the regimes in Brazil and Ukraine. In Turkey, party allegiances and important social cleavages coincided. The government's supporters were not among the protesters, and the government was confident that its supporters would not object to the use of violence against the protesters. Furthermore, the authors argue that the "Turkish government did not passively rely on their supporters to reject the protesters; it led its followers to interpret the uprising as a conspiracy against the nation, instigated from abroad."[17]

In the course of their analysis, the researchers investigate and rule out several rival explanations for divergent extrication strategies: They systematically compare the three countries with respect to democratic consolidation, decentralization, incomplete civilian control over the police, ideological orientation of the government, the nature of the threat posed by protesters, and the social class of protesters. These comparisons are shown in table 7-1, which you may remember from chapter 1.[18] The authors were particularly concerned about democratic consolidation as a rival explanation. The authors note that previous scholarly research on the response of democratic regimes to citizen protests concluded that transitional regimes, ones that are neither fully authoritarian nor consolidated democracies, are especially prone to violence against their populations. A consolidated democracy is one that is not expected to revert to authoritarianism. The authors selected countries that were similar in their level of democratic consolidation. In fact, Ukraine's level of democratic consolidation was slightly lower than Turkey's, yet Ukraine resolved its crisis peacefully. Thus, the authors argue that differences in the level of democratic consolidation cannot account for the difference in extrication strategies.

What are the implications of these findings? The authors present their research as a "plausibility probe" and state that it contributes to theory building about the relationship of democracy to governments' use of repression by demonstrating how electoral security shapes governments' responses to protest in democratic settings. They suggest that future cross-national research could test their claim that variation in electoral insecurity explains variation in the response to protests by governments in new democracies.

TABLE 7-1 ■ Extrication Strategies: Where the Cases Fall on Favored and Rival Explanations					
	Security of Office	Centralization	Democratic Consolidation	Control over the Police	Extrication Strategy
Turkey	High	High	Low	High	Repression
Brazil	Low	Low	High	High	Restraint
Ukraine	Low	High	Low	Medium	Restraint

	Ideology of Government	Nature of Threat	Social Class of Protesters	Extrication Strategy
Turkey	Conservative	Low	High	Repression
Brazil	Leftist	Medium	High	Restraint
Ukraine	Conservative	High	High	Restraint

Source: S. Erdem Aytaç, Luis Schiumerini, and Susan Stokes, "Protests and Repression in New Democracies," *Perspectives on Politics* 15, no. 1 (2017): table 4, pp. 74–75.

USING CASES TO EXPLORE CAUSAL MECHANISMS: PROCESS TRACING

Comparative case analysis with the purpose of testing hypotheses relies on a **counterfactual understanding of causation.** It is based on the idea of difference-making: by studying "whether the *absence* of the cause results in the *absence* of the outcome, all other things being equal," we can claim that the cause produced the outcome.[19] Some case studies, however, seek to delve into the connection between cause and outcome and do not rely on counterfactuals to establish causation. Instead, they are based on a **mechanistic understanding** of causation: "Difference-making provides evidence of the cross-case effects of changing values of a posited cause, whereas mechanistic evidence sheds light on causal process within individual cases."[20] Derek Beach and Rasmus Brun Pedersen see a single case study whose purpose is a "mechanism understanding" of causation as a significant method furthering a scientific understanding of political phenomena.[21]

Process tracing refers to case studies that "explicitly unpack mechanisms and engage in detailed empirical tracing of them."[22] Process tracing studies use deductive reasoning and ask, "If an explanation is true, what would be the specific process leading to the outcome?"[23] Process tracing case studies often involve only one case because of the copious amount of information and detail that is required to trace a causal mechanism and to show that rival explanations do not account for an outcome. Process tracing studies may differ from other types of case studies, especially idiographic case studies: due to their intense focus on tracing steps in the causal process and testing evidence, they may not provide a highly readable narrative of events, although the two are not mutually exclusive.

Process tracing depends on logic and has been compared to a detective sifting through evidence in order to solve a mystery. Evidence needs to be tested for its usefulness in reaching conclusions. Stephen Van Evera points out that a strong test of a hypothesis is one in which evidence is *uniquely* predicted by a theory and is *certain* or unequivocal in the prediction. Tests of evidence vary to the extent to which they make unique or certain predictions. From the four possible combinations of uniqueness (or not) and certainty (or not), Van Evera identifies four tests.[24] For simplicity's sake, let us assume we are trying to evaluate a suspect in a murder case in which the victim was shot. *Hoop tests* involve evidence that is certain, but not unique. Hoop tests are useful in weeding out suspects. Thus, we might ask, "Was the suspect in the vicinity of the crime?" Failing the hoop test disqualifies a suspect. How much passing the hoop test points to a particular suspect depends on how many people there were in the vicinity of the crime—if there were many, a suspect passing the hoop test does not greatly increase the probability that our suspect is the murderer. *Smoking-gun tests* provide unique evidence, but not certain evidence. If we find gunpowder residue on the hands of the suspect, this is fairly strong evidence that implicates the suspect. Yet, we cannot rule out a suspect if she does not have gunpowder residue on her hands—after all, she may have worn gloves and disposed of them right away. *Doubly decisive tests* provide both certain and unique evidence. If the police find CCTV footage that shows the suspect holding a gun in the alley where the victim was found, this is very strong evidence pointing to the suspect. *Straw-in-the-wind tests* provide evidence that is neither unique nor certain. Suppose the main suspects are the deceased's sisters and it is discovered that the deceased was planning to sell his share of a family-run business to an outside entity, something the sisters were known to oppose. This evidence provides a motive for the crime, but it doesn't indicate which sister, nor does having a motive prove that someone is a killer. Furthermore, other people may have had other motives for killing the deceased. Process studies frequently use Bayesian logic, which involves probability calculations, to evaluate evidence from tests and update beliefs about competing explanations.[25]

Researchers also talk about causal conditions in terms of whether they are necessary or sufficient. A **necessary cause** is a condition that must be present in order for the outcome to occur. A **sufficient cause** is a condition with which the outcome is always found. The presence of a necessary condition does not guarantee an outcome: A condition may be necessary, but not sufficient. For example, in order to be pregnant, one must be a female, but being a female is not sufficient for the pregnancy outcome. Similarly, a condition can be sufficient but not necessary: The outcome may also be found in the absence of that condition because there are other conditions that cause the outcome. For example, swimming for thirty minutes three times a week may be sufficient to ensure cardiovascular fitness, but it's not necessary. Other forms of exercise performed regularly also lead to fitness. Lastly, there are INUS conditions. An INUS condition is a condition that is an individually necessary part of an unnecessary, but sufficient, condition. For example, having access to a pool or body of water is a necessary condition for swimming, which is an unnecessary, but sufficient, condition for achieving physical fitness.

Let us take a look at the initial steps of a process tracing study by Elizabeth N. Saunders, who traces the effects of beliefs held by presidents on their behavior. Specifically, she hypothesizes that how presidents perceive threats to national security (their causal beliefs about the nature of the threat) shapes both their willingness to engage in international military interventions involving smaller nations and the nature of those interventions.[26] Her research illustrates several important features of process tracing. First, she defines two types of causal beliefs: *Externally focused leaders* believe "that threats are associated with other states' foreign and security policies or international orientation. Such leaders do not see a causal connection between the outcomes and the domestic institutions of smaller powers.[27] *Internally focused* leaders "believe that a smaller power's foreign and security policies are intimately connected to its domestic institutions."[28] Second, she clearly describes how presidents' causal beliefs are linked to military intervention decisions—that is, she outlines the causal mechanism as shown in figure 7-1.

Third, she identifies two competing, alternative explanations, one of which she labels the structural/material conditions hypothesis:

> Leaders evaluate intervention opportunities based on structural and material conditions in the international environment, within their own state, and within the potential intervention target. Given a set of conditions, leaders will make similar cost-benefit calculations about whether and how to intervene, regardless of their own personal beliefs.[29]

The other she labels the domestic competition hypothesis:

> Competition among domestic actors, including not only leaders but also the bureaucracy, the public, advisors, parties, and advocacy groups, drives intervention policy. Intervention decisions, including the choice of strategy, are a product of political interaction among these actors rather than leaders' preferences.[30]

Saunders does not argue that these alternative explanations don't matter; rather, she contends that they are insufficient to explain the intervention choices of presidents. Furthermore,

FIGURE 7-1   ■   How Leaders' Causal Beliefs Influence the Expected Utility of an Intervention Strategy

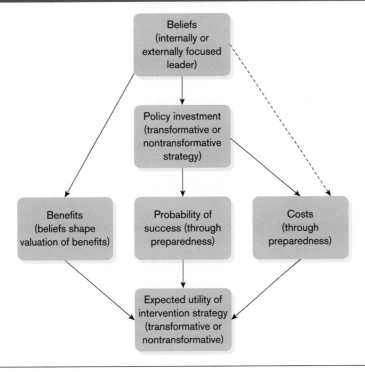

Source: Elizabeth N. Saunders, *Leaders at War: How Presidents Shape Military Interventions* (Ithaca, NY: Cornell University Press, 2011), fig. 2.1, p. 37.

as shown in table 7-2, she makes specific predictions based on the competing explanations about what she would expect to observe.

These predictions form the basis of tests and structure the evaluation of evidence.

Fourth, she clearly describes how she chooses a set of cases. She selects three presidents (Eisenhower, Kennedy, and Johnson) who provide variation in causal beliefs but who governed under similar international conditions: each governed "when the superpower conflict was well underway and the international system was relatively stable."[31] She then identifies cases of potential interventions and explains why she excludes others. For example, she excludes cases in which there was a risk of nuclear escalation. In essence, she is not claiming that her theory would hold up in such cases. She also clearly defines what constitutes an intervention. For each president, she selects one intervention and one nonintervention, closely spaced in time and within the same region. She also includes in her analyses the approaches of all three presidents to the Vietnam War. Finally, she develops a standard set of questions to be asked in each case and a standard set of indicators to code leaders' beliefs,

TABLE 7-2 ■ Summary of Predictions

	Structural/material conditions hypothesis	Domestic competition hypothesis	Causal beliefs hypothesis
Do leaders vary in how they make cost-benefit calculations?	No: Given a set of conditions, leaders make similar cost-benefit calculations.	Maybe, but not decisive: Cost-benefit calculations result from interaction among domestic actors.	Yes: Leaders' causal beliefs systematically influence their cost-benefit calculations.
Do leaders vary in threat perception and how they value benefits?	No: Threat perception and the valuation of benefits are driven by international security factors.	Maybe, but not decisive: Threat perception and the valuation of benefits result from interaction among domestic actors.	Yes: Leaders vary systematically in threat perception and how they value benefits.
Do attempted policy investments reflect causal beliefs?	No: Policy investments are driven by anticipated security needs.	Maybe, but not decisive: Policy investments are the product of competition among domestic actors.	Yes: Leaders attempt to invest in the capabilities that reflect their threat perception.
Does a leader's preferred strategy influence the decision to intervene?	No: Strategy may influence the decision to intervene but it is driven by structural and material factors.	Maybe, but not decisive: Leaders' preferences are only one input into domestic competition.	Yes: A leader will be more likely to intervene if he estimates his favored strategy to be feasible.
Do leaders' causal beliefs affect the choice of strategy?	No: Strategy is driven by the situation on the ground and available capabilities.	Maybe, but not decisive: Strategy is a product of interaction among domestic actors.	Yes: Internally focused leaders are more likely to intervene transformatively. Externally focused leaders are more likely to intervene nontransformatively.
If there are multiple crises, do leaders' causal beliefs affect intervention targets?	No: Target selection results from available capabilities, the target environment, and the security importance of targets.	Maybe, but not decisive: Target selection is a product of interaction among domestic actors.	Yes: Leaders choose targets based on threat perception and where they estimate their favored strategy to be more likely to succeed.
Do leaders considering the same ongoing crisis differ in their evaluations?	No: Any variation results from changes in capabilities or the situation on the ground.	Maybe, but not decisive: Any variation results from changes in interactions among domestic actors.	Yes: Leaders may not agree that there is a threat or may disagree about the source of the threat and choose different strategies.

Source: Elizabeth N. Saunders, *Leaders at War: How Presidents Shape Military Interventions* (Ithaca, NY: Cornell University Press, 2011), table 2.1, pp. 44–45.

policy investments, and intervention choices. To avoid confusing beliefs with behavior, her measurement of a president's beliefs is based on information about those beliefs *before* he became president. Each of these steps is essential to setting up a valid test of her claims.

GENERALIZING FROM CASE STUDIES

Process tracing studies can provide strong support for theories by specifying what evidence would need to be found to support a theory or rule it out and sifting through information for that evidence. In addition, process tracing studies offer the opportunity to make and test revisions to theories during the research process. But, to what extent can the relationships observed in process tracing case studies be generalized to other cases? Beach and Pedersen argue that in order to generalize to other cases from within-case causal analysis, the other cases must be causally homogeneous, not heterogeneous. A **causally homogeneous population** is "one in which a given cause can be expected to have the *same* causal relationship with the outcome across cases in the population," whereas a **causally heterogeneous population** is "one where a given cause might have many different effects across different cases or the same cause is linked to the same outcome through different causal mechanisms."[32] So, for example, as noted above, Saunders excludes cases involving the risk of nuclear escalations because she expects these cases to be causally different. The presence of the nuclear risk is expected to change the decision-making calculations of presidents, leaving less room for their personal beliefs about threats to play a role in decisions to intervene internationally. It would be interesting to expand her research to these cases. They would constitute a least likely test of her theory.

Generalization from individual case studies or case studies based on counterfactual reasoning may be limited, but this criticism does not mean the information gleaned from them is not important. In fact, as Robert K. Yin pointed out, the same criticism can be leveled against a single experiment: Scientific knowledge is usually based on multiple experiments rather than on a single experiment.[33] Yet people do not say that performing a single experiment is not worthwhile.

In addition to the issue of generalizing from case studies, there are two other drawbacks of case studies to consider. One is that case studies may require long and arduous efforts to describe and report the results owing to the need to present adequate documentation. (Think about the documentation that Saunders would need to present in her comparison of three presidents.) A related, and more serious, criticism is the potential problem of researcher bias and subjectivity in the selection of cases and interpretation of evidence. To better understand the potential for evidentiary bias, it is necessary to know more about the data collection techniques associated with qualitative research, which is the subject of chapter 8.

Despite these concerns, case study designs can be an informative and appropriate choice. Case study designs permit a deeper understanding of causal processes, the explication of general theory, and the development of hypotheses regarding difficult-to-observe phenomena. Much of our understanding of politics and political processes comes from case studies of individuals (presidents, senators, representatives, mayors, judges), statutes, campaigns, treaties, policy initiatives, political movements, democratization, countries, peace, and wars. The case study design should be viewed as complementary to, rather than inconsistent with, other experimental and nonexperimental designs.

CONCLUSION

In this chapter, we have discussed case study research designs, their purposes, and their important contribution to understanding political phenomena. The purpose of some case studies is simply to illustrate a political phenomenon or to provide an account of an event. Other case study designs aim to explore connections between causes and effects. Thus, this chapter included a discussion of the comparative method and the logic behind the method of difference and the method of agreement and the selection of cases for comparison. Case study research is particularly well suited to exploring causal mechanisms, which connect causes and outcomes. Process tracing involves testing hypothesized connections by explicitly unpacking causal mechanisms and systematically weighing evidence to see if it conforms to predictions based on theory and contradicts predictions based on competing explanations. Where to obtain evidence and how to present it are the subjects of the chapters to follow.

TERMS INTRODUCED

Case study design. A comprehensive and in-depth qualitative study of a single case or several cases. A nonexperimental design in which the investigator has little control over events.   135

Causally heterogeneous population. A population in which a given cause might have many different effects across different cases or the same cause is linked to the same outcome through different causal mechanisms.   145

Causally homogeneous population. A population in which a given cause can be expected to have the *same* causal relationship with the outcome across cases in the population.   145

Counterfactual understanding of causation. The logical argument that support for the claim that A causes B is demonstrated by a case in which A is absent and B does not occur.   140

Deviant case. A case that exhibits all of the factors thought to lead to a particular outcome, but in which the outcome does not occur.   139

Hypothesis-generating case study. A type of case study that attempts to develop from one or more cases some general theoretical propositions that can be tested in future research.   137

Hypothesis-testing case study. A type of case study that attempts to test hypothesized empirical relationships.   137

Idiographic case study. A type of case study that attempts to describe, explain, or interpret a singular historical episode with no intention of generalizing beyond the case.   137

Least likely case. A case in which it is expected that a theory is least likely to apply.   138

Mechanistic understanding of causation. An approach to demonstrating or understanding causation by focusing on the mechanism by which a cause leads to an outcome.   140

Method of agreement. A comparative strategy wherein the researcher selects cases that share the same outcome and identifies those conditions or causal factors that the cases also have in common.   138

Method of difference. A comparative strategy wherein the researcher selects cases in which the outcomes differ, compares the cases looking for the single factor that the cases do not have in common, and concludes that this factor is causal.   138

Most likely case. A case in which theory predicts an outcome is most likely to occur.   138

Necessary cause. A condition that must be present in order for the outcome to occur.   141

Plausibility probes. A case study that is not expected to provide a definitive test of the connection between a cause and an outcome, but is expected to contribute to conducting such a test in the future.   138

Process tracing. A case study in which a causal mechanism is traced from causal condition to final outcome.   141

Sufficient cause. A condition with which the outcome is always found.   142

SUGGESTED READINGS

Beach, Derek, and Rasmus Brun Pedersen. *Causal Case Study Methods: Foundations and Guidelines for Comparing, Matching, and Tracing.* Ann Arbor: University of Michigan Press, 2016.

Bennett, Andrew, and Jeffrey T. Checkel, eds. *Process Tracing: From Metaphor to Analytic Tool.* Cambridge, UK: Cambridge University Press, 2015.

Bennett, Andrew, and Colin Elman. "Complex Causal Relations and Case Study Methods: The Example of Path Dependence." *Political Analysis* 14, no. 3 (2006): 250–67.

George, Alexander L., and Andrew Bennett. *Case Studies and Theory Development in the Social Sciences.* Cambridge, MA: MIT Press, 2005.

Gerring, John. "Case Selection for Case-Study Analysis: Qualitative and Quantitative Techniques." In *The Oxford Handbook of Political Methodology*, edited by Janet M. Box-Steffensmeier, Henry E. Brady, and David Collier, 647–48. Oxford: Oxford University Press, 2008.

Mahoney, James. "The Logic of Process Tracing Tests in the Social Sciences." *Sociological Methods & Research* 41, no. 4 (2012): 570–97.

Van Evera, Stephen. *Guide to Methods for Students of Political Science.* Ithaca, NY: Cornell University Press, 1997.

NOTES

1. Michael Barnett, *Eyewitness to a Genocide: The United Nations and Rwanda* (Ithaca, NY: Cornell University Press, 2002).

2. Gerard Alexander, *The Sources of Democratic Consolidation* (Ithaca, NY: Cornell University Press, 2002).

3. Elisabeth Jean Wood, *Insurgent Collective Action and Civil War in El Salvador* (Cambridge, UK: Cambridge University Press, 2003).

4. S. Erdem Aytaç, Luis Schiumerini, and Susan Stokes, "Protests and Repression in New Democracies," *Perspectives on Politics* 15, no. 1 (2017): 62–82.

5. John D'Attoma, "Divided Nation: The North-South Cleavage in Italian Tax Compliance," *Polity* 49, no. 1 (January 2017): 66–99.

6. Alexander L. George and Andrew Bennett, *Case Studies and Theory Development in the Social Sciences* (Cambridge, MA: MIT Press, 2005), 153.

7. Ibid., 68.

8. Stephen Van Evera identifies five main purposes of case studies—testing theories, creating theories, identifying antecedent conditions, testing the importance of these antecedent conditions, and explaining cases of intrinsic importance—in his *Guide to Methods for Students of Political Science* (Ithaca, NY: Cornell University Press, 1997).

9. Jack S. Levy, "Case Studies: Types, Designs, and Logics of Inference," *Conflict Management and Peace Science* 25, no. 1 (2008): 1–18. For a more

elaborate typology, see John Gerring, "Case Selection for Case-Study Analysis," *The Oxford Handbook of Political Methodology*, ed. Janet M. Box-Steffensmeier, Henry E. Brady, and David Collier (Oxford: Oxford University Press, 2008), 647–48.

10. Levy, "Case Studies," 4.

11. Anthony Downs, "Up and Down with Ecology—the 'Issue Attention Cycle,'" *Public Interest* 28 (Summer 1972): 38–50; and John W. Kingdon, *Agendas, Alternatives, and Public Policies*, 2nd ed. (Boston: Pearson, 2011).

12. Levy, "Case Studies," 5.

13. Ibid., 6.

14. John Stuart Mill, *A System of Logic, Ratiocinative and Inductive: Being a Connected View of the Principles of Evidence and the Methods of Scientific Investigation* (New York: Harper, 1850), 225. Accessed February 15, 2019. Available at http://www.archive.org/details/systemoflogicrat01milliala.

15. Jeffrey L. Pressman and Aaron Wildavsky, *Implementation: How Great Expectations in Washington Are Dashed in Oakland; or, Why It's Amazing That Federal Programs Work at All, This Being a Saga of the Economic Development Administration as Told by Two Sympathetic Observers Who Seek to Build Morals on a Foundation* (Oakland: University of California Press, 1973).

16. Aytaç et al., "Protests and Repression in New Democracies."

17. Ibid., 76.

18. Ibid., 73–74.

19. Derek Beach and Rasmus Brun Pedersen, *Causal Case Study Methods: Foundations and Guidelines for Comparing, Matching, and Tracing* (Ann Arbor: University of Michigan Press, 2016), 28.

20. Ibid., 41.

21. Ibid., 31.

22. Ibid., 34. Beach and Pedersen distinguish between congruence studies, which provide only a minimalist understanding of mechanisms, and process tracing studies.

23. Ibid., 21. Induction is also an aspect of process tracing, as researchers may revise expectations about causal processes based on evidence discovered during the research process.

24. Van Evera, *Guide to Methods for Students of Political Science*, 31–32.

25. A discussion of Bayes' theorem is beyond the scope of this text. For an introduction to the application of Bayes' theorem to process tracing, see the appendix in *Process Tracing: From Metaphor to Analytic Tool*, ed. Andrew Bennett and Jeffrey T. Checkel (Cambridge, UK: Cambridge University Press, 2015). See also Andrew Bennett, "Process Tracing: A Bayesian Perspective," *The Oxford Handbook of Political Methodology*, ed. Janet M. Box-Steffensmeier, Henry E. Brady, and David Collier (Oxford: Oxford University Press, 2008), 702–21.

26. Elizabeth N. Saunders, *Leaders at War: How Presidents Shape Military Interventions* (Ithaca, NY: Cornell University Press, 2011).

27. Ibid., 30.

28. Ibid., 31.

29. Ibid., 27.

30. Ibid., 27–28.

31. Ibid., 14.

32. Beach and Pedersen, *Causal Case Study Methods*, 50–51.

33. Robert K. Yin, *Case Study Research: Design and Methods*, rev. ed., Applied Social Research Methods Series, vol. 5 (Newbury Park, CA: Sage, 1989), 21.

STUDENT STUDY SITE

SAGE edge for CQ Press

Give your students the SAGE edge!

SAGE edge offers a robust online environment featuring an impressive array of free tools and resources for review, study, and further exploration, keeping both instructors and students on the cutting edge of teaching and learning. Learn more at **edge.sagepub.com/johnson9e.**

8 MAKING EMPIRICAL OBSERVATIONS
Qualitative Analysis

Political scientists tend to use three broad types of empirical observations, or data collection methods, depending on the phenomena they are interested in studying: firsthand observation, document analysis, and interviews. The data obtained by these methods can be analyzed qualitatively or quantitatively. In this chapter, we give a general description of the types of empirical observations and factors affecting a researcher's choice of data collection method. The remainder of the chapter focuses on the data collection methods as they are used in qualitative research designs. In chapter 10, we discuss data collection methods as they are used in quantitative research designs. Each data collection method brings its own unique advantages and disadvantages and many choices for researchers. As we shall see, the validity and objectivity of measurement is of particular concern in qualitative research. Adhering to data accessibility and research transparency (DA-RT) principles introduced in chapter 2 and meeting obligations for the ethical treatment of people who are the subjects of some research pose a significant challenge to qualitative researchers. We begin with an overview of the three approaches and then discuss the application of these data collection methods in qualitative research.

CHAPTER OBJECTIVES

8.1 Identify different types of data collection techniques.

8.2 Discuss factors affecting choice of data collection methods.

8.3 Discuss ethical considerations of data collection and obligations of researchers.

8.4 Discuss data collection methods used in qualitative studies.

8.5 Discuss the ethical issues associated with observation.

8.6 Discuss the implications of calls for data accessibility and research transparency for qualitative research.

TYPES OF DATA AND COLLECTION TECHNIQUES

Interview data are derived from individuals. This type of data collection may involve surveying a representative cross section of the national adult population or a select group of political actors, such as leaders of nongovernmental organizations like the International Committee of the Red Cross. It may involve face-to-face interviews or interviews conducted over the phone or through the mail or internet. Researchers may use highly structured interviews in which a questionnaire is followed closely, while in some situations, interviews take the form of less-structured, open-ended discussions. Regardless of the particular type of interview setting, however, the essentials of the data collection method are the same: the data come from responses to the verbal or written cues of the researcher, and the respondent knows these responses are being recorded.

Document analysis as a source of data relies heavily on the record-keeping activities of government agencies, private institutions, interest groups, media organizations, and even private citizens. Political scientists use documents (newspapers, photographs, audiovisual clips, hearing testimony, press releases, letters, and diaries) as well as statistical data that exist in various archival records. We refer to these sources of data collectively as the **written record.** Also included in what we refer to as the written record are data first collected as interview data but then aggregated and reported in summary form for groups of individuals. For example, unemployment statistics are derived from the U.S. Census Bureau's Current Population Survey, a household survey conducted each month. What often sets document analysis apart from other data collection methods is that the researcher is usually not the original collector of the data and the original reason for the collection of the data may not have been to further a scientific research project.

The term **running record** is used to refer to materials collected systematically across time. These records are likely to be produced by organizations rather than by private citizens, carefully stored and easily accessed, and made available for long periods of time. Governmental organizations are by far the most common source of political document collections, and these records are both extensive and growing. The increasing worldwide availability of the internet has opened many sources of data that formerly may have been difficult or impossible to access without extensive travel. The running record is available for a wide variety of political topics. You can find a wealth of information related to foreign affairs from the United Nations. The UN collects and distributes data on most nations through its data website.[1] The UN maintains databases on major topical areas like crime, environment, labor, and many others. Alternatively, you could access data from regional data sources like the European Union. Students wishing to study the EU can quickly access data on a host of political, economic, social, and geographic data through the European Union Open Data Portal.[2] The portal is managed by the publications office of the EU and provides access to data provided by its member nations. Another popular source of the running record in world affairs is the Central Intelligence Agency's (CIA) *World Factbook.*[3]

Domestically, the data collection and reporting efforts of the U.S. government alone are impressive, and if you add to that the written records collected and preserved by state and local governments, interest groups, publishing houses, research institutes, and commercial concerns, the quantity of politically relevant written records increases quickly. Reports of the U.S. government, for example, now cover everything from electoral votes to electrical rates, and from taxes to taxicabs.

If you are interested in elections and campaigns, you can visit the Federal Election Commission at www.fec.gov and find financial records filed by candidates, interest groups, and political parties, or you can visit privately operated websites, like www.opensecrets.org, that offer processed reports in an easy-to-read and -use format. Or you might visit the websites administered by the secretaries of state to find state-level election returns or summaries of election law changes over time, or the America Votes series to find election results for national and some state and local elections. Alternatively, if you are interested in the lawmaking process, Congress makes the text and legislative histories of bills, committee reports, hearings, congressional votes, and the *Congressional Record* available at www .congress.gov, with a useful search engine to find needed documents. Or you can search for similar material through nongovernmental sources like the Inter-university Consortium for Political and Social Research archive or in print in the *CQ Almanac* or in CQ Press's *Politics in America*.

There is so much data available on the internet that it may be somewhat overwhelming to try to begin a search of the running record. A good starting point may be a more general data archive like Cornell University's Institute for Social and Economic Research.[4] Students can easily identify and access data directly from this archive on a host of topics and locations across time. As you can imagine, the references listed here represent only a small fraction of the available records. Each reference has its own advantages and disadvantages, and you should take care to understand exactly what is and what is not included in each reference before using it.

Records that are not part of an ongoing, systematic record-keeping program but are produced and preserved in a more casual, personal, and accidental manner are called **episodic records.** Good examples are personal diaries, memoirs, manuscripts, correspondence, and autobiographies; biographical sketches and other biographical materials; the temporary records of organizations; and media of temporary existence, such as brochures, posters, and pamphlets. The episodic record is of particular importance to political historians, since much of their subject matter can be studied only through these data.

There are three primary advantages to using the running record rather than the episodic record. The first is cost, in both time and money. Since the costs of collecting, tabulating, storing, and reporting the data in the running record are generally borne by the record keepers themselves, political scientists are usually able to use these data inexpensively. Researchers can often use the data stored in the running record by photocopying a few pages of a reference book, purchasing a government report or data file, or downloading data into a spreadsheet. In fact, the continued expansion of the data collection and record-keeping activities of national governments has been a financial boon to social scientists of all types.

A second, related advantage is the accessibility of the running record. Instead of searching packing crates, deteriorated ledgers, and musty storerooms, as users of the episodic record often must do, users of the running record more often rely on downloading data files and handling reference books and government publications. Many political science research projects have been completed with only the data stored in the reference books and government documents of a decent research library or through online archives.

A third advantage of the running record is that, by definition, it covers a more extensive period than does the episodic record. This permits the type of longitudinal analysis and before-and-after research designs discussed in chapter 9. Although the episodic record helps explain the origins of and reasons for a particular event, episode, or period, the running record allows the measurement of political phenomena over time.

The running record presents problems, however. One is that a researcher is at the mercy of the data collection practices and procedures of the record-keeping organizations themselves. Researchers are rarely in a position to influence record-keeping practices; they must rely instead on what organizations such as the U.S. Census Bureau, the European Union, and the Policy Agendas Project decide to do. A trade-off often exists between ease of access and researcher influence over the measurements that are made. Some organizations—some state and local governments, for example—do not maintain records as consistently as researchers may like.

Another, related disadvantage of the running record is that some organizations are not willing to share their raw data with researchers. The processed data that they do release may reflect calculations, categorizations, and aggregations that are inaccurate or uninformative. Access to public information is not *always* easy. More problems may be encountered when trying to obtain public information that shares some of the characteristics of the episodic record, for example, such as information on the effect of specific public programs and agency activities. Emily Van Dunk, a senior researcher at the Public Policy Forum, a nonpartisan, nonprofit research organization that conducts research on issues of importance to Wisconsin residents, noted that obtaining data from state and local government agencies can be difficult at times and offered tips for researchers.[5]

Finally, it is sometimes difficult for researchers to find out exactly what an organization's record-keeping practices are. Unless the organization publishes a description of its procedures, a researcher may not know what decisions have guided the record-keeping process. This can be a special problem when these practices change, altering in an unknown way the measurements reported.

Firsthand observation is the third method of data collection. Data may be collected by making observations in a field study or in a laboratory setting. In firsthand observation, the researcher collects data on political behavior by observing either the behavior itself (**direct observation**) or some physical trace of the behavior (**indirect observation**). Physical trace measures may be **accretion measures** (ones that measure the accumulation of material) or **erosion measures** (ones that measure wear or depletion of material). It involves firsthand examination of activities, behavior, events, relationships, or the like. It may even involve observing and recording speech, but unlike interviewing, this method of data collection does not rely solely on people's verbal responses to verbal stimuli presented by the researcher. Observation also may be structured or unstructured. In highly **structured observation**, the investigator looks for and systematically records the incidence of specific behaviors. This typically results in quantitative measures and analysis. The researcher will have decided, based on theory, the relevant behaviors before starting data collection. In **unstructured observation**, all behavior is considered relevant, at least at first, and recorded. Only later, upon reflection, will the investigator distinguish between important and trivial behavior. Open-ended, flexible observation is appropriate if the research purpose is one of description and exploration. For example, Richard Fenno explained that he began unstructured data collection in order to crystalize his thoughts on what was important to study about members of Congress in their districts. As Fenno explained, his visits with representatives in their districts

> were totally open-ended and exploratory. I tried to observe and inquire into anything and everything these members did. I worried about whatever they worried about. Rather than assume that I already knew what was interesting, I remained prepared to find interesting questions emerging in the course of the experience. The same with data. The research method was largely one of soaking and poking or just hanging around.[6]

Most of the time, as you might expect, researchers have a general idea of the phenomena they are interested in, although they are not sure exactly how it will be manifested. For example, Katherine Cramer and Benjamin Toff knew that they wanted to examine the forms or sources of knowledge people use in their conversations with others about political affairs: What do citizens consider to be "factual" knowledge? They discovered from listening to group discussions that people typically refer to personal experiences rather than to outside, recognized sources of factual information.[7]

Data collected through firsthand observation is just one example of **primary data**— that is, data recorded and used by the researcher making the observations. **Secondary data** refers to data used by a researcher who did not personally collect the data. We discuss issues related to the collection and use of primary and secondary data in this chapter.

Choosing among Data Collection Methods

A political scientist's choice of data collection method depends on many factors. One important consideration is the validity of the measurements that a particular method will permit. For example, a researcher who wants to measure the crime rate of different cities may feel that the crime rates reported by local police departments to the Federal Bureau of Investigation are not sufficiently accurate to support a research project. The researcher may be concerned that some departments overreport and some underreport various criminal acts or that some victims of crimes may fail to report the crimes to the police, hence rendering that method of collecting data and measuring the crime rate unacceptable. Therefore, the researcher may decide that a more accurate indication of the crime rate can be attained by interviewing a sample of citizens in different cities and asking them how much crime they have experienced themselves.

Also reflecting a concern over the validity of measurements, Susan J. Carroll and Debra J. Liebowitz noted that scholars of women and politics have criticized the use of survey research to study the political participation of women.[8] One problem is that existing conceptions of what is considered "political," and hence what is asked about in survey questions, may not fully capture the range of women's political activity. Carroll and Liebowitz suggested that researchers look at the issue inductively—that is, study women's activities and determine in what ways their activities are political. For this approach, observation and in-depth interviews, rather than structured questionnaires, are more appropriate data collection methods.

A political scientist is also influenced by the **reactivity** of a data collection method—the effect of the data collection itself on the phenomena being measured. When people know their behavior is being observed and know or can guess the purpose of the observation, they may alter their behavior. As a result, the observed behavior may be an unnatural reaction to the process of being observed. People may be reluctant, for example, to admit to an interviewer that they hold views or engage in behavior that is unpopular or embarrassing or even immoral or illegal. Thus, many researchers prefer unobtrusive or nonreactive measures of political behavior, because they believe that the resulting data are more accurate.

The population covered by a data collection method is another important consideration for a researcher. The population of interest determines whose behavior the researcher observes. One type of data may be available for only a few people, whereas another type may permit more numerous, interesting, and worthwhile comparisons. A researcher studying the behavior of political consultants, for example, may decide that relying on the published memoirs of a handful of consultants will not adequately cover the population of consultants (not to mention the validity problems of the data) and that it would be better to seek out a broad cross section of consultants and interview them. Or a researcher interested in political corruption may decide that interviewing a broad cross section of politicians charged with various corrupt practices is not feasible and that data (of a different kind) could be obtained for a more diverse set of corrupt acts from accounts published in the mass media.

Additionally, cost and availability are crucial elements in the choice of a data collection technique. Some types of data collection are simply more expensive than others, and some types of information are made more readily available than others. Large-scale interviewing, for example, is very expensive and time-consuming, and the types of questions that can be asked and behaviors that can be observed are limited. The cost of firsthand observation through the expenditure of time (if the researcher does it) or money (if the researcher pays others to do it) will generally be even higher. Data from archival records are usually much less expensive, since the record-keeping entity has borne most of the cost of collecting and publishing the data. With the increased use of computers, many organizations are systematically collecting data of interest to researchers. A disadvantage, however, may be that the data must be made available by the record-keeping organization, which can refuse a researcher's request or take a long time to fill it.

Availability becomes an issue affecting the use of direct observation as a method of empirical research for political scientists in that significant instances of political behavior are not accessible for observation. For example, high-level national security briefings are not open to the public, U.S. Supreme Court conferences are not open to anyone but the justices themselves, and authoritarian regimes often design institutions that are purposely difficult to access and reject the idea of public disclosure. Occasionally, physical traces of these private behaviors become public—such as the Watergate tapes of Richard Nixon's conversations with his aides. Typically, access is a major barrier to directly observing consequential political behavior.

On the whole, students at most institutions of higher education will have access to vast amounts of data from survey data, to databases of government and organizations' statistics and media output, to special collections of primary materials. Grants may be available to students working on a larger-scale project, like a thesis, allowing them to create and administer their own surveys or to spend time in the field observing and interviewing people. For example, a student of one of the authors spent a semester in a Latin American country interviewing people about community water projects for his senior thesis.

Last, but not least, researchers must consider the ethical implications of their proposed research. In most cases, the research topics you are likely to propose will not raise serious ethical concerns, nor will your choice of method of data collection hinge on the risk it may pose to human subjects. Nevertheless, you should be aware of the ethical issues and risks to others that can result from social science research, and you should be aware of the review process that researchers are required to follow when proposing research involving human subjects.

In accordance with federal regulations, universities and other research organizations require faculty and students to submit research proposals involving human subjects for review by an **institutional review board** (often called a human subjects review board). This is a requirement for both funded and unfunded research. There may be some variation in practice concerning unfunded research, but the proper course of action is to contact your institution's research office for information regarding the review policy on human subjects *before starting any research involving human subjects*. There are three levels of review: some research may be exempt, some may require only expedited review, and some research will be subject to full board review. Even if your research project seems to fit one of the categories of research exempt from review, you must request and be granted an exemption.[9]

Three ethical principles—respect for persons, beneficence, and justice—form the foundation for assessing the ethical dimensions of research involving human subjects. These principles were identified in the *Belmont Report*, a report of the National Commission for the Protection of Human Subjects of Biomedical and Behavioral Research.[10] The principle concerning *respect for persons* asserts that individuals should be treated as autonomous agents and that persons with diminished capacity are entitled to protection. *Beneficence* refers to protecting people from harm as well as making efforts to secure their well-being. The principle of *justice* requires researchers to consider the distribution of the benefits and burdens of research.

The principle of respect for persons requires that subjects be given the opportunity to choose what shall or shall not happen to them. **Informed consent** means that subjects are to be given information about the research, including the research procedure, its purposes, risks, and anticipated benefits; alternative procedures (where therapy is involved); how subjects are selected; and the person responsible for the research. In addition, each subject is to be given a statement offering him or her the opportunity to ask questions and to withdraw from the research at any time. This information and statement should be conveyed in a manner that is comprehensible to the subject, and the consent of the subject must be voluntary.

An assessment of risks and benefits relates directly to the beneficence principle by helping to determine whether risks to subjects are justified and by providing information useful to subjects for their informed consent. The justice principle is often associated with the selection of subjects insofar as some populations may be more likely to be targeted for study; one example is prison populations, particularly in the past.

DATA COLLECTION IN QUALITATIVE RESEARCH

Observation

Political scientists have used firsthand observation to study democratization, political participation, social movements, political campaigning, community politics, program implementation, judicial proceedings, lawmaking, and other topics. The term **ethnography** is often associated with firsthand observation. It refers to observation that goes beyond description of events or actions to reveal the "cultural constructions, in which we live."[11] The goal of ethnography is to make cultural interpretation through personal observation of everyday life. The method is commonly characterized as one of "thick description" that captures as many details as possible[12] or, as Lisa Wedeen defined ethnography, "immersion in the place and lives of people under study."[13] Observation studies conducted by political scientists, typically, are referred to as **field studies**—open-ended and wide-ranging observation in a natural setting. In field studies, researchers typically ask questions of the people they are observing; thus, field studies involve collection of interview data.

Field studies have several advantages. One advantage of observing people in a natural setting is that people generally behave as they would ordinarily. Researchers often observe people for lengthy periods so that interaction and changes in behavior may be studied, and to achieve a degree of accuracy or completeness that documents or recall data, such as those obtained in surveys, cannot provide. For example, Joan E. McLean suggested that researchers interested in studying the decision-making styles of women running for public office will obtain more valid information by spending time with campaigns in order to gather information as decisions are being made than by relying on postelection questionnaires or debriefing sessions.[14] Observing a city council or school board meeting or a public hearing on the licensing of a locally undesirable land use will allow you to know and understand what happened at the event far better than reading official minutes or transcripts.

A good example of a field study is Ya-Chung Chuang's study of democratization in Taiwan, *Democracy on Trial: Social Movements and Cultural Politics in Postauthoritarian Taiwan*, in which he examined the interaction among individuals in a community and between individuals and institutions.[15] To understand how individuals overcome complex problems, Chuang interviewed community and ethnic leaders, examined coalitions of community organizations, and interacted with residents in their communities. This method allowed Chuang to better understand a wide range of sociopolitical activities like community referendums for collective decision making and cultural walking tours in the community. Chuang's personal experiences and firsthand observations in local communities gave him a vantage point that could not be acquired otherwise.

Direct observation can be carried out as a participant or nonparticipant. Chuang made his observations as a participant observer—interacting with the people and institutions he was studying and participating in conversations and events as they unfolded. In **participant observation,** the investigator is "both an actor and a spectator"—that is, a regular participant in the activities of the group being observed.[16] In **nonparticipant observation,** the observer does not participate in group activities or become a member of the group or community. For example, an investigator interested in hearings held by public departments of transportation or city council meetings could observe those proceedings without becoming a participant.

Most field studies involve participant observation. An investigator cannot be like the proverbial fly on the wall, observing a group of people for long periods of time. Usually, he or she must assume a role or identity within the group under observation and participate in the activities of the group. Thus, in addition to interviewing influential Latinos in Boston, Carol Hardy-Fanta joined the community group Familias Latinas de Boston while conducting her research on Latina women and politics. As she pointed out, this strategy complemented her research interviews:

> Joining the community group Familias Latinas de Boston allowed me to gain
> an in-depth understanding of one community group over an extended period.
> Participating in formal, organized political activities such as manning the
> phone bank at the campaign office of a Latino candidate and attending political
> banquets, public forums, and conferences and workshops provided another means
> of observing how gender and culture interacted to stimulate—or suppress—
> political participation. I also joined protest marches and rallies and tracked down
> voter registration information in Spanish for a group at Mujeres Unidas en Acción.
> In addition, I learned much from informal interactions: at groups on domestic
> violence, during lunch at Latino community centers, and during spontaneous
> conversations with Latinos from many countries and diverse backgrounds. As
> I talked to people in community settings and observed how they interacted
> politically, the political roles of Latina women and the gender differences in how
> politics is defined emerged. Thus, multiple observations were available to check
> what I was hearing in the interviews about how to stimulate Latino political
> participation, and how Latina women and Latino men act politically.[17]

Another choice in direct observation is between overt and covert observations. In **overt observation,** those being observed are aware of the investigator's presence and intentions. In **covert observation,** the investigator's presence is hidden or undisclosed, and his or her intentions are disguised. For example, covert observation was used in a study to measure what percentage of people washed their hands after using the restroom.[18] The advantage of covert observation is that the researcher may be better able to observe unrestrained behavior. If people are aware that someone is watching and recording observations, they may behave differently than they normally would. Hence, by concealing observation, a researcher may be able to make more valid observations. One must be concerned about the ethical implications of covert observation. Research involving covert observation of *public* behavior of private individuals is not likely to raise ethical issues as long as individuals are not or cannot be identified and disclosure of individuals' behavior would not place them at risk. Note that elected or appointed public officials are not shielded by these limitations. Ethical standards and their application or enforcement have changed, and some earlier studies using covert observation would not receive approval from human subjects review boards today. For example, social scientists Mary Henle and Marian B. Hubble once hid under beds in students' rooms to study student conversations.[19]

Evaluating Field Studies

Unstructured participant observation also has been criticized as invalid and biased. A researcher may selectively perceive behaviors, noting some while ignoring others. The interpretation of behaviors may reflect the personality and culture of the observer rather than the meaning attributed to them by the observed themselves. Moreover, the presence of the observer may alter the behavior of the observed, no matter how skillfully the observer attempts to become accepted as a nonthreatening part of the community.

Fieldworkers attempt to minimize these possible threats to data validity by immersing themselves in the culture they are observing and by taking copious notes on everything going on around them, no matter how seemingly trivial. Events without apparent meaning at the time of observation may become important and revealing upon later reflection. Of course, copious note-taking leads to what is known as a "high dross rate"; much of what is recorded is not relevant to the research problem or question as it is finally formulated. It may be painful for the investigator to discard so much of the material that was carefully recorded, but it is standard practice with this method.

Note-taking is a demanding, yet essential, aspect of field study. It is especially important because the recorded observations in notes constitute the data in fieldwork. The narratives that researchers develop and the conclusions they make come directly from the field notes. The richness of detail in the notes leads to a fully developed, published product that relays to the reader a sense of what the researcher experienced. Note-taking is therefore the lifeblood of field research, as it records the observations and anecdotes that eventually find their way to the printed page. Notes can be divided into three types: mental notes, jotted notes, and field notes. Mental note-taking involves orienting one's consciousness to the task of remembering things one has observed, such as "who and how many were there, the physical character of the place, who said what to whom, who moved about in what way, and a general characterization of an order of events."[20] Because mental notes may fade rapidly, researchers use jotted notes to preserve them. Jotted notes consist of short phrases and keywords that will activate a researcher's memory later when the full field notes are written down. Researchers may be able to use tape recording equipment if they have the permission of those being observed.

"Full" field notes should include a running description of conversations and events. For this aspect of field notes, John Lofland advises that researchers should be factual and concrete, avoid making inferences, and use participants' descriptive and interpretative terms. Full field notes should include material previously forgotten and subsequently recalled. Lofland suggests that researchers distinguish between verbal material that is exact recall, paraphrased or close recall, and reasonable recall.[21]

Field notes should also include a researcher's analytic ideas and inferences, personal impressions and feelings, and notes for further information.[22] Because events and emotional states in a researcher's life may affect observation, they should be recorded. Notes for further information provide guidance for future observation—to fill in gaps in observations, call attention to things that may happen, or test out emerging analytic themes.

Full field notes should be legible and should be reviewed periodically, since the passage of time may present past observations in a new light to the researcher or reveal a pattern worthy of attention in a series of disjointed events. Creating and reviewing field notes is an important part of the observational method. Consequently, a fieldworker should expect to spend as much time on field notes as he or she spends on observation in the field.

Research based on fieldwork is often criticized as being too subjective because it is based on the researcher's interpretation of what the observed have said or done. Often, a researcher will present quotes from one or a few individuals being observed to illustrate or validate an interpretation. How do we know when we read an article based on fieldwork that the author's conclusions are actually supported by observations or whether the author has cherry-picked observations to fit with preconceived notions or preferred theory? Someone else might interpret the data differently. Thus, the data may be invalid and unreliable. One way to obtain more valid data is to allow the observed to read and comment on what the investigator has written and point out events and behaviors that may have been misinterpreted. Another is for researchers to make their data available to others, as envisioned by the DA-RT initiative described in chapter 2. This way, one can review field notes and interview transcripts to see if one agrees with the author's interpretation. Compliance with DA-RT requirements, however, may pose substantial challenges to researchers, including adhering to promises made to the observed regarding anonymity and the cost and time commitment to preparing field notes in a suitable format for sharing.[23]

Let's take a look at a recent example of participant observation to see how the researcher addressed these issues—Katherine Cramer Walsh's study of rural consciousness or how place matters among Wisconsin residents and how it affected residents' perspective on political issues.[24] Over a period of four years, Walsh studied public affairs conversations in thirty-seven groups across twenty-seven widely varying communities (urban, suburban, and rural). These groups met in local restaurants, cafés, or gas stations early on weekday mornings. Once she had identified community groups using a stratified purposeful sampling approach,[25] she approached each group and asked permission to sit with them. She explained that she was a public opinion researcher for the University of Wisconsin–Madison and that she wished to listen to their concerns about public affairs and the state's flagship public university, asked permission to record the conversations, and gave them tokens of her appreciation such as university football schedules. Two groups refused to have their conversations recorded. To protect the identity of group members, she does not mention the name of the communities except for the cities of Madison and Milwaukee in her research findings. She began by asking each group what were the big concerns for people in their community. She had a question protocol to make sure she covered the same questions with each group, although she adjusted the order and number as necessary. Here's how she described her data collection and analysis process:

I designed my interview protocol to generate talk about several topics that pilot studies suggested were likely to invoke economic considerations and references to social class: tax policy, immigration, higher education, and health care. To analyze my data, I used data displays and adjusted my collection as I proceeded to test the conclusions I was reaching. That is, as I collected transcripts from the conversations, I read through them, looking for patterns across groups with respect to the kinds of considerations people brought to bear in talking about public affairs. I displayed my data in a matrix in which the rows represented particular groups, and the columns represented different characteristics of the groups and the broader community.

As I proceeded, I wrote memos detailing the patterns I perceived. I analyzed what additional evidence I would need to observe in order to validate my conclusions (and altered my protocol accordingly), and used the visual displays to test whether the patterns were pervasive and whether they varied across group type. To further verify my conclusions, I considered how my presence affected the conversations, reexamined conversations I deemed inconsistent with the patterns observed, considered spurious relations, added additional groups to test for similar patterns among people of different demographic backgrounds, and sent detailed reports of my results to the groups I visited so they could comment on my conclusions.[26]

Based on her observation of conversations of community groups, Walsh concluded that rural residents possessed a "rural consciousness" rooted in a sense of place and how that place stands in relation to others in terms of power and resource allocation; a sense that their values and lifestyles are different; a sense of injustice and perception that rural residents are deprived relative to residents of urban and suburban areas, with political elites based in urban areas being at fault; and a lack of trust in government and alienation from the political system. Walsh argues that this rural consciousness explains why rural Wisconsin voters seem to political analysts to vote against their interests.[27]

Ethical Issues in Observation

Ethical dilemmas arise primarily when there is a potential for harm to the observed. The potential for serious harm to subjects in most observational studies is quite low. Observation generally does not entail investigation of highly sensitive, personal, or illegal behavior, because people are reluctant to be observed in those circumstances and would not give their informed consent. Nonetheless, harm or risks to the observed may result from observation. They include (1) negative repercussions from associating with the researcher because of the researcher's sponsors, nationality, or outsider status; (2) invasion of privacy; (3) stress during the research interaction; and (4) disclosure of behavior or information to the researcher resulting in harm to the observed during or after the study. Each of these possibilities is considered here in turn.

In some fieldwork situations, contact with outsiders may be viewed as undesirable behavior by an informant's peers. Cooperation with a researcher may violate community norms. For example, a researcher who studies a group known to shun contact with outsiders exposes informants to the risk of being censured by their group.

Social scientists from the United States have encountered difficulty in conducting research in countries that have hostile relations with the United States.[28] Informants and researchers may be accused of being spies, and informants may be exposed to harm for appearing to sympathize with "the enemy." Harm may result even if hostile relations develop after the research has been conducted. Military, CIA, or other government sponsorship of research may particularly endanger the observed.

A second source of harm to the observed results from the invasion of privacy that observation may entail. Even though a researcher may have permission to observe, the role of observer may not always be remembered by the observed. In fact, as a researcher gains rapport, there is a greater chance that informants may view the researcher as a friend and reveal to him or her something that could prove to be damaging. A researcher does not always warn, "Remember, you're being observed!" Furthermore, if a researcher is being treated as a friend, such a warning may damage rapport. Researchers must consider how they will use the information gathered from subjects. They must judge whether use in a publication will constitute a betrayal of confidence.[29] If this information is included in field notes, then sharing those notes (as per DA-RT) presents difficulties.

Elite Interviewing

We have discussed the use of interviewing (asking questions) as a data collection method in field studies. In some examples, such as Walsh's study of Wisconsin residents, the primary sources of data were conversations shaped by her questions. In contrast to highly structured surveys, discussed in chapter 10, in-depth, loosely structured interviews give the interviewer a chance to probe, to clarify, to search for deeper meanings, to explore unanticipated responses, and to assess intangibles such as mood and opinion intensity as well as develop an empathetic understanding of the interviewee's perspective. In this section, we focus on elite interviewing: the use of interviewing to glean information from elites—individuals with special knowledge about topics or events. These individuals are uniquely situated to possess information and perspectives critical to an accurate understanding of a research topic. On the one hand, anyone can be viewed as an elite insofar as he or she has information that the researcher does not have. On the other hand, only a small number of individuals may have firsthand knowledge, for example, about how a president reached a decision to go to war. How to approach these individuals and make the most of opportunities to talk to them warrants special consideration.

The Practicalities of Interviewing. There is a general consensus on the practicalities of interviewing regarding preparation, conducting, interpretation, and writing.[30] First and foremost, it is important to *be fully prepared before conducting any interviews.* Preparation should include reading all secondary sources on the subject, as well as primary sources if they are available, in order to determine what is known and what is not known. It will also help you identify key individuals to be interviewed. A solid review of the literature will yield hypotheses to explore. Being well prepared leads to more efficient interviews focusing on critical topics, with the researcher able to recognize in the midst of an interview important points to pursue. On an ethical basis, you should not take the time of someone (elite or otherwise) by asking about something you could have easily found out about before the interview. Professionally, an ill-prepared interviewer may not be taken seriously by the interviewee, who in turn may decide to be less helpful. Respondents are less likely to try to manipulate the conversation or give a slanted account if the researcher is well prepared and knowledgeable. If there is not much information available about a topic or event, begin by conducting exploratory interviews with lower-ranking respondents. Use exploratory or early interviews to build up a list of people to contact.

Design an appropriate method of initial contact so you can avoid making cold calls. An initial letter on professional letterhead or a letter of introduction from a local institution or person with standing in the community may facilitate access. In your letter, explain why the person is important to your research. You might mention who referred you to the person or people you have already interviewed (if you have their permission to identify them). Your initial letter should state your preference for recording the interview and that the conversation be on the record, but you should also state that respondents are not obligated to speak on the record. Suggest a wide time frame for scheduling an interview to make it harder for a person to avoid an interview.

Think about how you want to present yourself. You want to balance the need to establish that you are knowledgeable about your topic so that you will be taken seriously against appearing to try to impress the interviewee or to be so knowledgeable that you intimidate the interviewee. Consider how to use nonverbal cues to encourage an interviewee to elaborate further and tactful ways to get interviewees to consider different perspectives or to return to a question you think they have not answered fully.[31]

Record interviews if possible. This will allow you to concentrate on what the interviewee is saying and to think of follow-up questions. Having recordings enhances accuracy and reduces challenges regarding subjective interpretation. If individual respondents do not wish to be on the record, then ask for permission to quote them without identifying them by name. Come to the interview with a list of questions specifically designed for the person you are interviewing, but be prepared to deviate as needed to take advantage of the particular perspective and knowledge of the interviewee. Elites usually are able to easily detect a standardized list of questions and may object to being treated as standard rather than as someone with unique and valuable knowledge. Start with questions that allow you to *build up some rapport* before tackling more difficult questions, but make sure to get to your most important questions before time runs out. At the end of the interview, ask the interviewee if he or she is available for follow-up questions and for suggestions about whom else to talk to. If possible, *do not schedule too many interviews in a day* (no more than two per day). Take time to reflect on the interview, noting significant aspects while it is still fresh in your mind. These notes can be paired later with a transcript of the interview. It is also important to review what interviewees have said so that successive interviews build on each other. Examine the plausibility of statements, check for internal consistency, and identify statements that you want to corroborate with other interviewees.

Establishing the meaningfulness and validity of the interview data is important. Bias may come from both the interviewer and the interviewee. As noted earlier, advance preparation may help an interviewer recognize remarks that differ from established fact, thus guarding against interviewee bias. Yet, if a researcher is after facts, there is a very real possibility that a researcher's biases will affect which version of the truth to believe. As Jeffrey M. Berry points out,

> if the goal of interviews is to find out the truth about what happened—how was the bill passed, how was the deal cut, how was the judge chosen?—there is a very high risk of finding one interviewee more persuasive than the others and having that one interview strongly shape our understanding of the issue. It's easy to make oneself believe that one account is more accurate than another because a subject was more knowledgeable or more detailed in her answers, rather than admitting that we liked that person better or her story was closer to our own take on the situation.[32]

The potential for problems with error in which account is truthful is greater, the fewer the number of interviews conducted regarding any one event or topic. Recorded interviews leave no doubt about what has been said. Researchers often use selected quotes to illustrate key points, but care should be taken not to present quotes out of context.

Interviewing is a challenging form of data collection requiring skills as a conversationalist, listener, and prober of information, but it often provides a more comprehensive and complex understanding of phenomena than other methods of data collection.

Using Documents

Much political research relies on documents as a source of data. Let's look at two examples of research using documents. In chapter 1, we introduced the case study research by John D'Attoma in which he presents an explanation for the difference in tax compliance between northern and southern Italy. D'Attoma uses a historical institutionalist approach, which involves tracing the institutional settings in northern and southern Italy and their impact on political behavior from the unification of Italy in 1871 to the start of the Second Republic in the 1990s. He traces "the ways in which unification pitted the [Catholic] church against the state and the North against the South, providing a different experience with the state in the two regions and hence different preferences regarding taxation."[33] For much of the period of interest, observation and interviewing obviously are not possible data collection methods. Instead, he relies on secondary sources (histories of Italy written by others) and, in a few instances, primary sources (church documents). How can we evaluate the reliability and validity of his conclusions? What are the possible threats to their reliability? One potential problem would be if D'Attoma was selective in the sources he referenced or what he chose to use from those sources, such as only material that supported his line of argument. It is also possible that some of those sources, themselves, were slanted or incomplete in their coverage of Italian history. We could read each of the histories he cites to make sure he uses their content accurately, and we could investigate whether his list of sources was comprehensive. This would be a lot of work for the average reader of his article. Ultimately, we have to rely on the system of peer review of articles published in professional journals. We would expect the individuals to whom his article was sent for review to be experts in Italian political history so that they would be familiar with his sources. They would know which histories were most respected in the field and whether or not he was using material from his sources appropriately.

Elizabeth Saunders relied on primary documents to measure the concepts central to her hypothesis that presidential beliefs about the origin of threats posed by other countries had a causal impact on presidential decisions to intervene militarily in international affairs and the nature of that intervention.[34] She drew from archival and published document collections, including presidential libraries, to examine what the prepresidential documentary record indicated about presidents' beliefs. Among other documents, she read personal letters, letters to constituents, and transcripts of speeches. She used policy investments, such as staffing decisions, official policy on strategy, the defense posture, and the use of force, and budgetary allocations made by a president while in office as observable implications of causal beliefs. Information about these policy investments was available through public records—for example, the running record of federal budgets—as well as presidential papers. Documents from numerous federal agencies and offices such as the National Security Council also provided information about international interventions. Saunders goes to considerable lengths to explain the operationalization of the concepts central to her research, and she provides quoted material to support her interpretation of presidential beliefs and other concepts. Nevertheless, assessing the reliability of some of her measurements would be a difficult task.

Political scientists are devising strategies to respond to DA-RT guidelines for transparency, which would assist in this task. One strategy is the use of hyperlink citations to online sources, but as Andrew Moravcsik points out, hyperlink citations fail to "accommodate the majority of political science sources that are not found online or accessible under intellectual property law and human subject restrictions, as well as running up against the problem that links are surprisingly unstable over time."[35] He suggests the use of a "transparency index" to provide detailed information about any source used to support a contestable empirical claim. The information would include the full citation for the source, an excerpt from the source, an annotation explaining how the source supports the claim being made, and, optionally, an outside link to and/or a scan of the full source.[36]

CONCLUSION

Qualitative research is the backbone of many investigations into interesting and important political science phenomena. Once researchers have selected their case or cases, they then must collect data to test their research hypotheses. As evidenced by our discussion of observation, interviewing, and document analysis, qualitative research can be quite challenging in terms of gathering useful data as well as demonstrating its reliability and validity. Nevertheless, the investigative process can be exciting and rewarding.

TERMS INTRODUCED

Accretion measures. Measures of phenomena through indirect observation of the accumulation of materials.   152

Covert observation. Observation in which the observer's presence or purpose is kept secret from those being observed.   157

Direct observation. Actual observation of behavior.   152

Document analysis. The use of audio, visual, or written materials as a source of data.   150

Elite interviewing. Interviewing individuals who possess specialized knowledge about a political phenomenon.   161

Episodic records. Materials that are not part of a systematic and ongoing record-keeping effort.   151

Erosion measures. Measures of phenomena through indirect observation of selective wear of some material.   152

Ethnography. A type of field study in which the researcher is deeply immersed in the place and lives of the people being studied.   156

Field studies. Open-ended and wide-ranging (rather than structured) observation in a natural setting.   156

Firsthand observation. Method of data collection in which the researcher personally observes political behavior or some physical trace of it.   152

Indirect observation. Observation of physical traces of behavior.   152

Informed consent. Procedures that inform potential research subjects about the proposed research in which they are being asked to participate; the principle that researchers must obtain the freely given consent of human subjects before they participate in a research project.   155

Institutional review board. Panel to which researchers must submit descriptions of proposed research involving human subjects for the purpose of ethics review.   155

Interview data. Data that are collected from responses to questions posed by the researcher to a respondent.   149

Nonparticipant observation. Observation of activities, behaviors, or events in which the researcher does not participate.   157

Overt observation. Observation in which those being observed are informed of the observer's presence and purpose.   157

Participant observation. Observation in which the observer becomes a regular participant in the activities of those being observed.   157

Primary data. Data recorded and used by the researcher who is making the observations.   153

Reactivity. Effect of data collection or measurement on the phenomenon being measured.   154

Running record. Materials or data that are collected across time.   150

Secondary data. Data used by a researcher that were not personally collected by that researcher.   153

Structured observation. Systematic observation and recording of the incidence of specific behaviors.   152

Unstructured observation. Observation in which all behavior and activities are recorded.   152

Written record. Documents, reports, statistics, manuscripts, photographs, audio recordings, and other recorded materials available and useful for empirical research.   150

SUGGESTED READINGS

Feldman, Martha S. *Strategies for Interpreting Qualitative Data.* Thousand Oaks, CA: Sage, 1995.

Fenno, Richard F., Jr. *Home Style: House Members in Their Districts.* Boston: Little, Brown, 1978. See esp. the introduction and appendix, "Notes on Method: Participant Observation."

Golafshani, Nahid. "Understanding Reliability and Validity in Qualitative Research." *The Qualitative Report* 8, no. 4 (2003): 597–606. Accessed May 28, 2018. Available at http://www.nova.edu/ssss/QR/QR8-4/golafshani.pdf.

Jaggar, Alison M. *Just Methods: An Interdisciplinary Reader.* Boulder, CO: Paradigm, 2008.

Miles, Mathew B., A. Michael Huberman, and Johnny Saldana. *Qualitative Data Analysis: A Methods Sourcebook.* 4th ed. Thousand Oaks, CA: Sage, 2019.

Moravcsik, Andrew. "Transparency: The Revolution in Qualitative Research." *PS: Political Science and Politics* 47, no. 1 (2014): 48–53.

Piccolo, Francesco Lo, and Huw Thomas, eds. *Ethics and Planning Research.* Burlington, VT: Ashgate, 2009.

Rathbun, Brian C. "Interviewing and Qualitative Field Methods: Pragmatism and Practicalities." In *The Oxford Handbook of Political Methodology*, edited by Janet M. Box-Steffensmeier, Henry E. Brady, and David Collier, 685–701. Oxford: Oxford University Press, 2008.

Reason, Peter, and Hilary Bradbury, eds. *The SAGE Handbook of Action Research: Participative Inquiry and Practice.* 2nd ed. Thousand Oaks, CA: Sage, 2008.

Sieber, Joan E., and Martin B. Tolich. *Planning Ethically Responsible Research: A Guide for Students and Internal Review Boards.* 2nd ed. Applied Social Research Methods Series, vol. 31. Newbury Park, CA: Sage, 2013.

Smyth, Marie, and Emma Williamson, eds. *Researchers and Their "Subjects": Ethics, Power, Knowledge, and Consent.* Bristol, UK: Policy Press, 2004.

Wedeen, Lisa. "Reflections on Ethnographic Work in Political Science." *Annual Review of Political Science* 13, no. 1 (2010): 255–72.

Williamson, Vanessa, Theda Skocpol, and John Coggin. "The Tea Party and the Remaking of Republican Conservatism." *Perspectives on Politics* 9, no. 1 (2011): 25–43.

NOTES

1. United Nations Statistics Division. Accessed February 18, 2019. Available at http://data.un.org/Default.aspx.

2. European Union Open Data Portal. Accessed February 18, 2019. Available at https://open-data.europa.eu/en/data/.

3. Central Intelligence Agency, *The World Factbook*. Accessed February 18, 2019. Available at https://www.cia.gov/library/publications/resources/the-world-factbook/index.html.

4. Cornell Institute for Social and Economic Research. Accessed February 18, 2019. Available at https://cisermgmt.cornell.edu/go/PHPs/browse.php.

5. Emily Van Dunk, "Getting Data through the Back Door: Techniques for Gathering Data from State Agencies," *State Politics and Policy Quarterly* 1, no. 2 (2001): 210–18.

6. Ibid., xiv.

7. Katherine J. Cramer and Benjamin Toff, "The Fact of Experience: Rethinking Political Knowledge and Civic Competence," *Perspectives on Politics* 15, no. 3 (2012): 754–70.

8. Susan J. Carroll and Debra J. Liebowitz, "Introduction: New Challenges, New Questions, New Directions," in *Women and American Politics: New Questions, New Directions*, ed. Susan J. Carroll (Oxford: Oxford University Press, 2003), 1–29.

9. Exemption categories are as follows: "1. Research conducted in established or commonly accepted educational settings, involving normal educational practices, such as (a) research on regular and special education instructional strategies or (b) research on the effectiveness of or the comparison among instructional techniques, curricula, or classroom management methods.

2. Research involving the use of educational tests (cognitive, diagnostic, aptitude, achievement), survey procedures, interview procedures, or observation of public behavior, unless (a) information obtained is recorded in such a manner that human subjects can be identified, directly or through identifiers linked to the subjects, AND (b) any disclosure of the human subjects' responses outside the research could reasonably place the subjects at risk of criminal or civil liability or be damaging to the subjects' financial standing, employability, or reputation. 3. Research involving the use of education tests, survey procedures, interview procedures, or observation of public behavior that is not exempt under category 2, if (a) the human subjects are elected or appointed public officials or candidates for public office or (b) federal statute(s) requires without exception that the confidentiality of the personally identifiable information will be maintained throughout the research and thereafter. 4. Research involving the collection or study of existing data, documents, records, pathological specimens, or diagnostic specimens, if these sources are publicly available or if the information is recorded by the investigator in such a manner that subjects cannot be identified directly or through identifiers linked to the subjects. 5. Research and demonstration projects that are conducted by or subject to the approval of department or agency heads and that are designed to study, evaluate, or otherwise examine (a) public benefit or service programs, (b) procedures for obtaining benefits or services under those programs, (c) possible changes in or alternatives to those programs or procedures, or (d) possible changes in methods or levels of payment for benefits or services under those programs. 6. Taste and food quality evaluation and consumer acceptance studies, (a) if wholesome foods without additives are consumed or (b) if a food is consumed that contains a food ingredient at or below the level and for a use found to be safe, or agricultural chemical or environmental contaminant at or below the level found to be safe, by the Food and Drug Administration or approved by the Environmental Protection Agency or the Food Safety and Inspection Service of the U.S. Department of Agriculture." From United States Office of the Federal Register, *Code of Federal Regulations: Title 45, Public Welfare; Part 46,*

Protection of Human Subjects (Washington, DC: U.S. Government Printing Office, 1977), Part 46.101(b). These exemptions do not apply to research involving prisoners, fetuses, pregnant women, or human in vitro fertilization. Exemption 2 does not apply to children except for research involving observations of public behavior when the investigator does not participate in the activities being observed.

10. National Commission for the Protection of Human Subjects of Biomedical and Behavioral Research, *The Belmont Report: Ethical Principles and Guidelines for the Protection of Human Subjects of Research* (Washington, DC: U.S. Government Printing Office, 1979). Accessed February 18, 2019. Available at https://www.hhs.gov/ohrp/regulations-and-policy/belmont-report/index.html.

11. Brian A. Hoey, "A Simple Introduction to the Practice of Ethnographic Fieldnotes," *Marshall University Digital Scholar* (June 2014). Accessed February 18, 2019. Available at http://works.bepress.com/brian_hoey/12.

12. Clifford Geertz, *The Interpretation of Cultures* (New York: Basic Books, 1973).

13. Lisa Wedeen, "Reflections on Ethnographic Work in Political Science," *Annual Review of Political Science* 13, no. 1 (2010): 255–72. See also Eugene J. Webb, Donald T. Campbell, and Richard D. Schwarz, *Nonreactive Measures in the Social Sciences*, 2nd ed. (Boston: Houghton Mifflin, 1981).

14. Joan E. McLean, "Campaign Strategy," in *Women and American Politics: New Questions, New Directions*, ed. Susan J. Carroll (Oxford: Oxford University Press, 2003), 53–71.

15. Ya-Chung Chuang, *Democracy on Trial: Social Movements and Cultural Politics in Postauthoritarian Taiwan* (Hong Kong: The Chinese University Press, 2013).

16. Wedeen, "Reflections on Ethnographic Work in Political Science."

17. Carol Hardy-Fanta, *Latina Politics, Latino Politics: Gender, Culture, and Political Participation in Boston* (Philadelphia: Temple University Press, 1993), xiv.

18. Paul B. Allwood, "Handwashing among Public Restroom Users at the Minnesota State Fair." Accessed January 21, 2015, from http://www.health.state.mn.us/handhygiene/stats/fairstudy.pdf. See also

Minnesota Department of Health and Healthy Minnesota Partnership, "The Health of Minnesota: Statewide Health Assessment," April 2012. Accessed February 19, 2018. Available at https://www.health.state.mn.us/communities/practice/healthymn partnership/docs/1204healthofminnesota.pdf.

19. Mary Henle and Marian B. Hubble, "'Egocentricity' in Adult Conversation," *Journal of Social Psychology* 9, no. 2 (1938): 227–34.

20. John Lofland, *Analyzing Social Settings: A Guide to Qualitative Observation and Analysis* (Belmont, CA: Wadsworth, 1971), 102–103.

21. Ibid., 105.

22. Ibid., 106–107.

23. Kristen Renwick Monroe, "The Rush to Transparency: DA-RT and the Potential Dangers for Qualitative Research," *Perspectives on Politics* 16, no. 1 (2018): 141–48.

24. Katherine Cramer Walsh, "Putting Inequality in Its Place: Rural Consciousness and the Power of Perspectives," *American Political Science Review* 106, no. 3 (2012): 517–32.

25. Walsh used a stratified purposeful sampling procedure to select communities. She categorized Wisconsin counties into eight distinct regions, based on partisan leaning, median household income, population density, size of community, racial and ethnic heterogeneity, local industry, and agricultural background. Within each region, she chose the municipality with the largest population and randomly chose a smaller municipality. She included several additional municipalities to provide additional variation.

26. Ibid., 522.

27. Ibid., 521–22.

28. See Myron Glazer, *The Research Adventure: Promise and Problems of Field Work* (New York: Random House, 1972), 25–48, 97–124.

29. See Richard F. Fenno Jr., *Home Style: House Members in Their Districts* (Boston: Little, Brown, 1978), 272.

30. Brian C. Rathbun, "Interviewing and Qualitative Research Methods," in *The Oxford Handbook of Political Methodology*, ed. Janet M. Box-Steffensmeier, Henry E. Brady, and David Collier (Oxford: Oxford University Press, 2008), 685–701.

31. See Jeffrey M. Berry, "Validity and Reliability Issues in Elite Interviewing," *PS: Political Science and Politics* 35, no. 4 (2002): 679–82.

32. Ibid., 680.

33. John D'Attoma, "Divided Nation: The North-South Cleavage in Italian Tax Compliance," *Polity* 49, no. 1 (2017): 77.

34. Elizabeth N. Saunders, *Leaders at War; How Presidents Shape Military Interventions* (Ithaca, NY: Cornell University Press, 2011).

35. Andrew Moravcsik, "Transparency: The Revolution in Qualitative Research," *PS: Political Science and Politics* 47, no. 1 (2014): 50.

36. Ibid.

9

QUANTITATIVE RESEARCH DESIGNS

This chapter explores quantitative research designs. Quantitative designs are often called large *N* designs. Whereas qualitative designs generally examine one or a few cases, quantitative studies include more (sometimes many more) cases. Exactly how many more is not the important distinction, however. Rather, the difference pertains to the types of comparisons that are made and the use of summary statistics and other mathematical procedures to compare groups of cases. As we did with qualitative designs in chapter 7, we will focus on the extent to which the various designs allow the researcher to demonstrate causal relationships—that is, exhibit internal validity. External validity, the extent to which the relationships demonstrated by a particular example of research can be generalized beyond the population or context of the research study, is also considered. We start by discussing a number of experimental designs, then move on to a discussion of field and natural experiments. Next we discuss quasi-experimental designs—designs that lack random assignment to experimental and control groups—and conclude with a discussion of observational research designs in which there is not only no random assignment, but also no researcher control over the treatment variable. While political scientists regularly use all types of research designs, much political science research uses the cross-sectional design and, to a lesser extent, longitudinal research designs, both of which are observational designs.

RANDOMIZED EXPERIMENTAL DESIGNS

We discussed the classical randomized experiment in chapter 6. Here we consider several variations of randomized experiments. Each one represents a different attempt to retain experimental control over the experimental situation while dealing

CHAPTER OBJECTIVES

9.1 Understand the difference between the three main types of quantitative research designs (randomized experimental, quasi-experimental, and observational) and evaluate their internal and external validity.

9.2 Understand the distinctions between posttest-only, repeated-measurement, and multigroup experimental designs.

9.3 Discuss the use of field experiments and natural experiments in political science research and understand how they differ from laboratory experiments.

9.4 Describe the quasi-experimental design and its limitations.

9.5 Describe two types of observational research designs—cross-sectional designs and longitudinal designs—and explain how they contribute to our understanding of political phenomena.

with threats to internal and external validity. Although you may not have an opportunity to employ these designs, knowledge of them will help you understand published research and determine whether the research design employed supports the authors' conclusions.

Posttest Design

A simple variant, the posttest design, involves two groups and two variables, one independent and one dependent. As in the classic experiment, subjects are randomly assigned to one or the other of two groups. One group, the experimental group, is exposed to a treatment or stimulus, and the other, the control group, is not or is given a placebo. Then the dependent variable is measured for each group. The difference between this and the classical randomized experiment is that there is no pretest, so one cannot be certain that at the outset the two groups (experimental and control) have the same average levels on all relevant variables (see figure 9-1).

Nonetheless, researchers using this design can justifiably make causal inferences because they know that the treatment occurred prior to measurement of the dependent variable and that any difference between the two groups on the measure of the dependent variable is attributable to the difference in the treatment. Why? This design still requires random assignment of subjects to the experimental and control groups and, therefore, assumes that extraneous factors have been controlled for. It also assumes that, prior to the application of the experimental stimulus, both groups were equivalent with respect to the dependent variable. If the assignment to experimental or control groups is truly random, and the size of the two groups is large, these are ordinarily safe assumptions. However, if the assignment to groups is not truly random or the sample size is small, or both, then posttreatment differences between the two groups may be the result of pretreatment differences and not the result of the independent variable. Because it is impossible with this design to tell how much of the posttreatment difference is simply a reflection of pretreatment differences, a classical experimental research design is considered to be a stronger design.

Repeated-Measurement Design

Naturally, when an experiment uses both a pretest and a posttest, the pretest comes before the experiment starts, and the posttest afterward. But exactly how long before and how long

FIGURE 9-1 ■ Simple Posttest Experiment		
		Posttest
R Experimental Group	X	M_{exp}
R Control Group		$M_{control}$
X = Experimental manipulation		
M = Measurements		
R = Random assignment of subjects to groups		

afterward? Researchers seldom know for sure. Therefore, an experiment, called a repeated-measurement design, may contain several pretreatment and posttreatment measures, especially when researchers don't know exactly how quickly the effect of the independent variable should be observed or when the most reliable pretest measurement of the dependent variable should be taken. An example of a repeated-measurement experimental design would be an attempt to test the relationship between watching a presidential debate and support for the candidates. Suppose we started out by conducting a classical experiment, randomly assigning some people to a group that watches a debate and others to a group that does not watch the debate. On the pre- and posttests, we might measure the scores shown in table 9-1.

These scores seem to indicate that the control group was slightly less supportive of Candidate X before the debate (that is, the random assignment did not work perfectly), and that the debate led to a decline in support for Candidate X of 5 percent: $(60 - 50) - (55 - 50)$. Suppose, however, that we had the additional measures shown in table 9-2.

It appears now that support for Candidate X eroded throughout the period for both the experimental and control groups and that the rate of decline was consistently more rapid for the experimental group (that is, the two groups were not equivalent prior to the debate). Viewed from this perspective, it seems that the debate had no effect on the experimental group, since the rate of decline both before and after the debate was the same. Hence, the existence of multiple measures of the dependent variable, both before and after the

TABLE 9-1 ■ Pre- and Posttest Scores in Non-Repeated-Measurement Experiment

	Predebate Support for Candidate X	Treatment	Postdebate Support for Candidate X
Experimental group	60	Yes	50
Control group	55	No	50

Note: Hypothetical data.

TABLE 9-2 ■ Pre- and Posttest Scores in Repeated-Measurement Experiment

	Pretest				Posttest		
	First	Second	Third	Treatment	First	Second	Third
Experimental group	80	70	60	Yes	50	40	30
Control group	65	60	55	No	50	45	40

Note: Hypothetical data.

introduction of the independent variable, would lead in this case to a more accurate conclusion regarding the effects of the independent variable.

Multiple-Group Design

To this point, we have discussed mainly research involving one experimental and one control group. In a multiple-group design, more than one experimental or control group are created so that different levels of the experimental variable can be compared. This is useful if the independent variable can assume several values or if the researcher wants to see the possible effects of manipulating the independent variable in several different ways. Multiple-group designs may involve a posttest only or both a pretest and a posttest. They may also include repeated measurements.

Here is an example of a posttest-only, multigroup experiment. The proportion of respondents who return questionnaires in a mail survey is usually quite low. Consequently, investigators have attempted to increase response rates by including an incentive or token of appreciation inside the survey. Since incentives add to the cost of the survey, researchers want to know whether or not the incentives increase response rates and, if so, which incentives are most effective and cost-efficient. To test the effect of various incentives, we could use a multiple-group posttest design. If we wanted to test the effects of five treatments, we could randomly assign subjects to six groups. One group would receive no reward (the control group), whereas the other groups would each receive a different reward—for example, 25¢, 50¢, $1.00, a pen, or a key ring. Response rates (the posttreatment measure of the dependent variable) for the groups could then be compared. In table 9-3, we present a set of hypothetical results for such an experiment.

The experimental data indicate that rewards increase response rates and that monetary incentives have more effect than do token gifts. Furthermore, it seems that the dollar incentive is not cost-effective, since it did not yield a sufficiently greater response rate than the 50¢ reward to warrant the additional expense. Other experiments of this type could be conducted to compare the effects of other aspects of mail questionnaires, such as the use of prepaid versus promised monetary rewards or the inclusion or exclusion of a prestamped return envelope.

Note that in this example the posttest design is appropriate as measuring the dependent variable (whether or not a respondent returns a mail survey) before mailing the survey is not feasible. In general, posttest-only research designs have weaker internal validity than the classical experiment because the researcher assumes that the control and experimental groups start out equally with respect to the dependent variable rather than using a pretest to check if they are equal.

Randomized Field Experiments

As might be readily guessed, laboratory experiments, whatever their power for making causal inferences, cannot be used to study many of the phenomena that interest political scientists. Furthermore, laboratory experiments tend to be weak with respect to external validity. It would be better to demonstrate cause and effect in natural settings.

TABLE 9-3 ■ Mail Survey Incentive Experiment		
(Random Assignment)	Treatment	Response Rate (%)
Experimental Group 1	25¢	45.0
Experimental Group 2	50¢	51.0
Experimental Group 3	$1.00	52.0
Experimental Group 4	pen	38.0
Experimental Group 5	key ring	37.0
Control Group	no reward	30.2

Note: Hypothetical data.

The basic principles of experimental design can be taken into the field. Actually, the multigroup survey incentive experiment discussed above is an example of a field experiment: it did not take place in a laboratory. A **field experiment** adopts the logic of randomization and variable manipulation but applies these techniques in naturally occurring situations.[1] Let's look at an example.

Like many others, David Niven speculated about the effects of campaigning on electoral participation. He, too, was concerned about the lack of external validity of laboratory experiments.

> Various . . . studies inquire about intentions to vote, or candidate preferences, but none is equipped to measure actual resulting behavior. . . . Regardless of the rigor of the researchers or the ingenious nature of their design, the laboratory remains a difficult setting in which to demonstrate the effect of negative advertising on the real world behavior of turning out to vote.[2]

As a way around this inferential obstacle, he conducted an experiment on a sample of citizens of West Palm Beach, Florida:

> Voters in the sample were randomly assigned to either the control group (700 voters who would not receive any mailings) or to one of seven experimental groups (which varied in the number of negative mailings each would receive). . . . Subjects receiving the treatment were randomly assigned to one of seven groups which received either one, two, or three negative ads. . . . After the ads were distributed and the election had occurred, official voting records were consulted to determine who cast a ballot in the election.[3]

Niven found a positive effect: Turnout among the residents receiving the negative mailings was a bit higher (32.4 percent) than among those in the treatment condition (26.6 percent).[4] Hence, Niven comes down on the side of those who feel negative advertising might have a beneficial impact on voter turnout.[5]

Field experiments have limitations, however. This is especially true for the study of public policies and programs. Imagine trying to conduct an experiment to discover whether or not enrollment in a high-deductible health insurance plan ultimately leads to poorer health outcomes or higher health care costs because people with such plans try to avoid paying the deductible and delay seeking health care until the situation is serious. At a minimum, you would need to draw a random sample of individuals and families and then randomly assign some individuals and families to high-deductible health plans—the treatment—and others to a plan with a low or no deductible. (Typically, these plans have much higher monthly premiums.) That would be possible in theory but impossible in practice. Assuming that you paid the cost of the monthly premium for both types of plans, how would you force people to enroll in the high-deductible plan?

NATURAL EXPERIMENTS

In a **natural experiment,** "nature"—forces not under the investigator's control—assign individuals or units to "treatment" and "control" groups. Assignment to groups may involve true random assignment, or, in some cases, the assignment is "as-if" random. Researchers are able to observe but do not themselves manipulate the operation of the "experimental" factor.

Susan Hyde's research on the observer effect in international elections is a good example of a natural experiment with as-if random assignment of observer teams to polling stations.[6] Recall from our discussion of this research in chapter 1 that Hyde analyzed the effect of the assignment of international observers to polling stations during the 2003 presidential elections in Armenia. She argues:

> If election-day fraud occurs in any election, it should have the observable implication of increasing the vote share of the fraud-sponsoring candidate. In the case of Armenia, the incumbent sponsored the majority of election-day fraud. Therefore, if international observers have no effect on election-day fraud, then the incumbent should perform equally well in both groups of polling stations: those that were monitored and those that were not. If international observers reduce election fraud, the incumbent's average vote share should be lower in monitored polling stations than in unmonitored polling stations.[7]

Assignment of observers to polling stations was "functionally equivalent" to random assignment according to Hyde: Each team's assigned polling places were selected arbitrarily from a complete list of polling places; individuals making the assignments did not possess information about the polling places so that they could choose polling stations according to criteria that could have predicted voting patterns; observers were distributed across the entire country including both urban and rural areas; their lists did not overlap; and observers were instructed to go only to their assigned polling places. Furthermore, the list of polling stations was not preannounced so that cheaters couldn't limit their cheating to those polling stations where observers were not expected.

Because Armenian presidential elections took place in two stages and election observers were assigned using a separate assignment process for each stage, this natural experiment resulted in multiple treatment groups: polling places with observers for both stages, those with observers for the first stage only, those with observers for the second stage only, and those with no observers for either stage (the control group). Hyde was able to make numerous comparisons of the percentage of the vote received by the incumbent. The results are shown in table 9-4, which should look familiar to you as we also included it in chapter 1. The first column contains the control group (polling stations with no observation or less observation), and the second column contains the treatment group (polling stations with more observation compared to the control group). In each comparison, the percentage of votes received by the incumbent was lower in the treatment group; as would be expected, the presence of observers deterred election fraud. Notice, for example, that comparison 6 shows that the presence of observers in round 1 only had an effect on fraud in round 2.

Hyde was extremely fortunate in the conditions characterizing the elections. First, there was ample evidence that the incumbent and his supporters engaged in election fraud. If there had been none, then there would be no reason to expect the incumbent's share of the vote to vary by polling place in accordance with the presence of election observers. Second, the assignment of observer teams resembled random assignment (as-if random). Third, election results by polling place were available. One might expect, in countries where there is rampant election fraud, such transparency of election results would not occur. Was Hyde just lucky, or are social scientists likely to encounter other natural experiments?

Thad Dunning would argue it's both. There are known situations involving natural experiments. Knowing about these may help researchers to discover others.[8] Yet, there is some luck involved in discovering natural experiments. A selection of natural experiments identified by Dunning are shown in table 9-5, those involving random assignment are shown in table 9-6, and those with as-if randomization are shown in table 9-7.

Natural experiments, especially those with actual randomization, may possess high levels of internal validity. Because the researcher does not control the manipulation or application of the treatment variable, however, one needs to consider the possibility that the treatments were not identical for all units in the treatment group or that there was some bias in the application of the treatment variable. Also, because natural experiments take place outside the controlled environment of a laboratory, it is possible that some factor in the environment also influenced the dependent variable. These possibilities would lessen the internal validity of such experiments. Yet, natural experiments tend to possess a high degree of external validity because they *do* take place in the real world. One may still need to question whether the results would apply in different contexts or for different populations.

So far, we have discussed research designs involving random assignment or as-if random assignment. In some instances, the researcher had control over the manipulation of the treatment, while in others (natural experiments), someone else did. Now let us consider research designs in which there is no random assignment.

TABLE 9-4 ■ Difference of Means Tests Comparing "Treatment" and "Control" Groups

	Average Incumbent Vote Share among Polling Stations That Were . . .	vs.	Average Incumbent Vote Share among Polling Stations That Were . . .	Difference
1.	Not observed in R1 54.2% (R1 vote share)	vs.	Observed in R1 48.3% (R1 vote share)	5.9% $t(1762) = 5.92$ $P > \|t\| = 0.00$
2.	Not observed in R2 69.3% (R2 vote share)	vs.	Observed in R2 67.3% (R2 vote share)	2.0% $t(1761) = 2.47$ $P > \|t\| = 0.014$
3.	Never observed 70.7% (R2 vote share)	vs.	Observed in both R1 and R2 66.2% (R2 vote share)	4.5% $t(1116) = 4.48$ $P > \|t\| = 0.00$
4.	Never observed 62.8% (Average of R1 and R2 vote share)	vs.	Observed in both R1 and R2 57% (Average of R1 and R2 vote share)	5.8% $t(1116) = 5.36$ $P > \|t\| = 0.00$
5.	Never observed 62.7% (Average of R1 and R2 vote share)	vs.	Observed in one or both rounds 58.1% (Average of R1 and R2 vote share)	4.6% $t(1761) = 5.65$ $P > \|t\| = 0.00$
6.	Never observed 70.7% (R2 vote share)	vs.	Observed only in R1 66.3% (R2 vote share)	4.4% $t(1138) = 4.40$ $P > \|t\| = 0.00$
7.	Never observed 70.7% (R2 vote share)	vs.	Observed only in R2 68.7% (R2 vote share)	2.0% $t(1013) = 1.73$ $P > \|t\| = 0.084$
8.	Observed only in R2 68.7% (R2 vote share)	vs.	Observed in both R1 and R2 66.2% (R2 vote share)	2.5% $t(621) = 1.93$ $P > \|t\| = 0.054$
9.	Observed in both R1 and R2 66.3% (R2 vote share)	vs.	Observed only in R1 66.2% (R2 vote share)	.11% $t(746) = 0.094$ $P > \|t\| = 0.93$
10.	Observed only in R1 68.7% (R2 vote share)	vs.	Observed only in R2 66.3% (R2 vote share)	2.4% $t(643) = 1.83$ $P > \|t\| = 0.067$

• Reported results reflect two-sample *t* tests with equal variances.

Source: Susan Hyde, "The Observer Effect in International Politics: Evidence from a Natural Experiment," *World Politics* 60, no. 1 (2007): table 1, p. 53.

TABLE 9-5 ■ **Typical "Standard" Natural Experiments**

Source of natural experiment	Random or as-if random	Units in study group	Outcome variables
Lotteries	Random		
Military drafts		Soldiers	Earnings
Electoral quotas		Politicians	Public spending
Term lengths		Politicians	Legislative productivity
School vouchers		Students	Educational achievement
Prize lotteries		Lottery players	Political attitudes
Program roll-outs	Random	Municipalities, villages, others	E.g., voting behavior
Policy interventions	As-if random		
Voting locations		Voters	Turnout
Election monitors		Candidates	Electoral fraud
Property titles		Squatters	Access to credit markets
Number of police		Criminals	Criminal behavior
Jurisdictional borders	As-if random	Voters, citizens, others	Ethnic identification, employment
Electoral redistricting	As-if random	Voters, candidates	Voting behavior
Ballot order	Random or as-if random	Candidates	Voting behavior
Institutional rules	As-if random	Countries, voters, politicians	Economic development
Historical legacies	As-if random	Citizens, countries, regions	Public goods provision

Source: Thad Dunning, *Natural Experiments in the Social Sciences: A Design Based Approach* (Cambridge, UK: Cambridge University Press, 2012), 44.

TABLE 9-6   ■   Natural Experiments with Random Assignment

Authors	Substantive focus	Source of natural experiment	Country	Simple difference of means?
Angrist (1990a, 1990b)	Effect of military induction on later labor-market earnings	Randomized Vietnam-era draft lottery	US	Yes
Angrist et al. (2002); *Angrist, Bettinger, and Kremer* (2006)	Effect of private school vouchers on school completion rates and test performance	Allocation vouchers by lottery	Colombia	Yes[a]
Chattopadhyay and Duflo (2004)	Effect of electoral quotas for women	Random assignments of quotas for village council presidencies	India	Yes
Dal Bó and Rossi (2010)	Effect of tenure in office on legislative performance	Randomized term lengths in some sessions of legislature	Argentina	Yes
De la O (forthcoming)	Effect of length of time in conditional cash transfer program on voter turnout and support for incumbent	Comparison of early- and late-participating villages based on randomized roll-out program	Mexico	No[b]
Doherty, Green, and Gerber (2006)	Effect of lottery winnings on political attitudes	Random assignment of lottery winnings, among lottery players	US	No[c]
Erickson and Stoker (2011)	Effect of military conscription on political attitudes and partisan identification	Randomized Vietnam-era draft lottery	US	Yes
Galiani, Rossi, and Schargrodsky (2011)	Effect of military conscription on criminal behavior	Randomized draft lottery for military service in Argentina	Argentina	No
Ho and Imai (2008)	Effect of ballot position on electoral outcomes	Randomized ballot order under alphabet lottery in California	US	Yes
Titiunik (2011)	Effect of term lengths on legislative behavior	Random assignment of state senate seats to two- or four-year terms	US	Yes

Note: The table lists selected natural experiments with true randomization. The final column codes whether a simple difference-of-means test is presented, without control variables.

[a]The 2002 study includes a regression with cohort dummies.

[b]Nonoverlapping units of assignments and outcome lead to estimation of interaction models.

[c]The treatment variables are continuous.

Source: Thad Dunning, *Natural Experiments in the Social Sciences: A Design Based Approach* (Cambridge, UK: Cambridge University Press, 2012), 45.

TABLE 9-7 ■ Natural Experiments with "As-If" Randomization

Authors	Substantive focus	Source of natural experiment	Country	Simple difference of means?
Ansolabehere, Snyder, and Stewart (2000)	The personal vote and incumbency advantage	Electoral redistricting	US	Yes
Banerjee and Iyer (2005)	Effect of landlord power on development	Land tenure patterns instituted by British in colonial India	India	No[a]
Berger (2009)	Long-term effect of colonial taxation institutions	The division of northern and southern Nigeria at 7°10′ N	Nigeria	No
Blattman (2008)	Consequences of child soldiering for political participation	Abduction of children by the Lord's Resistance Army	Uganda	No
Brady and McNulty (2011)	Voter turnout	Precinct consolidation in California gubernatorial recall election	US	Yes
Cox, Rosenbluth, and Theis (2000)	Incentives of Japanese politicians to join factions	Cross-sectional and temporal variation in institutional rules in Japanese parliamentary houses	Japan	Yes
Di Tella and Schargrodsky (2004)	Effect of police presence on crime	Allocation of police to blocks with Jewish centers after terrorist attack in Buenos Aires	Argentina	No
Ferraz and Finan (2008)	Effect of corruption audits on electoral accountability	Public release of corruption audits in Brazil	Brazil	Yes[a]
Galiani and Schargrodsky (2004, 2010); also *Di Tella, Galiani, and Schargrodsky* (2007)	Effect of land titling for the poor on economic activity and attitudes	Judicial challenges to transfer of property titles to squatters	Argentina	Yes (*Galiani and Schargrodsky*, 2004); No (*Di Tella, Galiani, and Schargrodsky* 2007; *Galiani and Schargrodsky*, 2010)

(Continued)

TABLE 9-7 ■ (Continued)

Authors	Substantive focus	Source of natural experiment	Country	Simple difference of means?
Glazer and Robbins (1985)	Congressional responsiveness to constituencies	Electoral redistricting	US	No
Grogman, Brunell, and Koetzle (1998)	Midterm losses in the House and Senate	Party control of White House in previous elections	US	No
Grofman, Griffin, and Berry (1995)	Congressional responsiveness to constituencies	House members who move to the Senate	US	Yes
Hyde (2007)	The effect of international election monitoring on electoral fraud	Assignment of election monitors to polling stations in Armenia	Armenia	Yes
Krasno and Green (2008)	Effect of televised presidential campaign ads on voter turnout	Geographic spillover of campaign ads in states with competitive elections to some but not all areas of neighboring states	US	No[b]
Lyall (2009)	Deterrent effect of bombings and shellings	Allocation of bombs by drunk Russian soldiers	Chechnya	No
Miguel (2004)	Nation-building and public goods provision	Political border between Kenya and Tanzania	Kenya/ Tanzania	No
Posner (2004)	Political salience of cultural cleavages	Political border between Zambia and Malawi	Zambia/ Malawi	Yes
Snow ([1855] 1965)	Incidence of cholera in London	Allocation of water to different houses	UK	Yes
Stasavage (2003)	Bureaucratic delegation, transparency, and accountability	Variation in central banking institutions	Cross-national	No

Note: This table lists selected natural experiments with alleged as-if randomization. The final column codes whether a simple difference-of-means test is presented, without control variables.

[a] Includes state fixed effects.

[b] The treatment conditions are continuous in this study, complicating the calculation of difference of means.

Source: Thad Dunning, *Natural Experiments in the Social Sciences: A Design Based Approach* (Cambridge, UK: Cambridge University Press, 2012), 46–47.

NONRANDOMIZED DESIGNS: QUASI-EXPERIMENTS

A **quasi-experimental design** contains treatment and control groups, but the experimenter does not randomly assign individual units to these groups. The effects, if any, of putative treatments have to be inferred without the help of strong internal validity. To compensate for the lack of randomization, experimenters turn to judgment, theory, common sense, and statistical and mathematical tools to rule out spurious or confounding causes and make assumptions about how consistent or equal exposure to the treatment variable was. Any scientific activity requires some inference, but as one moves from randomized designs to quasi-experiments, inferences about causal effects demand more and more of the researcher's substantive knowledge and analytic skills.

Suppose we set up an experiment like the one exploring the effects of negative campaign ads on intention to vote, but we do *not* randomly assign individuals to the experimental and control groups. Instead, we use our judgment or, more likely, preexisting groups—perhaps two sections of Political Science 101 being taught at different times of the day in the same room. We show one section negative campaign ads, while the other section is shown bland commercials. Since we are going to measure intention to vote both before and after the experiment, we reason that under the circumstances, this plan provides a reasonable approximation of a classical experiment. But, because there is no randomization of assignment of students to the two sections, we cannot be sure that the groups were similar. The pretest will allow us to see if the groups had similar levels of intention to vote before being exposed to the ads, but we do not know if there is some other factor that differs between the groups that might affect the impact of exposure to negative campaign ads. If we find an ostensible or apparent effect—ads reduce motivation to vote—it might be because the ads really do have an effect, or because of the operation of some unmeasured or unobserved factor, or both. The problem is that we just don't know. The internal validity of an experiment without random assignment is suspect.

What is to be done? The investigator must look for and ensure that all other possible effects on the independent variable have been taken into account. In terms of the trade, this procedure is called "controlling" or "holding constant" variables. How? By judgment, careful observation, application of previous research, common sense and logic, and—in some cases, where appropriate—statistical adjustment, which we discuss in later chapters.

In our example, we might have access to course rosters and the instructors' records and be able to measure the average class level, gender, major, and so forth. We hope that there would be no appreciable variation between groups on these indicators, thereby increasing our confidence that treatment did indeed have the hypothesized effect (see table 9-8).

We see that at the start, both classes had roughly the same percentages on all the variables we were able to measure explicitly, including "intention to vote" in the next election. After the quasi-experiment, the dependent variable (*Y*) has decreased 10 points from 60 to 50 percent in the experimental group, while it has changed hardly at all among the control subjects (55 to 52 percent). As expected, the other variable averages have stayed the same. Consequently, we make two tentative conclusions: (1) The treatment (exposure to negative ads) is *associated with* a drop in voting, and (2) this decrease is *not* explained by changes in any

TABLE 9-8 ■ Results from Hypothetical Quasi-Experiment		
	Before Measurements	**Postmeasurements**
Experimental (negative ads)		
Percentage intending to vote	60	50
Percentage male	45	45
Percentage liberal arts majors	70	70
Percentage undeclared	40	40
Control (bland ads)		
Percentage intending to vote	55	52
Percentage male	50	50
Percentage liberal arts majors	65	65
Percentage undeclared	35	35

other measured variables, which have remained at their same levels. So, for example, the drop in expected turnout in the experimental group is presumably not due to changes in major or gender, which are constant. That leaves among the measured factors only the exposure–nonexposure difference. Alas, there are many other unmeasured factors that could have affected changes in intention to vote.

Naturally, this is not a very compelling example. But it reveals the logic behind most empirical studies in political science, whether or not they are quantitative: They use judgment and explicit measurement and controls to rule out the possibility that the treatment–effect relationship is not spurious. Even if quasi-experimental designs do not meet the standards of randomized experiments, they constantly lead to new knowledge.

OBSERVATIONAL STUDIES

The term **observational study** is used to describe designs in which the researcher neither manipulates experimental variables nor randomly assigns subjects to treatments but instead merely *observes* causal sequences and covariations. Furthermore, the researcher has no control over the environment of the units being studied and, without random assignment to control the impact of extraneous factors, must use statistical procedures to control for or take into consideration as many confounding factors as he or she can think of. Cross-sectional designs and longitudinal designs are two frequently used observational research designs.

Cross-Sectional Design

Perhaps the most common observational research design is cross-sectional analysis. In a **cross-sectional design**, measurements of the independent and dependent variables are taken all at the same time or approximately the same time,[9] and the researcher does not control or manipulate the independent variable, the assignment of subjects to treatment or control groups, or the conditions under which the independent variable is experienced. If the units of analysis are individuals, the study is often called a *survey* or poll; if the subjects are geographical entities, such as states or nations or other groupings of units, the term *aggregate analysis* is frequently applied. In either situation, attributes of the units are measured or observed, and the data recorded. In surveys, the respondents themselves report their exposure to various factors or their beliefs, opinions, and behaviors. In aggregate analysis, the investigator simply observes which units have what values on the variables. For example, one could use data collected by the United Nations to examine the relationship between per capita gross national income and infant mortality rates.[10] In both situations, the measurements are used to construct, with the help of statistical methods, posttreatment quasi-experimental and quasi-control groups that have occurred naturally, and the measurements of the dependent variable are used to assess the differences between these groups. Data analysis and logical assumptions (for example, about whether the independent variable occurred before the dependent variable), rather than physical manipulation of variables, are the bases for making causal inferences.

Although this approach makes it far more difficult to measure the causal effects that can be attributed to the presence or introduction of independent variables (treatments), it has the virtues of allowing observation of phenomena in more natural, realistic settings; increasing the size and representativeness of the populations studied; and allowing the testing of hypotheses that do not lend themselves easily to experimental treatment. In short, cross-sectional designs improve external validity at the expense of internal validity.

Assume we try to assess the effects of negative campaigning on the likelihood of voting by interviewing (that is, surveying) a sample of citizens and then dividing the respondents into different categories according to *their* answers to questions of this sort: "Did you happen to see or read any campaign ads? How many? How many seemed to attack the opponent?" We could then sort respondents by their self-reported level of exposure to negativity. Notice that since there is no random assignment, only self-reports, we do not control who is in each group by forcing people to view differing levels of negative advertising. The groups are simply observed. Because of our research design and our inability to ensure that those with less and those with more exposure were alike in every other way, we could not necessarily conclude that campaign tone determines the propensity to vote. And note that this is true no matter how large our sample is. With a survey design, then, we must include appropriate questions in the survey to measure potential confounders that may affect both the independent and dependent variables and then use statistics to hold them constant.

In essence, the limitations of the cross-sectional design—that is, lack of control over exposure to the independent variable and inability to form pure experimental and control groups—force us to rely on data analysis techniques to isolate the impact of the independent variables of interest. This process requires researchers to make their comparison groups equivalent by holding relevant extraneous factors constant and then observing the relationship between independent and dependent variables, procedures described more fully in chapters 13 and 14. Yet holding extraneous factors constant is problematic, since it is very difficult to be sure that all relevant variables have been explicitly identified and measured. It is important to stress that if a causal variable is not recognized and brought into the analysis, its effects are nonetheless still operative, even though we may not be aware of them.

Longitudinal (Time-Series) Designs

Longitudinal or **time-series designs** are characterized by the availability of measures of variables at different points in time. As with the other designs, the researcher does not control the introduction of the independent variable(s) and must rely on data collected by others to measure the dependent variable rather than personally conducting the measurements. On the other hand, time-series designs have two distinct advantages: (1) change in the level of variables or conditions can be measured and modeled, and (2) it is sometimes easier to decide time order or which comes first, X or Y.

Additional benefits of longitudinal studies include the fact that they can in principle estimate three kinds of effects: age, period (history), and cohort. **Age effects** can be considered a direct measure of (chronological) time and be assessed like other variables. As in cross-sectional work, an investigator may be interested in the effect of age on political predispositions or ideology. (It is commonly asserted that as people age, they become more politically conservative.) But in addition, in longitudinal analysis, a period (interval of time) may be thought of as an indicator of history during a period, and the consequences on individuals are **period effects**. It is the "history" that occurs during the period, not chronological age, that matters. During the late 1960s and early 1970s, for example, events such as Watergate and the Vietnam War adversely affected many citizens' trust in government, whether they were young or old. When that era passed, its effects on newer generations dissipated. So those who lived through those stormy times might have very different beliefs and opinions than do younger people.

Another way of interpreting period effects is to consider cohorts. A **cohort** is defined as a group of people who all experience a significant event in roughly the same time. A birth cohort, for instance, consists of those born in a given year or period; an "event" cohort is those who shared a common experience, such as their first entry into the labor force at a particular time. It is often hypothesized that individuals in one cohort will, because of their shared background, behave differently than individuals in a different cohort. To take one example, people born in the years immediately after World War II (the baby boomers) may have different political attitudes and affiliations than those who were born in the 1980s. Note that cohort, period, and age effects are inescapably related because "cohort (year of birth) = period (year of event) + age (years since birth)."[11]

There are, in short, a number of ways of understanding longitudinal research; the choice depends on the analyst's interests.

Intervention Analysis

In one version of a nonexperimental time-series design, called **intervention analysis** or "interrupted time-series analysis," measurements of a dependent variable are taken both before and after the "introduction" of an independent variable. Here we speak figuratively: As with the other nonrandomized designs, the occurrence of the independent variable is *observed*, not literally introduced or administered. We could observe, for instance, the annual poverty rate both before and after the ascension of a leftist party to see if regime change makes any difference on living standards. The premeasurements allow a researcher to establish trends in the dependent variable that are presumably unaffected by the independent variable so that appropriate conclusions can be drawn about posttreatment measures. Refer to figure 9-2. Panel (a) shows an increase in a dependent variable over time (suppose it is the poverty rate in metropolitan areas). At a specific moment or period, an intervention takes place (perhaps the enactment of a job-training program). But the trend line remains undisturbed: *Y* grows at the same rate before and after the "appearance" of the independent variable. In this case, the intervention did not interrupt or alter the trend. (We would conclude, for example, that the program did not affect the increase in poverty.) Now consider the second figure (b). It shows an increase in *Y* until the intervention occurs, at which point the growth in the trend begins to abate. In this instance, the introduction of the factor appears to have caused the trend to flatten (e.g., the advent of job training slowed the growth in poverty).

For a perhaps more realistic example, let us return briefly to the case Jacob S. Hacker and Paul Pierson made about the growth of business power and income inequality in the United States (see chapter 1).[12] Recall that the authors first documented an increase in the share of America's wealth going to the wealthiest individuals. Hacker and Pierson claimed that this phenomenon—the rich getting richer, leaving less for the middle and lower classes—does

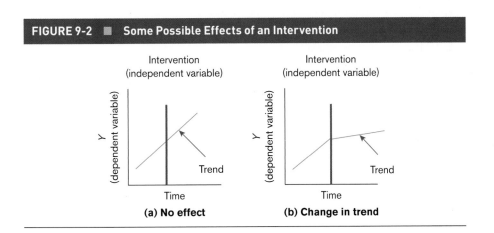

FIGURE 9-2 ■ Some Possible Effects of an Intervention

not result from mere economic change or happenstance but follows as a direct result of policy changes (e.g., tax rates and financial deregulation). They explained that

> [p]olicy—both what government has done and what, as a result of drift, it has failed to do—has played an absolutely central role in the rise of winner-take-all economic outcomes. . . . Moreover, in the main areas where the role of government appears most significant, we see a consistent pattern: active, persistent, and consequential action on the part of organized interests that stood to gain from a transformation of government's role in the American economy. A winner-take-all politics accompanied, and helped produce a winner-take-all economy.[13]

Hacker and Pierson dated the transformation from the mid-1980s, when the so-called conservative or Reagan "revolution" began. Policy shifts advantageous to the wealthy, however, have been sustained with the help of Democrats in the White House and Congress.[14]

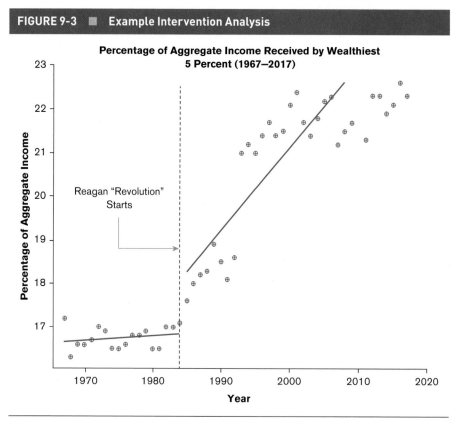

FIGURE 9-3 ■ Example Intervention Analysis

Source: U.S. Census Bureau, *Current Population Survey: Annual Social and Economic Supplements; Historical Income Tables—Income Inequality,* table H-2: Share of Aggregate Income Received by Each Fifth and Top 5 Percent of Households (All Races) 1967 to 2017. Retrieved March 4, 2019. Available at https://www.census .gov/data/tables/time-series/demo/income-poverty/historical-income-households.html.

It is a stretch, but we could analyze the argument with an intervention analysis. Figure 9-3 shows the share of aggregate income going to the richest 5 percent of American households each year from 1967 to 2017. (These data are called a "time series.") We see that this share remained around 17 percent until the mid-1980s. Beginning in the late 1970s and accelerating when Ronald Reagan took office in 1981, the federal government began to cut taxes and roll back regulations of the finance industry. We might conceptualize this change as a policy "intervention." We see its "effects" in the jump in income going to the top group after about 1984, when Reagan was reelected to a second term; after climbing to 21 percent in 1993, it has since stabilized. The straight lines—technically called "regression" lines—show that changes were relatively modest from 1967 to 1984 and then soared. There is, in statistical language, a shift in both the level (average) and slope (trend) in the series of income shares.

This analysis is, of course, vastly oversimplified. But it illustrates this nonexperimental design and its pitfalls. The data from Hacker and Pierson's study suggest that increasing concentration of wealth had a cause—namely, the tax and other conservative policies pushed by the corporate and financial sectors. But notice our use of the weasel word *suggest*. The conclusion rests on an inference that no other factors were at work to produce the observed changes. Since no one randomized the years to control and experimental groups, we have no assurance that other unmeasured variables were at work. And Hacker and Pierson's critics argue that many other factors were surely in play. Yet, as we stress throughout the book, it is incumbent on the skeptics to identify those alternative causes and show how they, not growing business power, account for the results.

In closing this example, we point out that a "real" intervention analysis involves the application of statistical techniques to, among other things, ensure that the observed shifts in level and trend are not merely the result of chance fluctuations in the time series. A more realistic study would require measuring other variables and adjusting the data to remove the effects of random error.[15]

Trend Analysis

Former congressman Lee H. Hamilton noted, "There's a funny thing going on in our national politics right now: Everyone deplores polarization, but it just keeps getting worse."[16] To know if Americans are becoming more polarized, we must answer three questions:

1. What does *polarized* mean?

2. Exactly who is polarized?

3. Has the division been growing?

A 2017 report by the Pew Research Center addresses all three questions. Since 1994, public opinion polls have asked a sample of American adults whether they agreed with a series of policy-related statements. So *polarized* in this case refers to differences in policy positions. The polls also asked for respondents' partisanship and demographic information, which gives us the who. Using this information, we can look to see if responses to the policy questions vary by partisan affiliation and demographic characteristics. To address the third question, we turn to **trend analysis**. As the term implies, the analysis of a trend starts with measurements or observations on a dependent variable of interest taken at different times and attempts to determine whether and why the level of the variable is changing. A simple approach for numeric data is to plot some appropriate summary measure of the dependent variable at different times. Figure 9-4 shows the percentage of respondents agreeing with a policy statement for ten policy areas from 1994 to 2017 for all respondents (the middle line) and for Republicans and Democrats.

As you can see, the differences between Republicans and Democrats have increased over the years, more sharply in issues related to assistance to the poor, blacks getting ahead, and immigration and slightly on the issues of homosexuality and corporate profits. The importance of partisanship to polarization is made clearer in figure 9-5, which shows the gap in responses by party and key demographic characteristics.

These graphs represent fairly simple and straightforward analyses of changes over time, but by themselves don't completely explain why the trends are occurring. In more complicated models of change, change in the dependent variable can be hypothesized to be a function of the past values of many independent variables. When data are measured at many different points, statistical procedures called *time-series analysis* are often employed.

FIGURE 9-4 ■ **Growing Gaps between Republicans and Democrats across Domains**

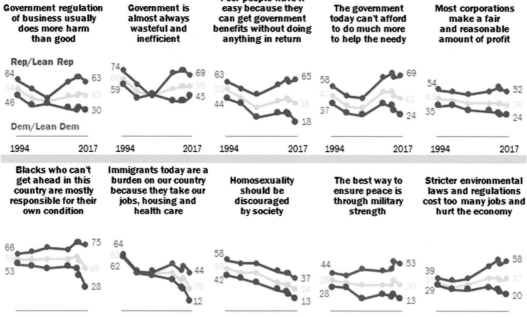

Source: Pew Research Center, "Partisan Divides over Political Values Widen," October 5, 2017. Accessed February 21, 2019. Available at http://www.people-press.org/2017/10/05/1-partisan-divides-over-political-values-widen/.

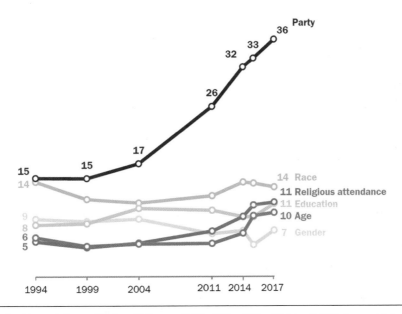

FIGURE 9-5 ■ As Partisan Divides over Political Values Widen, Other Gaps Remain More Modest

Average gap in the share taking a conservative position across 10 political values, by key demographics

Party
36
33
32
26
17
15   15
15
14   14 Race
11 Religious attendance
11 Education
10 Age
9
8   7 Gender
6
5

1994   1999   2004   2011 2014 2017

Source: Pew Research Center, "Partisan Divides over Political Values Widen," October 5, 2017. Accessed February 21, 2019. Available at http://www.people-press.org/2017/10/05/1-partisan-divides-over-political-values-widen/.

For that analysis, we need slightly more advanced statistical tools and more data. This type of analysis takes (roughly speaking) this form:

$$Y_t = f(Y_{t-1} + Y_{t-2} \ldots + Xs_t + Xs_{t+1} + Xs_{t+2} \ldots),$$

where the Ys and Xs are measures of the dependent (Y) and independent (X) variables at the current (latest) time (t) and at previous times ($t-1, t-2, \ldots$ etc.) and f means "is a function of" or "is produced by."[17] The equation for time-series analysis makes it clear that its primary purpose is to measure and predict the effects of causes. If the equation accurately models the impact of the independent variables on the dependent variable, then it may be used to predict the values of Y at a future time, $t+1$ for example. Note also that, although the previous examples pertain to changing proportions in samples of individuals, trends in aggregate variables (e.g., crime or poverty rates in urban areas) can also be investigated. But, as is the case with our other observational research designs, internal validity is a concern: We cannot be sure that we have identified the real causes of Y. There may be some other, yet unmeasured, variable(s) that render some of the independent variables spurious. External validity is strong, however, as the data are based on observing events in the real world.

CONCLUSION

In this chapter, we have discussed research designs for large *N* studies. These designs allow us to make causal assertions, with varying degrees of confidence. We presented three basic types of research designs—experimental, quasi-experimental, and nonexperimental or observational designs—along with a couple of variations of these approaches. We discussed their advantages and disadvantages. Experimental designs—which allow the researcher to exercise control over the independent variable, the units of analysis, and their environment—are often preferred over quasi-experimental and nonexperimental designs because they enable the researcher to establish sounder causal explanations due to their strength in internal validity. Natural experiments involve situations in which the researcher controls neither the assignment of units to treatment and control groups, nor the application of the treatment. Nevertheless, careful examination of the situation may satisfy concerns over random assignment and consistent application of treatments. Quasi-experimental designs lack random assignment, but do involve researcher manipulation of the treatment. Statistical procedures are used to test for the equivalence of treatment and control groups prior to the experimental treatment. Frequently, it may not always be possible or appropriate to use an experimental or quasi-experimental design. Instead, observational designs such as cross-sectional or longitudinal research designs are used to test hypotheses in a meaningful fashion and often in a way that increases the external validity of the results. In these instances, causal assertions rest on weaker grounds and frequently have to be approximated by statistical means (see chapters 13 and 14). No matter which design, however, the emphasis is on discovering the causes of political phenomena.

TERMS INTRODUCED

Age effects. Effects associated with the process of becoming older. 184

Cohort. A group of people who all experience a significant event in roughly the same time frame. 184

Cross-sectional design. A research design in which measurements of independent and dependent variables are taken at the same time; naturally occurring differences in the independent variable are used to create quasi-experimental and quasi-control groups; and extraneous factors are controlled for by statistical means. 183

Field experiment. Experimental designs applied in a natural setting. 173

Intervention analysis. A nonexperimental time-series design in which measurements of a dependent variable are taken both before and after the "introduction" of an independent variable. 185

Multiple-group design. Experimental design with more than one control and experimental group. 172

Natural experiment. A study in which there is random assignment or "as-if" random assignment of units to experimental and control groups but the researcher does not control the randomization process or the manipulation of the treatment factor. 174

Observational study. A nonexperimental research design in which the researcher simply observes differences in the dependent variable for naturally occurring treatment and control groups. 182

Period effect. An indicator or measure of history effect on a dependent variable during a specified time. 184

Posttest design. A research design in which the dependent variable is measured after, but not before, manipulation of the independent variable. 170

Quasi-experimental design. A research design that includes treatment and control groups to which individuals are not assigned randomly. 181

Repeated-measurement design. A plan that calls for making more than one measure or observation on a

dependent variable at different times over the course of the study. 171

Time-series design. A research design (sometimes called a longitudinal design) featuring multiple measurements of the dependent variable before and after experimental treatment. 184

Trend analysis. A research design that measures a dependent variable at different times and attempts to determine whether the level of the variable is changing and, if it is, why. 188

SUGGESTED READINGS

Beck, Nathaniel. "Time-Series Cross-Section Methods." In *The Oxford Handbook of Political Methodology*, edited by Janet M. Box-Steffensmeier, Henry E. Brady, and David Collier, 475–93. Oxford: Oxford University Press, 2008.

Campbell, Donald T., and Julian C. Stanley. *Experimental and Quasi-Experimental Designs for Research.* Chicago: Rand McNally, 1966.

Cook, Thomas D., and Donald T. Campbell. *Quasi-Experimentation: Design and Analysis Issues for Field Settings.* New York: Houghton Mifflin, 1979.

Gerber, Alan S., and Donald P. Green. "Field Experiments and Natural Experiments." In *The Oxford Handbook of Political Methodology*, edited by Janet M. Box-Steffensmeier, Henry E. Brady, and David Collier, 357–81. Oxford: Oxford University Press, 2008.

Hay, M. Cameron. *Methods That Matter: Integrating Mixed Methods for More Effective Social Science Research.* Chicago: University of Chicago Press, 2016.

King, Gary, Robert O. Keohane, and Sidney Verba. *Designing Social Inquiry: Scientific Inference in Qualitative Research.* Princeton, NJ: Princeton University Press, 1994.

Menard, Scott. *Longitudinal Research.* A Sage University Paper: Quantitative Applications in the Social Sciences no. 07–076. Newbury Park, CA: Sage, 1991.

Morton, Rebecca B., and Kenneth C. Williams. "Experimentation in Political Science." In *The Oxford*

Handbook of Political Methodology, edited by Janet M. Box-Steffensmeier, Henry E. Brady, and David Collier, 339–56. Oxford: Oxford University Press, 2008.

Murnane, Richard J., and John B. Willett. *Methods Matter: Improving Causal Inference in Educational and Social Science Research.* Oxford: Oxford University Press, 2011.

Perecman, Ellen, and Sara R. Curran. *A Handbook for Social Science Field Research: Essays & Bibliographic Sources on Research Design and Methods.* Thousand Oaks, CA: Sage, 2006.

Pevehouse, Jon C., and Jason D. Brozek. "Time-Series Analysis." In *The Oxford Handbook of Political Methodology*, edited by Janet M. Box-Steffensmeier, Henry E. Brady, and David Collier, 456–74. Oxford: Oxford University Press, 2008.

6, Perri, and Christine Bellamy. *Principles of Methodology: Research Design in Social Science.* Los Angeles: Sage, 2012.

Salkind, Neil J. *Encyclopedia of Research Design.* Thousand Oaks, CA: Sage, 2010.

Spector, Paul E. *Research Designs.* A Sage University Paper: Quantitative Applications in the Social Sciences no. 07–023. Beverly Hills, CA: Sage, 1981.

Vandaele, Walter. *Applied Time Series and Box-Jenkins Models.* New York: Academic Press, 1983.

NOTES

1. For an overview, see Thomas D. Cook and William R. Shadish, "Social Experiments: Some Developments over the Past Fifteen Years," *Annual Review of Psychology* 45, no. 1 (1994): 545–80.

2. David Niven, "A Field Experiment on the Effects of Negative Campaign Mail on Voter Turnout in a Municipal Election," *Political Research Quarterly* 59, no. 2 (2006): 204.

3. Ibid., 206.

4. Ibid., 207.

5. For similar studies, see Ted Brader, "Striking a Responsive Chord: How Political Ads Motivate and Persuade Voters by Appealing to Emotions," *American Journal of Political Science* 49, no. 2 (2005): 388–405. Accessed February 20, 2019. Available at http://www.uvm.edu/~dguber/POLS234/articles/brader.pdf; David Dreyer Lassen, "The Effect of Information on Voter Turnout: Evidence from a Natural Experiment," *American Journal of Political Science* 49, no. 1 (2005): 103–18; and David W. Nickerson, Ryan D. Friedrichs, and David C. King, "Partisan Mobilization Campaigns in the Field: Results from a Statewide Turnout Experiment in Michigan," *Political Research Quarterly* 59, no. 1 (2006): 85–97. Accessed February 21, 2019. Available at https://doi.org/10.1177/106591290605900108.

6. Susan Hyde, "The Observer Effect in International Politics: Evidence from a Natural Experiment," *World Politics* 60, no. 1 (2007): 37–63.

7. Ibid., 46–47.

8. Thad Dunning, *Natural Experiments in the Social Sciences: A Design Based Approach* (Cambridge, UK: Cambridge University Press, 2012).

9. Although the measurements may be taken over a period of days or even weeks, cross-sectional analysis treats them as though they were obtained simultaneously.

10. Data can be found at http://data.un.org/Default.aspx. Accessed October 27, 2018.

11. See Scott Menard, *Longitudinal Research*, A Sage University Paper: Quantitative Applications in the Social Sciences no. 07–076 (Newbury Park, CA: Sage, 1991), 7.

12. Jacob S. Hacker and Paul Pierson, "Winner-Take-All Politics: Public Policy, Political Organization, and the Precipitous Rise of Top Incomes in the United States," *Politics & Society* 38, no. 2 (2010): 152–204. Accessed February 20, 2019. Available at http://pas.sagepub.com/content/38/2/152.full.pdf.

13. Ibid., 196. See also Joseph E. Stiglitz, *The Price of Inequality* (New York: Norton, 2012), 82.

14. For example, "The shift toward a much more favorable tax regime for the wealthy has occurred largely through policy enactments. The bulk of these have occurred under Republican congressional majorities and Republican presidents (although often with significant Democratic support)" (ibid., 186).

15. The canonical source is G. E. P. Box and G. C. Tiao, "Intervention Analysis with Applications to Economic and Environmental Problems," *Journal of the American Statistical Association* 70, no. 349 (1975): 70–79. Accessed February 21, 2019. Available at https://www.tandfonline.com/doi/abs/10.1080/0162 1459.1975.10480264.

16. Lee H. Hamilton, "The Changes Necessary to Make American Politics Less Polarized," *Deseret News*, December 6, 2010. Accessed February 21, 2019. Available at http://www.deseretnews.com/article/700088722/The-changes-necessary-to-make-American-politics-less-polarized.html.

17. In practice, relationships of this sort are thought of as probabilistic, not deterministic, so a random error term would be added.

STUDENT STUDY SITE

for CQ Press

Give your students the SAGE edge!

SAGE edge offers a robust online environment featuring an impressive array of free tools and resources for review, study, and further exploration, keeping both instructors and students on the cutting edge of teaching and learning. Learn more at **edge.sagepub.com/johnson9e.**

10 QUANTITATIVE METHODS

In chapter 8, we discussed important Research design issues in regard to qualitative methods and analysis. In this chapter, we turn our attention to quantitative methods and data collection. We first illustrate the wide variety of quantitative methods by examining how one research topic drawn from chapter 1—the gender gap—can be studied using different quantitative methods. We then discuss two methods of data collection—content analysis and surveys—frequently used in quantitative research, noting issues of measurement reliability and validity and ethics. Finally, we conclude with a discussion of data management.

THE WIDE VARIETY OF QUANTITATIVE PROJECTS

In chapter 1, we introduced the book by examining a number of political science research topics, one of which was the gender gap. Each of the articles in the gender gap section investigates some aspect of the gender gap but asks slightly different research questions, tests different hypotheses, and uses different methods. Here we want to explore how researchers can use different quantitative methods to explore similar topics.

Richard L. Fox and Jennifer L. Lawless examined explanations for the gender gap in political ambition using a national random sample of nearly four thousand high school and college students.[1] In another article, Fox and Lawless investigated the political ambitions of nearly four thousand men and women in professions (lawyers, business leaders, educators, and political activists) typically thought of as recruitment grounds for candidates for public office.[2]

Tali Mendelberg, Christopher F. Karpowitz, and J. Baxter Oliphant researched the presence of elected women in legislative bodies and its effect on substantive as well as symbolic representation of women in legislatures. They wanted to know whether the number of women in a legislative body is the critical factor, or whether the rules governing deliberation in the legislature is also important.[3] To test their hypothesis, they conducted a randomized experiment with 94 five-member discussion groups composed of between 0 and 5 women, and randomly assigned each group to unanimous or majority rule. Each group was given the identical decision task except for the decision rule. The researchers observed (recorded) and analyzed the decision-making discussion in each group. They counted the number of times each person spoke and coded the number and tone (positive, neutral, or negative) of interruptions, the gender of the speaker, and the gender of the person interrupting.

Finally, Jennifer J. Jones investigated whether and when Hillary Clinton chose to "talk like a man" throughout her political career. She wanted to know if women in politics adopt masculine styles of communication in order to be effective in policy-making contexts governed by male norms.[4] Jones conducted a quantitative textual analysis of 567 interview transcripts and candidate debates between 1992 and 2013. She calculated a feminine to masculine ratio by coding feminine and masculine linguistic markers in each transcript.

This quick summary of each research project demonstrates that there are many different ways of using quantitative methods and they can be used to analyze similar topics. These articles used a cross-sectional research design and collected data using a survey; an experiment using nonparticipant observation looking for and counting instances of specific behaviors or interactions; and a time-series design with a textual analysis of documents collected and stored by someone other than the researcher. Each research design allowed the opportunity for the researcher(s) to record observations for use in a statistical analysis.

SOURCES OF DATA FOR QUANTITATIVE STUDIES

Making observations is similar in both qualitative and quantitative research as either approach can make use of firsthand observations or observations made by someone else. The basic difference is that in a quantitative project, the observations will have associated numeric scores, while in a qualitative analysis, the observations will not. Political scientists collect their quantitative measures using three approaches or sources: content analysis, surveys, and statistics available from the running record. In this section, we provide a broad overview of content analysis and surveys as use of the running record was discussed previously in chapter 8.

Content Analysis

As we discussed in chapter 8, qualitative document analysis uses the written record to explain political phenomena usually by extracting excerpts, quotations, or examples from documents to support an observation or relationship. In quantitative studies, aspects of the documents are systematically counted, and those counts are analyzed statistically. Consider a research project on the ideology of Supreme Court justices. A researcher may use a qualitative approach that identifies patterns across the writings of different justices by analyzing quotations from their written opinions on various questions about the role of government or social and economic issues that come before the Court. Alternatively, a researcher might take an approach that involves applying systematic measurement of justices' writings to create quantitative measures of justices' ideology. This use of the written record via systematic coding and classification of its contents is an example of **content analysis**.

Content Analysis Procedures

The first step in content analysis is to choose materials for analysis. This selection, of course, is guided by the topic, theory, existing research, and other measures. For example, if a researcher is interested in the political values of candidates for public office, position papers and campaign speeches might be suitable. Klaus Krippendorff referred to these materials as the "sampling units" and defined them as "units that are distinguished for selective inclusion in an analysis."[5] The list of materials germane to the researcher's subject thus makes up a "sampling frame." Once the appropriate sampling frame has been selected, then any of the possible types of samples described in chapter 5 can be used. It is also possible that the sampling frame corresponds to the population and that all units of the population will be studied. For example, you might analyze every State of the Union address.

The second task in any content analysis is to define the "recording or coding units"— that is, "the units that are distinguished for separate description, transcription, recoding, or coding."[6] For example, from a given document, news item, video clip, or other material, the researcher may want to code (1) each word or sentence fragment, (2) each character or actor, (3) each sentence, (4) each paragraph, or (5) each item in its entirety. The choice of the recording or coding unit depends on the categories of content to be measured. In choosing the recording unit, the researcher usually considers the correspondence between the unit and the content categories (stories may be more appropriate than words for determining whether crime is a topic of concern, whereas individual words or sentences rather than larger units may be more appropriate for measuring the traits of political candidates). Generally, if the recording unit is too small, it will be unlikely to possess any of the content categories. If the recording unit is too large, however, it will be difficult to measure the single category of a content variable that it possesses (in other words, the case will possess multiple values of a given content variable). For example, a paragraph or a story may contain both positive and negative evaluations of a candidate. The selection of the appropriate recording unit is often a matter of trial and error, adjustment, and compromise in the pursuit of measures that capture the content of the material being coded.

The third task, therefore, is to choose categories of content to be measured. These categories are the variables you want to focus on in your study. This process is in many respects the most important part of any content analysis, because the researcher must measure the content in such a way that it relates to the research topic and must define this content so that the measures of it are both valid and reliable. So, for example, researchers studying the prevalence of crime in the news might take a sample of the front pages of newspapers or half-hour nightly news programs and measure the percentage of the content that deals with crime. Exactly how this measurement is to be done must be explained. This is especially important if more than one person is involved in coding the stories. Often, researchers assess the tone of the coding unit. So, for example, campaign advertisements may be coded as positive, negative, or mixed. Or, news stories on unconventional oil and gas development may be coded as favorable, unfavorable, or neutral. The coding process involves the judgment of the coder. Researchers should test the reliability of their measurements by having more than one person code the item and checking to see if the measurements are the same.

Content analysis can be greatly improved in quality and efficiency by taking advantage of computer software designed to identify and code material. In its most basic form, researchers can identify keywords and phrases that define how a software package will identify relevant words, phrases, or sections of written documents—this is similar to a keyword search you might use with an internet search engine or your library's electronic catalog. Once keywords or passages have been identified, the software can be used to automatically code documents for use in quantitative analysis or allow the researcher to code identified passages manually. Some software can use examples of manually coded material and apply the examples to code additional material. Once coded, software can be used to analyze data and create graphical representations of relationships using charts, tables, and figures.[7] The downside to automatic coding of documents is that use of words, for example, may be taken out of context and affect the validity of measures.

To observe feminine and masculine linguistic styles, Jones operationalized feminine and masculine linguistic styles as "function words—articles, prepositions, pronouns, and auxiliary verbs—[that] shape and connect the content of our thoughts into meaningful forms of communication."[8] Table 1-1 demonstrates Jones's recorded differences in the use of pronouns, verbs, articles, social references, prepositions, emotion words, anger words, cognitive mechanisms, big words, tentative words, and swear words to establish masculine and feminine linguistic styles.[9] These linguistic markers were not designed on a whim, but drawn from examinations of linguistics in the scholarly literature.

Surveys

Surveys, in their most basic form, are a series of questions answered by respondents. Surveys can come in a variety of forms, and survey researchers face numerous challenges in collecting survey responses from a sample that is representative of the target population. There are many sources of survey data. Researchers often rely on existing survey data rather than designing and administering their own surveys. For example, John D'Attoma relied on public opinion data collected by the Quality of Government Institute at the University of Gothenburg, and S. Erdem Aytaç, Luis Schiumerini, and Susan Stokes used survey data collected by other organizations in Turkey and Ukraine in addition to conducting their own surveys in Turkey and Brazil. If you decide to create your own survey, there are many things to consider. Even if you are using existing surveys, you should be aware of what goes into creating a survey as the validity and reliability of responses can be affected by questionnaire design.

Questionnaire Design Issues

The term **questionnaire design** refers to the physical layout and packaging of the questionnaire. An important goal of questionnaire design is to make the questionnaire attractive and easy for the interviewer and the respondent to follow. Good design increases the likelihood that the questionnaire will be completed properly. Design may also make the transfer of data from the questionnaire to the computer easier.

Question Wording

The point of survey research is to accurately measure people's attitudes, beliefs, and behavior by asking them questions. Good questions prompt accurate answers; bad questions provide inappropriate stimuli and result in unreliable or inaccurate responses. Try to put yourself in the respondent's place when writing or analyzing survey questions. The basic rule of question wording is that *the target subjects must be able to understand and in principle have access to the requested information.* This means that questions should be written with simple language using words that most adults can comprehend.

Certain types of questions make it difficult for respondents to provide reliable, accurate responses. These include double-barreled, ambiguous, and leading questions. A **double-barreled question** is really two questions in one, such as "Do you agree with the statement that the federal government should increase fuel taxes and use the proceeds to pay for infrastructure improvements?" This is a problematic question because the answer could apply to increasing taxes, spending proceeds on infrastructure, or both. Thus, it is impossible to determine what the question is measuring, so it cannot be used as a valid measure. An ambiguous question is one that does not offer enough specificity. For example, "Did you vote in the last election?" is ambiguous because "the last election" is different across localities and respondents could be describing different elections. A **leading question** encourages respondents to choose a particular response because the question indicates that the researcher expects it. The question "Don't you think that global warming is a serious environmental problem?" implies that to think otherwise would be unusual, which could create bias in the answer.

Response categories may also contain leading or biased language and may not provide respondents with equal opportunities to agree or disagree. Response distributions may be affected by whether the researcher asks a **single-sided question**, in which the respondent is asked to agree or disagree with a single substantive statement, or a **two-sided question**, which offers the respondent two substantive choices. An example of a single-sided question is:

> Do you agree or disagree with the idea that the government should see to it that every person has a job and a good standard of living?

An example of a two-sided question is:

> Do you think that the government should see to it that every person has a job and a good standard of living, or should it let each person get ahead on his or her own?

With a single-sided question, a larger percentage of respondents tend to agree with the statement given. Forty-four percent of the respondents to the single-sided question given above agreed that the government should guarantee employment, whereas only 30.3 percent of the respondents to the two-sided question chose this position.[10] Presenting two substantive choices has been found to reduce the proportion of respondents who give no opinion.[11]

As you can see from these brief examples, question wording can be very complicated, and survey researchers must give due diligence to each question on a survey to reduce the possibility that the question wording will affect the responses. Attention to these basic guidelines for question wording increases the probability that respondents will interpret a question consistently and as intended, yielding reliable and valid responses. One of the big advantages of survey research is that questions can be recycled—you will find on the internet a great many survey questions written by survey professionals. These questions can be reused for your own purposes, and if they're written by professionals at a trusted corporate survey organization like Gallup, or a university organization like the University of Delaware's Center for Political Communication, you will save yourself a great deal of time and effort and benefit from well-written questions when collecting data.

HELPFUL HINTS
SAVE TIME: REUSE PROFESSIONAL SURVEY QUESTIONS

When writing your own survey questions, consider using questions written by survey professionals available from professional survey organizations. If you cannot find a question that is exactly what you are interested in, review similar questions and use them as a starting point. Starting with professionally written questions will save you a great deal of time and effort and contribute to a better final product. Sources for questions are plentiful on the internet if you know where to look. You might start with a library.

Princeton University Library has a useful collection of links to publicly available surveys and data sets focusing on U.S. public opinion (https://libguides.princeton.edu/politics/opinion) and international public opinion (https://libguides.princeton.edu/politics/opinion/international). It may take some time to find exactly what you are looking for from the various archives linked to on the library pages, but the time spent will be worthwhile.

The form or type of question as well as its specific wording is important. There are two basic types of questions: closed-ended and open-ended. A **closed-ended question** provides respondents with a list of responses from which to choose, while an **open-ended question** does not provide the respondent with any answers from which to choose. The main advantages of a closed-ended question are that selecting answer choices takes little time; the answers can be precoded, and the code then easily used in an analysis; the answers are easy to compare, since all responses fall into a fixed number of predetermined categories; and closed-ended questions may help clarify the question for the respondent, thus avoiding misinterpretations of the question and unusable answers for the researcher. The main advantage of open-ended questions is that unstructured, free-response questions allow respondents to state what they know and think. They are not forced to choose between fixed responses that do not apply. Open-ended questions allow respondents to tell the researcher how they define a complex issue or concept. Also, open-ended questions allow respondents to identify answers researchers did not think of in advance.

The order in which questions are presented to respondents may also influence the reliability and validity of answers. Researchers call this the **question-order effect**. In ordering questions, the researcher should consider the effect on the respondent of the previous question, the likelihood of the respondent's completing the questionnaire, and the need to select groups of respondents for certain questions. In many ways, answering a survey is a learning situation, and previous questions can be expected to influence subsequent answers. This presents problems as well as opportunities for the researcher.

Question Order

The first several questions in a survey are usually designed to break the ice. They are general questions that are easy to answer. Complex, specific questions may cause respondents to terminate an interview or not complete a questionnaire because they think it will be too hard. Questions on personal or sensitive topics usually are left to the end. Otherwise, some respondents may suspect that the purpose of the survey is to check up on them rather than to find out public attitudes and activities in general.

One problem to avoid is known as a **response set**, or straight-line responding. A response set may occur when a series of questions have the same answer choices. Respondents who find themselves agreeing with the first several statements may skim over subsequent statements and check "agree" on all. This is likely to happen if statements are on related topics. To avoid the response-set phenomenon, statements should be worded so that respondents may agree with the first, disagree with the second, and so on. This way, the respondents are forced to read each statement carefully before responding.

Additional question-order effects include saliency, redundancy, consistency, and fatigue.[12] Saliency is the effect that specific mention of an issue in a survey may have in causing a respondent to mention the issue in connection with a later question: The earlier question brings the issue forward in the respondent's mind. For example, a researcher should not be surprised if respondents mention crime as a problem in response to a general question on problems affecting their community if the survey earlier asked them about crime in the community. Redundancy is the reverse of saliency. Some respondents, unwilling to repeat themselves, may not say crime is a problem in response to the general query if earlier they had indicated that crime was a problem. Respondents may also strive to appear consistent. An answer to a question may be constrained by an answer given earlier. Finally, fatigue may cause respondents to give perfunctory answers to questions late in the survey. In lengthy questionnaires, response-set problems often arise due to fatigue.[13]

If there is no specific reason for placing questions in a particular order, researchers may vary questions randomly to control question-order bias.[14] Question order also becomes an important consideration when the researcher uses a **branching question**, which sorts respondents into subgroups and directs these subgroups to different parts of the questionnaire, or a **filter question**, which screens respondents from inappropriate questions. For example, a question on party identification may use a branching question to sort people into several groups by party. For each group, a different set of questions asking about party leaders may be appropriate. A filter question is typically used to prevent the uninformed from answering questions. For example, respondents in the 1980 American National Election Study were given a list of presidential candidates and asked to mark those names they had never heard of or did not know much about. Respondents were then asked questions only about those names that they had not marked.[15]

These physical design considerations are also very important for surveys. A survey with a confusing design or instructions may lead respondents to accidentally skip questions or fail to complete the survey out of frustration. A well-designed survey will move respondents from one question to the next without ambiguity about where to turn, with sufficiently large printing or font size in a printed form, and clearly marked interactive components, like buttons or text fields, in online surveys.

Survey Types

Surveys may be executed in person, over the phone, through mail, or using the internet. Regardless of how the survey is executed, there are always trade-offs of advantages and disadvantages. Some of the most prominent trade-offs involve cost, potential response rates, sample–population congruence, questionnaire length, and data-processing costs.

TABLE 10-1 ■ Types and Characteristics of Surveys					
Type of Survey	Overall Cost[a]	Potential Response Rate[b]	Sample–Population Congruence	Questionnaire Length[c]	Data-Processing Costs
Personal/face-to-face	High	High to medium	Potentially high	Long-medium	High
Telephone	Medium	Medium	Medium	Medium-short	High to low
Mail	Low	Low	Medium	Medium-short	Medium
Email	Low	Depends but low	Low	Medium-short	High to low
Internet	Low	Depends but low	Low	Medium-short	High to low
Group administration	Very low	High once group is convened	Depends on group selection process	Variable	High to low
Drop-off/pick-up	Very low	Low	Low	Short	Low

[a]Costs of design, administration, and processing.

[b]Assumes a general target population (see text): high = greater than 75 percent; medium = 30 to 75 percent; low = less than 30 percent.

[c]*Length* can refer to the number of questions or the time to complete (see text).

Table 10-1 demonstrates trade-offs among important survey characteristics. Any type of survey research takes time and incurs at least some expenses for materials, represented in the table by "cost." Among the factors determining survey costs are the amount of professional time required for questionnaire design, the length of the questionnaire, the geographical dispersion of the sample, callback procedures, respondent selection rules, and availability of trained staff.[16] **Sample–population congruence** refers to how well the individuals in a sample represent the population from which they are presumably drawn. Bias can enter through the initial selection of respondents, so proper attention must be paid to sampling technique. Bias can also originate through incomplete responses of those who agree to take part in the study. A **response rate** refers to the proportion of persons initially contacted who actually participate. As the response rate decreases, the likelihood that the sample will not resemble the population increases—this will lead to poor statistical inference as explained in chapter 5. A survey needs to include enough questions to gather the data necessary for the research topic, but a good rule of thumb is to keep the survey as short as possible because respondents can suffer fatigue that leads to inaccurate answers or failure to complete the survey. Questionnaire length is therefore crucial to consider. Finally, after the answered surveys have been collected, the answers still have to be recorded—and recording can be costly. Data processing is easier and less costly if survey answers are initially collected electronically, but costs soar when answers are handwritten or involve free response, due to issues of legibility and uncertainty over how to assign numerical codes to answers.

Looking at table 10-1, you can easily see a relationship between cost and survey quality, represented by sample–population congruence, and completion rate. Survey research can provide high-quality results, but those results are expensive. If you are considering your own survey project, these are important considerations.

We want to pay special attention to internet surveys as they are an increasingly important type of survey. Websites like YouGov have capitalized on the growing market for internet surveys and have carved out an important presence in polling the American public.[17] Internet surveys have become increasingly popular in part because of some important advantages over other types of surveys, including lower costs; the ability to question respondents about a wide variety of multimedia materials, like pictures or video segments; and the ability to allow respondents to answer questions when it is most convenient and at their own pace. But there are some significant issues associated with internet surveys that make them both interesting examples and vexing to survey researchers.

The biggest obstacle associated with internet surveys is twofold. First, while internet access has grown considerably over the last two decades, from an estimated 52 percent of American adults in 2000 to 89 percent in 2018, the internet is still not as widely adopted as the telephone.[18] That is a critical problem when trying to create a representative sample because internet use is correlated with important demographic indicators like age (98 percent of those aged eighteen to twenty-nine, but only 66 percent of those aged sixty-five and older, use the internet), income (98 percent of those with family incomes over $75,000, but only 81 percent of those with family incomes under $30,000, use the internet), and education (97 percent of college graduates, while only 65 percent of those who did not graduate from high school, use the internet).[19] Simply put, not everyone uses the internet, and if it were possible to randomly sample all internet users, that sample would not be representative of the U.S. population. Second, unlike telephone or mail surveys, where it is possible to assemble nearly complete lists of phone numbers or mailing addresses for identifying a population from which to sample, there is no comparable way to identify all internet users. Internet surveys are therefore limited to those that use select lists of email addresses or social media accounts, or those that collect responses from respondents who happen to see the survey on a website.

To overcome this obstacle, many survey researchers who want to use an internet survey because of its many advantages choose to identify a random sample by first contacting respondents via phone or mail. Respondents are asked to indicate if they have internet access, and a sample is then identified from these respondents. Many internet surveys could therefore be appropriately categorized as hybrid surveys because they make use of different survey methods to identify respondents and collect data. Other researchers rely on panels of respondents who answer multiple surveys on the internet over time. YouGov relies on panels of respondents who participate in multiple surveys enticed by participation points that can be exchanged for prizes.[20]

A major ethical consideration associated with survey research is the protection of personal information and identities. Data that include personally identifiable information like names, phone numbers, or addresses should be vigilantly safeguarded. When researchers collect data from individuals, they often collect the data in a confidential manner by intentionally not recording any personal identification in an electronic file. For example, a researcher collecting public opinion data will assign a unique and randomly generated identification number to each respondent, and that number is recorded in the data rather than a person's name, address, or telephone number. There may be a master list in which respondent information and identification numbers are linked. This permits researchers to send reminders to respondents who have not completed the survey. This master list must be kept in a secure location and destroyed once the data collection process has ended. In most cases in political science, it is better to record less rather than more personally identifiable information.

DATA MANAGEMENT

Because we already discussed many of these issues in chapter 8 with respect to qualitative methods, many of the terms should sound familiar. But you should pay special attention to how researchers think about concepts like reliability or validity in a different way, face different challenges, or benefit from different advantages when using quantitative methods rather than qualitative methods. Remember also that while distinct qualitative methods each have their own disadvantages and advantages, so do distinct quantitative methods. We will try to highlight these, and you should think about how qualitative and quantitative methods could be paired in a mixed methods approach to benefit from the advantages of each while compensating for the disadvantages of each.

At first, it can be a little overwhelming when you sit down and try to find and download data from the internet, or enter your own observations into a spreadsheet or statistical analysis program, as you will be confronted with nearly endless options and sometimes confusing processes and commands. In this section, we review some basic protocols for successful data management that will help you in finding, downloading, and managing data for use in your own analyses.

Finding and Downloading Data

If you decide to forgo making your own observations and collecting data firsthand, you will likely rely on publicly available data on the internet. The good news is that with a little digging you can likely find available data related to your research topic. It would be a good idea for you to review chapter 3 and our explanation of how you can find data sources while collecting sources in your literature review. In this chapter, we largely forgo step-by-step instructions on how to locate suitable data. Very briefly, you have a number of starting points for finding available data. First, consider data made available by political scientists on their personal websites or political-science-oriented data archives. You might also check out the data available from government sources or nongovernmental organizations. By using some of the same search tips we suggest in chapter 3, you can narrow your search field and start finding data related to your own research topic.

Once you have found a relevant data source, you will want to learn as much as you can about the data. Who collected the data? When was it collected? Which variables are included? How are the variables coded—what is the operational definition? What is the level of measurement? As every data set is different, you will want to spend some time finding the answers to these questions. Sometimes the answers are easy to find. Some data sources provide a codebook or manual that includes comprehensive answers to all of these questions and more. Other data will require more digging to find answers. For example, many data sets include variable descriptions somewhere in the data set, or variable descriptions may be found in the text of a published work that used the data. Finally, some data will be made available with little to no explanation as to the contents of the variables. In any case, you will need to pay special attention to the contents of publicly available data to make sure that you understand the contents and use the data appropriately. Remember our earlier discussion on validity? If you use secondhand data from the internet, you are at risk of using data that measure a different concept than the concept you defined in the context of your project. Invalid measures will necessarily lead to invalid conclusions.

Once you have found suitable data and the proper documentation to understand the contents of the variables, you will need to download a data file. Usually, data are made available in a text file format. The beauty of a text file is that just about any software program you might want to use can access the file. Unfortunately, the specific procedure for doing so varies by software program. You will want to consult with your professor to learn the commands to read the text file with your chosen program. In general, a text data file will include variable names and potentially variable descriptions in the first row, or the first number of rows, with the data associated with each variable located in the column below each variable name on each successive row for each observation or case.

Alternatively, you may find data available in a file formatted for a specific software program, like Excel, SPSS, or Stata. If this is the case, you will need the appropriate software program to open and use the data file.

Recording Data

If instead of relying on data available on the internet you intend to collect your own data by making your own observations, you will need to consider how to record your data in a data file. As noted in our previous discussion about using downloaded data, you will face different commands related to recording data in different programs. So, again, your professor is your best resource for learning these commands. That said, there are some general observations we can make. First, you will want to think about your data in terms of columns and rows. You will want to label a column with a name to represent each variable you have collected. You should try to label variables with names that make sense to you but are not too long. We also recommend taking notes on each variable so that you will have a record of the name and other important information about each variable in your data file. This is very important because it is easy to forget why you did what you did with a data file, especially if it is your first effort. Taking notes as you work will save you precious time when accessing and analyzing data at a later time, or when seeking help from your professor with your data file.

Once the columns are labeled with variables names, you will enter data for each observation or case in its own row. So, for example, you will enter the data for each variable, for the first observation or case, in the first row. You will then enter the data for each variable, for the second observation or case, in the second row, and so on, until you have entered data for all of the observations or cases.

Once you have created a data file, we are big believers in saving extra copies of data. You put a good bit of work into recording your data and do not want to make a mistake and lose your data. Creating backup files will save you a great deal of work and heartache.

Managing Data

Managing data largely consists of trying to organize and manipulate variables into a form that will allow you to analyze the data and test your hypotheses. As discussed in the previous sections, the specific commands necessary for data management and manipulation will vary by software package, and your best resource is your professor. There are, however, some basic commands on which you will often rely and that are generally available in every software package. The most basic and commonly used commands involve the following.

Sorting data by variable: Sorting data is simply instructing the computer to sort all of your cases based on the value of one or more variable(s). Sorting data is useful for getting a sense of how many observations are in a category within a nominal or ordinal variable or seeing the full range of scores on an interval or ratio variable.

Creating a new variable based on the values of an existing variable: You will often need to create new variables from old variables. For example, if you have an ordinal variable with too many categories, you might want to collapse the number of categories from, say, six to three, by combining the first two categories, and the next two, and the next two. Or, perhaps, you want to create an ordinal-level variable from a ratio-level variable. For this, you would need to create a new variable with, say, four categories, where each category includes one-fourth of the observations in the ratio-level variable.

Deleting cases or variables: Deleting cases and variables can be useful in cleaning up a data set, but be careful because you are playing with fire. Before deleting any data, we recommend saving a backup of your data file in case you make a mistake. Accidentally deleting data you need, and wasting time and effort to rebuild a data set, is no fun, so be careful. With that warning in mind, all statistics software includes a delete command with which you can delete variables, cases, and the contents of individual cells. Deleting variables can be useful if you have variables you no longer need, as a less cluttered data set will likely be easier to work with.

Deleting cases is another matter entirely. In some instances, you will wonder if it is appropriate to delete a case. We argue that it is generally not wise to delete cases. For example, in many data files made available by the United Nations, data are often incomplete for some small island nations and authoritarian regimes. If you have missing data for one case on a variable and use that variable in an analysis, software programs will drop that case from the analysis because there are no data. If you intend to analyze every country in the world, dropping a country means that you are no longer working with the whole population. You have a couple of options. You could try to find the missing data. Depending on the variable, you may be able to find missing data somewhere else. That is the best solution if you have the time. Alternatively, you could continue the analysis with missing data for one or more cases. It is good practice in this situation to include a footnote in the text or on a table reporting the missing cases and the reason why they are missing. There is usually no harm in leaving an incomplete case in your data file.

Selecting cases or variables for analysis: Most software programs include a simple command for selecting active cases. Cases identified as active will be used in analyses, while inactive cases still remaining in the data file will not. This is a useful command for describing groups individually with descriptive statistics or eliminating cases that do not fit a particular analytical requirement. For instance, if you have data for every country in the world but only want to analyze Middle Eastern countries, you could create a variable called "middle_east" coded as 1 = *Middle Eastern country* and 0 = *not.* You could then select active cases for analysis using this variable without deleting the other cases.

In addition to the specific commands for executing the above steps, you will want to focus on the level of measurement for each of your variables. As you enter data in your file, consider the level of measurement of each variable and the consequences for your analysis and how you can use each variable.

ETHICAL CONCERNS WITH QUANTITATIVE METHODS

Among the many goals we have in writing this textbook are teaching you to be better researchers and consumers of research. Qualitative and quantitative projects alike share many ethical concerns. In chapter 8, we discussed several important ethical concerns that apply to quantitative work as well, such as protecting the identity of survey respondents. We have additional ethical concerns about quantitative methods.

We begin with a quotation popularized by Mark Twain: "There are three kinds of lies: lies, damned lies, and statistics."[21] While the original author of this colloquial wisdom is uncertain, it captures an important notion about the use of quantitative methods. As we explained in the previous section, statistics can be a powerful tool in providing evidence to back an empirical claim. Unfortunately, statistics can also be misunderstood, misinterpreted, misreported, manipulated, or even intentionally falsified.

This truism alerts us to the power of numbers and reminds us to be ever vigilant when it comes to errors and deception. The most important point of advice on this score is that you should remember one of the central tenets of the scientific method—that you should be objective in accepting and reporting findings. In addition to reporting findings objectively, you should take care to properly report important information about statistics so a careful reader can correctly interpret results. Basic steps like properly labeling tables and figures with accurate descriptions, explaining every statistic in a table in the text, or providing a link where a reader will be able to find replication data can prevent many misunderstandings. Providing context and full explanations for data collection and analysis procedures will prevent even more. As a reader, you should seek out these explanations so you can assess the quality of a research report.

In chapter 3, we discussed the idea of "fake news." Here we want to stress that attention to methodological detail can help you uncover attempts at deception. A basic understanding of quantitative methods will help you a great deal in consuming political science research, reports, or communication from elected or appointed officials, interest group representatives, governmental and nongovernmental institutions and the like, and popular news sources. In this book, we have paid and will continue in subsequent chapters to pay special attention to how you can verify empirical claims. You will be in a better position to identify misleading or fraudulent claims if you understand quantitative research design. For example, having read chapter 5 on sampling, you will understand why poll results on cable news programs based on a sample of viewers who decided to participate should not be given much, if any, credence. Having read chapter 6, you will understand that in order to establish a causal relationship, one must have covariation, time order, and elimination of alternative explanations. If you read a claim about the root cause of a political outcome, you can determine if there is really a causal relationship or if the relationship falls short. Later, in chapter 11 when we discuss statistics, you will learn about important concepts like central tendency and dispersion and how to properly interpret and report statistical results. These new skills will be very valuable not only during your college career but in everyday life.

Special care should also be taken when using publicly available data. Projects using data made available on the internet, for example, should always include proper attribution to the original authors of the data. This proper attribution not only serves to inform readers where they too can find the data, but gives credit to those who collected and archived the data for public use.

CONCLUSION

In this chapter, we reviewed issues related to quantitative methods, including the wide variety of quantitative methods that can be used to study a similar research question, surveys and questionnaire design, content analysis, questions of validity and reliability related to surveys and content analysis, data management, and ethical considerations in using quantitative methods. Across the topics, we have seen that quantitative methods are quite flexible and can be used in combination with qualitative methods in a mixed methods approach to solve complex problems. In the following chapters, we address how to analyze quantitative data using a variety of statistical methods.

TERMS INTRODUCED

Branching question. A question that sorts respondents into subgroups and directs these subgroups to different parts of the questionnaire.   199

Closed-ended question. A question with response alternatives provided.   198

Content analysis. A systematic procedure by which records are transformed into quantitative data.   194

Double-barreled question. A question that is really two questions in one.   197

Filter question. A question used to screen respondents so that subsequent questions will be asked only of certain respondents for whom the questions are appropriate.   199

Leading question. A question that encourages the respondent to choose a particular response.   197

Open-ended question. A question with no response alternatives provided for the respondent.   198

Question-order effect. The effect on responses of question placement within a questionnaire.   199

Questionnaire design. The physical layout and packaging of a questionnaire.   196

Response rate. The proportion of respondents selected for participation in a survey who actually participate.   201

Response set. The pattern of responding to a series of questions in a similar fashion without careful reading of each question.   199

Sample–population congruence. The degree to which sample subjects represent the population from which they are drawn.   201

Single-sided question. A question in which the respondent is asked to agree or disagree with a single substantive statement.   197

Two-sided question. A question with two substantive alternatives provided for the respondent.   197

SUGGESTED READINGS

Aldridge, Alan, and Kenneth Levine. *Surveying the Social World*. Buckingham, UK: Open University Press, 2001.

Bradburn, Norman, Seymour Sudman, and Brian Wansink. *Asking Questions*. Rev. ed. San Francisco: Jossey-Bass, 2004.

Braverman, Marc T., and Jana Kay Slater. *Advances in Survey Research*. San Francisco: Jossey-Bass, 1998.

Converse, J. M., and Stanley Presser. *Survey Questions: Handcrafting the Standardized Questionnaire*. Beverly Hills, CA: Sage, 1986.

Dillman, Don A. *Mail and Electronic Surveys*. New York: Wiley, 1999.

Frey, James H., and Sabine M. Oishi. *How to Conduct Interviews by Telephone and in Person*. Thousand Oaks, CA: Sage, 1995.

Krippendorff, Klaus. *Content Analysis: An Introduction to Its Methodology*. 3rd ed. Thousand Oaks, CA: Sage, 2013.

Nesbary, Dale. *Survey Research and the World Wide Web*. Needham Heights, MA: Allyn & Bacon, 1999.

Newman, Isadore, and Keith A. McNeil. *Conducting Survey Research in the Social Sciences*. Lanham, MD: University Press of America, 1998.

Patten, Mildred L. *Questionnaire Research: A Practical Guide*. 2nd ed. Los Angeles: Pyrczak, 2001.

Rea, Louis M., and Richard A. Parker. *Designing and Conducting Survey Research*. San Francisco: Jossey-Bass, 1997.

Roberts, Carl W., ed. *Text Analysis for the Social Sciences: Methods for Drawing Statistical Inferences from Text and Transcripts*. Mahwah, NJ: Lawrence Erlbaum Associates, 1997.

Sapsford, Roger. *Survey Research*. Thousand Oaks, CA: Sage, 1999.

Tanur, Judith M., ed. *Questions about Questions*. New York: Russell Sage Foundation, 1992.

Van Dunk, Emily. "Getting Data through the Back Door: Techniques for Gathering Data from State Agencies." *State Politics and Policy Quarterly* 1, no. 2 (2001): 210–18.

Weisberg, Herbert F. *The Total Survey Approach*. Chicago: University of Chicago Press, 2005.

NOTES

1. Richard L. Fox and Jennifer L. Lawless, "Uncovering the Origins of the Gender Gap in Political Ambition," *American Political Science Review* 108, no. 3 (2014): 499–519.

2. Richard L. Fox and Jennifer L. Lawless, "Reconciling Family Roles with Political Ambition: The New Normal for Women in Twenty-First Century U.S. Politics," *The Journal of Politics* 76, no. 2 (2014): 398–414.

3. Tali Mendelberg, Christopher F. Karpowitz, and J. Baxter Oliphant, "Gender Inequality in Deliberation: Unpacking the Black Box of Interaction," *Perspectives on Politics* 12, no. 1 (2014): 18–44.

4. Jennifer J. Jones, "Talk 'like a Man': The Linguistic Styles of Hillary Clinton, 1992–2013," *Perspectives on Politics* 14, no. 3 (2016): 625–42.

5. Klaus Krippendorff, *Content Analysis: An Introduction to Its Methodology*, 2nd ed. (Thousand Oaks, CA: Sage, 2004), 98.

6. Ibid., 99.

7. For a discussion of computer-assisted text analysis, see Krippendorff, "Computer Aids," chap. 12 in *Content Analysis*; Daniel Riffe, Stephen Lacy, and Frederick G. Fico, "Computers," chap. 9 in *Analyzing Media Messages: Using Quantitative Content Analysis in Research*, 2nd ed. (Mahwah, NJ: Lawrence Erlbaum Associates, 2005), 208–24; and Roel Popping, "Computer Programs for the Analysis of Texts and Transcripts," in *Text Analysis for the Social Sciences: Methods for Drawing Statistical Inferences from Text and Transcripts*, ed. Carl W. Roberts (Mahwah, NJ: Lawrence Erlbaum Associates, 1997), 209–24.

8. Jones, "Talk 'like a Man,'" 630.

9. Ibid., 631.

10. Raymond L. Gordon, *Interviewing: Strategy, Techniques, and Tactics* (Homewood, IL: Dorsey, 1969), 18.

11. Lewis Anthony Dexter, *Elite and Specialized Interviewing* (Evanston, IL: Northwestern University Press, 1970), 17.

12. Norman M. Bradburn and William M. Mason, "The Effect of Question Order on Responses," *Journal of Marketing Research* 1, no. 4 (1964): 57–61.

13. A. Regula Herzog and Jerald G. Bachman, "Effects of Questionnaire Length on Response Quality," *Public Opinion Quarterly* 45, no. 4 (1981): 549–59. Accessed February 25, 2019. Available at https://doi.org/10.1086/268687.

14. William D. Perrault Jr., "Controlling Order-Effect Bias," *Public Opinion Quarterly* 39, no. 4 (1975): 544–51.

15. American National Election Studies, "1980 Time Series Study." Accessed February 25, 2019. Available at https://electionstudies.org/project/1980-time-series-study/.

16. Floyd J. Fowler, *Survey Research Methods*, rev. ed. (Newbury Park, CA: Sage, 1988), 68.

17. YouGov. Accessed February 23, 2019. Available at https://today.yougov.com/#/.

18. Pew Research Center, "Internet/Broadband Fact Sheet," February 5, 2018. Accessed February 25, 2019. Available at http://www.pewinternet.org/fact-sheet/internet-broadband/.

19. Ibid.

20. YouGov, "YouGov Panel Rewards." Accessed February 25, 2019. Available at https://pk.yougov.com/en-ur/account/panel-rewards/.

21. Department of Mathematics, University of York, "Lies, Damned Lies and Statistics," July 19, 2012. Accessed February 23, 2019. Available at https://www.york.ac.uk/depts/maths/histstat/lies.htm.

11 MAKING SENSE OF DATA
First Steps

Many students wonder why they spend a semester or more studying statistical methods. After all, topics such as current events, politics in general, law, foreign affairs, voting, and legislatures might be more interesting. Why bother with data collection and analysis? To repeat our sermon from chapter 1, we offer two compelling reasons. First, for better or worse, you need to understand a few basic statistical concepts and methods in order to understand the meaning behind numbers. Second, good citizenship requires an awareness of statistical concepts. To one degree or another, many issues and policies involve statistical arguments. A recent *New York Times* article reported on rising wages in Europe after ten years of wage stagnation. The author explained that while wages are rising

in Europe, economists have different viewpoints on why wages rise.[1] In order to understand those viewpoints, understand the data that support them, and have an informed opinion on how governments might improve wages, one needs to be able to understand simple statistics.

We proceed slowly because the concepts, though not excessively mathematical, do require thought and effort to comprehend. But it is worth the effort because the knowledge will make you not just a better political science student but also a better citizen.

THE DATA MATRIX

Most of the statistical reports you come across in both the mass media and scholarly publications show only the final results of what has been a long process of gathering, organizing, and analyzing a large body of data. But knowing what goes on behind the scenes is as important as understanding the empirical conclusions. Conceptually, at least, the first step is the arrangement of the observed measurements into a **data matrix**, which is simply an array of rows and columns that stores observed values of variables. Separate rows hold the data for each case or unit of analysis. If you read across one row, you see the specific values that pertain to that case. Each column contains the values of a single variable for all the cases.

The column headings list the variable names. To find out where a particular case stands with regard to a particular variable, just look for the row for that case and read across to the appropriate column.

Table 11-1 provides an example, using data from Western European countries. It is useful for finding information about individual countries, or even comparing two countries. The table is less useful if one wants to summarize information about multiple countries. So many numbers can overwhelm the eye, and it is difficult to identify interesting patterns or trends with so much data in one table. Imagine reading a much larger data matrix—one with, say, five thousand rows and fifty variables; the difficulties of interpretation are even worse.

Data Description and Exploration

To go from raw data to meaningful conclusions, you begin by summarizing and exploring the information in the matrix. Several kinds of tables, statistics, and graphs can be used for this purpose, but which ones are appropriate to use depends on the level of measurement of the variables. Different statistical procedures assume different levels of measurement. Recall the four broad types of measurement scales (with examples from table 11-1):

1. *Nominal:* Variable values are unordered names or labels. (Western European Country; Most Common Language)

TABLE 11-1 ■ Characteristics of Western European Countries						
Country	Western European Country	Unemployment (percent)	Population	Life Expectancy (years)	Average High Temperature (Celsius)	Most Common Language
Belgium	1	7	2	81	6	Dutch
France	1	10	3	82	7	French
Ireland	1	6	2	81	8	English
Luxembourg	1	6	1	82	2	Luxembourgish
Monaco	1	2	1	89	13	French
Netherlands	1	5	2	81	6	Dutch
United Kingdom	1	4	3	81	8	English

Source: Central Intelligence Agency, *World Factbook*. Last accessed August 7, 2018. Available at https://www.cia.gov/library/publications/resources/the-world-factbook/rankorder/rankorderguide.html; One World Nations Online, "Official and Spoken Languages of European Countries." Last accessed August 7, 2018. Available at https://www.nationsonline.org/oneworld/european_languages.htm; Current Results, "Average January Temperatures for Cities in Europe." Last accessed August 8, 2018. Available at https://www.currentresults.com/Weather/Europe/Cities/temperature-january.php.

Notes: Data rounded to whole numbers. Western European Country is a dichotomous variable where 1 = *Western European* and 0 = *otherwise*. Population is coded where 1 = *less than 10 million*; 2 = *between 10 and 20 million*; and 3 = *more than 20 million people*. The average high temperature was measured in each country's capital city in January.

2. *Ordinal:* Numbers may be assigned to categories to show ordering or ranking, but strictly speaking, arithmetical operations (e.g., addition) are inappropriate. (Population)

3. *Interval:* Numbers are assigned to objects so that interval differences are constant across the scale, but there is no true or meaningful zero point. (Average High Temperature)

4. *Ratio:* In addition to having the properties of interval variables, these scales have a meaningful zero value. (Unemployment; Life Expectancy)

In this chapter, we clarify which techniques apply to which kinds of variables.

In the following sections, we show how to summarize a large batch of numbers with

- tables (e.g., frequency distributions);
- a single number or range of numbers (e.g., descriptive statistics); and
- graphs (e.g., bar charts).

Frequency Distributions, Proportions, and Percentages

Table 11-2 illustrates a **frequency distribution** of 1,036 airports in Western Europe. The first column lists the countries of Western Europe. The second column simply records how many or the *frequency* of airports in each country (e.g., 464 airports in France). More useful indicators are **relative frequencies**, proportions and percentages that help put the raw

TABLE 11-2 ■ Frequency Distribution: Airports in Western European Countries

Country	Frequency	Proportion	Percentage	Cumulative Percentage
Belgium	41	.04	4	4
France	464	.45	45	49
Ireland	40	.04	4	53
Luxembourg	2	.00	0	53
Monaco	0	.00	0	53
Netherlands	29	.03	3	56
United Kingdom	460	.44	44	100
Totals	1,036	1.00	100	

Source: Central Intelligence Agency, *World Factbook.* Last accessed August 7, 2018. Available at https://www.cia.gov/library/publications/resources/the-world-factbook/rankorder/rankorderguide.html.

Note: Proportions are rounded to the hundredths place.

frequencies into perspective. A *proportion*—the ratio of a part to a whole—is calculated by dividing the number of observations in a category by the total number of observations.

HOW IT'S DONE
PROPORTIONS AND PERCENTAGES

Table 11-2 includes 1,036 total airports. France has 464 airports.

The proportion, or relative frequency, is

$$p = \frac{frequency}{total}$$

$$p = \frac{464}{1,036}$$

$$p = .45$$

The percentage is

$$p \times 100$$
$$.45 \times 100$$
$$45\%$$

The cumulative percentage frequency is

$$4 + 45 + 4 + 0 + 0 + 3 + 44 = 100$$

A *percentage* is found by multiplying a proportion by 100 or, equivalently, moving the decimal two places to the right. In the third column, which contains proportions, we see that France has nearly half of all of the Western European airports (.45, or 464 ÷ 1,036). In the fourth column, these proportions have been converted into percentages. Frequency tables may contain just percentages and not proportions. Finally, the last column shows the **cumulative percentages**. The percentages are added for each successive row, with a total of 100 percent.

It is important to note that missing data can drastically affect the interpretation of proportions and percentages. Table 11-2 reports that 45 percent of Western European airports are located in France. Imagine that we did not know how many airports were in the United Kingdom—these missing airports would be missing data in the table. Dividing 464 French airports by the total of 576 (1,036 − 460 UK airports) would result in a conclusion that 81 percent of Western European airports are located in France. The point is that missing data can drastically affect conclusions, and you must therefore make an effort to include as much data as possible, clearly report which data are missing and why, and make less certain conclusions when dealing with missing data.

DESCRIPTIVE STATISTICS

We now turn to another way of describing data—descriptive statistics. A **descriptive statistic** is a number that describes certain characteristics or properties of a batch of numbers. In this section, we describe statistics for measuring central tendency and dispersion. Central tendency and dispersion are presented together because that is how they are in many cases best used—together as complementary statistics. Central tendency describes the typical value of a variable while dispersion describes how the data are distributed around that typical case. We use the word *typical* to capture three different notions of central tendency: the most frequently observed, the middle, and the average. As with many other statistical procedures we will encounter in later chapters, the appropriate statistic to use depends on the level of measurement.

Measures of Central Tendency

Formally speaking, a measure of **central tendency** locates the middle or center of a distribution, but in a more intuitive sense, it describes a typical case. In this section, we apply three measures of central tendency to the Unemployment variable in table 11-1 to describe the typical unemployment level in the seven Western European countries.

The Mode

The **mode** is the value or category with the greatest frequency of recorded observations. As an example, start with table 11-1. The unemployment variable has a mode of 6 because 6 is the most frequently observed value. The mode is a great choice for any variable that employs categories like Most Common Language (nominal) or Population (ordinal) in table 11-1. The mode often has less utility in describing interval and ratio data than the median or mean, though it can still be used. The mode can be helpful in describing the *shape* of distributions of all kinds of variables.

When one category or range of values has many more cases than all the others, we describe the distribution as being *unimodal*, which is to say it has a single peak. But there can be more than one dominant peak or spike in a distribution, in which case we speak of *multimodal* distributions. For example, consider the most common language variable. This variable has three modal categories, Dutch, English, and French. We could refer to this variable as *rectangular*, because the distribution has roughly the same number or proportion of observations in each category. Graphs are often more useful than tables for investigating the "shape" of a distribution, as we will see later.

The Median

The median is a measure of central tendency that is fully applicable to ordinal as well as interval and ratio data. The **median** is a value that divides a distribution in half. That is, *half the observations lie above the median, and half below it.*

You can find the middle of an *odd* number of observations by arranging them from lowest to highest and counting the same number of observations from the top and bottom to find the middle. Figure 11-1 lists the ordered values of the Unemployment variable from the data matrix in table 11-1; we sorted the data like you would when calculating the median. In this example, counting down and up four observations in figure 11-1 will bring you to the middle observation, the fourth.

If you have many observations, an easy way to find the middle one is to apply the following formula to our sample data:

$$median = \frac{(n+1)}{2}$$

For the Unemployment example, this formula yields $(7 + 1) \div 2 = 4$, as it should. Note that the answer, 4, identifies the row number in figure 11-1, not the value of the unemployment variable. After finding the row number, you can then scan across the row for the median value—in this example, 6.

HOW IT'S DONE
THE MEDIAN

This procedure is practical if the number of cases is not large (say, fewer than thirty to forty):

1. Sort the values of the observations from lowest to highest.

2. If the number of cases is an odd number, locate the middle one and record its value. This is the median.

3. If the number of cases is an even number, locate the two middle values. Average these two numbers. The result is the median.

If, however, the number of observations is *even*, a modification is required because the middle observation number will contain a 0.5. What to do? Simply average the two middle values. Thus, if we added another country with 9 percent unemployment, we would have eight countries, and the middle observation would be $(8 + 1) \div 2 = 4.5$. The middle observations would be the fourth and fifth, and the median would be the average of the two countries corresponding to those cases: $(6 + 6) \div 2 = 6$.

FIGURE 11-1 ■ Median Unemployment in Western Europe

$n = 7$, so *median* $= \dfrac{(7 + 1)}{2} = 4$. Hence, the median is the fourth observation.

	Country	Unemployment
1	Monaco	2
2	United Kingdom	4
3	Netherlands	5
4	**Ireland**	**6**	⟵ Median = 6
5	Luxembourg	6
6	Belgium	7
7	France	10

Source: Table 11.1 data adapted from CIA World Factbook and Nationsonline.

The Mean

The third measure of central tendency is the mean, called the average in everyday conversation. The mean of a population is denoted by μ. For a sample, the mean is denoted by a bar above the letter representing the variable. If we are working with variable Y, we would note the sample mean as $\bar{Y}$ (read as "Y bar"). The mean is calculated by adding the values of a variable and dividing the sum by the number of values. For example, if we want the mean of the variable, Unemployment, for the seven countries in table 11-1, we just add the values and divide by seven, as we have done in the following box. Thus, we can say that, on average, the unemployment level in Western European countries is 5.71 percent.

HOW IT'S DONE
THE MEAN

The mean is calculated as follows:

$$\bar{Y} = \frac{\Sigma Y}{n}$$

$$\bar{Y} = \frac{40}{7}$$

$$\bar{Y} = 5.71,$$

where ΣY refers to the sum of all values of the variable Y and n refers to the sample size, or total number of observations.

The mean is most appropriate for interval and ratio variables, but it is sometimes applied to ordinal scales in which the categories have been assigned numbers. The mean cannot be used with a nominal-level variable. If we were to assign numerical values to the languages in table 11-1 (Dutch = 1, English = 2, etc.), we could compute a mean value, but the result would have no meaning.

Resistant Measures

One important concern when measuring central tendency is the presence of outliers. An outlier is a value that is far greater or smaller than the other values of a recorded variable. Consider the life expectancy variable in table 11-1. The mode is 81, the median is 81, and the mean is 82.43. What is the best choice to report central tendency? In this case, the mode or median would be a better choice than the mean. Why? Because six of the seven values are either 81 or 82. The mean is inflated because one country, Monaco, has a life expectancy of 89 years, which is an outlier because it is far greater than the other values. Both the mode and the median are known as resistant measures, because they are not sensitive to one or a few extreme values. In the end, you will want to choose a measure of central tendency that best describes the distribution of data.

Measures of central tendency are quite useful in describing data. Used alone, however, measures of central tendency can be misleading. Table 11-3 reports the number of study-abroad trips in Western Europe. Measures of central tendency would lead us to believe that the study-abroad trips to Western Europe at State University and State College are pretty much the same, as the mode, median, and mean are all 7 for both groups. One look at the distribution of the data, however, confirms that State University has much more variability across countries than State College. In the next section, we will see how measures of dispersion work and can help us distinguish between data with little variation and data with great variation.

Measures of Dispersion

We come now to a key concept in statistics: **dispersion**, or the differences among the units of a variable. Naturally, we want to know what a typical case in our study looks like. But equally important, we need to take stock of the variability among the cases. The point of many research projects is to understand why this variation arises.

Consider the Unemployment variable in table 11-1. The values are somewhat similar, but there is clearly variation between the smallest value, 2, and the largest value, 10. How do we measure this variation? Measures of dispersion allow us to express the exact amount of variation in a variable in a single summary number. Ideally, we would use that number in combination with a measure of central tendency to get a better sense of the distribution of data and potentially begin to explain political phenomena.

TABLE 11-3 ■ Number of Study-Abroad Trips in Western European Countries		
Country	State University	State College
Belgium	4	7
France	5	7
Ireland	7	7
Luxembourg	7	7
Monaco	7	7
Netherlands	9	7
United Kingdom	10	7
	Mode = 7 Median = 7 Mean = 7	Mode = 7 Median = 7 Mean = 7

Source: Hypothetical data.

Properties of Measures of Dispersion

The properties of measures of dispersion as described in this book can be summed up in three statements:

1. If there is *no* variability (all the scores have the same value), the measure will equal 0.

2. The measure will always be a positive number (there cannot be less than no variation).

3. The greater the variability in the data, the larger the numerical value of the measure.

The Range

The **range** is a particularly simple measure of variation: it is just the largest (maximum) value of a variable minus the smallest (minimum) value:

$$\text{Range} = \text{maximum} - \text{minimum}$$

Look carefully at the Unemployment variable in table 11-1. The largest value is 10 percent (France), and the smallest is 2 percent (Monaco). The range in unemployment is therefore $10 - 2$, or 8 percent. In plain language, an enormous disparity exists in unemployment. We can use this measure of dispersion in combination with the mean to conclude that the average unemployment in Western European countries is 5.71 percent with a range of 8 percent.

Next, consider the variable, Western European Country, coded as a 1 if the country is in Western Europe and a 0 if the country is not in Western Europe. Each of the countries in table 11-1 is, of course, in Western Europe, so each is recorded as a 1. As each of the seven countries is coded as a 1, there is no dispersion. If we were to calculate the range for Western Europe, we would calculate $1 - 1 = 0$, verifying that there is no dispersion in the data.

Interquartile Range

Another measure of variation, the interquartile range, is easily computed from data that are ordered from smallest to largest. Imagine that, after ordering your data, you divide them into four equal-sized batches. The first bunch would contain 25 percent of the cases, the next would have 25 percent, the next 25 percent, and the last the remaining 25 percent. The division points defining these groups are called quartiles, abbreviated Q. Now, find the range as before but use the third and first quartiles as the maximum and minimum. Their difference is the **interquartile range (IQR)**:

$$IQR = Q_3 - Q_1,$$

where Q_3 stands for the third quartile (sometimes it's called the seventy-fifth percentile because 75 percent of the cases lie below it), and Q_1 is the first quartile (or twenty-fifth percentile). Since the IQR, a single number, indicates the difference or distance between the third and first quartiles, the middle 50 percent of observations lie between these values.

Another way to think about the computation of the IQR is to obtain the median, which divides the data in half. Then find the medians of *each* half; these medians will be the first and third quartiles.

We will now calculate the IQR for the Unemployment variable in table 11-1. Figure 11-2 shows how the IQR is calculated for the seven countries in table 11-1. We first find the location of the median: $(n + 1) \div 2 = (7 + 1) \div 2 = 4$ (Luxembourg). Then we find the first quartile by taking the median of the first three observations: $(3 + 1) \div 2 = 2$, or the second case (United Kingdom). Its value is $Q_1 = 4$. Similarly, the third quartile is found by calculating the median of the largest three values: $Q_3 = 7$ (Belgium). The IQR is thus $7 - 4 = 3$. We can explain these numbers as saying that three-quarters of the Western European countries have unemployment levels between about 7 and 4 percent.

Quartiles, the range, and the IQR have the property that we have been calling resistance: Extreme or outlying values do not distort the picture of the majority of cases. This is a major advantage, especially in small samples. The next measures of dispersion reveal how data diverge from the mean.

Deviations from the Mean

We now turn to a different measure of variability. This approach compares departures or deviations from the mean using the variance and standard deviation. The key to understanding variance and standard deviation is understanding how data vary from the mean. Variance and standard deviation measure dispersion by measuring each case's variation from the mean. The Unemployment variable in Table 11-4 has a mean of 5.71, as we calculated earlier in the chapter. There are observations greater than the mean (Belgium, France, Ireland, and Luxembourg) and observations less than the mean (Monaco, United Kingdom, and Netherlands). Note that the column labeled Deviation from the Mean indicates how far each of these observations is from the mean by subtracting the mean from the observed value.

FIGURE 11-2 ■ The Quartiles and Interquartile Range

Rank	Country	Unemployment	
1	Monaco	2	
2	United Kingdom	4	← $Q_1 = 4$
3	Netherlands	5	
4	Luxembourg	6	← Median = 6
5	Ireland	6	
6	Belgium	7	← $Q_3 = 7$
7	France	10	

$$IQR = Q_3 - Q_1 = 7 - 4 = 3$$

TABLE 11-4 ■ **Deviations from the Mean**

Country	Unemployment Y	Deviation from the Mean $Y_i - \bar{Y}$
Monaco	2	−3.71
United Kingdom	4	−1.71
Netherlands	5	−0.71
Ireland	6	.29
Luxembourg	6	.29
Belgium	7	1.29
France	10	4.29
	$\bar{Y} = 5.71$	

Source: Table 11.1 data adapted from CIA World Factbook and Nationsonline.

The Variance

The **variance** is the average or *mean* of squared deviations, or the average of all the squared differences between each score and the mean. Denoted σ^2 for a population, the variance can be found by subtracting the mean (μ) from each observation of the variable (Y_i), squaring the result (a squared deviation), adding up all the squared deviations, and dividing by N. Note that when calculating the variance for a sample, denoted as $\hat{\sigma}^2$, the denominator is adjusted to $n-1$.

Variance for a population:

$$\sigma^2 = \frac{\Sigma(Y_i - \mu)^2}{N}$$

Variance for a sample:

$$\hat{\sigma}^2 = \frac{\Sigma(Y_i - \bar{Y})^2}{n-1}$$

The variance and sample variance follow the rules of a measure of variation: The greater the dispersion of data around the mean, the higher the value of the variance. If all the values are the same, variance equals zero. And it is always nonnegative. The variance is a fundamental concept in mathematical and applied statistics.

HOW IT'S DONE
THE VARIANCE FOR A SAMPLE

The sample variance is calculated as follows:

$$\hat{\sigma}^2 = \frac{\Sigma\left(Y_i - \bar{Y}\right)^2}{n-1},$$

where Y_i stands for each individual value of variable Y, $\bar{Y}$ is the sample mean of the variable Y, and n is the sample size.

Using the Unemployment variable in table 11-4, the first step is to solve for the mean and the numerator of the equation:

i	Y	$Y_i - \bar{Y}$	$\left(Y_i - \bar{Y}\right)^2$
1	2	−3.71	13.76
2	4	−1.71	2.92
3	5	−0.71	0.50
4	6	0.29	0.08
5	6	0.29	0.08
6	7	1.29	1.66
7	10	4.29	18.40
$n=7$	40		37.40

$$\bar{Y} = \frac{\Sigma Y}{n}$$

$$\bar{Y} = \frac{40}{7}$$

$$\bar{Y} = 5.71$$

$$\hat{\sigma}^2 = \frac{\Sigma\left(Y_i - \bar{Y}\right)^2}{n-1}$$

$$\hat{\sigma}^2 = \frac{37.40}{7-1}$$

$$\hat{\sigma}^2 = \frac{37.40}{6}$$

$$\hat{\sigma}^2 = 6.23$$

As you can see in the equations above, the sample mean, $\bar{Y}$, is 5.71. The sample mean is then used to calculate the numerator in the equation, and the sample variance, $\hat{\sigma}^2$, is 6.23. As you work through this calculation, work from left to right, from data matrix, to calculation of the mean, to calculation of the variance.

We can now describe unemployment in Western European countries as an average of 5.71 percent with a variance of 6.23. The difficulty is that because we squared the deviations, we cannot interpret the variance in the unit of the mean, percent unemployed. We can rectify that shortcoming by using the standard deviation.

The Standard Deviation

The most commonly calculated measure of variation is the **standard deviation**, which we denote by σ for a population and by $\hat{\sigma}$ for a sample. The standard deviation is simply the square root of the variance.

Standard deviation for a population:

$$\sigma = \sqrt{\frac{\Sigma\left(Y_i - \mu\right)^2}{N}}$$

Standard deviation for a sample:

$$\hat{\sigma} = \sqrt{\frac{\Sigma\left(Y_i - \bar{Y}\right)^2}{n-1}}$$

HOW IT'S DONE
THE STANDARD DEVIATION FOR A SAMPLE

The standard deviation is calculated as follows:

$$\hat{\sigma} = \sqrt{\frac{\Sigma\left(Y_i - \bar{Y}\right)^2}{n-1}},$$

where Y_i stands for each individual value of variable Y, $\bar{Y}$ is the sample mean of the variable Y, and n is the sample size.

Using the data in table 11-4, the first step is to solve for the mean and the numerator of the equation, then complete the standard deviation equation:

i	Y	$Y_i - \bar{Y}$	$\left(Y_i - \bar{Y}\right)^2$
1	2	–3.71	13.76
2	4	–1.71	2.92
3	5	–0.71	0.50
4	6	0.29	0.08
5	6	0.29	0.08
6	7	1.29	1.66
7	10	4.29	18.40
$n=7$	40		37.40

$$\bar{Y} = \frac{\Sigma Y}{n}$$

$$\bar{Y} = \frac{40}{7}$$

$$\bar{Y} = 5.71$$

$$\hat{\sigma} = \sqrt{\frac{\Sigma\left(Y_i - \bar{Y}\right)^2}{n-1}}$$

$$\hat{\sigma} = \sqrt{\frac{37.40}{7-1}}$$

$$\hat{\sigma} = \sqrt{\frac{37.40}{6}}$$

$$\hat{\sigma} = \sqrt{6.23}$$

$$\hat{\sigma} = 2.50$$

Because we are using the same data we used for the calculation of the sample variance, the answers are very similar. The sample mean, $\bar{Y}$, is 5.71. We use the sample mean to calculate the numerator of the sample variance equation, and the sample variance, $\hat{\sigma}^2$, is 6.23, but after taking the square root, we get the standard deviation, $\hat{\sigma}$, of 2.50 percent.

Having calculated the standard deviation, we can now expand our interpretation of the unemployment variable. We can say that the average unemployment in Western European countries is 5.71 percent with a standard deviation of 2.50 percent. Unlike with the variance, we can use the unit of the mean, percent unemployed, with the standard deviation because we have taken the square root of the squared deviations. Next, examine table 11-5 to get a sense of how the standard deviation works with the mean to describe a variable.

We can interpret the magnitude of the standard deviation relative to the mean. The mean for Unemployment is about twice the size of its standard deviation. The mean for Life Expectancy is 28 times the size of its standard deviation. Comparing the Unemployment and Life Expectancy variables, we can see that there is much more variation in the Unemployment variable than in the Life Expectancy variable. The important point here is that the scale of the variable matters in interpretation. The values for the Life Expectancy variable are all in the 80s, but the standard deviation is in the low single digits. This means that there is not a great deal of variation across the values of the variable. The values of the Unemployment variable, however, are in the single digits, so a standard deviation of 2.50

TABLE 11-5 ■ Descriptive Statistics for Select Variables

Variable	$\bar{Y}$	$\hat{\sigma}$
Western European Country	1	0
Unemployment	5.71	2.50
Life Expectancy	82.43	2.93
Average High Temperature	7.14	3.29

Source: Authors' calculations.

suggests a good bit of variation relative to the size of the values for the variable. To further drive the point home, consider the Western European Country variable. Remember that this variable was recorded as 1 for each of the seven cases, meaning that there is no variation across cases. The standard deviation of 0 for this variable reflects this lack of dispersion.

More on the Interpretation of the Standard Deviation

The significance of the standard deviation in statistics is illustrated by considering a common situation. Suppose a large set of data has a distribution approximately like the one shown in figure 11-3. Figure 11-3 features a "bell-shaped" distribution called a **normal distribution**, which has the following features:

- The bulk of observations lie in the center, where there is a single peak.

- More specifically, in a normal distribution, half (50 percent) of the observations lie *above* the mean, and half lie *below* it.

- The mean, median, and mode have the same numerical values.

- Fewer and fewer observations fall in the tails of the distribution.

- The spread of the distribution is symmetric: one side is the mirror image of the other.

If data have such a distribution, the proportion of cases lying between the mean and a number of standard deviations above and below the mean can be described this way:

- Approximately 68 percent of the data lie between $\mu - \sigma$ and $\mu + \sigma$. Read this as "68 percent of the observations are between plus and minus one standard deviation of the mean." For example, if the mean of a variable is 100 and its standard deviation is 10, then about 68 percent of the cases will have scores somewhere between 90 and 110.

● Approximately 95 percent of the cases will fall between $\mu - 2\sigma$ and $\mu + 2\sigma$. In the first example, 95 percent or so would be between 80 and 120.

● Almost all of the data will be between $\mu - 3\sigma$ and $\mu + 3\sigma$.

This feature of the standard deviation and the normal distribution has an important practical application. For all suitably transformed normal distributions, the areas between the mean and the various distances above and below it, measured in standard deviation units or z scores, are precisely known and have been tabulated in what is called a "z table" (see appendix A).

How do we know these percentages? Because mathematical theory proves that normal distributions have this property. Of course, if data are not perfectly normally distributed, the percentages will only be approximations. Yet many naturally occurring variables do have nearly normal distributions, or they can be transformed into an almost normal distribution.[2] In the next chapter, we introduce z scores, which will allow you to understand even more about the standard deviation and the normal distribution. We conclude this section with table 11-6, which summarizes the descriptive statistics discussed in this chapter.

We cannot emphasize enough the importance of carefully exploring data with summary statistics and looking out for cases that may unduly sway the interpretation of the results. The lesson in all of this is that you should not rely on a single number to summarize or describe your data. Rather, use as much information as is reasonable and take your time interpreting each variable. Computers spit out results, but they never interpret them.

FIGURE 11-3 ■ Properties of a Normal Distribution

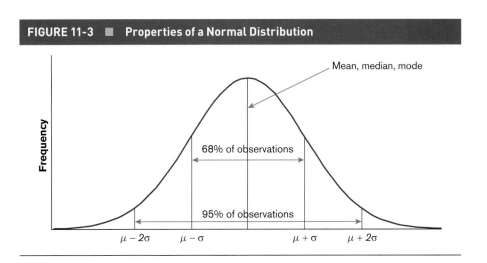

TABLE 11-6 ■ Summary of Descriptive Statistics

Statistic	Symbol (if any)	Description (what it shows)	Resistant to Outliers	Most Appropriate for . . .
Measures of central tendency				
Mean	$\bar{Y}$ (for sample) μ (for population)	Arithmetic average: identifies center of distribution	No	Interval, ratio scales
Median	Median	Identifies middle value: 50% of observations lie above, 50% below	Yes	Interval, ratio, ordinal scales; ranks
Mode	Mode	Identifies the category (or categories) with highest frequencies	Yes	Categorical (nominal, ordinal) scales
Measures of variation				
Range	Range	Maximum − minimum	No	Interval, ratio scales
Interquartile range	IQR	Middle 50% of observations	Yes	Interval, ratio scales
Variance	σ^2 for population $\hat{\sigma}^2$ for sample	Average of squared deviations	No	Interval, ratio scales
Standard deviation	σ for population $\hat{\sigma}$ for sample	Square root of average of squared deviations	No	Interval, ratio scales

GRAPHS FOR PRESENTATION AND EXPLORATION

We have already discussed the difficulty of using a large data matrix and the need to condense information to a few descriptive numbers. Graphs can be used to present large amounts of data in a report, on a website, or in a book and can also be used to explore and analyze data. These visual tools may lead you to see aspects of the data that are not revealed by tables or a single statistic, and they assist with developing and testing models.[3]

In particular, for a data matrix, a well-constructed graph can answer several questions at one time:

- *Central tendency:* Where does the center of the distribution lie?

- *Dispersion or variation:* How spread out or bunched up are the observations?

- *The shape of the distribution:* Does it have a single peak (one concentration of observations within a relatively narrow range of values) or more than one?

- *Tails:* Approximately what proportion of observations is in the ends of the distribution or in its tails?

- *Symmetry or asymmetry (also called skewness):* Do observations tend to pile up at one end of the measurement scale, with relatively few observations at the other end? Or does each end have roughly the same number of observations?

- *Outliers:* Are there values that, compared with most, seem very large or very small?

- *Comparison:* How does one distribution compare to another in terms of shape, spread, and central tendency?

- *Relationships:* Do values of one variable seem related to those of another?

Figure 11-4 illustrates some ways a variable (*Y*) can be distributed. Panel A displays a symmetric, unimodal (one-peak) distribution, which we previously called bell-shaped or normal. Panel B depicts a rectangular distribution; in this case, each value or range of values has the same number of cases. Panel C shows a distribution that, although unimodal, is **negatively skewed** or skewed to the left. In other words, there are a few observations on the left or low end of the scale, and most observations are in the middle or high end of the scale. Finally, panel D represents the opposite situation: There are comparatively few observations on the right or high end of the scale. The curve is skewed to the right or **positively skewed**. These are ideal types. No empirical distribution will look exactly like any one of them. Yet if you compare these shapes with the graphs of your own data, you can quickly approximate the kind of distribution you have.

FIGURE 11-4 ■ Shapes of Distributions

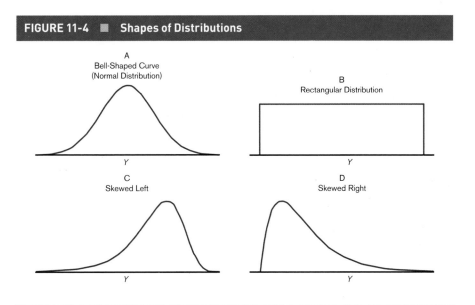

Designing and Drawing Graphs

A graph is supposed to provide the viewer with a visual description of the data, but the inclusion of too many extra features, such as three-dimensional bars or icons, can obfuscate the data. It is usually best to keep lines and areas as simple as possible so that readers can easily understand the data. More important, the essence of successful graphing is to ensure that the viewer can accurately perceive the data and any relations among variables.[4]

Many statisticians and social scientists regard a graph as a story about data. Like any story, it should be well told but not drone on and on.

Here are some general tips.

- Graphs can provide a succinct summary emphasizing trends or patterns in data.

- A table (e.g., frequency distribution), rather than a graph, is often a better way to present small amounts of data.

- Pick an appropriate type of graph. Some graphs are better suited for categorical variables (nominal and ordinal) while others are best for quantitative variables (interval and ratio). A mixture of variable types (one ordinal and one ratio, for example) may require special attention.

- Think carefully about the axes and how they relate to the scale of the data. There are two considerations: the range of data values and how they are measured on the graph and the physical dimensions of the plot. Consider the data's maximum and minimum before setting the axes' limit(s). Both axes should be proportional to the data's limits. Scale the axes to show trends in a reasonable way.

- Clearly label axes and graphical elements (e.g., bars or lines). Note the measurement units in labels, titles, and legends (e.g., "Population [in thousands]").

- Use sufficient tick marks so the reader can quickly estimate quantities.

- Make sure to include extreme values as part of the data. In some narrow cases, it is necessary to exclude an outlier, but make sure the reader understands what you are excluding and why.

- Only label the most interesting or extreme values, as labeling all of them may overwhelm the reader. Sparingly use text to point out interesting features of the data.

- Independent variables usually (but not always) appear on the x- or horizontal axis. A common exception is when comparing categories of nominal or ordinal factors in terms of a quantitative variable (interval or ratio). In this case, analysts frequently list the classes along the y- or vertical axis and extend bars or boxes into the graph (from left to right) to show magnitudes along the horizontal scale.

- The size of the graphical elements should be proportional to the data they represent. Only use the size of a graphical element, such as a bar or circle, to show differences in data; keep these elements the same size otherwise.

- If you are using bars to represent data, it helps to arrange them in a logical order. For example, if the variable is ordinal, then list the categories from lowest to highest.

- Avoid 3-D effects and other unneeded decorations.

- Always include a title.

- Indicate the source and date of the data if possible.

- Points are usually better than icons.

- Colors can be useful to show different categories but may not work well if printed in black and white. Furthermore, do not use more colors than data values.

- A rule of thumb: when it comes to graphing, the less ink on the page, the better.

As an example of some of these issues, consider the debate about global warming and the associated graphs in figure 11-5. Figure 11-5 shows the trend in CO_2 emissions, in parts per million (ppm), over the past half-century or so. The first graph appears to have a flat trend line that suggests that emissions have not really changed that much over nearly sixty years while the second graph reports a steep increase in emissions. The reason for this difference is found in the scale of the graphs. The first graph has a wider scale on the *y*-axis, from 0 to 450, while the second graph has a more narrow scale, from 300 to 420. So even though the graphs were produced using the same data, the scales can change the interpretation.

Bar Charts

Numerical information can be presented in many ways, the most common of which are bar charts. A **bar chart** is a series of bars in which the height of each bar represents the proportion or percentage of observations in the category. Figure 11-6 presents a bar chart of unemployment in Western Europe. The bar chart summarizes the data and tells the story of how unemployment varies across Western Europe.

These types of graphs are most useful when the number of categories or values of a variable is relatively small and the number of cases is large. They most commonly display percentages or proportions. Be careful about constructing a bar chart when you have, say, a dozen or more categories. You should make sure the graphical elements (bars in this case) are proportional to the data. Unless there is a substantive reason to do otherwise, keep miscellaneous and missing value categories out of the picture.

Exploratory Graphs

The graphs in this section display empirical frequency distributions for different types of variables. They can be presented in formal reports but are often used behind the scenes to explore the properties of a batch of numbers in one picture.

FIGURE 11-5   ■   CO₂ Concentration, 1959–2017: Dramatic Climate Change?

a

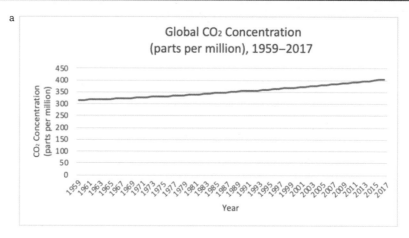

b

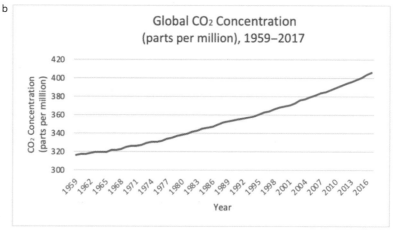

Source: Hannah Ritchie and Max Roser, "CO₂ and Other Greenhouse Gas Emissions," *Our World in Data*, May 2017. Accessed February 27, 2019. Available at https://ourworldindata.org/co2-and-other-greenhouse-gas-emissions#co2-emissions-global-and-regional-trends.

Dot Chart

A dot chart displays *all* of the observed values in a batch of numbers as dots along a horizontal or vertical line that represents the variable. Since it shows the entire data set, the number of observations should be relatively small—for example, fewer than fifty. The great advantage of this plot is that it presents the main features of a distribution. To construct a simple dot chart, draw a horizontal line that stands for the variable. Below the line, print a reasonable number of values of the variable. Finally, using the data scores to position the dots, draw one dot above the line for each observation.

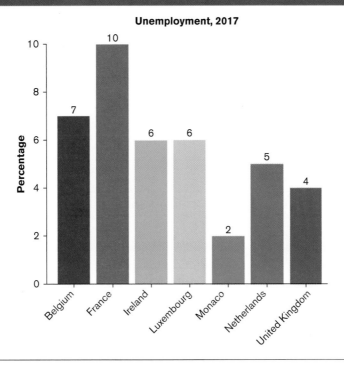

FIGURE 11-6 ■ **Bar Chart of Unemployment in Western Europe, 2017**

Unemployment, 2017

Source: Central Intelligence Agency, *World Factbook*. Last accessed August 7, 2018. Available at https:// www.cia.gov/library/publications/resources/the-world-factbook/rankorder/rankorderguide.html. See also Table 11-1.

HELPFUL HINTS
INSPECT GRAPHS FIRST

Participants in debates frequently use graphs to bolster their arguments. In most instances, it's a good idea to scan a graph before reading the author's claims about what it says. The application of data analysis to real-world problems is at least as much a matter of good judgment as it is an exact science. A researcher, who will have a lot invested in demonstrating a point, may see great significance in a result, whereas your independent opinion might be "big deal." You can maintain this independence by first drawing your own conclusions from the visual evidence and then checking them against the writer's assessments. If you do not study the information for yourself, you become a captive, not a critic, of the research.

Figure 11-7 shows a simple dot chart of unemployment rates in Western Europe. It shows at a glance which countries have low and high unemployment. We can quickly deduce that Monaco has the lowest, and France the highest, level of unemployment. We can see that the other countries are very close to each other in the middle.

FIGURE 11-7 ■ Dot Chart of Unemployment in Western Europe, 2017

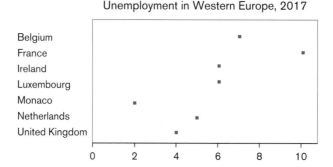

Unemployment in Western Europe, 2017

Source: Table 11.1 data adapted from CIA World Factbook and Nationsonline.

The dot chart is actually quite versatile, and depending on available software, it can display combinations of categorical factors against a quantitative dependent variable. (In this simple example, the independent variable is Country, and the category labels are just the country names.) It is common practice, for example, to sort the values of the dependent variable from lowest to highest and display the ordered data. Or one can use symbols and colors to highlight important features.

Histogram

A **histogram** is a type of bar graph in which the height and area of the bars are proportional to the frequencies in each category of a nominal or ordinal variable or of a continuous variable in intervals. If the variable is continuous, such as age or income, construct a histogram by dividing the variable into intervals, counting the number of cases in each interval, and then drawing the bars to reveal the proportion of total cases falling in each interval. If the variable is nominal or ordinal with a relatively few discrete categories, just draw bar sizes so as to reflect the proportion of cases in each class.

A histogram, like other descriptive graphical devices, reduces a data matrix in such a way that you can easily see important features of the variable. For example, you can quickly see modes if there are any, the shape of the distribution (that is, whether or not it is skewed), and even extreme values. It helps to annotate your exploratory graphs with summary statistics so that you have everything required for analysis in one place.

Figure 11-8 shows a histogram of women's ages from the 2004 American National Election Study. Although a couple of spikes can be observed in this distribution, the overall appearance is very roughly normal or bell-shaped. The graph succinctly sums up the more than 600 female respondents in the sample. Notice among other things that the middle of the distribution, as measured by both the mean and the median, is just about 47. The "location" statistics (Q_1, median, and Q_3) are instructive: 50 percent of the women are somewhere between 33 and 60 years old, and fully 25 percent are older than 60 years.

Histograms are helpful, as we have indicated, because they summarize both the spread of the values and their average magnitude. They are, however, quite sensitive to the delineations or definitions of the cut points. By *sensitive*, we mean that the shape of the distribution can be affected by the number and the width of the intervals.

Boxplot

Perhaps the most useful graphical device for summarizing and exploring interval- and ratio-level data is the boxplot. It does not display individual points but does explicitly and simultaneously let you see several descriptive statistics: Q_1, the median, Q_3, the minimum, and the maximum. Boxplots are sometimes called box-and-whisker plots because they appear to have a whisker at each end of a box.

Constructing a boxplot is relatively simple:

1. Find the maximum and minimum, the first and third quartiles, the interquartile range (IQR), and the median.

2. Draw a horizontal line to indicate the scale of the variable. Mark off intervals of the variable. Be sure to fully label the scale.

3. Above the line, say about half an inch or so, draw a small vertical line to indicate the median. It should correspond to the appropriate value on the scale.

4. Next, draw short vertical lines of the same size above the scale to indicate Q_1 and Q_3.

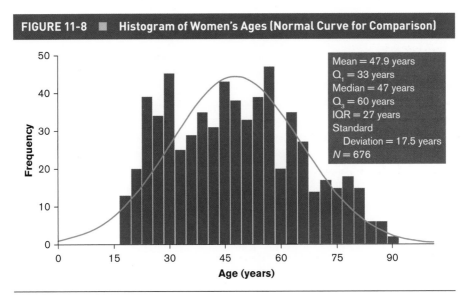

FIGURE 11-8 ■ Histogram of Women's Ages (Normal Curve for Comparison)

Mean = 47.9 years
Q_1 = 33 years
Median = 47 years
Q_3 = 60 years
IQR = 27 years
Standard
 Deviation = 17.5 years
N = 676

Source: The American National Election Studies ("http://www.electionstudies.org" www.electionstudies .org). These materials are based on work supported by the National Science Foundation under grant numbers SES 1444721, 2014-2017, the University of Michigan, and Stanford University.

5. Sketch a rectangle with the two quartiles (Q_1 and Q_3) at the ends. The median will be in the box somewhere. The height of the rectangle does not matter.

6. Draw a vertical line at the minimum for the "lower whisker." Call this quantity LW for short.

7. Draw a line a distance LW from the left end (Q_1) of the box.

8. Do the same for the "upper whisker." This time, however, you will use the maximum of the variable. Call the result UW. Alternatively: Instead of using the minimum and maximum, you can use a function of the IQR, like 2 times the IQR, for the whiskers and place points or symbols to indicate the actual location of extreme values. These should be labeled with the observation name or number.

9. Draw a line from the third quartile (Q_3) to the point UW.

10. Give the graph a title and properly label the *x*-axis.

While there are quite a few steps described above, they are quite simple if you follow them carefully. Consider the example boxplot in figure 11-9 for unemployment in Western Europe, using the same data we have been working with from table 11-1. The bottom scale is measured in percentages. The solid line in the middle of the box represents the median of 6. The lines at the end of the box, marked Q_1 and Q_3, are the first and third quartiles, 4 and 7 respectively. The lower and upper whiskers show the location of the minimum, 2, and maximum, 10. We now have a graphical summary of the Unemployment variable.

FIGURE 11-9 ■ Boxplot of Unemployment in Western Europe

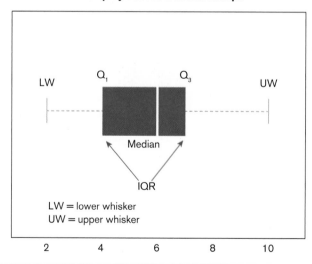

Unemployment in Western Europe

Source: Table 11.1 data adapted from CIA World Factbook and Nationsonline.

Time-Series Plot

Political scientists frequently work with variables that have been measured or collected at different points in time. In a time-series plot, the *x*-axis marks off time periods or dates, whereas the *y*-axis represents the variable. These sorts of plots frequently appear in newspapers and magazines and could well be described as a type of presentation graph. However, they are also helpful in exploring trends in data in preparation for explaining or modeling them.

The time-series plot in figure 11-10 shows the share of total income held by the wealthiest 1 percent of Americans each year from 1913 to 2013. As you can see, the rich had about 18 percent in 1913; that portion dropped to 7.74 percent in 1973 and then began rising sharply after the late 1970s. By 2012, the percentage had increased to close to 20. It is data like these that convince many analysts that economic inequality is on the increase in the United States.

Table 11-7 summarizes the kinds of graphs we have discussed and offers a few tips on their proper use.

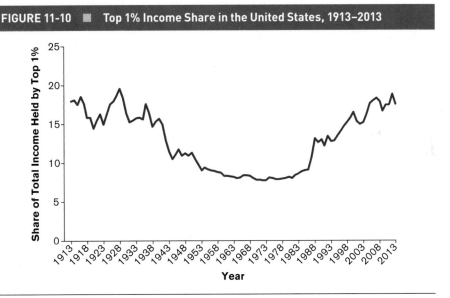

FIGURE 11-10   ■   Top 1% Income Share in the United States, 1913–2013

Source: The World Top Incomes Database, World Inequality Report 2018, http://topincomes.parisschool ofeconomics.eu/#Database.

CONCLUSION

In this chapter, we introduced some basic tools for describing and exploring data. We began with a discussion of the data matrix political scientists use to organize and present data in table form. We then moved on to describing data with descriptive statistics. Measures of central tendency like mode, median, and mean can bse used to describe the typical case in a data set. Measures of dispersion like the range, variance, and standard deviation can be used

TABLE 11-7 ■ Typical Presentation and Exploratory Graphs				
Type of Graph	What Is Displayed	Most Appropriate Level of Measurement	Number of Cases	Comments
Bar chart	Relative frequencies (percentages, proportions)	Categorical (nominal, ordinal)	3–10 categories	Common presentation graphic
Dot chart	Frequencies, distribution shape, outliers	Quantitative (interval, ratio)	*Fewer than* 50 cases	Displays actual data values
Histogram	Distribution shape	Quantitative	$N > 50$ cases	Essential exploratory graph for interval or ratio variables with a large number of cases
Boxplot	Distribution shape, summary statistics, outliers	Quantitative	$N > 50$ cases	Can display several distributions; actual data points, an essential exploratory tool
Time-series plot	Trends	Quantitative (percentages, rates)	$10 < N < 100$	Common in presentation and exploratory graphics

Note: Entries are guidelines, not hard-and-fast rules.

to describe how the data are distributed around the typical case. Hence, by using measures of central tendency and dispersion together, you will have a better understanding of the data than if you were to use only either central tendency or dispersion. We also explained how you can present data graphically using boxplots, bar charts, histograms, and more. Combined, these tools can assist you in clearly describing data to an audience, and you will be in a better position to understand data presentations.

TERMS INTRODUCED

Bar chart. A graphical display of the data in a frequency or percentage distribution.   229

Central tendency. The most frequent, middle, or central value in a frequency distribution.   215

Cumulative percentage. The total percentage of observations at or below a value in a frequency distribution.   214

Data matrix. An array of rows and columns that stores the values of a set of variables for all the cases in a data set.   211

Descriptive statistic. A number that, because of its definition and formula, describes certain characteristics or properties of a batch of numbers.   214

Dispersion. The distribution of data values around the most frequent, middle, or central value.   218

Frequency distribution. The number of observations per value or category of a variable.   213

Histogram. A type of bar graph in which the height and area of the bars are proportional to the frequencies in each category of a nominal variable or intervals of a continuous variable.   232

Interquartile range (IQR). The difference between the third and first quartiles.   219

Mean. The sum of the values of a variable divided by the number of values.   217

Median. The category or value above and below which one-half of the observations lie.   215

Mode. The category with the greatest frequency of observations.   215

Negatively skewed. A distribution of values in which fewer observations lie to the left of the middle value and those observations are fairly distant from the mean.   227

Normal distribution. A distribution defined by a mathematical formula and the graph of which has a symmetrical, bell shape; in which the mean, the mode, and the median coincide; and in which a fixed proportion of observations lies between the mean and any distance from the mean measured in terms of the standard deviation.   224

Outlier. A value that is far greater or smaller than other values in a recorded variable.   217

Positively skewed. A distribution of values in which fewer observations lie to the right of the middle value and those observations are fairly distant from the mean.   227

Range. The distance between the highest and lowest values or the range of categories into which observations fall.   219

Relative frequencies. Percentages or proportions of total numbers of observations in a frequency distribution that have a particular value.   213

Resistant measure. A measure of central tendency that is not sensitive to one or a few extreme values in a distribution.   217

Standard deviation. A measure of dispersion of data points about the mean for interval- and ratio-level data.   222

Variance. A measure of dispersion of data points about the mean for interval- and ratio-level data.   221

SUGGESTED READINGS

Abelson, Robert P. *Statistics as Principled Argument.* Hillsdale, NY: Lawrence Erlbaum Associates, 1995.

Agresti, Alan. *An Introduction to Categorical Data Analysis.* New York: Wiley, 1996.

Agresti, Alan, and Barbara Finlay. *Statistical Methods for Social Sciences.* Upper Saddle River, NJ: Prentice Hall, 1997.

Cleveland, William S. *Visualizing Data.* Summit, NJ: Hobart Press, 1993.

Jacoby, William. *Statistical Graphics for Univariate and Bivariate Data.* Thousand Oaks, CA: Sage, 1997.

Lewis-Beck, Michael. *Data Analysis: An Introduction.* Thousand Oaks, CA: Sage, 1995.

Tufte, Edward R. *Beautiful Evidence.* Cheshire, CT: Graphics, 2006.

Tufte, Edward R. *The Visual Display of Quantitative Information.* 2nd ed. Cheshire, CT: Graphics, 2001.

Velleman, Paul, and David Hoaglin. *Applications, Basics, and Computing of Exploratory Data Analysis.* Pacific Grove, CA: Duxbury Press, 1983.

NOTES

1. Jack Ewing, "Wages Are Rising in Europe. But Economists Are Puzzled," *The New York Times*, July 25, 2018. Accessed July 26, 2018. Available at https://www.nytimes.com/2018/07/25/business/europe-ecb-wages-inflation.html?rref=collection%2Fsectioncollection%2Fworld&action=click&contentCollection=world&region=stream&module=stream_unit&version=latest&contentPlacement=9&pgtype=−sectionfront.

2. For example, some numbers can be converted to logarithms, which might be normally distributed.

3. The literature on this topic is vast. For guidelines for presenting accurate and effective visual presentations, Edward Tufte is indispensable. His *The Visual Display of Quantitative Information* (Cheshire, CT: Graphics, 1983) is a classic. For an introduction to graphical data exploration, see William Jacoby, *Statistical Graphics for Univariate and Bivariate Data* (Thousand Oaks, CA: Sage, 1997).

4. Kevin J. Keen, *Graphics for Statistics and Data Analysis with R* (Boca Raton, FL: CRC Press, 2010), 11. Chapter 1 of this book succinctly describes the "principles of statistical graphics."

STUDENT STUDY SITE

for CQ Press

Give your students the SAGE edge!

SAGE edge offers a robust online environment featuring an impressive array of free tools and resources for review, study, and further exploration, keeping both instructors and students on the cutting edge of teaching and learning. Learn more at **edge.sagepub.com/johnson9e.**

12 TESTING RELATIONSHIPS

Imagine that you wanted to determine whether interest in politics is related to the decision to vote. The first step might be to take a random sample of the population and divide it into two groups: Group 1 includes those with interest in politics; group 2 includes those without interest in politics. On average, group 1's turnout rate was 80 percent, and group 2's turnout rate was 20 percent. This is a situation in which the relationship is pretty clear; interest in politics is associated with strong voting tendencies. But, let us imagine that group 1's turnout rate was 56 percent and group 2's turnout rate was 53 percent. Clearly, those interested in politics were voting at a higher rate, but is there enough difference between groups 1 and 2 for us to assert the difference is meaningful rather than the result of a random process?

In this chapter, we demonstrate how you can use statistics to do just that: to help you decide if there is enough of a difference between two groups to establish a meaningful relationship. We first explore the normal distribution and its properties along with z scores. We then move to a discussion of confidence intervals, using z scores to learn about data, and testing hypotheses using z and t tests. After learning about these basic statistics, you will be ready to begin your own basic analyses of data, and be in a better position to read and understand quantitative political science work because you understand how hypothesis testing works.

CHAPTER OBJECTIVES

12.1   Define normal distribution and z scores.

12.2   Explain confidence intervals and confidence levels.

12.3   Understand difference of means hypothesis testing with population data: z tests.

12.4   Understand difference of means hypothesis testing with sample data: t tests.

12.5   Explain hypothesis testing for a proportion.

12.6   Understand statistics with two samples.

THE NORMAL DISTRIBUTION AND z SCORES

We begin our discussion of testing relationships with the normal distribution. You will remember our preliminary discussion of the normal distribution in chapter 5 in regard to sampling and again in chapter 11 with respect to descriptive statistics. It will likely be helpful for you to review those discussions on pages 105–107 and pages 224–227.

The normal distribution is often referred to as a bell curve because it is shaped like a bell, with most of the observations in the thick middle portion under the curve and fewer observations in the tails.[1] As we explained in chapter 5, statistical theory tells us that we can use the normal distribution with any variable in political science—gross domestic product (GDP), education, ideology, or another measure—because every variable has the same sampling distribution, which is distributed normally. In this chapter, we expand our use of the normal distribution, beginning with some of the properties of the normal distribution and how we can make use of those properties in statistical applications.

The graph of the standard normal distribution is a unimodal, symmetrical (bell-shaped) curve. This particular distribution has a mean of 0 and a standard deviation of 1. You have seen the normal distribution in chapter 11 in figure 11-3, but we show it again here in figure 12-1. There are many important features to note. First, the mean, median, and mode are all found in the center of the distribution and share the same numerical value. Second, the distribution is symmetrical; the right side of the distribution has the same shape as the left side. Third, notice that on the x-axis of the figure, we have included labels for the number of standard deviations from the mean, with positive counts of one and two standard deviations above the mean, and negative counts of one and two standard deviations below the mean. Finally, in the center of the figure, you will see that 68 percent of observations lie within one standard deviation above and below the mean, and that 95 percent of observations fall within two standard deviations above and below the mean. How do we know this to be true?

Turning to appendix A, you will find a table of probabilities for the right tail of the normal distribution. In the first column, labeled z, you will find a z score in each row, from 0.0 to 5.0. A z score represents the number of standard deviations from the mean. Notice that in the first row, the z-score value is 0.0. A z score of 0.0 tells us that we are at the mean—and since we are zero standard deviations away from the mean, it makes good common sense that the z-score value is zero. As we move away from the mean, toward the right tail, the number of standard deviations increases. As you work your way down the column of

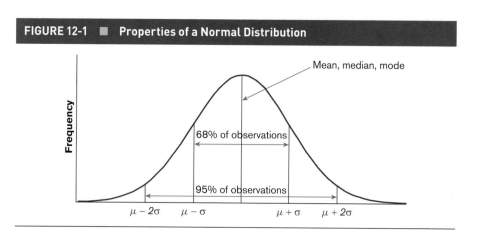

FIGURE 12-1 ■ Properties of a Normal Distribution

z scores, you will notice that the numbers incrementally increase, representing more distance from the mean. A z score close to 0.0 is near the mean while a large z score is far into the right tail.

Next, let us examine the other columns of the table. Each additional column in the table, with the headings .00 through .09, represents the hundredths place of a z score. In order to use the table, you will need to add this hundredths place to the z score in the first column. So, if we start with the 1.0 row, we have a series of z scores—1.00 in the second column, 1.01 in the third column, 1.02 in the fourth column, and so on—until we get to the end of the row with a z score of 1.09 in the eleventh column. Each of the z scores is associated with a probability value in the main body of the table. The probability values reported in the table describe the proportion of observations associated with a portion of the area under the curve. For example, a z score of 0.0 is located at the mean. The associated probability is .5000. This makes sense because we know that the probability describes the observations under the curve to the right of the z score. As panel A in figure 12-2 demonstrates, half of the distribution (.5000) lies to the right of the mean. Consider another example: When we have a z score of 1.00, the associated probability is .1587. As panel B in figure 12-2 demonstrates, 15.87 percent of the observations lie to the right of a z score of 0.00 in the shaded area. We can also make use of the hundredths columns. A z score of 1.55 has an associated probability value of .0606. This is reported in panel C in figure 12-2.

FIGURE 12-2   ■   Using the Standard Normal Distribution

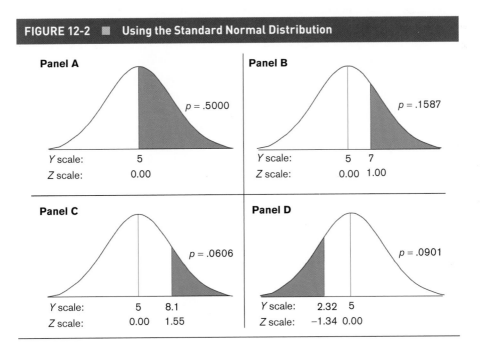

What about negative z scores in the left tail? Because the distribution is symmetrical (the right and left sides of the curve are identical) and probability values must always be positive (you cannot have a negative probability), we can use the same table from appendix A to find probabilities in the left tail. We begin by taking the absolute value of the z score. So, if we want to find the probability associated with a z score of −1.34, we look up 1.34 on the table and find a probability of .0901. That probability tells us that 9.01 percent of the observations are to the left of a z score of −1.34. You will find this example in panel D in figure 12-2.

When working with the probability values in the normal distribution, notice that the values decrease in size from .5000 to near zero with a large z score of 5.0. You should be able to understand that as we move further and further into the tail, the probability of observing an observation gets infinitesimally small.

As figure 12-2 demonstrates, we can include multiple scales on a distribution figure. The Y scale indicates the values of the variable Y, and the Z scale indicates the z scores associated with the values of Y. You can think of a z score as translating the value of a variable into the language of the normal distribution. Instead of describing a numerical value for a variable in terms of its unit—GDP, ideology, education, or another measure—we can describe it in terms of a z score: the number of standard deviations the value of the variable is from the mean. This is helpful in thinking about how extreme values are with reference to the mean given the variability of the data. As this example demonstrates, we found a z score for each listed value of Y. How did we do that? That is the next step.

Now that you understand the relationship between standard deviations, z scores, probabilities, and the area under the curve, we can use this information to calculate and interpret z scores. The formula for calculating a z score is

$$z = \frac{(Y_i - \mu)}{\sigma},$$

where z is a z score, Y_i is an individual value of the variable Y, μ is the population mean, and σ is the population standard deviation. If you do not recognize these symbols, or need a refresher on their meaning and use, refer to chapter 11, pages 221–223.

We can apply this formula in an example. Suppose we are interested in generals and their uniforms. We would like to know the percentage chance of observing a general wearing five or more medals. We can calculate a z score using the following data, where Y is the number of medals worn in a population of generals, to determine the percentage chance.[2] First, we find the mean and standard deviation for the population. We then use the standard deviation and mean to find the z score and use the z score to find a probability value. We can then convert the probability value into a percentage and answer the question: there is an 18.94 percent chance of observing a general wearing five or more medals. See the How It's Done box for the calculation.

HOW IT'S DONE
CALCULATING z SCORES

i	Y	$Y_i - \mu$	$(Y_i - \mu)^2$
1	4	1	1
2	2	−1	1
3	2	−1	1
4	5	2	4
5	7	4	16
6	1	−2	4
7	0	−3	9
$N=7$	21		36

$$\mu = \frac{\Sigma Y}{N}$$

$$\mu = \frac{21}{7}$$

$$\mu = 3$$

$$\sigma = \sqrt{\frac{\Sigma(Y_i - \mu)^2}{N}}$$

$$\sigma = \sqrt{\frac{36}{7}}$$

$$\sigma = \sqrt{5.14}$$

$$\sigma = 2.27$$

$$z = \frac{(Y_i - \mu)}{\sigma}$$

$$z = \frac{(5-3)}{2.27}$$

$$z = \frac{(2)}{2.27}$$

$$z = .88$$

$$p = .1894$$

Using the same data and the same formula, we can determine the percentage chance of observing a general wearing two medals or fewer (33 percent) and even the percentage chance of observing a general wearing between three and five medals (48.06 percent). To find this last area under the curve, we simply subtract .1894 and .3300 from 1, before converting to a percentage, because the entire distribution includes all of the possible observations (1) and we subtract the values of the tails we do not need to answer the question, leaving us with the area under the middle of the curve, .4806. See figure 12-3 for a graphical representation.

$$z = \frac{(Y_i - \mu)}{\sigma}$$

$$z = \frac{(2-3)}{2.27}$$

$$z = \frac{(-1)}{2.27}$$

$$z = -.44 \qquad p = .3300$$

CONFIDENCE INTERVALS

Population Confidence Intervals

Recall from chapter 5 that if we take an infinite number of samples to obtain estimates of a population parameter, our estimates will be normally distributed and cluster around the

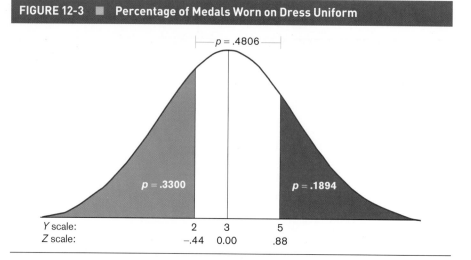

FIGURE 12-3 ■ Percentage of Medals Worn on Dress Uniform

true value of the population parameter. We concluded that, on average, $\bar{Y}$ is on target, but for any individual sample, we assume that there may be sampling error causing our estimation to be slightly off target: $\mu = \bar{Y} + sampling\ error$. In this section, we want to figure out how confident we are in our estimation of the population parameter.

Confidence intervals are probability estimates of the true parameter value in terms of its occurrence between constructed boundaries. In other words, a confidence interval is an estimate of a range in which the population mean will likely be found.

We can calculate a confidence interval using two different equations: one equation when using a population standard deviation (σ) and one when using a sample standard deviation ($\hat{\sigma}$). We first explain how to calculate the population confidence interval, then move on to the sample confidence interval:

$$PCI = \bar{Y} \pm \left(z_{\alpha/2}\right)\left(\frac{\sigma}{\sqrt{n}}\right)$$

This equation may look difficult at first glance, but once you understand the individual components and their purpose, you will find the formula much easier to work with. PCI stands for population confidence interval. The confidence interval is calculated using three parts, $\bar{Y}$, the sample mean; $z_{\alpha/2}$, the critical value; and $\frac{\sigma}{\sqrt{n}}$, the standard error of the mean. We already know what the sample mean represents, but the other terms are new to us. The critical value indicates how much confidence we want in the confidence interval by using a confidence level. We are free to choose any confidence level. We could decide that we want 99 percent confidence or 10 percent confidence. Of course, 10 percent confidence seems absurdly low, so most political scientists stick to a confidence level of 90 percent or higher. We will use 95 percent confidence as our standard. We can calculate the value that represents a 95 percent confidence level by using the equation, $z_{\alpha/2}$. The first step is to subtract .95 from 1, the value that captures the probability of an observation in the normal distribution (see our earlier discussion of z scores). Subtracting .95 from 1 leaves us with .05, or our alpha level, α. The formula next tells us to divide α by 2, giving us .025. This represents the two tails of the distribution, with .025 in each tail. The next step is to look up the probability value .025 in appendix A to find an associated z score. You will find .025 at the intersection of row 1.9 and column .06—a z score of 1.96. The z score of 1.96 is our critical value and represents 95 percent confidence.

HOW IT'S DONE
THE CONSTRUCTION OF CONFIDENCE INTERVALS

Calculate the confidence interval for population mean, μ, based on a sample size, n, and level of significance, α:

1. Obtain the sample mean, $\overline{Y}$, as an estimate of the population mean, μ.

2. Obtain the population standard deviation, σ, or the sample standard deviation, $\hat{\sigma}$.

3. Determine the critical value, z for a population or t for a sample, based on α the desired level of significance.

4. Multiply the critical value by the standard error of the mean.

5. Add and subtract this product from the sample mean, $\overline{Y}$.

The next term in the equation is the *standard error of the mean*. The standard error of the mean captures uncertainty in the data. The standard deviation tells us about variation around the mean—more variation and a larger standard deviation mean less certainty, while less variation and a smaller standard deviation mean more certainty. Likewise, the sample size tells us about certainty—we have more certainty in a large sample size and less certainty in a small sample size.

Multiplying the critical value by the standard error of the mean yields the confidence limit. The confidence limit is used to find the upper and lower boundaries that form the confidence interval. By adding the confidence limit to the mean and subtracting the confidence limit from the mean, we can establish the confidence interval. The last step is to note the confidence level we used to calculate the confidence interval, because a different choice of confidence level will in turn affect the size of the confidence interval. Consider the following example.

We have hypothetical data on the number of times individuals contributed money to a political campaign and are interested to know about the precision of our estimate. We can construct a population confidence interval using data, where Y is the number of contributions, and the following equation to estimate the range in which we are likely to find the population mean:

HOW IT'S DONE
POPULATION CONFIDENCE INTERVAL

Given:

$\bar{Y} = 5$

$\sigma = 2.5$

$n = 100$

Calculated above:

Confidence level $= 95\%$

$\alpha = 1 - .95$

$\alpha = .05$

$\frac{\alpha}{2} = .025$

$z = 1.96$

$PCI = \bar{Y} \pm \left(z_{\alpha/2}\right)\left(\frac{\sigma}{\sqrt{n}}\right)$

$PCI = 5 \pm \left(1.96\right)\left(\frac{2.5}{\sqrt{100}}\right)$

$PCI = 5 \pm \left(1.96\right)\left(\frac{2.5}{10}\right)$

$PCI = 5 \pm \left(1.96\right)\left(.25\right)$

$PCI = 5 \pm .49$

$PCI = (4.51 < \mu < 5.49), .05$

First, we substituted the mean, the population standard deviation, and the sample size in the equation. We also substituted the critical value of 1.96, as we calculated that for a 95 percent confidence level above. Second, we followed the order of operations to calculate the population confidence interval. The standard error of the mean is .25, the confidence limit is .49, and the confidence interval is $PCI = (4.51 < \mu < 5.49), .05$. We can interpret this as "We are 95% confident that the population mean lies between the lower limit of 4.51 and the upper limit of 5.49."

To stress the importance of choice of confidence level, using the same data, consider the following calculations using a 90 percent confidence level $(\alpha = .1)$ and a 99 percent confidence level $(\alpha = .01)$. Notice that when we require less confidence (90 percent), the interval is narrower, and when we require more confidence (99 percent), the interval is wider. A

FIGURE 12-4 ■ Comparison of Population Confidence Intervals

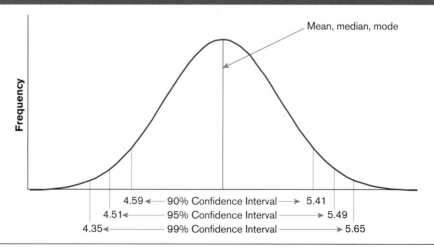

Mean, median, mode

Frequency

4.59 ◄— 90% Confidence Interval —► 5.41

4.51 ◄— 95% Confidence Interval —► 5.49

4.35 ◄— 99% Confidence Interval —► 5.65

wider interval extends further into the tail of the distribution, including more observations, as you can see in figure 12-4. Figure 12-4 is useful in conceptualizing why confidence intervals expand or contract with a larger or smaller confidence level.

HOW IT'S DONE
THE EFFECT OF THE CONFIDENCE LEVEL ON CONFIDENCE INTERVALS

With 90 percent confidence

$$PCI = \bar{Y} \pm \left(z_{\alpha/2}\right)\left(\frac{\sigma}{\sqrt{n}}\right)$$

$$PCI = 5 \pm \left(1.65\right)\left(\frac{2.5}{\sqrt{100}}\right)$$

$$PCI = 5 \pm \left(1.65\right)\left(\frac{2.5}{10}\right)$$

$$PCI = 5 \pm \left(1.65\right)\left(.25\right)$$

$$PCI = 5 \pm .41$$

$$PCI = \left(4.59 < \mu < 5.41\right), .10$$

With 99 percent confidence

$$PCI = \bar{Y} \pm \left(z_{\alpha/2}\right)\left(\frac{\sigma}{\sqrt{n}}\right)$$

$$PCI = 5 \pm \left(2.58\right)\left(\frac{2.5}{\sqrt{100}}\right)$$

$$PCI = 5 \pm \left(2.58\right)\left(\frac{2.5}{10}\right)$$

$$PCI = 5 \pm \left(2.58\right)\left(.25\right)$$

$$PCI = 5 \pm .65$$

$$PCI = \left(4.35 < \mu < 5.65\right), .01$$

Sample Confidence Intervals

So far, we have been working with a known population standard deviation. We can also calculate a confidence interval using a sample standard deviation. The equation for the sample confidence interval (SCI) is similar to the population confidence interval with some notable differences:

$$SCI = \bar{Y} \pm \left(t\right)\left(\frac{\hat{\sigma}}{\sqrt{n}}\right)$$

The first difference is in the critical value. We used a critical value from the normal distribution in the population confidence interval equation because we were using a population standard deviation and a sufficiently large sample size to do so. When we do not have a population standard deviation and a sufficiently large sample size, we instead draw a critical value from the Student's t distribution (t distribution).

The t distribution is a special case of the normal distribution for use with small samples. As sample sizes decrease, we have less certainty in the data. This uncertainty is captured by the t distribution, which changes shape with the sample size. With a sufficiently large sample, the t distribution has the same shape and properties of the normal distribution. As the sample size decreases, the shape of the t distribution changes—observations move into the tails, causing the distribution to get flatter and wider as if a heavy weight is pressing down on the middle crown of the distribution.

Like the z table, we can use the t table to find critical values. We include a t table in appendix B. The t table requires three pieces of information to find a critical value. The first is the degrees of freedom (df). The degrees of freedom are calculated differently for different statistics and in different contexts. For now, we will calculate degrees of freedom as

$df = n - 1$. We subtract 1 from the sample size because, in theory, we would need to make at least one change to a sample to match a population from which the sample is drawn. The second piece of information is to choose one tail or two tails. For now, we are working with two tails in a confidence interval. Finally, we must choose an alpha level. Remember that $\alpha = 1 -$ confidence level. We will use the standard of 95 percent confidence, so $\alpha = .05$. If we had a sample size of 10, with two tails and $\alpha = .05.$, we would find a t value of 2.262. With 20 cases, we would find a t value of 2.093. Because we have more cases in a sample of 20, the t value decreases in size. Now, look all the way down at the bottom of the two-tailed, .05-level column. You will find that with a sufficiently large sample size, noted as ∞, the t value is 1.960. With a sufficiently large sample size, the t distribution is identical to the normal distribution, so the t value with 95 percent confidence is the same as the z value with 95 percent confidence. Likewise, the t values of 1.645 and 2.576, respectively, equate the z values we used earlier with 90 percent and 99 percent confidence.

The last difference is that we are now using a sample standard deviation rather than a population standard deviation. With these differences in mind, we are ready to move on to calculating the sample confidence interval.

For this example, we begin with a raw data set of observations drawn from a random sample. We will be analyzing hypothetical data where Y is a variable that measures the number of times voters watched speeches by the head of state. For this problem, we use the two-tailed test and 95 percent confidence.

The first step is to calculate the mean, $\bar{Y}$. We then use the mean to calculate the sample standard deviation, $\hat{\sigma}$. Finally, we use the mean and standard deviation to calculate the

HOW IT'S DONE
SAMPLE CONFIDENCE INTERVAL

Here we calculate the sample confidence interval. You can follow the calculation by working from left to right in the data table and through the calculations from sample mean, to sample standard deviation, to sample confidence interval.

i	Y	$Y_i - \bar{Y}$	$(Y_i - \bar{Y})^2$
1	4	0	0
2	5	1	1
3	5	1	1
4	3	−1	1
5	8	4	16
6	1	−3	9
7	2	−2	4
$n = 7$	28		32

$$\bar{Y} = \frac{\Sigma Y}{n}$$

$$\bar{Y} = \frac{28}{7}$$

$$\bar{Y} = 4$$

$$\hat{\sigma} = \sqrt{\frac{\Sigma(Y_i - \bar{Y})^2}{n-1}}$$

$$\hat{\sigma} = \sqrt{\frac{32}{7-1}}$$

$$\hat{\sigma} = \sqrt{\frac{32}{6}}$$

$$\hat{\sigma} = \sqrt{5.33}$$

$$\hat{\sigma} = 2.31$$

$$SCI = \bar{Y} \pm (t)\left(\frac{\hat{\sigma}}{\sqrt{n}}\right)$$

$$SCI = 4 \pm (2.447)\left(\frac{2.31}{\sqrt{7}}\right)$$

$$SCI = 4 \pm (2.447)\left(\frac{2.31}{2.65}\right)$$

$$SCI = 4 \pm (2.447)(.87)$$

$$SCI = 4 \pm 2.13$$

$$SCI = (1.87 < \mu < 6.13), .05$$

sample confidence interval. To find the critical value, $t = 2.447$, we access the t table in appendix B and choose the .05 column under two-tailed test, with 6 degrees of freedom. We calculate the standard error of the mean by dividing the standard deviation by the square root of the sample size. Multiplying the critical value by the standard error of the mean gives us the confidence limit, and the confidence interval is $SCI = (1.87 < \mu < 6.13), .05$. We can interpret this confidence interval the same way as for the population confidence interval: "We are 95% confident that the population mean lies between the lower limit of 1.87 and the upper limit of 6.13." It bears repeating, because it is so vitally important, that if we were to use a different confidence level, the sample confidence interval would be different.

We can see how confidence intervals are used in analyzing political outcomes in figure 12-5. Figure 12-5 includes a graphic from the popular website FiveThirtyEight.com with 80 percent confidence intervals drawn around the average predicted national popular vote percentage for 2016 presidential candidates Hillary Clinton, Donald Trump, and Gary Johnson. A casual look at the graphic indicates that FiveThirtyEight's model predicted Clinton winning 48.5 percent of the popular vote with Trump garnering 44.9 percent of the vote and Johnson coming in a distant third at only 5.0 percent. But because you now understand confidence intervals, you will notice that the markers indicating Clinton and Trump's average support in the model are surrounded by confidence intervals indicating that there is uncertainty about those predictions, and it is possible that either or both outcomes are in fact higher or lower. Even more importantly, you will notice that the Clinton and Trump confidence intervals overlap on the vote percentage scale with the averages for each candidate nearly falling within the *other candidate's confidence interval* as well. As a discerning student of political science, you now understand that even though the average prediction had Clinton ahead, the uncertainty in the model, demonstrated by the confidence intervals, meant that it was possible that Trump would end up with a higher percentage of the popular vote than Clinton. Furthermore, these results suggested that while the model's best prediction was that Clinton would win 48.5 percent of the vote, it was certainly in the realm of possibility that she would win over 50 percent. Meanwhile, given that the 50 percent mark was far in the right tail of the Trump distribution, Trump winning over 50 percent of the vote was most unrealistic. In the actual election results, Clinton won 48.2 percent of the popular vote, and Trump won 46.1 percent.[3]

Now that we have a clear understanding of the normal and t distributions and how to construct confidence intervals to estimate a range of values around a sample mean, we will next move on to testing hypotheses. These initial hypothesis tests are quite simple, but can serve as a powerful tool in undergraduate research when trying to establish causal relationships.

HYPOTHESIS TESTING

Types of Hypotheses

Statistical hypotheses are statements about the value of a population parameter or about the relationship between two or more variables. There are two types of statistical hypotheses: null hypotheses and alternative or research hypotheses. A **null hypothesis**, commonly

| FIGURE 12-5 | ■ | Confidence Intervals in Political Analysis |

Who's winning the popular vote

Our model produces a distribution of outcomes for the national popular vote. The curves will get narrower as the election gets closer and our forecasts become more confident.

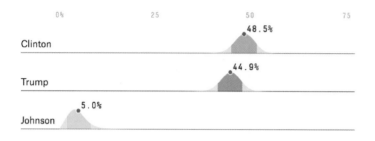

Note: 80% confidence intervals around average popular vote outcome for each candidate, last updated November 8, 2016.

Source: FiveThirtyEight.com, "2016 Presidential Election Forecast." Last accessed September 13, 2018. Available at https://proj ects.fivethirtyeight.com/2016-election-forecast/.

recorded as H_0, can be used to describe the absence of a statistical relationship between two or more variables. A null hypothesis could state that the mean (μ) approval ratings were the same for strong Republicans and strong Democrats:

$$H_0 : \mu_{SR} = \mu_{SD}$$

You will also often see a null hypothesis describe a lack of variation from a specified value— usually the population mean, or zero, but any value could be specified. For example, we could write a null hypothesis that the value of the sample mean is the same as the population mean, 7:

$$H_0 : \bar{X} = 7$$

Or, we could write a null hypothesis about the difference (X) between the average family income for female-headed households and average family income for the population is $0:

$$H_0 : X = \$0$$

As we will see in the coming examples, these null hypotheses are stated in such a manner that data plus statistical theory allow us to reject them with a known degree of confidence that we are not making a mistake.

In addition to stating a null hypothesis, researchers state another hypothesis called the **alternative hypothesis** or **research hypothesis**, represented by H_A. Researchers usually hope that they will be able to reject the null hypothesis in favor of their research hypothesis. Again, there are several ways a research hypothesis might be stated. We could pair with our earlier null hypothesis a research hypothesis that the approval rating for strong Republicans (SR) is different from the approval rating for strong Democrats (SD):

$$H_A : \mu_{SR} \neq \mu_{SD}$$

Or, we might instead hypothesize that the approval rating for strong Republicans is greater than the approval rating for strong Democrats:

$$H_A : \mu_{SR} > \mu_{SD}$$

One could also write a research hypothesis about the difference (X) in average family income for female-headed households from the rest of the population:

$$H_A : X < 0$$

Obviously, the null and research hypotheses cannot both be true. Deciding which to accept and which to reject involves the possibility of making a mistake or error.

Types of Errors in Statistical Inference

To paraphrase dictionary definitions, inference refers to reasoning from available information or facts to reach a conclusion. The end product, however, is not guaranteed to be true. It might in fact turn out to be incorrect. This possibility certainly arises in the case of statistical inference, in which values of unknown population characteristics such as means or proportions are estimated and hypotheses about those characteristics are tested.

In hypothesis testing—that is, making a decision about a null hypothesis—two kinds of mistakes are possible, as illustrated in figure 12-6. The first type of mistake is to reject a true null hypothesis. Statisticians call this mistake a **type I error**. The probability of making a type I error, and rejecting the null hypothesis (H_0) when it is actually true, is designated by alpha(α). In the example in figure 12-6, if it is actually true that there is no difference in support among Democrats and Republicans, then we would make a type I error by rejecting the null hypothesis.

FIGURE 12-6 ■ Type I and Type II Errors

H_0: There **is no difference** in support for a law among Democrats and Republicans.
H_A: There **is a difference** in support for a law among Democrats and Republicans.

Type I Error

State of the world: The null hypothesis (H_0) is actually true.

Incorrect rejection of null hypothesis (H_0)

Incorrect acceptance of research hypothesis (H_A)

Type II Error

State of the world: The null hypothesis (H_0) is actually false.

Incorrect acceptance of the null hypothesis (H_0)

Incorrect rejection of the research hypothesis (H_A)

Another possible mistake is failing to reject a null hypothesis that is false. In this example, if there were in fact a difference between support among Democrats and Republicans, we would make a **type II error** by accepting the null hypothesis (H_0). The probability of committing a type II error is normally designated with the lowercase Greek letter beta, β.[4]

The convention for testing hypotheses is to focus on the probability of making a type I error. A **test of statistical significance** calculates this probability. When researchers claim that their results are "statistically significant," they are claiming that the null hypothesis has been rejected with a specified probability of making a type I error.

Levels of Significance

The term *level of statistical significance* is used to refer to the probability of making a type I error. The most common level of **statistical significance** in political science is .05. You will often see additional levels of significance, including .10, .01, and .001, but it is really up to the researcher (and you) to decide how great a chance to take of making a type I error (remember that these were the alpha levels in the earlier discussion of confidence intervals). You are likely to encounter a statement such as "The result is significant at the .05 level." This statement means that a researcher has set up a null hypothesis, drawn a sample, calculated a sample statistic or estimator, and found that its particular value will occur by chance at most only 5 percent of the time, if the null hypothesis is true.

Steps for Hypothesis Testing

The process for testing statistical hypotheses involves several steps. Let's review these before we work with some examples.

1. State a null hypothesis—for example, H_0: $\mu = 80$.

2. State an alternative hypothesis—for example, H_A: $\mu \neq 80$, or $\mu > 80$, or $\mu < 80$ (choose only one of these alternatives).

3. Make a decision rule. This involves deciding the maximum probability of making a type I error you are willing to accept (level of statistical significance). This level of statistical significance is represented by α and called the "alpha" level.

4. Determine whether you are conducting a "one-tailed" or "two-tailed" test of statistical significance. If you are predicting that your sample statistic is different from the population parameter, but you are not predicting whether it is smaller or larger, you will be conducting a two-tailed test. If you are predicting that the sample statistic is larger (or smaller) than the population parameter, you will be conducting a one-tailed test.

5. Choose an appropriate test statistic and sampling distribution. The appropriate test statistic and sampling distribution will depend on the type of population parameter you are estimating and the size of your sample. Remember, a sampling distribution is a mathematical function that indicates the probability of different values of the

sample statistic or estimator occurring.[5] Think of a sampling distribution as a picture of the variability of sample results.

6. Determine the critical value of the test statistic. The critical value is the value of the test statistic that must be obtained in order to reject the null hypothesis at the specified alpha level.

7. Calculate the sample statistic or estimator of the population parameter.

8. Calculate the observed value of the test statistic. The general formula for calculating this value is:

$$\text{Observed test statistic} = \frac{\left(\text{Sample estimate} - \text{Hypothesized population parameter}\right)}{\text{Estimated standard error of sample statistic}}$$

9. Compare the observed value of the test statistic to the critical value of the test statistic.

The decision to reject or not reject the null hypothesis depends on the comparison between the observed test statistic and the critical value.

- Two-tailed test: Reject H_0 if the *absolute value* of the observed test statistic is greater than or equal to the critical value.

- One-tailed test: Check to make sure the sample estimate is consistent with H_A. If so, reject H_0 if the *absolute value* of the observed test statistic is greater than or equal to the critical value.

Difference of Means Tests

In this section, we test hypotheses using difference of means tests. We introduce the difference of means test for use with population data (z test), followed by a test for use with sample data (t test). In each test, we are using the same logic—we want to know whether two means are of different magnitude, and whether the difference in magnitude is statistically significant. Furthermore, in some cases, we want to determine if the difference in magnitude is in the hypothesized direction (one mean hypothesized to be larger, or smaller, than the other).

All difference of means tests—and there are many varieties—test hypotheses using the same logic. The basic logic is that we want to determine if the difference between two means is great enough for us to conclude that there is a substantive and statistically meaningful difference. We will use the z test, a difference of means test for population data, as an example to explain the basic logic.

The z-test formula is

$$z_{obs} = \frac{(\bar{Y} - \mu)}{\sigma / \sqrt{n}}$$

where $\bar{Y}$ is the sample mean, μ is the hypothesized population mean, σ is the population standard deviation, and n is the sample size. You should recognize these terms from earlier in the chapter. In the numerator, we are taking the difference between two means—here we label them as a sample mean and a population mean, but you can take the difference between any two mean values. This *difference of the means* is where we get the hypothesis test name. The denominator is the standard error of the mean—familiar to us from the confidence interval examples above. If you need a quick refresher on how the standard error of the mean captures uncertainty in the data, go back to page 245 and then return before you proceed. In combination in the formula, we are measuring the distance between two means and using the standard error of the mean to determine if the difference between the means is large enough for us to make a claim that there is a statistically significant difference between the means. Statistical significance is determined by relying on the z-observed value from this calculation in comparison with a critical value from the normal distribution table in appendix A.

We can see how this works by adding an example. Suppose that we have a null hypothesis that the average number of pages read in a single day on internet news sites by college students is the same as for the rest of the population. Using hypothetical data, we know that the population mean is 6 stories per day with a standard deviation of 2. We then collected a sample of 500 students and determined that the sample mean is 6.3 stories per day. Clearly, 6.3 is in fact different from 6, but do we have a real difference, or is there not enough difference between 6 and 6.3? We can use the z test to find out.

HOW IT'S DONE
THE Z TEST

$$z_{obs} = \frac{(\bar{Y} - \mu)}{\sigma/\sqrt{n}}$$

$$z_{obs} = \frac{(6.3 - 6)}{2/\sqrt{500}}$$

$$z_{obs} = \frac{(.3)}{2/22.36}$$

$$z_{obs} = \frac{(.3)}{.09}$$

$$z_{obs} = 3.33$$

$H_0 : \bar{Y} = \mu$

Two-tailed test

95% confidence level $(\alpha = .05)$

$z_{critical} = 1.96$

$|3.33| > 1.96$

Reject Null Hypothesis (H_0)

In this z test, we subtract the population mean from the sample mean to find the difference of means, then divide by the standard error of the mean to find a z-observed value of 3.33. We use this z-observed value to determine statistical significance by using information from the normal distribution table in appendix A. Like we did with confidence intervals, we begin with the confidence level—this time 95 percent confidence, which is associated with an alpha level of .05.

For this example, we hypothesized that the means will be different but did not hypothesize a direction (whether one mean is larger or smaller). In this case, we use what is known as a two-tailed test. A two-tailed test uses both the left and right tails of the distribution with half of the probability associated with a confidence level in the left tail and half in the right tail. In this case, with $\alpha = .05$, .025 is located in the left tail, and .025 is located in the right tail, because we did not make a prediction about positive or negative, right tail or left tail.

We know from our earlier work with confidence intervals that the two-tailed z score associated with $\alpha = .05$ is 1.96. Look at row 1.9 and column .06 in appendix A to find half of the alpha level (.025). It is half because the table only describes the right tail.

The last step in the hypothesis test is to compare the z-observed value and the z-critical value. If the absolute value of the z-observed value is greater than or equal to the z-critical value, we can say that there is a statistically significant difference between the two means and reject the null hypothesis.

Next, let us move on to the difference of means test for a sample, the t test. The formula is strikingly similar to the formula for a difference of means test with population data:

$$t_{obs} = \frac{(\bar{Y} - \mu)}{\hat{\sigma}/\sqrt{n}}$$

The only difference, aside from the label (z_{obs} vs. t_{obs}), is we are now using a sample standard deviation instead of a population standard deviation. Because we have less certainty with a sample standard deviation, and if we have a small sample, we rely on the t distribution rather than the normal distribution to test hypotheses. You will remember the difference between these distributions from our earlier discussion of confidence intervals.

For this example, we will assess the null hypothesis that the mean number of times that college students participated in politics in the last year is no different from the mean number of times the rest of the population did so. Our research hypothesis is that college students participate less than the rest of the population. We begin with a sample of 7 randomly selected college students and compare the mean with the mean of 8 for the rest of the population.

HOW IT'S DONE
THE t TEST

i	Y	$Y_i - \bar{Y}$	$\left(Y_i - \bar{Y}\right)^2$
1	10	5	25
2	1	−4	16
3	3	−2	4
4	2	−3	9
5	6	1	1
6	8	3	9
7	5	0	0
$n = 7$	35		64

$$\bar{Y} = \frac{\Sigma Y}{n}$$

$$\bar{Y} = \frac{35}{7}$$

$$\bar{Y} = 5$$

$$\hat{\sigma} = \sqrt{\frac{\Sigma\left(Y_i - \bar{Y}\right)^2}{n-1}}$$

$$\hat{\sigma} = \sqrt{\frac{64}{7-1}}$$

$$\hat{\sigma} = \sqrt{\frac{64}{6}}$$

$$\hat{\sigma} = \sqrt{10.67}$$

$$\hat{\sigma} = 3.27$$

$$t_{obs} = \frac{(\bar{Y} - \mu)}{\hat{\sigma}/\sqrt{n}}$$

$$t_{obs} = \frac{(5 - 8)}{3.27/\sqrt{7}}$$

$$t_{obs} = \frac{(-3)}{3.27/2.65}$$

$$t_{obs} = \frac{(-3)}{1.23}$$

$$t_{obs} = -2.44$$

After calculating the sample mean of 5, it appears that perhaps we will reject the null hypothesis and accept the research hypothesis—after all, the mean for the population is 8 while the mean for the sample is only 5. But is this enough difference given the uncertainty associated with our very small sample size? We use the mean to calculate the sample standard deviation and then plug both into the *t*-test formula. Dividing the difference of the mean by the standard error of the mean, we get a *t*-observed value of −2.44.

The next step is to find a *t*-critical value in similar fashion to how we did so for a sample confidence interval earlier in the chapter. Turning to the *t* table in appendix B, we will use the one-tailed test because we have hypothesized a direction (that the sample mean is smaller than the population mean). We have 6 degrees of freedom ($df = n - 1$), and we choose the .01 level because we want 99 percent confidence. The *t*-critical value is 3.143. The absolute value of the *t*-observed value is not greater than the *t*-critical value, so we cannot reject the null hypothesis, but we do reject the research hypothesis. It turns out that even though the sample mean appeared to be different from the population mean, given the uncertainty of a small sample size and large standard deviation, we cannot assert statistical significance.

$$H_0 : \bar{Y} = \mu; H_A : \bar{Y} < \mu$$

One-tail test

99% confidence level ($\alpha = .01$)

6 degrees of freedom

$t_{critical} = 3.143$

$$\left| -2.44 \right| < 3.143$$

Accept Null Hypothesis (H_0)

Testing Hypotheses about Proportions

In this section, we address statistical hypotheses about proportions. Suppose, for example, we want to estimate the proportion of citizens who donate money to political organizations and causes. After asking our question of a randomly drawn sample, we could record the responses as 0 for *No* and 1 for *Yes*. After the surveys have been tallied, we could find the average, which would just be the total of the scores divided by the sample size:

$$\frac{(0+0+0+\ldots+1+1+1\ldots)}{n} = \frac{\text{total number of 1s}}{n} = p$$

This equation is the proportion of respondents coded 1, or the proportion saying yes. The test that p equals a particular value follows the same procedure used for the difference of the mean.

As with difference of the mean tests, sample distributions of proportions depend on the sample size: For small samples (the rule of thumb is roughly $n < 30$), the *t* distribution is appropriate, while for larger samples, the z or standard normal distribution takes over. We calculate the standard error of the proportion:

$$\hat{\sigma}_p = \sqrt{\frac{p(1-p)}{n-1}},$$

where p is the sample proportion, $1 - p$ is the proportion *not* in the category of interest, and n is the sample size. We use this to find t observed:

$$z_{obs} = \frac{\text{sample proportion} - \text{hypothesized proportion}}{\text{standard error of the proportion}}$$

$$z_{obs} = \frac{p - P}{\hat{\sigma}_p}$$

As an example, we use data on political contributions, where those who did not make a financial contribution in the last year were recorded as a 0 and those who did were recorded as a 1. The estimated proportion across 1,000 respondents is $210 \div 1{,}000 = .21$. Imagine that we believe the real proportion is .30. Do we have reason to believe that our sample result differs (meaningfully) from the hypothesized value, $P = .30$?

Since the true value could be larger or smaller than .3, the alternative hypothesis is that P is either less or greater than .3, which leads to a two-tailed test. First, we calculate the standard error as

$$\hat{\sigma}_p = \sqrt{\frac{(.21)(1-.21)}{1000-1}}$$

$$\hat{\sigma}_p = \sqrt{\frac{.17}{999}}$$

$$\hat{\sigma}_p = .01$$

So the test statistic is

$$Z_{obs} = \frac{(p - P)}{\hat{\sigma}_p}$$

$$Z_{obs} = \frac{(.21-.3)}{.01}$$

$$Z_{obs} = \frac{-.09}{.01}$$

$$Z_{obs} = -9$$

9 is greater than the critical value of 1.96 at the .05 level. A small-sample test of a proportion follows the same procedure but uses the t distribution in place of the standard normal distribution.

Reinforcing Interpretation of Hypothesis Testing

Perhaps the most important lesson to remember about hypothesis testing is that substantive interpretation is just as important as, if not more important than, statistical interpretation.

Finding statistical support for a hypothesis is of no value if the hypothesis is drawn from a logically incoherent theory or the substantive effect is so minimal that there is no substantive value.

To reinforce interpretation, remember that there are conditions that must be met in order to reject a null hypothesis and accept a research hypothesis. Consider the hypotheses listed in table 12-1. The first set of hypotheses, labeled example 1, includes a research hypothesis that does not specify direction, simply that $\bar{Y}$ is different from μ. As such, to reject the null and accept the research hypothesis, you need only to establish that $|t_{obs}| \geq t_{critical}$. The research hypothesis in example 2 indicates that we expect $\bar{Y}$ to be greater than μ. In order that we can accept the research hypothesis, we must establish statistical significance, $|t_{obs}| \geq t_{critical}$, and that $\bar{Y}$ is greater than μ. Unless we satisfy both conditions, we cannot accept the research hypothesis.

Table 12-2 presents a chance to assess whether or not we accept the research hypothesis in each example. In example 1, we can accept the research hypothesis because the absolute value of t observed is greater than the t-critical value. In example 2, even though the absolute value of t observed is greater than the t-critical value, we cannot accept the research hypothesis because the hypothesis was that $\bar{Y}$ is greater than μ, but the negative t score indicates that $\bar{Y}$ is less than μ.

TABLE 12-1 ■ Assessing Difference of Means Test Results

Example	Hypotheses	Statistical significance	Direction
1	$H_0 : \bar{Y} = \mu$ $H_A : \bar{Y} \neq \mu$	$|t_{obs}| \geq t_{critical}$	H_A does not specify direction
2	$H_0 : \bar{Y} = \mu$ $H_A : \bar{Y} > \mu$	$|t_{obs}| \geq t_{critical}$	H_A specifies direction

TABLE 12-2 ■ Do We Accept the Research Hypothesis?

Example	Hypothesis	t_{obs}	$t_{critical}$
1	$H_0 : \bar{Y} = \mu$ $H_A : \bar{Y} \neq \mu$	−2.20	2.086
2	$H_0 : \bar{Y} = \mu$ $H_A : \bar{Y} > \mu$	−2.20	1.725

Note: 95 percent confidence, $\alpha = .05$, df = 20.

Another important fact to keep in mind when interpreting hypotheses is tests of statistical significance rest on specific assumptions and procedures, and making meaningful generalizations from samples depends on how thoroughly these assumptions and procedures are satisfied. In the difference of means tests and the tests of proportions presented here, the biggest factor is the difference between the values in the numerator—means or proportions. The simple fact is, the wider the difference between the two values, the more likely you will find statistical significance. Hopefully, this makes good logical sense.

A second major factor is the sample size. All other things being equal, the larger the sample, the easier it is to find significance—that is, to reject a null hypothesis. Why? A small sample size provides less certainty than a larger sample size, all other things being equal. Imagine that you have a sample of five Nigerians. A sample of 5 introduces a great deal of uncertainty because you could easily have no men, or no women, in a sample of just 5. But if you increase the sample to 1,500, certainty increases, as it is very unlikely that a sample of 1,500 would drastically misrepresent the underlying population—see chapter 5.

A third major factor is the size of the standard deviation, capturing variability in the data. More variation around the mean represents more uncertainty, and we will be less likely to find statistical significance. A small standard deviation, derived from data tightly distributed around the mean, will increase the likelihood of finding statistical significance. The reason has to do with certainty. Less variation is associated with more certainty.

To demonstrate the point, suppose a null hypothesis is $H_0: \mu = 100$. Further, assume the sample mean is $\bar{Y} = 105$ with a sample standard deviation of $\hat{\sigma} = 10$ In the t-test calculations below, we vary the sample size from 5 to 15 to 25. The observed t values are as follows:

HOW IT'S DONE
HOW SAMPLE SIZE AFFECTS STATISTICAL SIGNIFICANCE

$$t_{obs} = \frac{(\bar{Y} - \mu)}{\hat{\sigma}/\sqrt{n}}$$

$$t_{obs} = \frac{(105 - 100)}{10/\sqrt{5}}$$

$$t_{obs} = \frac{(5)}{10/2.24}$$

$$t_{obs} = \frac{(5)}{4.46}$$

$$t_{obs} = 1.12$$

$$t_{obs} = \frac{(\bar{Y} - \mu)}{\hat{\sigma}/\sqrt{n}}$$

$$t_{obs} = \frac{(105 - 100)}{10/\sqrt{15}}$$

$$t_{obs} = \frac{(5)}{10/3.87}$$

$$t_{obs} = \frac{(5)}{2.58}$$

$$t_{obs} = 1.94$$

$$t_{obs} = \frac{(\bar{Y} - \mu)}{\hat{\sigma}/\sqrt{n}}$$

$$t_{obs} = \frac{(105 - 100)}{10/\sqrt{25}}$$

$$t_{obs} = \frac{(5)}{10/5}$$

$$t_{obs} = \frac{(5)}{2}$$

$$t_{obs} = 2.5$$

In this example, a small change in sample size from 5 to 15 to 25 changed the observed t score enough that the result went from not being statistically significant at the 95 percent level (two-tailed test) with either 5 or 15 cases to being statistically significant with 25 cases. Likewise, notice that if we manipulated the numerator of the equation, to make the difference between the means smaller or larger, or if we decreased or increased the size of the standard deviation, we would change the likelihood of statistical significance. Plug in new numbers for the difference of the mean or the standard deviation and see for yourself. The lesson is that you must understand the statistics behind the claims if you are going to be an adept consumer of the political science literature, news media reporting, or government reports. Understanding how concepts like sample size affect interpretation is vital. A cynic might say, "You can *always* prove something if you take a large enough sample." A less cynical view is that "statistical significance is not the same thing as substantive significance."

TESTING A RELATIONSHIP WITH TWO SAMPLES

In the last section, we explored statistics using one sample. You will remember that in each example we had one sample size and one standard deviation. In this section, we introduce how you can test relationships with two samples. The statistics in this section are similar to those described in the previous section when working with one sample, and we will draw heavily on the logic explained in the earlier section.

What do we mean by two samples? Imagine that you hypothesize about the difference between the mean in a pretest and the mean in a posttest in an experimental context. Or, imagine that you have randomly sampled from two different groups—men and women—and want to hypothesize about the difference between the means of the groups. In each of these cases, you would need statistics that account for two samples. In this section, we introduce hypothesis tests for two samples as well as how we would estimate confidence intervals.

Difference of Means with Related Samples

Suppose that we are interested in how voters learn about national security issues. To answer this question, we have devised an experiment in which randomly selected participants answer a series of factual questions assessing knowledge about national security in a pretest before watching a documentary on national security issues and subsequently answering the same series of factual questions in a posttest.

In this example, we have two related samples—a sample for the pretest and a sample for the posttest—from the same respondents. We can use the following difference of means test to determine if we accept the null hypothesis $(H_0 : \bar{Y}_1 = \bar{Y}_2)$ or the research hypothesis $(H_A : \bar{Y}_1 < \bar{Y}_2)$, where $\bar{Y}_1$ is the mean of the pretest and $\bar{Y}_2$ is the mean of the posttest. In the following data matrix, we have listed the data from the pre- and posttests. The first step is to take the difference between the pre- and posttests. We subtracted $\bar{Y}_1$ from $\bar{Y}_2$ so that positive numbers would indicate an increase in scores from pre- to posttest. We then used the

HOW IT'S DONE
CALCULATING A t TEST WITH RELATED SAMPLES

i	Y_1	Y_2	d	$(d_i - \bar{d})$	$(d_i - \bar{d})^2$
1	6	7	1	0	0
2	3	4	1	0	0
3	0	2	2	1	1
4	4	4	0	−1	1
5	5	5	0	−1	1
6	5	6	1	0	0
7	1	3	2	1	1
$n = 7$			7		4

$$\bar{d} = \frac{\Sigma d}{n}$$

$$\bar{d} = \frac{7}{7}$$

$$\bar{d} = 1$$

$$\hat{\sigma} = \sqrt{\frac{\Sigma(d_i - \bar{d})^2}{n-1}}$$

$$\hat{\sigma} = \sqrt{\frac{4}{7-1}}$$

$$\hat{\sigma} = \sqrt{\frac{4}{6}}$$

$$\hat{\sigma} = \sqrt{.67}$$

$$\hat{\sigma} = .82$$

$$t_{obs} = \frac{(\bar{d})}{\hat{\sigma}/\sqrt{n}}$$

$$t_{obs} = \frac{(1)}{.82/\sqrt{7}}$$

$$t_{obs} = \frac{(1)}{.82/2.65}$$

$$t_{obs} = \frac{(1)}{.31}$$

$$t_{obs} = 3.23$$

difference (d) as the data for the hypothesis test—we calculate the mean of d and the standard deviation of d to calculate a t score like we did in the previous t-test example earlier in the chapter.

The result is a t observed of 3.23. The absolute value of 3.23 is larger than the t-critical value of 1.943 (one-tailed test, .05 level, 6 degrees of freedom) so we can reject the null hypothesis and accept the research hypothesis. In other words, we can say that watching the documentary caused an increase in knowledge about national security.

Difference of Means with Independent Samples

Next, let us suppose that we want to answer the same question, but with different data. This time, rather than using related samples, we will use independent samples. In order to answer the same question about knowledge of national security, we randomly sampled two different groups. We sampled a group of first-year college students and a group of second-year college students. Our thinking is that second-year college students are more knowledgeable about national security than first-year college students. In more formal terms, we have a null hypothesis $(H_0 : \bar{Y}_1 = \bar{Y}_2)$ and a research hypothesis $(H_A : \bar{Y}_1 < \bar{Y}_2)$, where $\bar{Y}_1$ is the mean of the first-year college students and $\bar{Y}_2$ is the mean of the second-year college students. Each group has its own mean score, of course, but complicating this problem is that we also have different group sizes and standard deviations because these are independently drawn samples.

As you can see below, the first-year students had a mean of 3.5 while the second-year students had a mean of 4. Is the difference enough to find statistical significance given the sample sizes and standard deviations? Using the following equation, we can calculate a t score.[6]

HOW IT'S DONE
CALCULATING A *t* TEST WITH INDEPENDENT SAMPLES

This equation looks difficult at first glance, but we have included the needed information (mean, sample size, and standard deviation for samples 1 and 2) and color coded the equations so you can more easily follow along.

$$\bar{Y}_1 = 3.5$$
$$n_1 = 15$$
$$\hat{\sigma}_1 = 1.5$$

$$\bar{Y}_2 = 4$$
$$n_2 = 20$$
$$\hat{\sigma}_2 = 2$$

$$t = \frac{\left(\bar{X}_1 - \bar{X}_2\right)}{\sqrt{\left(\frac{(n_1 - 1)\hat{\sigma}_1^2 + (n_2 - 1)\hat{\sigma}_2^2}{(n_1 + n_2 - 2)}\right)\left(\frac{1}{n_1} + \frac{1}{n_2}\right)}}$$

$$t = \frac{(3.5 - 4)}{\sqrt{\left(\frac{(15 - 1)1.5^2 + (20 - 1)2^2}{(15 + 20 - 2)}\right)\left(\frac{1}{15} + \frac{1}{20}\right)}}$$

$$t = \frac{(-.50)}{\sqrt{\left(\frac{(14)2.25 + (19)4}{(33)}\right)(.07 + .05)}}$$

$$t = \frac{(-.50)}{\sqrt{\left(\frac{31.5 + 76}{(33)}\right)(.12)}}$$

$$t = \frac{(-.50)}{\sqrt{\left(\frac{107.5}{(33)}\right)(.12)}}$$

$$t = \frac{(-.50)}{\sqrt{(3.26)(.12)}}$$

$$t = \frac{(-.50)}{\sqrt{.39}}$$

$$t = \frac{(-.50)}{.62}$$

$$t = -.81$$

If we examine the individual components that make up the larger statistic, we will see, as for all of the *z* and *t* tests discussed previously, that we have the difference of the means in the numerator and the standard error of the mean in the denominator. The numerator, in fact, is identical to previous difference of means tests. For ease of reading, we have color coded two segments of the standard error of the mean in the denominator. The blue segment captures the same terms we have seen before in the standard error of the mean, *standard deviation* and *sample size*, but because we have two samples, there are two of each. The red segment is a term that adjusts for the relative sizes of the samples—essentially weighting the statistic to account for the larger sample of second-year college students.

The blue segment is made easier to comprehend if you think about each part of the equation. First, we are subtracting 1 from each sample size—this gives us the degrees of freedom for each sample. Next, we are squaring the standard deviation for each sample—squaring the standard deviation gives us the variance of each sample (see chapter 11). Then we multiply the variance of each sample by its respective degrees of freedom. Next, we add the information from sample 2 to sample 1. Finally, we divide by the combined degrees of freedom—when we add both sample sizes and subtract 2, 1 for each sample.

In the red segment, we are accounting for the different sample sizes by dividing 1 by each sample size and adding the terms together. We then multiply the blue (3.26) and red (.12) terms. The final step is to take the square root to undo our earlier squaring of the standard deviation. The result is the same standard error of the mean we have discussed and calculated before. Dividing the difference of the mean by the standard error of the mean produces a t score that we can use to test our hypotheses just as we have done before, with one difference. Because we have two samples, we will use the combined degrees of freedom, 33. At the .05 level, using a one-tailed test and 33 degrees of freedom, the t-critical value is 1.697. Because 33 degrees of freedom is not listed in the table, we have a choice between 30 and 40 degrees of freedom. We do not have 40 degrees of freedom, so we use the value for 30 instead.

While the direction of the t-observed value is consistent with the research hypothesis that second-year college students know more about national security than first-year college students, the absolute value of the t score, .81, is not larger than the t-critical value, so we accept the null hypothesis and reject the research hypothesis.

Confidence Interval with Two Samples

Next we turn to calculating a confidence interval with two samples, and we are going to test the same hypotheses as in the previous two examples: We have a null hypothesis $(H_0 : \bar{Y}_1 = \bar{Y}_2)$ and a research hypothesis $(H_A : \bar{Y}_1 < \bar{Y}_2)$, where $\bar{Y}_1$ is the mean of the first-year college students and $\bar{Y}_2$ is the mean of the second-year college students. We are also going to use the same data as the previous example.

HOW IT'S DONE
TESTING A HYPOTHESIS WITH A CONFIDENCE INTERVAL WITH INDEPENDENT SAMPLES

$\bar{Y}_1 = 3.5$
$n_1 = 15$
$\hat{\sigma}_1 = 1.5$

$\bar{Y}_2 = 4$
$n_2 = 20$
$\hat{\sigma}_2 = 2$

$$SCI = d \pm t \left(\sqrt{\frac{(n_1 - 1)\hat{\sigma}_1^2 + (n_2 - 1)\hat{\sigma}_2^2}{n_1 + n_2 - 2}} \right) \left(\sqrt{\frac{1}{n_1} + \frac{1}{n_2}} \right)$$

$$SCI = -.5 \pm 1.697 \left(\sqrt{\frac{(15 - 1)1.5^2 + (20 - 1)2^2}{15 + 20 - 2}} \right) \left(\sqrt{\frac{1}{15} + \frac{1}{20}} \right)$$

$$SCI = -.5 \pm 1.697 \left(\sqrt{\frac{(14)2.25 + (19)4}{33}} \right) \left(\sqrt{.07 + .05} \right)$$

$$SCI = -.5 \pm 1.697 \left(\sqrt{\frac{31.5 + 76}{33}} \right) \left(\sqrt{.12} \right)$$

$$SCI = -.5 \pm 1.697 \left(\sqrt{\frac{107.5}{33}} \right) (.35)$$

$$SCI = -.5 \pm 1.697 \left(\sqrt{3.26} \right) (.35)$$

$$SCI = -.5 \pm 1.697 (1.81)(.35)$$

$$SCI = -.5 \pm 1.697 (.63)$$

$$SCI = -.5 \pm 1.07$$

$$SCI = (-1.57 < \mu < .57), .05$$

Like in the previous example, we have color-coded the different segments of the standard error of the mean. Because this uses the same data and virtually the same calculation of the standard error of the mean, we will rely on the previous explanation. After calculating the standard error of the mean, we create a 95 percent confidence interval. The t-critical value is 1.697 just like in the previous example and for the same reasons. In the same fashion as we did previously with one sample, we have calculated the confidence limit and added and subtracted the limit to the difference of the means (d).

We can use this confidence interval to test the null hypothesis. The null hypothesis ($H_0 : \bar{Y}_1 = \bar{Y}_2$) states that there is no difference between the two groups, first-year and second-year college students. If this hypothesis is true, we expect the difference between the groups to be 0: $d = 0$. If 0 is inside the confidence interval, and 0 is found between −1.57 and .57 in this interval, then we cannot reject the null hypothesis with 95 percent confidence. If, alternatively, 0 were found outside the confidence interval, we could reject the null hypothesis with 95 percent confidence. Confidence intervals are routinely used to test hypotheses in political science, and you will see them frequently used this way in books and journal articles.

CONCLUSION

We began this chapter with a discussion of the normal distribution and the closely related Student's t distribution. The information in the associated z and t tables is invaluable in analyzing data as it allows us to calculate z scores and confidence intervals and test hypotheses with z and t tests. The bulk of the chapter was dedicated to calculating and interpreting z scores, confidence intervals, and z and t tests. These basic tools will allow you to make interesting analyses of your own data as well as understand basic analysis in the political science literature. As a consumer of statistics, you should now have the ability to read results from academic, media, or government reports and understand what is meant by statistical significance. We stressed in this chapter that while the ability to compute these statistics is a useful skill, understanding how the statistics work, and how small changes in sample size or standard deviation can alter results and interpretation, is perhaps even more important. With this understanding, you will know not only how to use these statistics, but also why you are doing so and how they work.

TERMS INTRODUCED

Alternative hypothesis. A statement about the value or values of a population parameter. A hypothesis proposed as an alternative to the null hypothesis, represented by H_A.   250

Confidence interval. The range of values into which a population parameter is likely to fall for a given level of confidence.   244

Confidence level. The degree of belief or probability that an estimated range of values includes or covers the population parameter.   244

Null hypothesis. A statement that a population parameter equals a single or specific value. Often a statement that the difference between two populations is zero.   250

Research hypothesis. A statement about the value or values of a population parameter. A hypothesis proposed as an alternative to the null hypothesis, represented by H_A.   250

Statistical hypotheses. Two types of hypotheses essential to hypothesis testing: null hypotheses and research or alternative hypotheses.   249

Statistical significance. The probability of making a type I error.   252

Test of statistical significance. A convention for testing hypotheses that focuses on the probability of making a type I error.   252

Type I error. Error made by rejecting a null hypothesis when it is true.   251

Type II error. Error made by failing to reject a null hypothesis when it is not true.   252

z score. The number of standard deviations by which a score deviates from the mean score.   240

SUGGESTED READINGS

Abelson, Robert P. *Statistics as Principled Argument.* Hillsdale, NY: Lawrence Erlbaum Associates, 1995.

Agresti, Alan. *An Introduction to Categorical Data Analysis.* New York: Wiley, 1996.

Agresti, Alan, and Barbara Finlay. *Statistical Methods for Social Sciences.* Upper Saddle River, NJ: Prentice Hall, 1997.

Agresti, Alan, and Christine Franklin. *Statistics: The Art and Science of Learning from Data.* Upper Saddle River, NJ: Prentice Hall, 2007.

Lewis-Beck, Michael. *Data Analysis: An Introduction.* Thousand Oaks, CA: Sage, 1995.

Velleman, Paul, and David Hoaglin. *Applications, Basics, and Computing of Exploratory Data Analysis.* Pacific Grove, CA: Duxbury Press, 1983.

NOTES

1. For the technically disposed reader, an important theorem in statistics states that, given random samples of size 30 or more cases, the distribution of the sample means of a variable Y is approximately a normal distribution with a mean equal to μ (the mean of the population from which the sample was drawn) and a standard deviation of $\hat{\sigma}_{\bar{Y}} = \hat{\sigma} / \sqrt{N}$, also known as the *standard error* of the mean. It measures how much variation (or imprecision) there is in the sample estimator of the mean.

2. It is important to note that we are claiming that the data are normally distributed in the sampling distribution in order to use the normal distribution.

3. Federal Election Commission, "Official 2016 Presidential General Election Results," January 30, 2017. Last accessed September 13, 2018. Available at https://transition.fec.gov/pubrec/fe2016/2016presgeresults.pdf.

4. The probability of making a type II error depends on how far the true value of the population parameter is from the hypothesized one. In addition, for a fixed α, the probability of a type II error (β) decreases as the sample size increases. The probability of detecting and thus rejecting a false null hypothesis is called the power of the test and equals $1 - \beta$. Power is an extremely important issue in statistics. Many commonly used inferential tests may have relatively low power. Excellent introductions to the topic are Jacob Cohen, *Statistical Power Analysis for the Behavioral Sciences*, 2nd ed. (Hillsdale, NJ: Lawrence Erlbaum Associates, 1988); and Jacob Cohen, "A Power Primer," *Psychological Bulletin* 112, no. 1 (1992): 155–59. Accessed February 28, 2019. Available at https://www.ncbi.nlm.nih.gov/pubmed/19565683.

5. Building statistical inference on the idea of repeated samples initially makes students uneasy since it is indeed a difficult concept. Even more interesting is that it bothers many researchers in the field. For a readable introduction to this debate, see Bruce Western,

"Bayesian Analysis for Sociologists," *Sociological Methods and Research* 28, no. 1 (1999): 7–11.

6. We present here the formula for use when we assume that variances are equal. There is a separate equation for the case when we assume that variances are unequal. There are tests for equality of variances, but none performs especially well in all circumstances.

See Alan Agresti and Barbara Finlay, *Statistical Methods for the Social Sciences* (Upper Saddle River, NJ: Prentice Hall, 1997), 220–24. For a more technical discussion, see Richard J. Larsen and Morris L. Marx, *An Introduction to Mathematical Statistics and Its Applications* (Englewood Cliffs, NJ: Prentice Hall, 1981), 329–33.

STUDENT STUDY SITE

for CQ Press

Give your students the SAGE edge!

SAGE edge offers a robust online environment featuring an impressive array of free tools and resources for review, study, and further exploration, keeping both instructors and students on the cutting edge of teaching and learning. Learn more at **edge.sagepub.com/johnson9e.**

13 ANALYZING RELATIONSHIPS FOR CATEGORICAL DATA

In this chapter and in chapter 14, we examine a number of techniques to describe and measure the association between two variables (bivariate analysis) and between more than two variables (multivariate analysis). In these chapters, we also continue the discussion begun in chapter 12 regarding the testing of statistical hypotheses. In this chapter, we present methods for analyzing and reporting relationships between variables when the independent variable is categorical (a nominal- or ordinal-level measure) and the dependent variable is either categorical or numerical (an interval- or ratio-level measure). In addition to demonstrating how to use tables and graphs to show relationships, we discuss measures of association (statistics that summarize or measure the strength of a relationship) and tests of statistical significance for categorical data.

THE BASICS OF IDENTIFYING AND MEASURING RELATIONSHIPS

Determining how the values of one variable are related to the values of another is one of the foundations of empirical social science inquiry. This determination touches on several matters that we consider in the following sections:

- The level (or scale) of measurement of the variables: Different kinds of measurement necessitate different techniques.

- The "form" of the relationship: One can ask if changes in X move in lockstep with increases (or decreases) in Y or whether there is a more complicated connection.

- The strength of the relationship: It is possible that some levels of X will *always* be associated with certain

CHAPTER OBJECTIVES

13.1 Describe how to begin exploring the relationship between categorical variables.

13.2 Describe the shapes or types of bivariate relationships.

13.3 Explain how to construct and interpret bivariate contingency tables.

13.4 Understand how measures of association measure the strength of relationships between variables.

13.5 Understand how to choose an appropriate measure of association.

13.6 Introduce the chi-square statistic to test hypotheses involving categorical data.

13.7 Explain how to interpret contingency tables once a third (control) variable is introduced.

13.8 Describe the analysis of the difference between means for more than two means.

values of Y; more commonly, though, there is only a tendency for the values to covary, and the weaker the tendency, the less the "strength" of the relationship.

- Numerical summaries of relationships: Social scientists strive to boil down all the different aspects of a relationship to a single number that reveals the type and strength of the association. These numerical summaries, however, depend on how relationships are defined.

Level of Measurement

Just as the level of measurement of a variable was important in the selection of appropriate descriptive statistics, so too is it important in selecting the appropriate method for investigating relationships between variables. Procedures for measuring relationships are summarized in table 13-1[1]. These procedures are discussed in this chapter and in chapter 14.

Types of Relationships

A relationship between two variables, Y and X, can take one of several forms.

- General association: The values of one variable—Y, say—tend to be associated with specific values of the other variable, X. This definition places no restrictions

TABLE 13-1 ■ Levels of Measurement and Statistical Procedures: A Summary		
Type of Dependent Variable	**Type of Independent Variable(s)**	**Procedure**
Quantitative[a]	Dichotomous[b]	Difference of means, boxplots
Quantitative	Categorical[c] More than two categories	One-way analysis of variance (ANOVA) Boxplots
Categorical	Categorical	Cross-classification (contingency) tables analysis: measures of association
Quantitative	Quantitative and/or categorical	Linear regression Scatterplots
Dichotomous[b]	Quantitative and/or categorical (nominal and/or ordinal)	Logistic regression

[a]Ratio- or interval-level variables.

[b]A dichotomous variable has two categories.

[c]Nominal- or ordinal-level variables.

on how the values relate; the only requirement is that knowing the value of one variable helps to know or predict the value of the other. For example, if religion and party identification are associated, then certain members of certain sects should tend to identify with certain political parties. Discovering that a person is Catholic should say something about his or her partisanship. If there is no connection at all between the values of Y and X, we assert that they are *independent* of one another.

- Monotonic correlation:
  - Positive: High values of one variable are associated with high values of the other, and, conversely, low values are associated with low values. On a graph, $X–Y$ values drift upward from left to right (see figure 13-1a). A line drawn through the graph will be curved but *never goes down once it is on its way up*.
  - Negative: High values of Y are associated with low values of X, and—equally—low values of Y are associated with high values of X. In figure 13-1b, a graph of $Y–X$ pairs drifts downward from left to right and *never turns back up*.

- Linear correlation: In this particular type of monotonic relationship, plotted $Y–X$ points fall on (or, at least, close to) a straight line. (Figure 13-1c shows an example of a positive linear correlation.) If the plotted values of Y and X fall on a straight line that slopes downward from left to right, the relation is called a negative correlation (see figure 13-1d).

Variables may vary together in other patterns, as when values of X and Y increase together until some threshold is met and then decline. Since these curvilinear patterns of association are hard to analyze, we set them aside in this book.

TABLE SUMMARIES OF CATEGORICAL VARIABLE ASSOCIATIONS

A **cross-tabulation** or **contingency table** shows the joint or bivariate relationship between two categorized (nominal and/or ordinal) variables. Contingency refers to the idea that we are investigating whether the value of the dependent variable is contingent upon the value of the independent variable. We show how to construct a cross-tabulation table in the How It's Done box on page 271.

Let's start out using this procedure to investigate a hypothesis: "The greater one's party loyalty, the greater one's willingness to spend time and money on politics." Here the independent variable, level of partisanship, taps into the degree or intensity of partisan feelings, not their political direction. Hence, "Independents" are coded 1; "leaning Democrats or Republicans" get 2; those who simply identify with either party, but not strongly, receive scores of 3; and, finally, the strong partisans of either party (those who said they "strongly" identified with their party) are 4. This is an ordinal scale that extends from 1, *least partisan*, to 4, *most partisan*, with (we hope) more or less equally spaced psychological levels in between.

FIGURE 13-1 ■ **Types of Correlation**

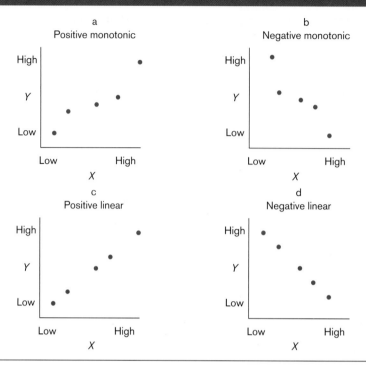

The data in table 13-2 provide a simple test of the hypothesis that partisanship is related to political activity—in this case, donating money to a political organization or cause. "Reading" the table is straightforward. The sample consists of 134 nonpartisans, those who state no preference for either party. Similarly, there are 141 "weak" partisans who lean toward one or the other party but do not identify with either; 359 moderates (Democrats or Republicans); and 322 highly partisan individuals, those who use the adjective *strong* to describe their party affiliations. (See the row labeled "Totals.") Next consider how the Independents are distributed on the dependent variable, donated or not. We see that 123, or about 92 percent (123 ÷ 134 = .92), of them report not having contributed in the last year. By the same token, fewer than 9 percent did donate. (Look at the next row down marked "Yes, donated.") Going across the "Yes" row, it is apparent that as partisanship increases, so too does the proportion of respondents who contribute. In fact, we find a 24-percentage-point difference between strong and nonpartisan: 8 percent versus 32 percent. The behavior of those in the middle partisan categories fits the pattern, except that for some reason the "weak" group gives more than the "moderates" do. (These sorts of anomalies arise all the time in survey research and invite us to think carefully about our measurements and data analysis. Did we make a coding mistake, for instance?) Overall, then, we could conclude that the research hypothesis is tenable. We might even say there is a positive monotonic correlation (with the exception just noted).

Notice how we use the numbers in the table to talk about the relationship. Because there are only two categories of the dependent variable, we look at one category ("Yes, donated") of the dependent variable and compare the percent of people in the first category of the independent variable (nonpartisan) who donated to the percent of people in the last category (strong partisans) who donated. Why? Because level of partisanship is an ordinal-level measure and we would expect the largest differences between categories of the independent variable to be between the categories at the ends of the scale. We tentatively conclude the bigger the difference, the bigger the relationship. We also look at the percentages for categories in between to see if they fall in between the two end values and if the increase was monotonic as we would expect. In this case, as noted, there was one "blip."

HOW IT'S DONE
BUILDING A CROSS-TABULATION

Suppose you have a dependent or response variable (Y) with two categories, A and B, and an independent variable (X) with three levels, L, M, and H. To construct a cross-tabulation, find each observation's scores on Y and X and the cell in a table that corresponds to these values. Mark the observation's position with a tally mark ("/"). Do the same for all N cases and write the totals in each cell. Add across the rows and then down the columns to obtain the row and column *marginal* totals.

Now comes the step that is critical in obtaining useful results: The numbers in each cell must be converted *correctly* to percentages. If the categories of the independent variable are column categories

(as they are in this example), calculate the percentage of cases in each cell based on the total number of cases in the column. Doing this for the first column in the top cell, we would get 7 divided by 9, or 77.8 percent. For the next cell, we get 2 divided by 9, or 22.2 percent. These percentages add to 100 for the column. Rarely do researchers construct a cross-tabulation table by hand. Instead, statistical packages are used, but you will have to choose whether the percentages are calculated by column or by row. In this example, we have calculated them by column as is correct when the independent variable categories are the column labels.

Categories of variable Y	Categories of variable X			Totals of row tallies
	L	M	H	
A	*//// //* 7 77.8%	*//// //// //* 12 66.7%	*////* 5 38.5%	24 60.0%
B	*//* 2 22.2%	*//// /* 6 33.3%	*//// ///* 8 61.5%	16 40.0%
Totals of column tallies	9 100%	18 100%	13 100%	40 100%

TABLE 13-2 ■ Level of Partisanship: Donating Money				
Donated Money?	**Nonpartisan (Independent)**	**Weak**	**Moderate**	**Strong**
No, did not donate	91.8%	71.6%	87.5%	68.0%
	(123)	(101)	(314)	(219)
Yes, donated	8.2%	28.4%	12.5%	32.0%
	(11)	(40)	(45)	(103)
Totals	100%	100%	100%	100%
	(134)	(141)	(359)	(322)

Question: "During the last 12 months, have you done any of the following? Donated money to a political organization or group."

Note: Cell entries are percentages and (frequencies).

Source: United States Citizenship, Involvement, Democracy Survey, 2006.

HELPFUL HINTS
CATEGORIES WITH "TOO FEW" CASES

A widely accepted rule of thumb asserts that percentages based on twenty or fewer observations are not reliable indicators and should not be reported or should be reported with "warning signs." Suppose, for example, we were looking at the relationship between ethnicity and partisanship and a survey contained only fifteen Asian American respondents who identified as strong Republicans. This estimate is based on such a small number (15) that many readers and analysts may not have confidence in it. Two possible solutions come to mind. First, use a symbol (for example, †) to indicate "too few cases." Alternatively, where appropriate, a category with too few cases may be combined with another one to increase the total frequency.

Now let's use another example to point out some other aspects of using contingency tables. In this example, we examine the relationship between gender and party identification (see table 13-3)—is there a gender gap?

If we compare males and females, we can see that 21.4 percent of females identify as strong Democrats, almost 6 percentage points more than males (15.6 percent). Females also tend to identify as weak Democrats 4 percentage points more than males. For Independent-leaning Democrats, the difference between males and females is smaller and in the opposite direction (18.5 percent versus 16.3 percent). Males are slightly more likely than females to identify as Independents (12.9 percent versus 10.2 percent). With the exception of Independent-leaning Republicans where males identify 4.5 percentage points more than

TABLE 13-3 ■ Cross-Tabulation of Gender by Party Identification (7 categories)		
	Gender	
Party Identification Response Category	**Male**	**Female**
Strong Democrat	15.6% (162)	21.4% (270)
Weak Democrat	13.0% (135)	17.1% (216)
Independent-leaning Democrat	18.5% (192)	16.3% (206)
Independent	12.9% (134)	10.2% (128)
Independent-leaning Republican	14.0% (146)	9.5% (120)
Weak Republican	12.9% (134)	12.5% (157)
Strong Republican	13.2% (137)	12.9% (163)
Total N = 2,300	100.0% (1,040)	100.0% (1,260)

Source: 2008 American National Election Study.

Note: Numbers in parentheses are frequencies.

females, there is very little difference between males and females in identification with the Republican Party. So, what might we conclude? There is a slight gender gap when it comes to identifying with the Democratic Party.

What would happen if we used fewer categories of partisan identification? Some information would be lost, but perhaps we would be able to see any differences between males and females more clearly if we looked at their identification as Democrats, Independents, and Republicans. This is shown in Table 13-4. (For the moment, ignore the information at the base of the table.)

With only three categories of party identification, we can see that females identify with the Democratic party 10 percentage points more than males (38.6 percent versus

TABLE 13-4 ■ Cross-Tabulation of Gender by Party Identification (3 categories)		
	Gender	
Party Identification Response Category	**Male**	**Female**
Democrat	28.6% (297)	38.6% (486)
Independent	45.4% (472)	36.1% (454)
Republican	26.1% (271)	25.4% (320)
Total N = 2,300	100% (1,040)	100% (1,260)

$\lambda = .02$; Somers' $D = -.079$; tau-$c = -.078$; $\gamma = -.120$; chi-square = 29.28, df = 2, $p = .000$.

Source: 2008 American National Election Study

Note: Numbers in parentheses are frequencies.

28.6 percent), that males are more likely than females to be Independents (45.4 percent versus 36.1 percent), and males and females are very similar to each other when it comes to identifying with the Republican Party. The lesson here is that it may be useful to work with fewer categories to get a general impression of the relationship, then dig further by looking at differences within strengths of identification with parties.

In each of the contingency tables we have presented so far, the independent variable has been the column variable with the categories of the independent variable displayed across the top of the table. Percentages are calculated for each cell based on the number of cases in each column so that the column percentages add to 100 for each column. This is the convention, but in some instances, it may make sense to have the categories of the independent variable displayed down the side (perhaps to make a table fit better on a page). In this situation, the independent variable becomes the row variable, and the percentages must be calculated on the row so that the percentages add up to 100 for each row.

In most statistical packages, you must request whether you want row percentages or column percentages: If this is the case, you want to be very sure that you ask for the right ones. Let's look at how asking for row percentages in the table with gender and party identification will change things. Table 13-5 suggests what might result, and the possible difficulties of interpretation. If you were not careful, you might conclude that there was a huge gender difference on "Democrat," 38 percent versus 62 percent. But this is not what the numbers mean. There are 782 Democrats in the sample (look in the last column), of which 38 percent

TABLE 13-5 ■ Row Percentages Are Not the Same as Column Percentages

Party Identification Response Category	Gender		
	Male	Female	Total
Democrat	38%	62%	100%
	(297)	(485)	(782)
Independent	51%	49%	100%
	(472)	(454)	(926)
Republican	46%	54%	100%
	(271)	(319)	(590)
Totals	45.3%	54.7%	100%
	(1,040)	(1,258)	(2,298)

Source: 2008 American National Election Study.

Note: Numbers in parentheses are frequencies.

are men and 62 percent women. It would be reasonable to say that Democrats tend to be women, whereas Independents are about half male and half female. Still, if in your mind one variable (e.g., party identification) depends on another variable (e.g., gender) and you want to measure the effect of the latter on the former, make sure the percentages are based on the independent variable category totals.

MEASURING STRENGTH OF RELATIONSHIPS IN TABLES

Do the data in table 13-4 support the hypothesis of a "gender gap"? Well, yes to some degree. There is a difference between genders in their identification as Democrats or Independents, but not as Republicans. To put our findings into perspective, what would a "strong" relationship look like?

The strength of an association refers to how different the observed values of the dependent variable are in the categories of the independent variable. In the case of cross-classified variables, the strongest relationship possible between two variables is one in which the value of the dependent variable for every case in one category of the independent variable differs from that of every case in another category of the independent variable. We might call such a connection a *perfect relationship*, because the dependent variable is perfectly associated with the independent variable; that is, there are no exceptions to the pattern. If the results can be applied to future observations, a perfect relationship between the independent and dependent variables enables a researcher to predict accurately a case's value on the dependent variable given a known value of X.

Assume we want to know if a connection exists between people's region of residency and attitudes about immigration. (The hypothesis might be that southerners and westerners are less favorable than citizens in other parts of the country.) An example of a perfect relationship is shown in table 13-6. Notice that 100 percent of the easterners and midwesterners favor comprehensive change, whereas 100 percent of the southerners and westerners do not.

A weak relationship would be one in which the differences in the observed values of the dependent variable for different categories of the independent variable are slight. In fact, the weakest observed relationship is one in which the distribution is identical for all categories of the independent variable—in other words, one in which no relationship appears to exist.

The percentages in table 13-7 show no relationship between the independent and dependent variables. The relative frequencies (that is, percentages) are identical across all categories of the independent variable. Another way of thinking about nil relationships is to consider that knowledge of someone's value on the independent variable does not help predict his or her score on the dependent variable. In table 13-7, 48 percent of the northerners "favor

TABLE 13-6 ■ Example of a Perfect Relationship between Region and Comprehensive Immigration Reform

Opinion	Region			
	East	Midwest	South	West
Favor immigration reform	100%	100%	0%	0%
Do not favor immigration reform	0%	0%	100%	100%
Total	100%	100%	100%	100%

Note: Hypothetical responses to the question, "Do you favor comprehensive immigration reform?"

TABLE 13-7 ■ Example of a Nil Relationship between Region and Opinions about Comprehensive Immigration Reform

Opinion	Region			
	East	Midwest	South	West
Favor immigration reform	48%	48%	48%	48%
Do not favor immigration reform	52%	52%	52%	52%
Total	100%	100%	100%	100%

Note: Hypothetical responses to the question, "Do you favor comprehensive immigration reform?"

reform," but so do 48 percent of the respondents in each of the other regions. The conclusions are that (1) slightly more than half of the respondents in the survey want changes in immigration laws, and (2) there is *no* difference among the regions on this point. Consequently, the hypothesis that region affects opinions would not be supported by this evidence.

Most observed contingency tables, like table 13-4, fall between these extremes. That is, there may be a slight (but not nil) relationship, a strong (but not perfect) relationship, or a "moderate" relationship between two variables. Deciding which is the case requires the analyst to examine carefully the relative frequencies and determine if there is a substantively important pattern. When asked "Is there a relationship between *X* and *Y*?" the answer will usually not be an unequivocal yes or no. Instead, the reply rests on judgment. If you think yes is right, then make the case by describing differences among percentages between categories of the independent variable. If, however, your answer is no, then explain why you think any observed differences are more or less trivial. A little later in the chapter, we present some additional methods and tools that help measure the strength of relationships.

Direction of a Relationship

In addition to assessing the strength of a relationship, one can examine its "direction." The **direction of a relationship** shows which values of the independent variable are associated with which values of the dependent variable. This is an especially important consideration when the variables are ordinal or have ordered categories such as *high, medium,* and *low* or *strongly agree* to *strongly disagree*, or the categories can reasonably be interpreted as having an underlying categorical spectrum, such as "least" to "most" liberal.

Table 13-8 displays the relationship between a scale of education (call it *X*) and a measure of interest in the presidential campaign (*Y*). Both variables have an inherent order. The education variable runs from least to most, while responses to the question about interest in the presidential campaign go from most to least interest.

Take a moment to study the numbers in the table. Start with the lowest education category. About one-third of respondents in this category (37.6 percent) say they are highly interested. Next look at those in the middle education category. Here, more (39.1 percent) say their interest is high. Finally, looking at the highest education category, you see that the percentage of respondents with high interest is even higher (54.7 percent) than the previous two categories of education. So, as education increases, so does campaign interest. Looking at the percentages in the "low interest" row, notice that the pattern is reversed. As education increases, those saying they have "low interest" declines from 28.7 percent to 24.3 percent to 9.6 percent. So, low education is associated with low interest, and high education is associated with high interest, although the relationship is not perfect.

Assessing both the strength and type (direction) of a relationship in contingency tables requires looking at the percentages cell by cell, and that is good practice. But statisticians have developed sophisticated methods for distilling the frequencies down to a single number that indicates the strength of a relationship and, where appropriate, its direction.

TABLE 13-8 ■ Interest in Presidential Campaign by Level of Education

	Education (X)			
Campaign Interest (Y)	0–11 years	12 years	13 or more years	Total
High	37.6%	39.1%	54.7%	47.8%
	(118)	(267)	(720)	(1,105)
Moderate	33.8%	36.6%	35.8%	35.7%
	(106)	(250)	(471)	(827)
Low	28.7%	24.3%	9.6%	16.5%
	(90)	(166)	(126)	(382)
Total	100%	100%	100%	100%
	(314)	(683)	(1,317)	(2,314)

Tau-b = −.186; γ = −.30; Somers' D = −.193; chi-square = 122.898, df = 4, p = .000.

Source: 2008 American National Election Study.

MEASURES OF ASSOCIATION: STATISTICS FOR REPORTING THE STRENGTH OF RELATIONSHIPS IN TABLES

A **measure of association** describes in a single number the kind and strength of a relationship between the values of two variables. A **correlation coefficient** is also a measure of the strength of a relationship, but the term is generally reserved for use with linear relationships. As we have demonstrated, interpreting relationships using contingency tables is challenging, especially if the relationships are not really weak or really strong and the tables contain many cells. Comparing the strength of relationships between tables may be particularly difficult. Measures of association can simplify this process, but just as we cautioned in chapter 11 about the need to understand the calculation of statistics summarizing the values of a single variable, it is imperative to develop a feel for what measures of association do (and do not!) say about possibly complex relationships.

Essentially all measures of association assess the extent to which knowledge about an independent variable helps us to predict the value of the dependent variable. It is important to note at the outset that these coefficients (1) assume a particular level of measurement—nominal, ordinal, interval, or ratio—and (2) rest on a specific conception of association. Stated differently, each coefficient measures a specific type of association, and to interpret (translate) its numerical value into everyday language, you have to grasp the kind of association it is measuring. Two variables can be associated strongly according to one coefficient and weakly (or not all) by another. Therefore, whenever we describe a measure such as the correlation coefficient, we need to explain what kind of relationship it is intended to measure.

Here are some important properties of commonly used coefficients:

- Null value: Usually, zero indicates no association, but there are important exceptions to this rule of thumb.

- Maximum value: Some coefficients do not have a maximum value; they can be in theory very large. Many, however, are bounded: Normally, their upper and lower limits are 1.0 and −1.0. When a coefficient attains a bound, variables are said to be perfectly associated according to the coefficient's definition.

- Strength of relationship: Subject to lower and upper boundaries, a coefficient's absolute numerical value increases with the strength of the association. So, for example, a coefficient of .6 would indicate a stronger relationship than one of .3. (But the relationship would not necessarily be twice as strong. It all depends on how the statistic is defined.)

- Level of measurement: As indicated above, nominal, ordinal, and quantitative (ratio and interval) variables each require their own type of coefficient. You can, of course, pretend that ordinal scales are numeric and calculate a statistic intended for quantitative data—plenty of people do—but since lots of research has gone into measures of association for different levels of measurement and satisfactory alternatives exist, you should be able to find one or two that will fit your data.

- Symmetry: The numerical magnitude of some indices depends on which variable, Y or X, is considered independent. These are asymmetric measures. The value of a coefficient calculated with Y as dependent may very well differ from the same indicator using X as the dependent variable. A symmetric measure keeps the same value no matter which variable is treated as dependent or independent.

- Standardized or unstandardized: The measurement scale on which variables are measured affects the numerical value of some measures, whereas others are not so affected.

A Coefficient for Nominal Data

When one or both of the variables in a cross-tabulation are nominal, Goodman and Kruskal's lambda (λ) is commonly used. Another measure of association that can be used, instead of lambda, is phi (ϕ). We will discuss its calculation later in the chapter. Lambda is a proportional-reduction-in-error (PRE) measure. Some of the most useful measures of association rest on a PRE interpretation. Let's examine the logic behind lambda. Suppose you know how many people out of a given population support a proposed gun control measure and how many do not. You are asked to predict a randomly selected person's position on the issue. Absent any information about the randomly selected person, what would your prediction be? Your best guess would be to pick the category (oppose or support) most frequently observed in the population. Let's call this making a prediction using rule 1. Now suppose that rule 2 lets you know the person's score on a second variable, which you now take into account in making the prediction (e.g., you now know if the individual is a member of the National Rifle Association). Since you are guessing in both situations, you can expect to make some errors, but *if* the two variables are associated, then using the second rule should lead to fewer errors than following the first.

How many fewer errors depends on how closely the variables are related. If there is no association at all, the expected number of errors should be roughly the same, and the reduction will be minimal. If, on the other hand, the variables are perfectly connected, in the sense that there is a one-to-one connection between the categories of the two variables, you would expect no errors by following rule 2. Lambda (λ) can be represented as

$$\lambda = \frac{(E_1 - E_2)}{E_1}$$

where E_1 is the number of errors made using rule 1 and E_2 is the number made under rule 2.

Let us calculate lambda for the data in Table 13-9, which investigates the relationship between living in a coastal region (East, Gulf, West) or not and concern about climate change. Region is the independent variable, and concern about climate change is the dependent variable.

Step 1: Calculate E_1. Your best prediction about a person's concern about climate change without knowing where the person lives is "concerned" as this is the modal category (285), but your predictions would be wrong 195 times.

$$E_1 = 195$$

Step 2: Calculate E_2. Now we base our predictions on knowing in what region a person resides. For someone living on the East Coast, your best prediction is "concerned," but you would make forty errors. Your best prediction for someone living on the Gulf Coast is "concerned," making thirty-five errors. For someone living on the West Coast, the best prediction is again

TABLE 13-9 ■ Cross-Tabulation of Region and Concern about Climate Change					
	East	**Gulf**	**West**	**Not coastal**	**Totals**
Concerned	80	85	75	45	285
	67%	71%	63%	38%	60%
Not concerned	40	35	45	75	195
	33%	29%	37%	62%	40%
Totals	120	120	120	120	480

Note: Hypothetical data.

"concerned," with forty-five errors made. For someone not living in one of the coastal regions, your best prediction is "not concerned," with forty-five errors.

$$E_2 = 40 + 35 + 45 + 45 = 165$$

Step 3: Substitute E_1 and E_2 into the equation.

$$\lambda = \frac{(E_1 - E_2)}{E_1}$$

$$\lambda = \frac{(195 - 165)}{195}$$

$$\lambda = \frac{30}{195}$$

$$\lambda = .15$$

So, knowing where a person resides allows us to improve our predictions by 15 percent—an improvement, but a very modest one.

Lambda does have an important limitation or flaw, however. Consider table 13-10. There is a 15-percentage-point difference between the views of coastal and noncoastal residents, so there is a relationship, but in this case $\lambda = 0$. This is because the modal category of the dependent variable is the same for both categories of the independent variable. This is a prime example of why you should always look at the distributions in a contingency table and not just rely on a measure of association to tell you about the relationship between variables. Also it is best to look at more than one measure of association appropriate for the data you are analyzing.

One further note on the use of lambda: It definitely should be used when the independent variable is a nominal-level variable with more than two categories and the dependent variable is measured at the nominal or ordinal level. If, however, the independent variable is a dichotomous nominal-level variable (one that has only two values or categories) *and* the dependent variable is a dichotomous nominal-level variable or an ordinal variable, measures of association for ordinal-level measures can be used. Why is this? Because with only two categories, one

---

TABLE 13-10   ■   Cross-Tabulation Demonstrating Misleading Value of Lambda

	Coastal	Noncoastal	Totals
Concerned	150	120	270
	75%	60%	67.5%
Not concerned	50	80	130
	25%	40%	32.5%
Totals	200	200	400

$E_1 = 130$, $E_2 = (50 + 80) = 130$, $\lambda = (130 - 130) \div 130 = 0$.

category is the absence of (less than) the characteristic being measured. So, in this sense, there is an order to the categories. Let's now turn to measures of association that are used when both the independent and dependent variables are ordinal-level measures.

Coefficients for Ordinal Variables

There are several measures of association to choose from for ordinal-level measures. Among the most common statistics are Kendall's tau-*b*, Kendall's tau-*c*, Somers' *D* (two versions), and Goodman and Kruskal's gamma—named after the individuals who developed them. They are similar, but not identical, in how they summarize the contents of a two-way frequency table. The formulae for the statistics are shown in the How It's Done box on page 286.

HELPFUL HINTS
CHECK OUT HOW CATEGORICAL VARIABLES ARE CODED

Computer statistical packages assume that an ordinal variable coded as a 1 represents a lower value of the variable than when it is coded as a 2 or some other higher number. Check out the values of your variables to see if they correspond to this assumption.

Sometimes the creator of a data set will reverse the order so that a 1 represents the highest-ranked category. You may want to recode the variable to make interpretation of measures of association easier.

TABLE 13-11 ■ Table with Concordant, Discordant, and Tied Pairs

Variable Y	Variable X		
	Low	Medium	High
Low	Ike Jasmine	Fay	Carl
Medium	Hera	Ernesto	
High	Gus	Dawn	Alex

All of the ordinal coefficients of association (tau-*b*, tau-*c*, Somers' *D*, and gamma) use the number of pairs of cases of different kinds to summarize the relationship in a table. There are three types of pairs: "concordant," "discordant," and "tied." Take a look at table 13-11. It contains nine individuals (cases).

- A *concordant pair* is a pair in which one case is *higher* on *both* variables than the other case. Fay is concordant with Alex. Hera is concordant with Dawn and

Alex, and Ernesto is concordant with Alex. Ike and Jasmine are concordant with Ernesto, Dawn, and Alex because Ernesto, Dawn, and Alex are higher on both X and Y compared to Ike and Jasmine.

- A *discordant pair* is one in which one case is *lower* on one of the variables but *higher* on the other. Carl, for example, has a higher score on X but a lower score on Y compared to either Ernesto, Hera, Gus, or Dawn. Therefore, these pairs "violate" the expectation that as one variable increases, so does the other.

- A *tied pair* is a pair in which both observations have the same value on one or both variables. There are lots of tied pairs in this table: Alex and Dawn are tied on Y (they both are in the "high" category), Alex and Carl are tied on X (but not Y), and Ike and Jasmine are tied on both X and Y. (There are several other tied pairs in the table.)

The basic comparison made is between the number of concordant and discordant pairs. If both types of pairs are equally numerous, the statistic will be zero, indicating no relationship. If concordant pairs are more numerous, the coefficient will be positive; if discordant pairs outnumber concordant pairs, the statistic will be negative. The degree to which concordant or discordant pairs predominate, or one kind of pair is more frequent than the other, affects the magnitude of the statistic. Hence, if only the main diagonal were filled with observations, all the pairs would be concordant, and the statistic would be +1—a perfect, positive relationship (see Table 13-12a). If only the minor (opposite) diagonal were filled with observations, all the pairs would be discordant, and the statistic would be −1—a perfect, negative relationship (see Table 13-12b).

As you can see in the How It's Done box (page 286), the coefficients differ in whether they consider the presence of ties. Gamma (γ), for example, is defined as

$$\gamma = \frac{(C - D)}{(C + D)}$$

It considers only concordant and discordant pairs. Gamma can attain its maximum (1 or −1) even if not all of the observations are on the main diagonal because it ignores all tied pairs. The other measures "discount the strength of the relationship by the number of ties in the table."[2] Hence, the absolute value of gamma will always be greater than or equal to that of any of the others.

Let's calculate gamma for the data in table 13-13. These are the same data as in table 13-8, except that the categories of the dependent variable, campaign interest, have been reordered so that they go from low to high, rather than high to low. We'll have more to say about this in a moment.

First let's calculate the number of concordant pairs. Start in the upper left cell, which has 90 respondents. We would pair them with other respondents in all cells that are down and to the right. Why? Because these other respondents have higher levels of education *and* higher levels of campaign interest, just as our hypothesis predicted. Move across the top row to the second cell. There are 166 respondents in this cell. We would pair them with

TABLE 13-12 ■ Perfect Positive and Negative Relationships			
	a. Every pair concordant (perfect positive monotonic relationship)		
	Variable X		
Variable Y	**High**	**Medium**	**Low**
High	Arthur		
Medium		Candy	
Low			Ed
	b. Every pair discordant (perfect negative monotonic relationship)		
	Variable X		
Variable Y	**High**	**Medium**	**Low**
High			Faith
Medium		Guy	
Low	Hilary		

TABLE 13-13 ■ Interest in Presidential Campaign by Level of Education				
	Education (X)			
Campaign Interest (Y)	**0–11 years**	**12 years**	**13 or more years**	**Total**
Low	28.7% (90)	24.3% (166)	9.6% (126)	16.5% (382)
Moderate	33.8% (106)	36.6% (250)	35.8% (471)	35.7% (827)
High	37.6% (118)	39.1% (267)	54.7% (720)	47.8% (1,105)
Total	100% (314)	100% (683)	100% (1,317)	100% (2,314)

respondents in the cells down and to the right. If we move to the third cell in the top row, we find there are no cells down and to the right. So, we move to the second row and repeat the pairing process. When we are finished, we will get the following value for C:

$$C = 90(250 + 471 + 267 + 720) + 166(471 + 720) + 106(267 + 720) + 250(720) = 636{,}048$$

To calculate the number of discordant pairs, start in the upper right cell of the table (126 respondents) and make pairs with respondents who are in cells down and to the left. Continue this pairing process to get all of the discordant pairs:

$$D = 126(106 + 250 + 118 + 267) + 166\ (106 + 118) + 471(118 + 267) + 250(118) = 341{,}385$$

Substituting C and D into the formula for gamma, we get this:

$$\gamma = (636{,}048 - 341{,}385) \div (636{,}048 + 341{,}385) = (294{,}663 \div 977{,}433) = .30$$

Interpreting measures of association is not straightforward. A rule of thumb is that absolute values of .3 or less represent weak relationships. If any of them reaches .4 or .5 in absolute value, there is an association worth paying attention to. But by themselves, the measures are not sufficient to assess how and how strongly one variable is related to another. You should ask the software to calculate all the coefficients, choose the appropriate ones for your table, *and* spend time visually inspecting the relative frequencies in the table.[3] Our calculation of gamma for table 13-13, therefore, shows a moderate relationship.

Now, look back to the bottom of table 13-8, where you will see that the values of several measures of association are reported. Here $\gamma = -.30$. Why does it have a negative sign? Computer programs assume that both variables will be ordered from lowest to highest. A positive measure of association will occur if the observations in a contingency table tend to fall along the diagonal going from upper left to bottom right. The sign will be negative if the observations fall along the diagonal going from bottom left to upper right.

Therefore, while the data are the same in tables 13-8 and 13-13 and examining the percentages within the contingeny tables will lead you to the same conclusion, the computer-generated statistics are different, and it is up to you to interpret them correctly. In this case, a negative sign for γ in table 13-8 does not mean there is a negative relationship between education and campaign interest. It is positive: campaign interest increases with education. The negative sign is simply the result of how the the data are coded and appear in the table.

Some other features of ordinal measures of association are worth noting. Tau-b is used for square tables (same number of rows and columns) whereas tau-c is used for rectangular tables. Somers' D is an "asymmetric" measure because its value depends on which variable is considered dependent. Therefore, there are really two possible versions: one, D_{YX}, has Y as the dependent variable, while the other, D_{XY}, treats X as dependent. *It is important that you know which is your independent variable and which is your dependent variable.*

HOW IT'S DONE
COMPUTING ORDINAL MEASURES OF ASSOCIATION

Let C = number of concordant pairs,

D = the number of discordant pairs,

T_X = the number of pairs tied only on X,

T_Y = the number of pairs tied only on Y,

T_{XY} = the number of pairs tied on both X and Y, and

m = the minimum of I or J, where I and J are the numbers of categories of Y and X, respectively.

Gamma: $\gamma = \dfrac{(C - D)}{(C + D)}$

Tau-b: $\tau_b = \dfrac{(C - D)}{\sqrt{(C + D + T_Y)}\sqrt{(C + D + T_X)}}$

Tau-c: $\tau_c = \dfrac{(C - D)}{N^2 \left[\dfrac{(m - 1)}{2m}\right]}$

Somers' D: $D_{YX} = \dfrac{(C - D)}{C + D + T_Y}$

The last point is worth emphasizing. None of the ordinal-level coefficients is appropriate if the relationship "curves," in the sense that as X increases, so does Y up to a certain point when an increase in X is accompanied by a decrease in Y. Consider table 13-14, which contains four observations. There is a "perfect" association: You tell me a person's value on X, and I will predict exactly her score on Y. Yet the number of concordant pairs (3) equals the number of discordant ones (3), so their difference is zero. This difference ($C - D$) appears in the numerator of all the coefficients, so they are all zero, implying no relationship. But there is an association; it's just not a correlation.

Let's go back and look at a contingency table that we discussed earlier. Table 13-4 (see page 274) includes several measures of association at the bottom of the table. They all show a very weak relationship. Lambda is very close to zero, and gamma has the highest value, with the values of Somers' D and tau-c in between. These are all appropriate measures to use for this table. Lambda is used when the independent variable is nominal and the dependent variable is either nominal or ordinal. But, because gender is a dichotomous variable, we can also use ordinal measures. Notice Somers' D, tau-c, and gamma all have negative

TABLE 13-14 ■ Perfect but Not Monotonic Relationship

Variable Y	Variable X			
	Very high	Medium high	Medium low	Very low
Very high				Doris
Medium high	Adele			
Medium low		Barbara		
Very low			Connie	

signs—why is this, and what does it mean? In calculating ordinal measures of association, male is the lower gender category, and Democrat is the lowest partisan category. In this table, high values of the independent variable (female) are associated with low values of the dependent variable (Democrat). Again, *it is important to take a look at how the values of the variables are arrayed in a table before jumping to a conclusion about the meaning of the sign of directional measures of association.*

CHI-SQUARE TEST FOR INDEPENDENCE

In chapter 12, we discussed tests for statistical significance when comparing means or proportions based on sample estimates. We can use the **chi-square (χ^2) statistic** to determine statistical significance for categorical data. This statistic essentially compares an observed result—the table produced by sample data—with a "hypothetical" table that would occur if, in the population, the variables were statistically independent. The chi-square measures the discrepancy between frequencies actually observed and those we would expect to see if there was *no* population association between the variables. When each observed cell frequency in a table equals the frequency expected under the null hypothesis of independence, chi-square will equal zero. Chi-square increases as the departures of observed and expected frequencies grow. There is no upper limit to how big the difference can become, but if it passes a certain point—a critical chi-square value, similar to the critical z and t values we worked with in chapter 12—we can reject the null hypothesis that the variables are independent.

To demonstrate chi-square, we will consider a null hypothesis that there is no difference between first- and second-year college students in regard to how well prepared they feel to debate national security. Table 13-15 reports a hypothetical distribution of student responses. The observed frequencies are shown in bold in the cross-tabulation. Expected frequencies in each cell of the table are found by multiplying the row and column marginal totals, and dividing by the sample size. As an example, consider the first cell in table 13-15. That cell is in the first row, first column of the table, so multiply the row total, 1,010, by the column total, 1,000, and then divide by 2,000, the total sample size in this table. The result is

$$\frac{1,010 \times 1,000}{2,000} = 505$$

This is the *expected* frequency in the first cell of the table; it is what we would expect to get in a sample of 2,000 with 1,010 answering "well prepared" and 1,000 first-year college students, *if there is statistical independence in the population.* This is more than we actually have in the cell, so there is a difference. What about the other cells? We performed the same calculation for each of the other five cells in the table, and report the expected frequency in italics under the observed counts that are in bold.

We want to stress that this procedure can be interpreted as measuring the adequacy of a simple model (the model of no association) to these observed data. If the adequacy or fit is good, we say the model partially explains the data, which in turn is a manifestation of the

TABLE 13-15 ■ Feelings of Preparedness to Debate National Security by Year in College			
How well prepared do you feel?	First-Year Student	Second-Year Student	Totals
Well prepared	**410**	**600**	**1,010**
	505	*505*	
Uncertain	**300**	**250**	**550**
	275	*275*	
Not well prepared	**290**	**150**	**440**
	220	*220*	
Totals	**1,000**	**1,000**	**2,000**

Note: Numbers in **bold** font are observed frequencies; those in *italics* are expected frequencies under the hypothesis of statistical independence.

real world. If the assumption of independence is not supported, we would not anticipate that the expected frequencies would equal the observed frequencies except by chance.

The overall measure of fit—the observed test statistic—is found by, in effect, comparing observed and expected frequencies. If the sum of differences is relatively small, we do not reject the hypothesis of no association. But, if in the aggregate the discrepancy between observed and expected numbers is large, then the model upon which the expected frequencies are calculated is not a summary of the data, and the decision will be to reject the null hypothesis. As with other tests of statistical significance, how large the discrepancy must be to reject the null hypothesis depends on the α level chosen. The first step in using the chi-square test is to calculate the observed chi-square value, which is the sum of the squared differences between observed and expected frequencies, divided by the expected frequency for each cell. Using the information in Table 13-15, we get this:

$$\chi^2 = \frac{(410-505)^2}{505} + \frac{(600-505)^2}{505} + \frac{(300-275)^2}{275} + \frac{(250-275)^2}{275} + \frac{(290-220)^2}{220} +$$
$$\frac{(150-220)^2}{220}$$
$$\chi^2 = \frac{(-95)^2}{505} + \frac{(95)^2}{505} + \frac{(25)^2}{275} + \frac{(-25)^2}{275} + \frac{(70)^2}{220} + \frac{(-70)^2}{220}$$
$$\chi^2 = \frac{9025}{505} + \frac{9025}{505} + \frac{625}{275} + \frac{625}{275} + \frac{4900}{220} + \frac{4900}{220}$$
$$\chi^2 = 17.87 + 17.87 + 2.27 + 2.27 + 22.27 + 22.27$$
$$\chi^2 = 84.82$$

This observed chi-square is 84.82, which we compare to a critical value to help decide whether or not to reject the null hypothesis. The chi-square test is always one-tailed. We reject the null hypothesis if the observed chi-square equals or exceeds the critical chi-square—that is, if $\chi^2_{obs} \geq \chi^2_{critical}$. Otherwise, do not reject the null. The null hypothesis for this example is that the two variables are independent. The alternative is that they are not. Before we can use the chi-square table in appendix C to do this, we need to pick a level of significance and calculate degrees of freedom. Here we will use $\alpha = .01$ level of significance. The degrees of freedom for the chi-square distribution equal the number of rows (R) minus 1 times the number of columns (C) minus 1, or $(R-1)(C-1)$. In this example, df $= (3-1)(2-1)$, or 2.

Now we have all the information we need to find the critical chi-square value. Using the chi-square table in appendix C, read down the first column (df) until you find the degrees of freedom (2 in this case), and then go across to the column for the desired level of significance. With 2 degrees of freedom, the critical value for the .01 level is 9.21. Since the observed chi-square is greater than the critical chi-square value, we reject the null hypothesis of statistical independence.

Large values of chi-square occur when the observed and expected tables are quite different and when the sample size upon which the tables are based is large. A weak relationship in a large sample may attain statistical significance, whereas a strong relationship found in a small sample may not. The lesson to be drawn is that when dealing with large samples (say, $n > 1,500$), small, inconsequential relationships can be statistically significant.[4] As a result, we must take care to distinguish between statistical significance and substantive importance or strength of the relationship.

In addition to the measures of association we described earlier in this chapter, there is one more, **phi** (ϕ), which is based on chi-square. It divides the observed chi-square statistic by n and takes the square root of the quotient. In ideal situations, phi varies between 0 and 1, but in many bivariate distributions, it can exceed 1.

HOW IT'S DONE
THE PHI COEFFICIENT

$$\phi = \sqrt{\frac{\chi^2}{n}},$$

where n is the sample size.

So far, we have discussed how to construct and interpret contingency tables to examine relationships between two categorical variables, how to use and interpret measures of association to assess the strength of a relationship, and how to use the chi-square test of statistical significance. But explaining political phenomena is never so simple as to involve only one independent variable. So now we turn to the task of analyzing categorical data with more than one independent variable.

MULTIVARIATE ANALYSIS OF CATEGORICAL DATA

Suppose that we have hypothesized a relationship between attitudes toward government spending and presidential voting. Our hypothesis is that "the more a person favors a decrease in government spending, the more likely he or she is to vote Republican." Table 13-16 seems to confirm the hypothesis, since 64 percent of those who favored decreased spending voted Republican, whereas only 46 percent of those who favored keeping spending the same or increasing it voted Republican. This difference of 18 percentage points among a sample of 1,000 suggests that a relationship exists between attitudes toward government spending and candidate preferences.

At this point, you might ask, "Is there a causal relationship between opinion and vote [see the upper arrow diagram in figure 13-2], or does another factor, such as socioeconomic status (e.g., family income), create the apparent relationship?" Or, even if you are not interested in causality, a question arises: "Can the explanation of presidential voting be increased by including another variable?" After all, 36 percent of those who favored decreased spending (Democrats) voted contrary to the hypothesis, as did 46 percent of those in favor of maintaining or increasing spending levels (Republicans). Perhaps it would be possible to provide a better explanation for those voters' behavior. This is where **multivariate analysis**, data analysis techniques designed to test hypotheses involving more than two variables, come in to play.

A second independent variable that might affect presidential voting is personal income. People with higher earnings might favor decreased government spending because they feel they gain little from most government programs.[5] Those with higher incomes might also be

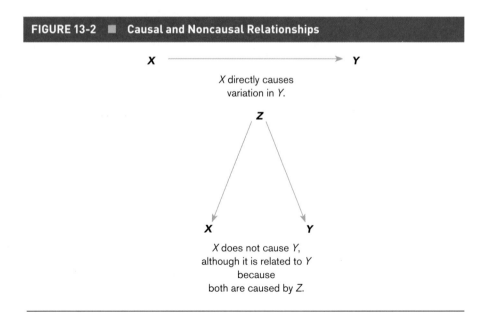

FIGURE 13-2 ■ Causal and Noncausal Relationships

X ⟶ Y

X directly causes
variation in Y.

Z

X   Y

X does not cause Y,
although it is related to Y
because
both are caused by Z.

TABLE 13-16 ■ Relationship between Attitudes toward Government Spending and Presidential Vote			
	Independent Variable: Attitudes toward Government Spending		
Dependent Variable: Presidential Vote	Decrease spending	Keep spending the same or increase it	(N)
Republican	64%	46%	(555)
Democratic	36%	54%	(445)
Total	100%	100%	
(N)	(550)	(450)	(1,000)

Note: Hypothetical data.

more likely to vote Republican because they perceive the Grand Old Party as supporting decreases in government spending. By the same token, people having lower incomes might feel both that increased government spending would help them *and* that Democrats generally support their interests. Therefore, income might influence both attitudes toward government spending and presidential voting, thus creating the appearance of a relationship between the two.

To consider the effect of income, we need to bring it explicitly into the analysis and observe the resulting relationship between attitudes and voting. In a **multivariate cross-tabulation**, we **control** for a third variable **by grouping**; that is, we group the observations according to their values on the third variable and then observe the relationship between opinions on spending and voting within each of these groups. In our example, each group consists of people with more or less the same income. Therefore, if a relationship between opinions on spending and voting in these groups remains, it cannot be due to income.

Table 13-17 shows what might happen were we to control for income by grouping respondents into three income levels: high, medium, and low. Notice that it contains three contingency tables: one for each category of income, the control variable. Within each of the categories of income, there is now *no* relationship between spending attitudes and presidential voting. Regardless of their attitudes on spending, 80 percent of respondents with high incomes voted Republican, 60 percent with medium incomes voted Republican, and 30 percent with low incomes voted Republican. Once the variation in income was removed by grouping those with similar incomes, the attitude–vote relationship disappeared. Consequently, income is a possible alternative explanation for the variation in presidential voting.

The original relationship, then, was spurious. Remember that a spurious relationship is one in which the association between two variables is caused by a third. Note, however, that these remarks do not mean that there is *no* relationship between spending attitudes and presidential voting, for there is such a relationship, as table 13-16 shows. But this original relationship occurred only because of the variables' relationships with a third factor, income. Thus, spending attitudes cannot be a cause of presidential voting because within income groups, they make no difference whatsoever. (See the lower arrow diagram in figure 13-2.)

Because we have been using hypothetical data, we can easily illustrate other outcomes. Suppose, for instance, the control variable had absolutely no effect on the relationship between attitudes and voting. The result might look like the outcomes in table 13-18. We now see that the strength and direction of the relationship between attitudes and voting are the same at all levels of income. In this situation, members of the upper-income group behave just like those in the lower levels. Given these data, we might be tempted to support the argument that attitudes toward government spending are causally related to candidate

TABLE 13-17 ■ Spurious Relationship between Attitudes and Presidential Voting When Income Is Controlled			
Control Variable: Income	Independent Variable: Attitudes toward Government Spending		
Dependent Variable: Presidential Vote	Decrease spending	Keep spending the same or increase it	(N)
High income			
Republican	80%	80%	(240)
Democratic	20%	20%	(60)
Total	100%	100%	
(N)	(250)	(50)	(300)
Medium income			
Republican	60%	60%	(210)
Democratic	40%	40%	(140)
Total	100%	100%	
(N)	(200)	(150)	(350)
Low income			
Republican	30%	30%	(105)
Democratic	70%	70%	(245)
Total	100%	100%	
(N)	(100)	(250)	(350)

Note: Hypothetical data.

choice. But, of course, a critic could always say, "But you didn't control for Z." That would be a valid statement, if the skeptic provided a plausible reason why Z would have an effect on the original relationship. A randomized controlled experiment, in contrast to an observational study, theoretically eliminates all alternative explanatory variables at one fell swoop.

These hypothetical data illustrate ideal situations. Consider, then, an actual multivariate cross-tabulation. Political pundits and campaign strategists, for example, are preoccupied with geographical variation in attitudes and voting. They talk of "blue" (Democratic)

TABLE 13-18 ■ Relationship between Attitudes and Presidential Voting after Income Is Controlled			
Control Variable: Income			
	Independent Variable: Attitudes toward Government Spending		
Dependent Variable: Presidential Vote	**Decrease spending**	**Keep spending the same or increase it**	**(N)**
High income			
Republican	64%	46%	(183)
Democratic	36%	54%	(117)
Total	100%	100%	
(N)	(250)	(50)	(300)
Medium income			
Republican	64%	46%	(197)
Democratic	36%	54%	(153)
Total	100%	100%	
(N)	(200)	(150)	(350)
Low income			
Republican	64%	46%	(179)
Democratic	36%	54%	(171)
Total	100%	100%	
(N)	(100)	(250)	(350)

Note: Hypothetical data.

and "red" (Republican) states to describe typical voting patterns in these areas. Let's investigate regional differences regarding an ongoing "cultural" or social issue, prayer in public schools. To start, we created a "region" variable by combining respondents in the 2008 General Social Survey (GSS) into four groups: (1) the "coasts," which include the Pacific, New England, and mid-Atlantic states; (2) the "industrial" upper midwestern states; (3) the traditional or Deep South; and (4) a conglomeration of south Atlantic and mountain states, which we label simply the "extended Sun Belt." The first two generally support Democrats for president and are thought to be centers of "liberalism." The remaining two are commonly identified with conservative and Republican voting patterns. (Needless to say, there is a lot of heterogeneity in these groupings; we use them merely for illustrative purposes.) Table 13-19 shows how people in different regions think about Supreme Court rulings limiting prayer in public schools. (For simplicity's sake, we have recoded the responses to "yes, favor" and "no, do not favor" prayer in the classroom.) The variation in the percentages saying "no" suggests an effect of region on public opinion. More than half of those on the coasts approve of the Court's decision, while only a quarter of those in the South do. The other regions fall in between. What, if anything, accounts for these differences?[6]

More precisely, is there something about a geographical area that induces people to think one way or another? Or—more likely—do different regions contain different kinds of voters, and do these characteristics—not geography, per se—explain variation in opinions? Since the South stands out so much and we are dealing with a religious issue, an obvious candidate variable to add to the mix is some kind of indicator of religiosity. After all, the Deep South was familiarly known as the "Bible Belt," and even today it is thought of as a stronghold of Christian conservatism. Therefore, let's include "fundamentalism" in the analysis. The GSS contains an item, "Fundamentalism/liberalism of respondent's religion," to which responses are coded *fundamentalist*, *moderate*, and *liberal*; the latter

TABLE 13-19 ■ Total Relationship between Region and School Prayer				
Prayer in public schools okay?	**Generally Democratic (Blue) States**		**Generally Republican (Red) States**	
	East and West Coast	*Industrial North Central*	*Extended Sun Belt*	*Traditional South*
Yes	46.4%	59.8%	59.7%	75.8%
No	53.6%	40.2%	40.3%	24.2%
	100%	100%	100%	100%
	(386)	(275)	(423)	(199)

$N = 1,283$; chi-square = 47.9, 3 df; $p = .000$; phi = 0.19.

Question: "The United States Supreme Court has ruled that no state or local government may require the reading of the Lord's Prayer or Bible verses in public schools. What are your views on this—do you approve or disapprove of the court ruling?"

Source: James A. Davis, Tom W. Smith, and Peter V. Marsden, *General Social Surveys*, 1972–2008, Roper Center for Public Opinion Research, University of Connecticut/Ann Arbor, MI: Inter-university Consortium for Political and Social Research.

category presumably includes atheists, agnostics, and skeptics, as well as religious people who nevertheless do not take sacred texts literally. Table 13-20 shows a multiway table in which the original region–opinion relationship is examined for each of the three levels of fundamentalism.

To make sense of the data, we need to explore each subtable individually and carefully. Look first, then, at the fundamentalists (table 13-20a). The overwhelming majority of respondents in *each* region favor allowing prayer in schools. The percentages run from 67 to more than 80 percent. There are differences, to be sure—the fundamentalists on the "coasts" appear to be a bit more secular than their counterparts elsewhere. Nonetheless, the relationship is rather weak. The same is true for moderates (the middle table), although the proportions saying "no" are somewhat larger. Finally, we see that the region–attitude association is strongest and clearest in the last category, "liberals." Except in the South, a majority of respondents oppose organized prayer reading in public education. But opposition declines as one moves across the table.[7] Further insight is achieved by looking at the chi-square statistics in each table and as compared to the overall chi-square in table 13-19. They seem to indicate a weak to nil association in the first two levels of fundamentalism and a moderate one in the third table. We see, for instance, that there is solid backing for school prayer (67 percent) even among nonfundamentalists in the South, but not so on the coasts, where the opposition exceeds 70 percent. So our overall conclusions might be that (1) there are regional differences in attitudes, and (2) these differences are partly explained by one's degree of religious commitment.

Using summary statistics such as categorical measures of association or observed chi-square statistics helps because we can quickly average them across tables. The overall chi-square for Table 13-19 is 47.9 with 3 degrees of freedom; the weighted (by number of cases in each subtable, N_j) average of chi-squares in table 13-20 is 12.2, again with 3 degrees of freedom. So the "controlled" relationship seems weaker than the total association. The average of the phi coefficients (remember that phi is the square root of the observed chi-square divided by the sample size) is a tad smaller than the value in the main table (.17 versus .19).[8]

Admittedly, this sort of analysis requires absorbing a lot of numbers and trying to discern patterns among them. Here are some guidelines, although in a moment we present a more formal procedure. (Figure 13-3 may help.)

Keep separate in your mind the original, uncontrolled relationship, $X–Y$. The goal is to see what happens to it when additional variables are introduced.

- If at each level or value of the conditioning variable, Z, there are approximately the same kind and degree of connection between X and Y as appear in the original, then Z may not be relevant to the $X–Y$ association.

- Are the controlled relationships on average weaker or smaller than the original? If so, Z may be a (partial) spurious cause of the $X–Y$ relationship, *or* there may be a spurious relationship or maybe a "causal sequence": that is, $X \rightarrow Z \rightarrow Y$. (Controlling for Z in either case reduces or eliminates the $X–Y$ association.)

TABLE 13-20 ■ **Controlled or Contingent or Conditional Relationships**

a. Religiosity = fundamentalist				
Prayer in public schools	The "Coasts"	Industrial North	Sun Belt	Traditional South
No	32.9%	15.4%	25.2%	20.0%
Yes	67.1%	84.6%	74.8%	80.0%
	100%	100%	100%	100%
	(51)	(64)	(143)	(85)

$N = 343$; chi-square = 5.68, 3 df; $p = .13$; phi = 0.13.

b. Religiosity = moderate				
Prayer in public schools	The "Coasts"	Industrial North	Sun Belt	Traditional South
No	47.1%	39.9%	41.8%	26.0%
Yes	52.9%	60.1%	58.2%	74.0%
	100%	100%	100%	100%
	(181)	(117)	(125)	(75)

$N = 498$; chi-square = 9.92, 3 df; $p = .02$; phi = 0.15.

c. Religiosity = liberal				
Prayer in public schools	The "Coasts"	Industrial North	Sun Belt	Traditional South
No	73.0%	59.3%	52.2%	32.6%
Yes	27.0%	40.7%	47.8%	67.4%
	100%	100%	100%	100%
	(132)	(89)	(140)	(34)

$N = 395$; chi-square = 23.06, 3 df; $p = .000$; phi = 0.24.

Source: Table 13-19.

- Is the relationship between X and Y strong at some levels of Z but not others? If so, there may be statistical **interaction**. Interaction means that the strength, direction, and nature of the X–Y relationship depend on levels of the control variable. At the high end of the Z scale, there may be little or no connection between X and Y, while in the middle there is a negative correlation and there is a modest negative

FIGURE 13-3 ■ How to Interpret Conditional Relationships

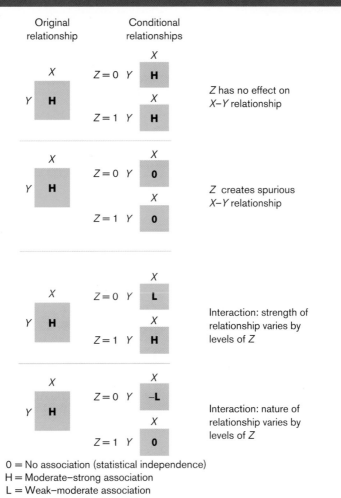

Legend:
0 = No association (statistical independence)
H = Moderate–strong association
L = Weak–moderate association

relationship for those cases with low values on Z. If interaction exists, the impact of X on Y depends on another variable and merits careful scrutiny. Such activity is sometimes referred to as "specifying" the relationship.

Sometimes graphs can be very helpful in sorting out relationships and the effects of controlling for another variable. Figure 13-4 looks at the relationship between age and partisan identification, controlling for gender. The lines show very clearly that identification with the Democratic Party increases with age for males (there is a monotonic relationship). The pattern for females is definitely not monotonic. Support for the Democratic Party among females is highest among females in the 41–50 and 61–older age groups, quite a bit higher than the other age groups. The line graph also allows us to look at the gender gap. Females identify with the

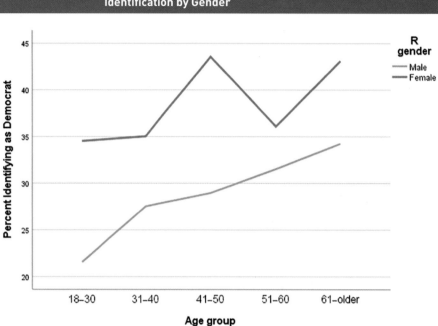

FIGURE 13-4 ■ Line Graph Showing Relationship between Age and Partisan Identification by Gender

Democratic Party more than males for all age groups. You can see that the gender gap is greatest for the 41–50 age group, followed by the 18–30 age group.

We conclude this section by comparing the analysis of cross-tabulations with the randomized experimental design discussed in chapter 6. The goal of the latter is to see if one factor causes another. By randomly assigning individuals to treatment (experimental) and control groups, the investigator (in theory at least) can scrutinize a relationship between X and Y uncontaminated by other variables, such as Z. In most research settings, however, randomization is simply not possible. Given a hypothesis about voter turnout and social class, for instance, how could a researcher randomly place someone in a particular occupation and then wait to see what effect this placement had on the person's behavior? Therefore, instead of using randomization to get rid of potentially contaminating variables, it is necessary to try to control for them manually. That is, the investigator has to explicitly identify variables (for example, Z) that might be influencing the X–Y relationship, measure them, and then statistically control for them just as we did in table 13-20. In that case, we looked at the association between the variables *within* levels of the third factor. This approach is possible if the control factor is categorical and the total number of cases is large. Controlling for more than one variable at a time is difficult because the number of tables generated becomes unwieldy. Therefore, other techniques are used when multiple variables are controlled for. These techniques are discussed in chapter 14.

ANALYSIS OF VARIANCE: ANALYZING THE DIFFERENCE BETWEEN MEANS FOR MORE THAN TWO MEANS

Analysis of variance, or **ANOVA**, extends the method of analyzing the difference between means (which we discussed in chapter 12) to the comparison of more than two means. In this section, we present a measure of association as well as a test of statistical significance used when we are comparing more than two means. As before, the dependent variable (Y) is quantitative. The independent or explanatory variable (X) is categorical and consists of several (more than two) categories. ANOVA treats the observations in the separate categories as independent samples from populations. If the data constitute random samples (and certain other conditions are met), you apply ANOVA to test a null hypothesis such as H_0: $\mu_1 = \mu_2 = \mu_3$ and so on, where the μs are the population means of the groups formed by X.

Suppose, for example, that you have a variable (X) with three categories—A, B, and C—and a sample of observations within each of those categories. For each observation, there is a measurement on a quantitative dependent variable (Y). Thus, for each of the categories or groups, you can find the mean of Y. ANOVA digs into such data to discover (1) if there are any differences among the means, (2) which specific means differ and by how much, and (3) assuming the observations are sampled from a population, whether the observed differences have arisen by chance or reflect real variation among the categories or groups in X.

Explained and Unexplained Variation

In statistics, the variation from all sources is frequently called the total variance. In an observed batch of data, the total variance of a variable is measured by the total sum of squares (TSS), which is the summation of the squared deviation of each observation from the mean. Symbolically,

$$TSS = \Sigma(Y_i - \bar{Y})^2$$

Identified and measured independent variables explain some of this overall variation; the explained part is called, naturally, the explained variation. What's left over is the unexplained variation. Figure 13-5 may help clarify this point. It shows the data in table 13-21 as a dot chart of individual values. Notice first the considerable variation among the points. By looking at the graph carefully, you may see two kinds of variation. For example, the members of group or category A differ from members of categories B and C. But these observations also vary among themselves—that is, within a group. In all three groups, four out of five observations lie above or below their category means. (The mean in A, for instance, is 14, and two scores are above and below it.)

In ANOVA parlance, two types of variation add up to the overall variation, or **total variance**. If we denote the overall variance as *total*, the within-category variance as *within* (or *unexplained*), and the between-group variance as *between* (or *explained*), then the fundamental ANOVA relationship is as follows:

Total variance = Within variance + Between variance

The term *between* or *explained* refers to the fact that some of the observed differences seem to be due to "membership in" or "having a property of" one category of X. That is, on average, the As differ from the Bs. Knowing that a case has characteristic A tells us roughly what its value on Y will be. Our best prediction for this case would be the mean of the As. The prediction will not be perfect, however, because of the internal variation among the As. Yet, if we could numerically measure these different sources of variability, we could determine what percentage of the total was explained:

$$\text{Percent explained} = \left(\frac{Between}{Total} \right) \times 100$$

This discussion should sound familiar. It is the basis of calculating a PRE measure of association. In the context of ANOVA, the percent variation explained is called **eta-squared** (η^2). It varies between zero, which means the independent variable (statistically speaking) explains nothing about Y, to 1, which means it accounts for all of the variation.

Y	$(Y_i - \bar{Y})$	$(Y_i - \bar{Y})^2$
10	−14	196
12	−12	144
14	−10	100
16	−8	64
18	−6	36
20	−4	16
22	−2	4
24	0	0
26	2	4
28	4	16
30	6	36
32	8	64
34	10	100
36	12	144
38	14	196
$\bar{Y} = 24$		$\Sigma (Y_i - \bar{Y})^2 = 1{,}120$

Let's calculate eta-squared for the data in table 13-21.
Step 1: Calculate the total variance (TSS).

$$\text{TSS} = \Sigma \left(Y_i - \bar{Y} \right)^2 = 1{,}120$$

Step 2: Calculate the within variation (WSS).

Group A			Group B			Group C		
Y_i	$Y_i - \bar{Y}_A$	$\left(Y_i - \bar{Y}_A \right)^2$	Y_i	$Y_i - \bar{Y}_B$	$\left(Y_i - \bar{Y}_B \right)^2$	Y_i	$Y_i - \bar{Y}_C$	$\left(Y_i - \bar{Y}_C \right)^2$
10	−4	16	20	−4	16	30	−4	16
12	−2	4	22	−2	4	32	−2	4
14	0	0	24	0	0	34	0	0
16	2	4	26	2	4	36	2	4
18	4	16	28	4	16	38	4	16
$\bar{Y}_A = 14$		$\Sigma \left(Y_i - \bar{Y}_A \right)^2 = 40$	$\bar{Y}_B = 24$		$\Sigma \left(Y_i - \bar{Y}_B \right)^2 = 40$	$\bar{Y}_C = 34$		$\Sigma \left(Y_i - \bar{Y}_C \right)^2 = 40$

$$\text{WSS} = \left(\left(\Sigma \left(Y_i - \bar{Y}_A \right)^2 \right) + \left(\Sigma \left(Y_i - \bar{Y}_B \right)^2 \right) + \left(\Sigma \left(Y_i - \bar{Y}_C \right)^2 \right) \right)$$
$$\text{WSS} = (40 + 40 + 40) = 120$$

Step 3: Calculate the between variation (BSS).

$$\text{BSS} = \text{TSS} - \text{WSS}$$
$$\text{BSS} = 1{,}120 - 120$$
$$\text{BSS} = 1{,}000$$

Step 4: Substitute values into the equation for eta-squared.

$$\eta^2 = \frac{\text{BSS}}{\text{TSS}}$$
$$\eta^2 = \frac{1{,}000}{1{,}120}$$
$$\eta^2 = .89$$

Thus, 89 percent of the variation in Y is explained by X.

Now look at figure 13-6. It shows two things: The means of A, B, and C are all the same, and the observations differ among themselves but not because they belong to one or another group. Each level of X has the same mean. So, the total variance in scores has nothing to do with levels of the factor. There is no difference among means and hence no explained or between variation:

$$\text{Percent explained} = \frac{Explained}{Total} = \frac{0}{Total} = 0$$

TABLE 13-21 ■ **Measurements on *Y* within Three Categories of *X***

	Categorical Variable (*X*)		
	A	**B**	**C**
	10	20	30
	12	22	32
	14	24	34
	16	26	36
	18	28	38
Number of cases: *n*	5	5	5
Mean: $\overline{Y}_i$	14	24	34
Standard deviation: $\hat{\sigma}$	3.16	3.16	3.16

Overall "grand" mean = 24

Significance Test for Analysis of Variance

The *F* test is used to test the hypothesis that *K* subpopulation means are equal (H_0: $\mu_1 = \mu_2 = \mu_3 \ldots = \mu_K$). It rests on several assumptions, especially that the observations in one group are independent of those in the other groups. In addition, we assume large N_s for each subpopulation and equal subpopulation variances (that is, $\sigma_1^2 = \sigma_2^2 = \sigma_3^2 = \ldots \sigma_K^2$). Test results are most often organized and summarized in an ANOVA table like table 13-22.

FIGURE 13-5 ■ **Dot Chart of *Y* by Categories of *X*: Means Differ**

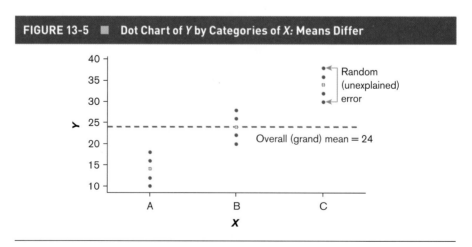

Note: Variation in *Y* is due to differences in *X* and "error."

FIGURE 13-6 ■ Dot Chart of *Y* by Categories of *X*: Means Do Not Differ

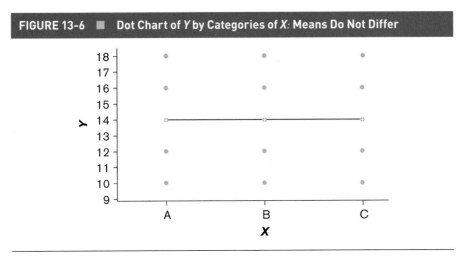

Note: *X* does not "explain" any variation in *Y*.

TABLE 13-22 ■ Typical ANOVA Table Format

Source of Variation	Sum of Squares	Degrees of Freedom	Mean Square	Observed *F*
Between (explained)	BSS	$df_{between} = K - 1$	BMS = BSS/$df_{between}$	$F_{obs} = \dfrac{BSS/(K-1)}{WSS/(N-K)} = \dfrac{BMS}{WMS}$
Within (unexplained or error)	WSS	$df_{within} = N - K$	WMS = WSS/df_{within}	
Total	TSS	$df_{total} = N - 1$		

Note: Assume *X* has *K* categories.

The terms inside the table may seem intimidating at first, but the numbers are straightforward. We have already demonstrated how to calculate the sums of squares BSS and WSS. Each sum of squares has an associated degree of freedom, *df*. They are easy to calculate: the between degree of freedom is the number of categories (*K*) of the independent variable minus 1, or $K - 1$; and the within degree of freedom is *N*, the total sample size, minus the number of categories, or $N - K$. Together they sum to the degrees of freedom for the total sum of squares, or $(K - 1) + (N - K) = N - 1$.

Whenever a sum of squares is divided by its degrees of freedom, the quotient is called a mean square. These are shown in the fourth column in table 13-22. The between-mean square is divided by the within-mean square to obtain an observed test statistic called the *F* statistic.

TABLE 13-23 ■ ANOVA Results				
Source of Variation	Degrees of Freedom (df)	Sum of Squares	Mean Squares	Observed F
Between X	2	1,000	500.0	50.0
Within	12	120	10.0	
Total	14	1,120		
p level ≈.000				

Source: Table 13-21.

Like the other statistics we have discussed, the observed F has a distribution. Three F tables are found in appendix D. Each one corresponds to an alpha level (.05, .01, and .001). Choose an alpha level, then use both degrees of freedom, one for the between component and one for the within component, to find F_{crit}. A decision about the null hypothesis of equal population means is made by comparing F_{obs} to F_{crit}.

Suppose we use the hypothetical data in Table 13-21 to test the hypothesis that $\mu_A = \mu_B = \mu_C$ against the alternative that at least two of them differ. (Technically, we should have larger samples, but this is just an illustration.) For this test, we choose the .001 level of significance. The critical F (with 2 and 12 df) at the .001 level is 12.97. Table 13-23 shows the results. The F_{obs} is 50, which exceeds F_{crit}. Thus, the null hypothesis is rejected at the .001 level. Indeed, if the null hypothesis were in fact true, the p value (.000) would tell us we have obtained a very improbable result.

What does all this mean? It tells us that it is safe to conclude that two or more population means are unequal. In this case, by looking at the scatterplot in figure 13-6, we can tell that all three of the population means are different from one another.

CONCLUSION

We have covered a lot of material in this chapter. We have shown you how to construct contingency tables used when both independent and dependent variables are categorical data. We have also demonstrated how to interpret contingency tables when a control variable has been introduced. We also introduced the use of measures of association to measure the strength of a relationship between two variables. Measures of association simplify the discussion about the strength of a relationship because they represent the strength using a single number. Yet, we have cautioned that care must be taken in selecting the appropriate measure to use with your data and that nothing can take the place of looking at the percentages within the cells of a contingency table. We also introduced the chi-square test of statistical significance, which is used with contingency tables. While contingency table analysis is limited by the inability to introduce multiple control variables, it is an excellent method for looking at relationships between two variables with one control variable at a time. Finally we introduced eta-squared, a measure of association to measure the strength of a relationship when comparing two or more means, and the F test of statistical significance to use when comparing more than two means. We turn in chapter 14 to the topic of regression analysis, one of whose strengths is to investigate causal relationships taking into account multiple independent variables.

TERMS INTRODUCED

Analysis of variance (ANOVA). A technique for measuring the relationship between one nominal- or ordinal-level variable and one interval- or ratio-level variable. 299

Chi square (χ^2) statistic. A statistic used to test whether a relationship is statistically significant in a cross-tabulation table. 287

Control by grouping. A form of statistical control in which observations identical or similar to the control variable are grouped together. 291

Correlation coefficient. In regression analysis, a measure of the strength and direction of the linear correlation between two quantitative variables; also called product-moment correlation, Pearson's r, or r. 278

Cross-tabulation or **contingency table.** Also called a cross-classification, this array displays the joint frequencies and relative frequencies of two categorical (nominal or ordinal) variables. 269

Direction of a relationship. An indication of which values of the dependent variable are associated with which values of the independent variable. 277

Eta-squared (η^2). A measure of association used with the analysis of variance that indicates what proportion of the variance in the dependent variable is explained by the variance in the independent variable. 300

Goodman and Kruskal's gamma (γ). A measure of association between ordinal-level variables. 282

Goodman and Kruskal's lambda (λ). A measure of association between one nominal- or ordinal-level variable and one nominal-level variable. 279

Interaction. The strength and direction of a relationship depend on an additional variable or variables. 296

Kendall's tau-b. A measure of association between ordinal-level variables. 282

Kendall's tau-c. A measure of association between ordinal-level variables. 282

Measures of association. Statistics that summarize the relationship between two variables. 278

Multivariate analysis. Data analysis techniques designed to test hypotheses involving more than two variables. 290

Multivariate cross-tabulation. A procedure by which cross-tabulation is used to control for a third variable. 291

Phi (ϕ). An association measure that adjusts an observed chi-square statistic by the sample size. 289

Proportional-reduction-in-error (PRE) measure. A measure of association that indicates how much knowledge of the value of the independent variable of a case improves prediction of the dependent variable compared to the prediction of the dependent variable based on no knowledge of the case's value on the independent variable. Examples are Goodman and Kruskal's lambda, Goodman and Kruskal's gamma, eta-squared, and R-squared. 279

Somers' D. A measure of association between ordinal-level variables. 282

Total variance. A numerical measure of the variation in a variable, determined by summing the squared deviation of each observation from the mean. 299

SUGGESTED READINGS

Agresti, Alan. *Categorical Data Analysis.* Hoboken, NJ: Wiley-Interscience, 2002.

Agresti, Alan. *An Introduction to Categorical Data Analysis.* Hoboken, NJ: Wiley-Interscience, 2007.

Fienberg, Stephen E. *The Analysis of Cross-Classified Categorical Data.* New York: Springer, 2007.

Rudas, Tamās. *Lectures on Categorical Data Analysis.* New York: Springer, 2018.

NOTES

1. In reality, there are many techniques for analyzing relationships at a given level of measurement. The ones presented in this chapter are the most common and least complicated.

2. You might think of ties as a "penalty" for the imprecise measurement classification involves. But, however they are interpreted, tied pairs count against all the measures except gamma in the sense that the more ties, the smaller the numerical value of the coefficient. See H. T. Reynolds, *The Analysis of Cross-Classifications* (New York: Free Press, 1977), 69–79.

3. Partly because these coefficients do not generally describe the complexities of relationships between categorical variables, they have fallen out of favor with many social scientists. Sociologists and statisticians have developed methods for modeling the multiplicity of interactions often found among categories in a table. We touch on a few techniques later in the chapter but leave the bulk of them to more advanced texts.

   A good introduction is Alan Agresti, *Analysis of Ordinal Categorical Data* (New York: Wiley, 1984).

4. Note, however, that small effects can in some circumstances have theoretical or substantive importance.

5. See Benjamin I. Page, Larry Bartels, and Jason Seawright, "Democracy and the Policy Preferences of Wealthy Americans," *Perspectives on Politics* 11 (March 2013): 51–73.

6. Totals do not add exactly across tables because (1) some observations have missing values on religiosity, as well as opinion on prayer in public schools, and (2) weighted data were used in the analysis and small rounding errors occur.

7. Notice that lambda in this table is zero. Recall that lambda will equal zero whenever the modal marginal category of *Y* is also the mode in each level of *X*.

8. There are techniques for "partitioning" a slightly different version of the chi-square into components—one for each table—that add up to the total chi-square.

STUDENT STUDY SITE

for CQ Press

Give your students the SAGE edge!

SAGE edge offers a robust online environment featuring an impressive array of free tools and resources for review, study, and further exploration, keeping both instructors and students on the cutting edge of teaching and learning. Learn more at **edge.sagepub.com/johnson9e.**

14 REGRESSION

In chapters 12 and 13, we discussed different approaches to measuring association for nominal-, ordinal-, and ratio-level variables and we discussed testing for statistical significance. In this chapter, we bring the two concepts, association and statistical significance, together with **regression analysis**. Using regression, you can measure the association between two or more variables and at the same time determine whether the relationship(s) you find are statistically significant. The basic regression logic and tools you will learn in this chapter will allow you to not only perform such calculations yourself, but also read the bulk of the quantitative political science literature. While many political science articles you read may employ more advanced forms of regression, understanding the basics introduced in this chapter will allow you to read and interpret results in tables and follow along with the basic narrative of the analysis.

LOGIC OF REGRESSION

We begin with an explanation of how ordinary least squares (OLS) regression works. To begin with, we are relying on regression to make causal assertions, rather than assertions about correlation. To make such assertions, we rely on **regression coefficients**—estimates of the unobserved population parameters. How is it justifiable to make causal assertions with regression? Why are those estimates trustworthy? To answer these questions, we turn to the ten classic assumptions of linear regression models.

The Classical Assumptions of Linear Regression Models

Table 14-1 lists the ten classical assumptions. When the model we are using satisfies these ten assumptions, the estimates generated in regression should be better than from any other linear model. We should, on average, end up with estimates that are relatively on target without systematic bias.

CHAPTER OBJECTIVES

14.1 Understand the logic behind an ordinary least squares (OLS) regression.

14.2 Describe how to calculate a bivariate regression.

14.3 Explain how to interpret bivariate regression results and test hypotheses.

14.4 Describe why one would include multiple independent variables in a regression to control for other sources of variation.

14.5 Explain how to interpret multivariate regression results and test hypotheses.

14.6 Understand the logic behind a maximum likelihood analysis.

14.7 Explain how to interpret logistic regression results and test hypotheses.

TABLE 14-1 ■ The Ten Classical Linear Regression Assumptions

Assumption	Explanation
1. The regression model is linear.	The expected value of the dependent variable is a linear function of the independent variable(s). This means that the regression model fits a linear pattern (a straight line instead of a line that bends or curves when plotting a bivariate regression, for example).
2. Values of the independent variable are fixed.	Values of the independent variable are assumed to be fixed, or nonstochastic, in repeated samples.
3. The error term has a population mean of zero.	The error component, which represents the effects of omitted causes of Y, measurement errors in Y, and "natural" variation among subjects, must be truly random in the sense that the errors cancel.
4. The error term should have a constant variance.	The variation in errors should be equal for each observation of a given X. In other words, as the value of the independent variable increases or decreases, the variance of the errors should remain equal. Constant variance is called homoscedasticity (equal spread), and correlated errors are called heteroscedasticity (unequal spread).
5. Observations of the error term should not be correlated.	The error associated with one observation should not be correlated with the next observation, positively or negatively (autocorrelation). The errors should instead be random.
6. The independent variable(s) are uncorrelated with the error term.	The independent variable and the error term should not covary. The error term is supposed to explain variation that is not explained by the independent variable. If the error term is correlated with one or more independent variables, it will create biased estimates.
7. Sample size should be greater than parameters.	The sample size must be larger than the number of variables. We need at least one observation for each unknown parameter in the regression model.
8. There must be variability in all independent variables.	Without variation in an independent variable, it is a constant, and constants do not explain variation.
9. The model must be properly specified.	All of the important variables must be included in the model, and the model should not include unnecessary variables (variables that do not systematically affect variation in the dependent variable).
10. No independent variable is a perfect linear function of other independent variables.	If two variables move together in unison, positively or negatively, then regression is not possible. If high levels of correlation are present, regression is possible, but suffers reduced precision due to multicollinearity.

Note: For a comprehensive explanation of these assumptions and the consequences of violation, see Damodar N. Gujarati, *Basic Econometrics* (New York: McGraw-Hill, 1995).

The assumptions in table 14-1, if violated, can have serious consequences for regression results. Violations of these assumptions, and tools used to identify them, are beyond the scope of this text. Thus, we generally proceed as if the assumptions were true.

Scatterplots

Regression analysis begins with the identification of associations, or correlations, between pairs of variables, and graphs provide the best first step.

One common graph is the **scatterplot**. Intended for quantitative data, a scatterplot contains a horizontal axis representing one variable and a vertical axis (drawn at a right angle) for the other variable. The usual practice is to place the values of the independent variable along the *x*-axis and the values of the dependent variable along the *y*-axis. The scales of the axes are in units of the particular variables, such as percentages or thousands of dollars. The *X* and *Y* values for each observation are plotted using this coordinate system. The measurements for each case are placed at the point on the graph corresponding to the case's values on the variables.

As an example, figure 14-1 shows five *Y* and *X* values and how they are plotted on a scatterplot. Each case is located or marked at the intersection of the line extending from the *x*- and *y*-axes. The first pair of observations, 5 and 10, appears at the point *Y* = 5 and *X* = 10.

Scatterplots are handy because they show at a glance the form and strength of relationships. In this example, increases in *X* tend to be associated with increases in *Y*. Indeed, we have drawn a straight line on the graph in such a fashion that most observations fall on it or very near to it. In the language introduced in chapter 13, this pattern of points indicates a strong "positive linear correlation."

FIGURE 14-1   ■   Construction of a Scatterplot

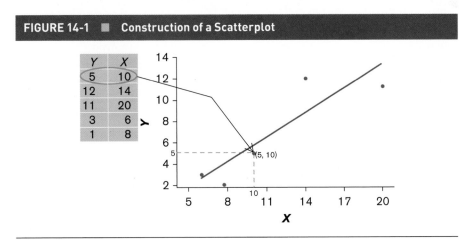

Source: Hypothetical data.

HELPFUL HINTS
A TIP AND A WARNING

If you have a large batch of quantitative data (say, more than 500 cases), you can obtain clearer, more interpretable results if you ask your software to first select a sample of the data (25 to 75 cases) and plot those numbers. If the sample is truly representative, the plot will reveal the important features of the relationship. Creating a scatterplot from an entire data set may produce a picture filled with so many dots

that nothing intelligible can be detected. Furthermore, scatterplots are suitable only for quantitative variables; they are not intended for categorical (nominal and ordinal) data. If you tried, for instance, to get your software to plot party identification by gender, the result would be two parallel lines that tell you nothing.

MINIMIZING THE SUM OF THE SQUARED ERROR

We are, however, interested in more than just correlation in this chapter. We want to establish a causal relationship between the independent and dependent variables. Establishing causal relationships is about the mean and variation from the mean. If the mean of the dependent variable were 5, and all observations of the dependent variable were 5, we would not need any independent variables to explain the dependent variable. When all observations equal 5, the variable has no variation and appears to be a constant. But, what if there were variation on the dependent variable? What if we collected additional observations of the dependent variable with values of 2, or −9, or 7? What explains why some observations equal the mean, 5, while other observations are below or above the mean? We want to explain that variation. We can explain variation from the mean of the dependent variable with an independent variable. We can hypothesize that variation in an independent variable causes variation in the dependent variable—a concept you have seen many times in previous chapters. In a bivariate regression (a regression with one independent variable and one dependent variable), we can plot a regression line that represents the relationship between the independent and dependent variables. We will get to the equation in a bit, but for now, just assume that it is possible and take a look at figure 14-2. Here you will see an x-axis and a y-axis representing the scale of the independent and dependent variables, respectively. You will also see a blue line running parallel to the x-axis, and labeled $\bar{Y}$, the mean of Y. If the dependent variable never varied, we would see all of the observations, no matter the value of the independent variable, lining up on the blue line, the mean. If there were variation from the mean on the dependent variable, and if variation on the independent variable *perfectly* explained that variation, we would see data points only on the regression line—the purple line in the figure.

Any data point that lands on the regression line is perfectly explained by the regression. In that case, the observed value of Y_i, the value observed in data collection, is the same value as the predicted value of the dependent variable, $\hat{Y}_i$. Notice that there is one data

FIGURE 14-2 ■ Predicted and Observed Values of Y

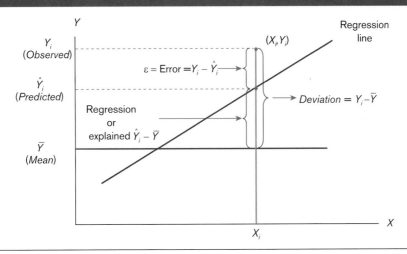

point in this figure that is not on the blue line or on the purple line—this is because not all data points will be perfectly explained in a regression. This data point is labeled X_i, Y_i at the intersection of Y_i on the y-axis and X_i on the x-axis. This observation has variation from the mean of the dependent variable that is not explained by the independent variable (because the observation is not on the regression line). We have labeled three distances on the red line representing different kinds of variation. First, the entire distance between the mean and the data point is labeled deviation, for deviation from the mean, calculated as $Y_i - \bar{Y}$. The second distance is one portion of the deviation from the mean—the distance between the mean and the regression line—and is labeled as the explained variation, calculated as $\hat{Y}_i - \bar{Y}$. This distance is variation explained by variation in the independent variable. Given the value of the independent variable, we would expect the observation to fall on the regression line so the distance between the mean and the regression line is explained by the regression. The third distance is the distance between the regression line and the data point, labeled as error, and calculated as $Y_i - \hat{Y}_i$. This distance is unexplained by the variation in the independent variable. After all, we would expect the observation to land on the regression line, but it lies even further from the mean. This distance is an error, because the distance is not explained.

This last distance, the unexplained variation, is the key to understanding regression. If we were to add additional data points to the figure, like in figure 14-3, we could go through the same exercise and determine each of the three distances for each data point. In the end, we would find that some errors are positive (data points above the regression line) and some errors are negative (data points below the regression line). In figure 14-3, the explained variation is marked with an orange line, and the unexplained variation is marked with a green line. Data point 5 lands on the regression line, so there is only explained variation associated with that point. Data point 4 is located above the regression line. Variation from the mean

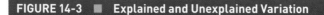

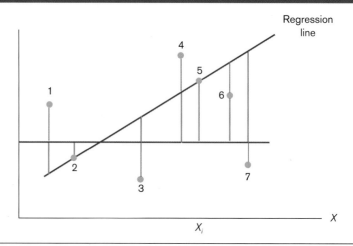

FIGURE 14-3 ■ Explained and Unexplained Variation

to the regression line is explained, and the additional variation above the regression line is unexplained, and so forth for each additional point.

If we summed all of the positive and negative values indicated by the green lines, we would get zero. The regression line creates equal positive and negative errors. But if we square the errors, they will all be positive. Summing the squared errors gives a positive number—and the regression line minimizes those squared errors. You cannot draw a line that produces a smaller sum of the squared errors. To drive the point home, minimizing the sum of the squared errors means that the regression is producing estimates that reduce deviations from the predictions of the regression and the actually observed values of the dependent variable.

So, the regression equation estimates the relationship between the independent and dependent variables by minimizing the sum of the squared errors. We next turn to the regression formula to see how to calculate a regression. Seeing the equations behind regression will hopefully make this discussion of the logic of regression even clearer.

THE LINEAR REGRESSION MODEL

You should remember from algebra that the equation for a straight line has this general form:

$$Y = a + bX$$

In this equation, X and Y are variables. The letter a is called the **regression constant** and equals the value of Y when X equals zero. It is also called the intercept because if the graph of the equation is plotted, a is the point where the line crosses the y-axis. The letter b stands for the slope of the line, which indicates how much Y changes for each one-unit increase in X.

When we have a positive b, or slope, if we move up the X scale one unit, b indicates how much Y increases. Likewise, if b is negative, b indicates how much Y decreases as we move up the X scale one unit. If there is no relationship between the two variables, the slope of the line is zero, and its graph is horizontal and parallel to the x-axis.

Regression

Regression analysis applies these ideas to two variables, where the dependent variable, Y, is a ratio-level variable.

When we have two variables, an independent variable, X, and a dependent variable, Y, we can use the following regression equation:

$$Y = a + bX + \varepsilon$$

This equation is very similar to the slope of a line, but you will notice that there is an extra term at the end of the equation. The ε represents error, or variation in the dependent variable, Y, that is not explained by variation in the independent variable, X. An example will help explain the error term.

Imagine that you want to assess the relationship between income earned and taxes paid. For simplicity, let us assume that we are analyzing data from a lightly taxed country, Fredonia, where citizens pay 10 percent of their earned income in taxes, regardless of the size of their earned income. If variation in earned income, X, perfectly explained variation in taxes paid, Y, then all of the data points (taxpayers) would line up in a straight line with a positive slope, and all the points would fall on the regression line.

Now imagine that while we have an accurate accounting of earned income in our data, the government does not, because some taxpayers report a lower income than they actually earn. As such, those individuals would pay a smaller amount of tax, and the scatterplot of income and taxes would reveal some data points that are not on the regression line. These data points, those plotted off the regression line, are unexplained error—variation in the dependent variable that is not explained by the independent variable (the green lines in figure 14-3). The regression equation accounts for this unexplained variation by adding it at the end of the equation with the ε term.

The problem we as data analysts face is that we do not know the true value of ε. Perhaps there are dishonest taxpayers, or maybe some made arithmetic errors when calculating their income, or maybe others misplaced financial documents—we just cannot say for certain why there is unexplained variation or how much there is.

Given this problem, if we want to use the regression equation to plot the relationship between two variables, we need to use an equation that does not include unknown terms like ε. The following equation solves this problem. This regression equation predicts the value of the dependent variable based on the value of the independent variable to plot a regression line:

$$\hat{Y} = a + bX$$

The key difference between this equation and the earlier equation for plotting a line is the inclusion of $\hat{Y}$ instead of Y. We do not need an error term in this equation because $\hat{Y}$ is the predicted value of the dependent variable given only the information that we know—the independent variable.

Before we can calculate the regression equation to plot a line, we need to calculate the intercept, a, and the slope, b. The equation for the slope is as follows:

$$b = \frac{\sum\left(X_i - \bar{X}\right)\left(Y_i - \bar{Y}\right)}{\sum\left(X_i - \bar{X}\right)^2}$$

After calculating the slope, we can use the slope to calculate the intercept using this equation:

$$a = \bar{Y} - b\bar{X}$$

Let us turn to an example to see how we can use this equation to plot a regression line, measure the relationship between an independent and dependent variable, establish the statistical significance of that relationship, and test a hypothesis.

We will use hypothetical data to test a hypothesis about the relationship between an independent variable, X = the number of close friends who are interested in politics, and a dependent variable, Y = the number of political discussions. Our hypothesis is that there is a positive relationship between the number of close friends who are interested in politics and the number of political discussions. As you can see in table 14-2, we have five observations of the two variables, X and Y. You can follow the calculations in the How It's Done box on page 315 from left to right as we calculate first the slope, then the intercept, and use both the slope and intercept to calculate predicted values of the dependent variable, $\hat{Y}$, for use in plotting the regression line. You should be able to follow the order of operations as we move through the example calculation as each column in the table is labeled with the same description used in the equations.

TABLE 14-2 ■ Bivariate Regression Calculation

i	X	Y	$X_i - \bar{X}$	$Y_i - \bar{Y}$	$(X_i - \bar{X})(Y_i - \bar{Y})$	$(X_i - \bar{X})^2$	$\hat{Y}$
1	3	6	0	1	0	0	5.00
2	0	1	−3	−4	12	9	2.45
3	2	5	−1	0	0	1	4.15
4	6	6	3	1	3	9	7.55
5	4	7	1	2	2	1	5.85
n = 5	$\bar{X}$ = 3	$\bar{Y}$ = 5			17	20	

HOW IT'S DONE
CALCULATING THE REGRESSION SLOPE, INTERCEPT, AND PREDICTED VALUES OF THE DEPENDENT VARIABLE, Y

$$b = \frac{\sum(X_i - \bar{X})(Y_i - \bar{Y})}{\sum(X_i - \bar{X})^2}$$

$$b = \frac{17}{20}$$

$$b = .85$$

$$a = \bar{Y} - b\bar{X}$$
$$a = 5 - .85(3)$$
$$a = 5 - 2.55$$
$$a = 2.45$$

$$\hat{Y} = a + b(X)$$
$$\hat{Y} = 2.45 + .85(3) = 5.00$$
$$\hat{Y} = 2.45 + .85(0) = 2.45$$
$$\hat{Y} = 2.45 + .85(2) = 4.15$$
$$\hat{Y} = 2.45 + .85(6) = 7.55$$
$$\hat{Y} = 2.45 + .85(4) = 5.85$$

Here we are calculating predicted values to discover the value of the dependent variable we would expect to see with a given value of the independent variable. Take, for example, the first observation, where $X = 3$. Given that the independent variable equals three close friends, we would expect to see five political discussions. In the data, we observed six discussions rather than five.

Having calculated the predicted values, $\hat{Y}$, we are now ready to plot the regression line. Figure 14-4 includes a plot of the regression line based on these results. All that is needed to plot a line is two points. You can easily verify that the regression line connects the y-intercept, a, at $X = 0$ and $Y = 2.45$ and one other predicted value from the $\hat{Y}$ column in table 14-2 at $X = 3$ and $Y = 5$. The slope of the regression line is positive, representing a positive relationship between the independent and dependent variables.

We can interpret the slope of .85 as a coefficient value. The coefficient tells us that as X, the number of close friends interested in politics, increases by one friend, the dependent variable increases by .85 political discussions. This result is consistent with the hypothesis that having more close friends interested in politics causes an increase in the number of political discussions.

It is important to note that you can interpret both the direction and the magnitude of the coefficient. The direction of the relationship is positive because the coefficient is positive. If the coefficient were negative, the direction of the relationship would be negative.

The magnitude of the coefficient is important because it indicates the size of the effect of the independent variable on the dependent variable. The magnitude can help us decide if the effect is substantively important. If the magnitude is large enough, we can conclude that the effect of the independent variable on the dependent variable is an important result. If the magnitude of the coefficient is too small, even if the relationship is statistically significant, then we can conclude that the effect is not that important. The magnitude is dependent on the scale of the independent and dependent variables in the relationship. When analyzing

FIGURE 14-4 ■ Regression of Political Discussions on Close Friends

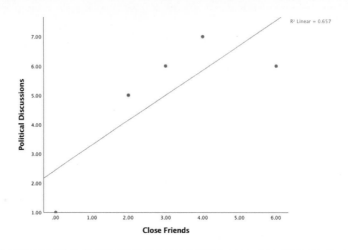

variables on a scale in the single digits, a coefficient of 2 might be substantively significant, but with a scale in the millions, the same coefficient of 2 would seem rather unimportant.

We cannot yet reject or accept the hypothesis because the coefficient alone cannot be used to determine statistical significance. Next, we will calculate the standard error of the coefficient in order to determine if the relationship between X and Y is statistically significant and if we can accept or reject our hypothesis.

In chapter 12, we discussed tests of statistical significance using difference of means tests. In those tests, we divided the difference of the means by the standard error of the mean. We can use similar logic to test for statistical significance in a regression by dividing a coefficient by its standard error. The equation is

$$SE = \frac{\hat{\sigma}}{\sqrt{\sum\left(X_i - \bar{X}\right)^2}}$$

where

$$\hat{\sigma} = \sqrt{\frac{\sum\left(Y_i - \hat{Y}\right)^2}{n - 2}}$$

In this equation, SE stands for standard error. In Table 14-3, we calculate the terms needed for the standard error equation. Note that this table is based on Table 14-2 in which we already calculated some of this information. In Table 14-3, we begin with the observed values of Y and the predicted values of Y. Notice that there is a difference between these two values for each

TABLE 14-3 ■ Standard Error of the Coefficient Calculation

i	X_i	Y_i	$(X_i - \bar{X})^2$	$\hat{Y}$	$Y_i - \hat{Y}$	$(Y_i - \hat{Y})^2$
1	3	6	0	5.00	1.00	1.00
2	0	1	9	2.45	−1.45	2.10
3	2	5	1	4.15	0.85	0.72
4	6	6	9	7.55	−1.55	2.40
5	4	7	1	5.85	1.15	1.32
$n = 5$	$\bar{X} = 3$	$\bar{Y} = 5$	20			7.54

Source: Table 14-2.

observation. The first step is to subtract the predicted values of Y from the observed values. We then square that difference and sum, giving us 7.54, the numerator of the standard deviation portion of the standard error equation (see the How It's Done box on page 315 for the calculations). The standard deviation is the standard deviation of the difference between the observed and predicted values. We then divide by the degrees of freedom, $n - 2$, in the denominator. The degrees of freedom are calculated as n minus the number of variables in regression.

HOW IT'S DONE
CALCULATING A t SCORE FOR USE IN TESTING A HYPOTHESIS WITH REGRESSION

$$\hat{\sigma} = \sqrt{\frac{\sum \left(Y_i - \hat{Y}\right)^2}{n-2}}$$

$$\hat{\sigma} = \sqrt{\frac{7.54}{3}}$$

$$\hat{\sigma} = \sqrt{2.51}$$

$$\hat{\sigma} = 1.58$$

$$SE = \frac{\hat{\sigma}}{\sqrt{\sum \left(X_i - \bar{X}\right)^2}}$$

$$SE = \frac{1.58}{\sqrt{20}}$$

$$SE = \frac{1.58}{4.47}$$

$$SE = .35$$

$$t = \frac{b}{SE}$$

$$t = \frac{.85}{.35}$$

$$t = 2.43$$

one-tailed test
.05 level
df $= n - 2$

$t_{critical} = 2.353$

We calculate the standard error of the coefficient as .35. In order to test our hypothesis, we need to calculate a t score. To do so, we divide the coefficient, b, by its standard error, SE. Dividing .85 by .35 gives us a t score of 2.43. We find the t-critical value in the same way as described in detail in chapter 12. As you can see, the *t*-score is more than than the *t*-critical value with 3 degrees of freedom at the .05 level, found in appendix B. We can, therefore, accept our hypothesis because the relationship is positive, as predicted; the magnitude of the relationship is large enough to make it substantively significant; and the relationship is statistically significant.

Measuring Correlation: Pearson's *r*

A statistic related to regression, as you will see in the following equation, is Pearson's *r*, the correlation coefficient. Pearson's *r* indicates the level of association between two variables. The equation for Pearson's *r* is

$$r = \frac{\sum(X_i - \bar{X})(Y_i - \bar{Y})}{\sqrt{\sum(X_i - \bar{X})^2} * \sqrt{\sum(Y_i - \bar{Y})^2}}$$

Pearson's *r* measures correlation on a scale of −1 (perfect negative correlation) to 1 (perfect positive correlation) with 0 at the midpoint (no correlation). While there are no hard cut-points in interpreting the amount of correlation, a Pearson's *r* value of around .4 or greater is generally considered to be a strong, positive correlation in the political science literature. Likewise, −.4 would be considered a strong, negative correlation. See chapter 13 to review positive and negative correlation. We will now calculate Pearson's *r* using the political discussion data (see table 14-4).

$$r = \frac{\sum(X_i - \bar{X})(Y_i - \bar{Y})}{\sqrt{\sum(X_i - \bar{X})^2} \times \sqrt{\sum(Y_i - \bar{Y})^2}}$$

$$r = \frac{17}{\sqrt{20} \times \sqrt{22}}$$

$$r = \frac{17}{4.47 \times 4.69}$$

$$r = \frac{17}{20.96}$$

$$r = .81$$

As you can see, Pearson's *r* indicates that there is a strong, positive correlation between the independent and dependent variables, consistent with the regression coefficient.

Measuring the Fit of a Regression Line: *R*-Squared

We can further use Pearson's *r* to calculate another statistic called **R-squared**, or R^2. R-squared is a commonly reported statistic interpreted as the percentage of variation in *Y* that can be explained by the variation in the independent variable. *R*-squared is a useful way to quickly report or determine how well a regression model fits data.

To calculate *R*-squared, one need only square Pearson's *r*. Pearson's *r* is on a scale of −1 (perfect negative correlation) to 1 (perfect positive correlation) with 0 at the midpoint (no

TABLE 14-4   ■   Pearson's r Calculation

i	X	Y	$X_i - \bar{X}$	$Y_i - \bar{Y}$	$(X_i - \bar{X})(Y_i - \bar{Y})$	$(X_i - \bar{X})^2$	$(Y_i - \bar{Y})^2$
1	3	6	0	1	0	0	1
2	0	1	−3	−4	12	9	16
3	2	5	−1	0	0	1	0
4	6	6	3	1	3	9	1
5	4	7	1	2	2	1	4
n = 5	$\bar{X} = 3$	$\bar{Y} = 5$			17	20	22

Source: Table 14-2.

correlation). When Pearson's r is squared, for R-squared, the scale is from 0 to 1. When multiplied by 100, a zero can be interpreted as follows: Variation in the independent variable explains 0 percent of the variation in the dependent variable. With an R-squared value of 1, we could say that variation in the independent variable(s) explains 100 percent of the variation in the dependent variable. In this example, by squaring $r = .81$, we get $R^2 = .66$. We can interpret this result as follows: The variation in the independent variable explains 66 percent of the variation in the dependent variable.

Multivariate Regression

In the previous section, we saw why we would want to use a regression with two variables, how to calculate a regression, and how to interpret the results.

We can, however, include many independent variables in a regression. Why would we want to include more than one independent variable? Consider political contributions. We could try to predict how much individuals contribute to political organizations with a single variable like age. We could hypothesize that as people get older, they contribute more money to political organizations. For this example, we have two variables, age, the independent variable, measured in years, and contributions, the dependent variable, measured in dollars.

The bivariate regression results reported in table 14-5 support the hypothesis. The table includes a coefficient value for the constant and the independent variable with standard errors in parentheses. The coefficient value, 56.09 for age, means that when age increases by one year, contributions increase by $56.09. The coefficient is in the hypothesized direction (positive), the relationship is of a sufficiently large magnitude to be substantively important, and the relationship is statistically significant (the t-critical value is 1.645 with a one-tailed test at the .05 level).

TABLE 14-5 ■ Bivariate Model Financial Contributions to Political Organizations	
Variable	Coefficient
constant	.34
	(.05)
age	56.09
	(23.78)

Source: Hypothetical data.

Notes: Dependent variable = contributions. $n = 1,500$. Standard errors in parentheses.

Perhaps this explanation, though, does not make sense. We might question this result on theoretical grounds and think that, perhaps, we could find a better explanation for contributions. We might instead think about a hypothesis that people with a higher income are more likely to donate more money. We can add a variable to the regression, income, measured in dollars. When we do so, we are controlling for another factor that might explain variation in the dependent variable. Table 14-6 reports the results. Lo and behold, when we account for income, age is no longer statistically significant.

A **multivariate regression analysis** uses more than one independent variable to estimate the effect of each independent variable on the dependent variable at the same time. This means that the regression analyzes the effect of each independent variable controlling

TABLE 14-6 ■ Multivariate OLS Regression of Financial Contributions to Political Organizations	
Variable	Coefficient
constant	.13
	(.09)
age	13.37
	(29.01)
income	.02
	(.01)

Source: Hypothetical data.

Notes: Dependent variable = contributions. $n = 1,500$. Standard errors in parentheses.

for the other independent variables in the model. In this model, we have two independent variables, age and income. We could pair each of these variables with a **multivariate regression coefficient** in a multivariate regression equation:

$$\hat{Y} = a + b_1 X_1 + b_2 X_2,$$

where $\hat{Y}$ is the predicted value of the dependent variable contributions; a is the constant; b_1 is the coefficient for the first independent variable, age; and b_2 is the coefficient for the second independent variable, income. If we added an additional independent variable, we would simply add an additional term, $b_3 X_3$, at the end of the equation. If we added even more variables, we would add more sequentially numbered terms.

Turning back to interpretation, consider the first independent variable. The effect of age on contributions, controlling for income, is 13.37. When age increases by one year, contributions increase by $13.37, but the coefficient is not statistically significant. Dividing the coefficient for age by its standard error gives us a t score of .46, and that is not greater than the t-critical value of 1.645 (one tail at the .05 level). So when we control for income, age is not a statistically significant variable.

Moving to the second independent variable, income, we find a coefficient value of $0.02. At first glance, this coefficient size may not be very impressive, but remember that the magnitude of the coefficient is relative to the scale of the independent and dependent variables. We interpret this coefficient value as a $1 increase in income, controlling for age, causing a $0.02 increase in contributions. In the context of the variables, a two-cent increase in contributions for every dollar of income would actually be quite substantively important if we were working with real data. The result is statistically significant.

By including two competing explanations for contributions, we were able to determine the explanatory power of each controlling for the other. In most political science analyses using multivariate regression, you will find more than two independent variables in an effort to fully specify the model and understand the effect of different factors controlling for the others.

Calculating a multiple regression by hand is beyond the scope of this text. Instead, we will focus on understanding the importance of using multiple independent variables to control for other sources of variation in the dependent variable and interpretation of multivariate regression tables.

Interpreting Regression Tables

In this section, we briefly reinforce interpretation of results from reported tables. You are likely to see regression results in this format in political science journal articles and books in class and when working on research projects.

In table 14-7, we reproduce select results from Atkeson and Rapoport's analysis of attitude expression. We can interpret these results in a similar fashion as in the previous example. The regression coefficients indicate the direction (negative or positive) and magnitude of the relationship between the independent variables and the dependent variable, controlling for the presence of the other independent variables. We will not interpret all of the

TABLE 14-7 ■ OLS Regression of Political Comments on Likes and Dislikes of Parties and Candidates	
Variable	Coefficient
Female	−1.11(.09)*
Education	1.22 (.03)*
Income	.54(.04)*
Married	.12(.1)
Homemaker	−.17(.11)
Black	−.52(.13)*
Age	.05(.00)*
Constant	−1.60(.4)*
Adjusted R^2	.19

Source: Adapted from table 1 in Lonna Rae Atkeson and Ronald B. Rapoport, "The More Things Change the More They Stay the Same: Examining Gender Differences in Political Attitude Expression, 1952–2000," *The Public Opinion Quarterly* 67, no. 4 (2003): 495–521.

Notes: Dependent variable = comments on likes and dislikes of parties and candidates in survey responses; * $p < .001$; standard errors in parentheses.

variables here, but provide a couple of examples. First, an increase in female (from *otherwise* = 0 to *female* = 1) caused a statistically significant decrease of 1.11 comments controlling for education, income, martial status, homemaker status, race, and age. Second, an increase in income caused a statistically significant increase of .54 comments controlling for gender, education, martial status, homemaker status, race, and age. We could interpret all of the other variables in a similar fashion.

Take a look at the reported value for adjusted R^2 in table 14-7. R^2 can be interpreted in a similar fashion in a multiple regression as in a bivariate regression: The variation in the independent variables explains 19 percent of the variation in the dependent variable. The reason R^2 is labeled as adjusted in a multiple regression has to do with the nature of correlation. Adding more variables to a regression model has the effect of artificially inflating the value of Pearson's *r*: The more variables you add, the greater the inflation. To account for this, we use adjusted R^2, which adjusts for the artificial inflation.

Another way we can interpret the results is to make use of predicted scores. We can restate the results in table 14-7 in equation form:

$$\hat{Y}_i = a + b_1 X_1 + b_2 X_2 + b_3 X_3 + b_4 X_4 + b_5 X_5 + b_6 X_6 + b_7 X_7$$

This equation can be read as follows: The predicted value of Y equals the sum of the constant, a, and the product of each coefficient multiplied by the value of its independent variable. We can include variable labels in the equation:

$$\hat{Y}_i = -1.6 + (-1.11 \times \text{Female}) + (1.22 \times \text{Education}) + (.54 \times \text{Income}) + (.12 \times \text{Married}) +$$
$$(-.17 \times \text{Homemaker}) + (-.52 \times \text{Black}) + (.05 \times \text{Age})$$

We can then use this formula to calculate the predicted value for a person with a specific set of characteristics or values for each variable. For example, we could calculate the predicted value for a man (*female* = 0), with a college education (4 on a scale of 1–4 for education), income in the 50th percentile (3 on a scale of 1–5), married (*married* = 1), not a homemaker (*homemaker* = 0), not black (*black* = 0), and age 45. In the following equation, we substitute these specific values for each variable and then finish the calculation.

$$\hat{Y}_i = -1.6 + (-1.11 \times 0) + (1.22 \times 4) + (.54 \times 3) + (.12 \times 1) + (-.17 \times 0) +$$
$$(-.52 \times 0) + (.05 \times 45)$$
$$\hat{Y}_i = -1.6 + (0) + (4.88) + (1.62) + (.12) + (0) + (0) + (2.25)$$
$$\hat{Y}_i = 7.27$$

The predicted value for this set of characteristics is 7.27 comments. The value of finding such predicted values is that we could examine theoretically interesting combinations and predict the outcome.

Categorical Independent Variables

In the previous regression example, you will find several categorical independent variables including female, black, homemaker, and married. These variables are categorical because they use categories. In each case, the categorical variable is dichotomous—*married* (1) or *not* (0), for example. But what if we want to include a categorical variable with more than two categories? We will consider adding an additional variable to Atkeson and Rapoport's analysis of attitude expression: military service. Atkeson and Rapoport's original data captures military service with a nominal-level variable with the following coding: *no service* (0), *enlisted* (1), *officer* (2). Adding this variable as is to the regression model would not be appropriate because a one-unit increase in the variable between 0 and 1 is not the same as a one-unit increase between 1 and 2—it is a nominal-level variable, after all.

Instead, we could first create new dichotomous variables (often called dummy variables) and add all but one to the model. As described in figure 14-5, we could create a new dichotomous variable, officer, coded as *officer* (1), *otherwise* (0); a new dichotomous variable, enlisted, coded as *enlisted* (1), *otherwise* (0); and a new dichotomous variable, service, coded as *service* (1), *otherwise* (0). We could then include two of these dichotomous variables in the regression model. We cannot include the third because if we did, there would be perfect correlation between the three independent variables and that would violate the regression

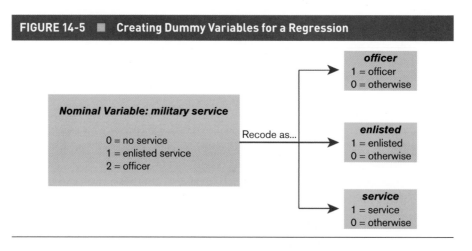

FIGURE 14-5 ■ Creating Dummy Variables for a Regression

assumptions presented in table 14-1. Therefore, we use one category (one dichotomous variable) as a reference category and exclude it from the equation. In this case, it makes sense to use service as the reference category and to include officer and enlisted in the model. When you think about it, we do not need to include service in the equation: Any observation with a 0 for military service likewise has a 0 for both officer and enlisted, and any observation with service will be either 1 for *enlisted* or 1 for *officer.*

We could then interpret regression results including these dichotomous variables in comparison to the excluded category—no service. If the officer variable had a coefficient of 2.3, we would interpret the coefficient as follows: Service as an officer increased attitude expression by 2.3 comments in comparison to no military service, controlling for the presence of the other independent variables. Likewise, if the coefficient for enlisted were −.45, we could interpret the coefficient as follows: Enlisted service decreased attitude expression by .45 comments in comparison to no military service, controlling for the presence of the other independent variables. Using this procedure, you can vastly expand the concepts you can include in a regression.

MAXIMUM LIKELIHOOD MODELS FOR DICHOTOMOUS DEPENDENT VARIABLES

Up to this point, we have been discussing regression in the context of a continuous, ratio-level dependent variable. For numerous reasons that are beyond the scope of this text, most political scientists choose to use a different kind of statistical analysis when analyzing a categorical dependent variable. In this chapter, we are most interested in explaining how you can interpret maximum likelihood results from an analysis of one particular kind of categorical dependent variable: the dichotomous dependent variable, like whether a country is at war or not, the choice to vote or not, or the presence or absence of a treaty. For dichotomous dependent variables, analysts rely on maximum likelihood models that predict the likelihood of observing one of the two possibilities: 1 if the condition is present, and 0 otherwise. While there are different maximum likelihood models analysts can use to analyze dichotomous dependent variables, we will only discuss results from one: logistic regression, also known as logit.

The Logic of Maximum Likelihood

Explaining the logic behind **maximum likelihood estimation** and expanding on the complicating factors that lead to numerous different kinds of models for specific data circumstances would be a separate book. But maximum likelihood models are used with such regularity in political science research that we feel that students should at the very least be able to interpret maximum likelihood results in a table or figure. So, with this disclaimer, we will endeavor to explain basic result interpretation.

One can use an OLS regression to estimate coefficients that describe the linear relationship between an independent variable and a dependent variable. Because the model describes a linear relationship, the effect is the same regardless of the independent variable's observed value, no matter how small or large.

A maximum likelihood model is quite different. Maximum likelihood models describe the probability of observing a condition: calling for a snap election, choosing a candidate for whom to vote in an election, or any categorical outcome. As you are aware, probability is bound between 0 and 1 and is always positive; we cannot observe a negative probability. Maximum likelihood models must therefore work differently than regression to account for the limited range in the dependent variable. Rather than minimizing the sum of the squared error, as done in OLS regression, maximum likelihood models choose the value for parameters for which the probability of observing an outcome is highest. The practical implication of this difference, for us, is that you cannot interpret a maximum likelihood model in the same way that you interpret regression. As we mentioned previously, we are interested in explaining how to interpret results from one particular kind of maximum likelihood model for use with a dichotomous dependent variable, a **logistic regression**, or logit for short. Consider table 14-8 describing civil war recurrence using a logit.

Interpreting a Logistic Regression Table

The results in table 14-8 include variable names, coefficients, and standard errors in parentheses. We can interpret the direction of the **logistic regression coefficient**, positive or negative, to understand whether the independent variable has a positive or negative relationship with the dependent variable, civil war recurrence, controlling for the other independent variables. We can also divide the coefficient by the standard error to calculate a t score to test statistical significance, similar to the earlier regression examples. So far, this is the same as for OLS regression results. The difference between interpreting logit results and interpreting OLS regression results is that we cannot interpret the magnitude of the coefficient.

A quick examination of the table indicates some interesting substantive findings. Rebel victory, army size, population, and years since last war have a negative effect on civil war recurrence, controlling for other factors. Likewise, fatalities and infant mortality have a positive effect on civil war recurrence, controlling for other factors. Each of the independent variables is statistically significant at various levels, reported in the table with asterisks indicating the specific level of significance. In this table, the reported *p* values equate to alpha levels as described in chapter 12.

Examining each variable individually, you could make some conclusions. Rebel victory is a dichotomous variable where a rebel victory in a civil war is coded as a 1 and any other condition is coded as a 0. Moving from other conditions to a rebel victory causes a decrease in the likelihood of civil war recurrence. Another interesting result is that as the infant mortality rate increases in the postwar environment, recurrence of civil war is more likely. The authors postulate that this variable captures both economic inequality and well-being for the population. You could make more conclusions from this table for each of the variables, interpreting them in a similar manner.

TABLE 14-8 ■ Logistic Regression of Civil War Recurrence

Variable Name	Coefficient
Rebel Victory	−1.09*
	(.84)
Fatalities	.43**
	(−.21)
Army Size	−.27
	(.17)
Infant mortality	.02**
	(.01)
Population	−.47
	(.22)
Years since last war	−.11***
	(.03)
Constant	7.58
	(4.33)

Source: Adapted from table 1 in J. Michael Quinn, T. David Mason, and Mehmet Gurses, "Sustaining the Peace: Determinants of Civil War Recurrence," *International Interactions* 33, no. 2 (2007): 167–93.

Notes: One-tailed *t* tests; *** $p < .01$; ** $p < .05$; * $p < .10$

$n = 116$ in both models. Standard errors in parentheses. Other control variables included in the original table are not reported here.

Predicted Probabilities

Because we cannot interpret the magnitude of the coefficients in maximum likelihood models, political scientists turn to various tools for additional interpretation beyond the coefficients. Generally, these tools rely on predicted probabilities. Earlier in the chapter, we discussed how you can use the slope and intercept in a bivariate regression to calculate predicted values for the dependent variable. In maximum likelihood models, you can use a similar but mathematically more complex procedure to calculate the predicted probability of observing a 1 on the dependent variable given values for each of the independent variables. These predicted probabilities can be reported in a table or used to generate various graphical representations.

Turning to table 14-9, we can assess the impact the independent variables in Table 14-9 have on the probability of observing civil war recurrence. Table 14-9 reports some of the predicted probabilities Quinn, Mason, and Gurses included in table 2 in their article. These predicted probabilities demonstrate the likelihood of observing a 1, *recurrence of civil war*, but only under the specific conditions specified. These specified conditions are vital in interpreting the predicted probabilities. In this case, Quinn et al. held each continuous variable in the model constant at its mean value and held each dichotomous variable in the model constant at 0. If the authors had chosen to hold any of the variables constant at a different value, the predicted probabilities would be different. In essence, the results reported here are just one set of possible results. The important job political scientists must do here is to choose theoretically interesting values to make the interpretation of predicted probabilities interesting and useful.

TABLE 14-9 ■ Predicted Probabilities

Variable	Probability of recurrence
Rebel victory	
no	.63
yes	.36
Change in probability	−.27
Infant mortality rate	
minimum	.15
maximum	.98
Change in probability	.83

Source: Adapted from table 2 in J. Michael Quinn, T. David Mason, and Mehmet Gurses, "Sustaining the Peace: Determinants of Civil War Recurrence," *International Interactions* 33, no. 2 (2007): 167–93.

With this in mind, we can interpret the results in table 14-9 by examining the predicted probabilities for two variables, rebel victory and infant mortality rate. The predicted probability for rebel victory is reported under two conditions: "no," the rebels did not win; and "yes," the rebels did win. The .63 listed after "no" can be interpreted as follows: With continuous variables held at their mean values and dichotomous variables held at 0, the predicted probability of recurrence of civil war is .63, or a 63 percent chance, when the rebels did not win. Likewise, the .36 listed after "yes" can be interpreted as follows: With continuous variables held at their mean values and dichotomous variables held at 0, the predicted probability of recurrence of civil war is .36, or a 36 percent chance, when the rebels did win. We can make one more interpretation by examining the marginal effect of the two outcomes— the difference between the predicted probabilities of the two conditions, rebel victory and otherwise. The change in probability from otherwise to a rebel victory is a decrease of .27— that is a substantively important difference. One might conclude that a rebel victory is important if one wants to avoid recurrence.

We can interpret the predicted probabilities for the second variable in a similar manner. The predicted probability for infant mortality rate is reported under two conditions: "minimum," the lowest observed value of post–civil war infant mortality in the data; and "maximum," the highest observed value in the data. The .15 listed after "minimum" can be interpreted as follows: With continuous variables held at their mean values and dichotomous variables held at 0, the predicted probability of recurrence of civil war is .15, or a 15 percent chance, when the infant mortality rate is at the minimum. Likewise, the .98 listed after "maximum" can be interpreted as follows: With continuous variables held at their mean values and dichotomous variables held at 0, the predicted probability of recurrence of civil war is .98, or a 98 percent chance, when infant mortality is at the maximum. Examining the marginal effect of the two outcomes—the difference between the predicted probabilities of the two conditions, minimum and maximum infant mortality—we find that the change in probability from minimum to maximum infant mortality is an increase of .83, a substantively important difference. One might conclude that economic inequality and well-being as captured through infant mortality is vitally important if one wants to avoid recurrence. When the population is suffering great hardship, the likelihood of recurrence is much greater.

CONCLUSION

In this chapter, we explored regression analysis. Regression is an important tool in the political science toolbox because it allows us to analyze the causal relationship between two or more variables while establishing the direction of the relationship (negative or positive), the magnitude of the relationship, and statistical significance while potentially accounting for alternative causes of variation in the form of other independent variables. When reading political science articles and books, you will frequently encounter various regression models. Some of these will be rather simple in form, like those described in this chapter, such as a bivariate or, more likely, multivariate OLS regression. You will likely find more elaborate regressions as well, but remember, the same basic underlying logic applies to all linear regression models, and will help you understand the results of even the most complex linear regression models.

While linear regression is best used with a continuous, ratio-level dependent variable, political scientists usually use a very different kind of regression model for dichotomous dependent variables. Political scientists use maximum likelihood models to predict the likelihood of observing one of two conditions of the dependent variable, a 1 or a 0. While these models are more sophisticated and more complex, the guidance we provide for interpreting a logit model can help you interpret the results from many different kinds of maximum likelihood models. With these basic regression skills in hand, you are ready to read and understand the bulk of the political science literature that employs quantitative data analysis.

TERMS INTRODUCED

Logistic regression. A nonlinear regression model that relates a set of explanatory variables to a dichotomous dependent variable.   325

Logistic regression coefficient. A multiple regression coefficient based on the logistic model.   325

Maximum likelihood estimation. A class of estimators that chooses a set of parameters that provides the highest probability of observing a particular outcome.   325

Multivariate regression analysis. A technique for measuring the mathematical relationships between more than one independent variable and a dependent variable while controlling for all other independent variables in the equation.   320

Multivariate regression coefficient. A number that tells how much Y will change for a one-unit change in a particular independent variable, if all the other variables in the model have been held constant.   321

Regression analysis. A technique for measuring the relationship between two interval- or ratio-level variables.   307

Regression coefficient. A statistic that tells how much the dependent variable changes per unit change in the independent variable.   307

Regression constant. Value of the dependent variable when all the values of the independent variables in the equation equal zero.   312

R-squared (R^2). The proportion of the total variance in a dependent variable explained by an independent variable.   318

Scatterplot. A graph that plots joint values of an independent variable along one axis (usually the x-axis) and a dependent variable along the other axis (usually the y-axis).   309

SUGGESTED READINGS

Achen, Christopher. *Interpreting and Using Regression.* Sage University Paper Series on Quantitative Applications in the Social Sciences, no. 29. Beverly Hills, CA: Sage, 1982.

Agresti, Alan. *An Introduction to Categorical Data Analysis.* New York: Wiley, 1996.

Agresti, Alan, and Barbara Finlay. *Statistical Methods for the Social Sciences*. 3rd ed. Upper Saddle River, NJ: Prentice Hall, 1997.

Anderson, T. W. *Introduction to Multivariate Statistical Analysis*. 3rd ed. New York: Wiley, 2003.

Berk, Richard A. *Regression Analysis: A Constructive Critique*. Thousand Oaks, CA: Sage, 2004.

Draper, Norman R., and Harry Smith. *Applied Regression Analysis*. 3rd ed. New York: Wiley, 1998.

Faraway, Julian J. *Linear Models with* R. New York: Chapman & Hall/CRC, 2005.

Fox, John. *Applied Regression Analysis and Generalized Linear Models*. 2nd ed. Los Angeles: Sage, 2008.

Lewis-Beck, Michael S., ed. *Basic Statistics*. Vol. 1. Newbury Park, CA: Sage, 1993.

Long, J. Scott. *Regression Models for Categorical and Limited Dependent Variables*. Thousand Oaks, CA: Sage, 1997.

Pampel, Fred C. *Logistic Regression: A Primer*. Sage University Paper Series on Quantitative Applications in the Social Sciences, no. 132. Thousand Oaks, CA: Sage, 2000.

Velleman, Paul, and David Hoaglin. *The ABC's of EDA: Applications, Basics, and Computing of Exploratory Data Analysis*. Duxbury, MA: Duxbury Press, 1981.

STUDENT STUDY SITE

for CQ Press

Give your students the SAGE edge!

SAGE edge offers a robust online environment featuring an impressive array of free tools and resources for review, study, and further exploration, keeping both instructors and students on the cutting edge of teaching and learning. Learn more at **edge.sagepub.com/johnson9e.**

15

THE RESEARCH REPORT
An Annotated Example

In the preceding chapters, we described important aspects of conducting a scientific investigation of political phenomena. In this chapter, we discuss the culmination of a research project: writing a research report. A complete and well-written research report that covers each component of the research process will contribute to the researcher's goal of creating transmissible, scientific knowledge.

This chapter examines how one researcher conducted and reported his research. We evaluate how well the author performed each component of the research process and how adequately he described and explained the choices he made during the investigation. As we conducted this evaluation, we used the following sets of questions:

1. Does the researcher clearly specify the main research question?

2. Does the researcher state the value and significance of the research questions and indicate how his research findings will contribute to scientific knowledge about his topic?

3. Has the researcher reviewed the relevant literature? Is his review organized around key themes related to his research question?

4. Has the researcher proposed clear explanations for the political phenomena that interest him? Does he discuss any alternative explanations?

5. What are his hypotheses? Are they empirical, general, and plausible?

6. Are the independent and dependent variables identified? If so, what are they? Are alternative or control variables considered? If so, what are they?

7. Are the concepts in the hypotheses clearly defined? If so, what are they? Are the operational definitions given for the variables valid and reasonable? What is the level of measurement for each of the variables?

8. What is the unit of analysis? Has the researcher made empirical observations about the units of analysis specified in the hypothesis?

9. What method of data collection is used to make the necessary observations? Are the observations valid and the measures reliable?

10. If a sample is used, what type of sample is it? Does the type of sample used seriously affect the conclusions that can be drawn from the research? Does the researcher discuss this?

11. What type of research design is used? Does the research design adequately test the hypothesized relationships?

12. Are the statistics used appropriate for the level of measurement of the variables?

13. Are the research findings presented and discussed clearly? Is the basis for deciding whether a hypothesis is supported or refuted clearly specified?

Keep these questions in mind as you read the research article.

ANNOTATED RESEARCH REPORT EXAMPLE

THE POLARIZING EFFECT OF THE MARCH FOR SCIENCE ON ATTITUDES TOWARD SCIENTISTS

Matthew Motta, *University of Minnesota*

Note: Colored icons have been placed next to paragraphs containing material related to the list of questions presented above. At the end of the article, we reveal which color corresponds with which question. We'd like you to read through the article and match the content to the questions by yourself before looking at the color coding that has been provided.

ABSTRACT Americans' attitudes toward scientists have become more negative in recent years. Although researchers have considered several individual-level factors that might explain this change, little attention has been given to the political actions of scientists themselves. This article considers how March for Science rallies that took place across the United States in late April 2017 influenced Americans' attitudes toward scientists and the research they produce. An online panel study surveying respondents three days before and two days after the March found that liberals' and conservatives' attitudes toward scientists polarized following the March. Liberals' attitudes toward scientists became more positive whereas conservatives' attitudes became more negative. However, the March appears to have had little effect on the public's attitudes about scientific research. In addition to answering questions about the March's political impact, this research calls attention to the possibility that the political actions of scientists can shape public opinion about them.

In recent years, Americans' attitudes toward scientists and other experts have become more negative. Trust in the scientific community, for example, has declined steadily on the ideological right since the mid-1990s (Gauchat 2012) and has remained only moderately positive on the ideological left (Mullin 2017). This increased negativity has important implications for American political life by shaping citizens' preferences for anti-science political candidates and encouraging disbelief in scientific consensus (Motta 2017).

An important line of scholarly research focuses on individual-level factors that might explain why some Americans hold negative attitudes toward scientists. For example, several studies investigated the effects of citizens' knowledge about science, ideological conservatism, and the interaction between the two on attitudes toward scientists and science more broadly (Blank and Shaw 2015; Bolsen, Druckman, and Cook 2015; Gauchat 2012; Gauchat, O'Brien, and Mirosa 2017; Hofstadter 1963; Kahan et al. 2012; McCright et al. 2013; Sturgis and Allum 2004). Americans' religious preferences, perceptions of scientific consensus and understanding, and attitudes toward modernization also have been linked to their attitudes toward scientists (Gauchat 2008; 2012; Hofstadter 1963; McCright, Dunlap, and Xiao 2013; Nichols 2017).

Much less attention, however, has been given to scientists and experts themselves, especially regarding their involvement in politics (see Cofnas, Carl, and Woodley of Menie 2017 for a review). This is a notable shortcoming in the literature because President Trump's skepticism toward science and interference with scientific research (Tobias 2017) have led scientists to organize on behalf of their political interests.

This raises an important question: When scientists organize politically, and visibly, do their actions influence public opinion? The March for Science events taking place across the country in late April 2017 offered a unique opportunity to answer this question.

Leveraging online panel data from three days before and two days after the events, I found that liberals' and conservatives' attitudes about scientists and experts polarized immediately following the March for Science. Liberals and conservatives were divided before the March about their attitudes toward scientists and experts, and the March appears to have exacerbated these differences. It is interesting that whereas liberals and conservatives also were divided in their attitudes toward scientific research before the March, the events did not appear to polarize these attitudes. The results suggest that, in this case, "mobilized science" can have polarizing effects on the public's affect for scientists and experts but does not necessarily impact their attitudes toward the research that these individuals produce.

Mobilized Science and Public Opinion

Although scholars have made important strides in understanding how individual-level factors affect attitudes toward science, fewer works consider how the political actions of scientists themselves might shape public opinion (however, see Brulle's 2018 critical reflection on the effectiveness of the March for Science). I refer to the public efforts of scientists, academics, and experts more broadly to advance their collective political interests as mobilized science. I conceptualize *mobilized science* as a general term to describe the efforts of these groups to draw attention to or take action on matters relevant to their shared goals.

The March for Science events taking place in April 2017 can be considered an example of mobilized science. It was organized by dozens of scientists and academics (March for Science 2017) in partnership with several preexisting interest groups devoted to the advancement of scientific interests (e.g., American Association for the Advancement of Science). Through an extensive social media campaign (March for Science 2017), the group organized 610 semi-autonomous "satellite" marches across the country (and the world). Today, the organization continues to operate by soliciting donations, supporting community organization efforts, and creating platforms by which interested visitors to their website can contact policy makers.

Critically, the marches received substantial attention in the popular press. The flagship March for Science in Washington, DC, had several celebrity hosts and guests (Gibson 2017) and even received Twitter attention from President Trump. High levels of popular attention to the March raise the possibility—at least in theory—that it may have had an impact on public opinion.

This article explores the possibility that the March for Science may have influenced the public's attitudes about science, research, and expertise. I suspect that it may have polarized opinion along ideological lines, potentially taking one of the following forms.

The first possibility is the Affective Polarization Hypothesis. Fundamentally, the "public face" of the March for Science is the *people* participating. Although they gathered in support of several common goals—some of which concerned academic and scientific research (e.g., federal funding for research and hiring practices)—media coverage about the March itself was focused primarily on

(Continued)

(Continued)

who was doing the marching (Nyhan 2017; Smith 2017). Consistent with this view, some scientists voiced concern (before the March) that the events might encourage the public to view scientists as a "liberal constituency" (Mullin 2017).

A second possibility is the Generalized Polarization Hypothesis. According to this model, the March for Science was a broadly polarizing event, encouraging conservatives (or liberals) to view both scientists and their research more negatively (or positively). Like the Affective Polarization Hypothesis, this view recognizes that the March may have polarized public opinion about scientists. However, consistent with recent insight on how citizens formulate political judgments (Lodge and Taber 2013), negative feelings toward these individuals might subsequently spill over to shape citizens' attitudes about related concepts (e.g., scientific research).

Although these expectations are exploratory, I suspect that the Affective Polarization Hypothesis is a particularly good candidate for explaining potential change in public opinion following the March for Science. Given the significant media attention given to it in an increasingly polarized political landscape (Abramowitz 2010), the March's personal focus on those doing the protesting creates a clear possibility for polarization on the basis of affect toward scientists and experts.

Three additional notes bear mentioning. First, this study concerns the polarization of attitudes about scientists as a group. Whereas it is certainly possible that liberals (or conservatives) evaluate some types of scientists differently than others (McCright et al. 2013), recent survey research found that conservatives tend to be more distrusting of scientists *writ large* than liberals (Blank and Shaw 2015). Second, this study focuses on ideological polarization in an effort to speak directly to extant literature on the subject (Gauchat 2008; 2012). Given the strong correspondence between ideological self-placement and partisan identification, however, I consider whether the March polarized partisans on these issues in the supplementary materials. Third, it is an important caveat that this study is only a first step in understanding how mobilized science shapes public opinion. Future

research should explore the dynamics of elite polarization on mobilized science and how media coverage of it might influence opinion formation about scientists and their research (for more on this general phenomenon, see Bolsen and Druckman 2015 and Druckman, Peterson, and Slothuus 2013).

The Panel Study

To test these hypotheses, I fielded a two-wave panel study measuring public support for scientists, experts, and their research immediately before and after the March for Science. My purpose was to exploit how change in the saliency of the March might alter opinions about scientists and research at the individual level for the same individuals.

This design can best be thought of as quasi-experimental. In a true natural experiment, respondents would be assigned to naturally occurring treatment and control groups. Here, I alternatively used what Shadish, Cook, and Campbell (2002) referred to as a "one-group (within-participants) pretest-posttest design," which means that all panel participants had the opportunity to be "treated by" (i.e., exposed to information about) the March. Consequently, I used tests designed not to assess the raw treatment effects of the March but rather the *conditional* treatment effects across ideological subgroups (identified before the treatment took place).

Data

To construct a pre–post-March panel, I first surveyed 428 workers on Amazon's Mechanical Turk (MTurk) on April 19, 2017, exiting the field two (full) days before the March for Science on April 22. I then recontacted all 428 individuals (using Turk Prime's recontact feature) and invited them to participate in a second survey, taking place from 10 a.m. (CST) on April 24 to 10 a.m. on April 25. The second wave of the study produced a recontact rate of 83% and a completion rate of 82%, with a final N of 350.

I fielded the study on these dates to assess respondents' opinions at a time in which media coverage of the March for Science was low (Wave 1), followed by a time in which media coverage

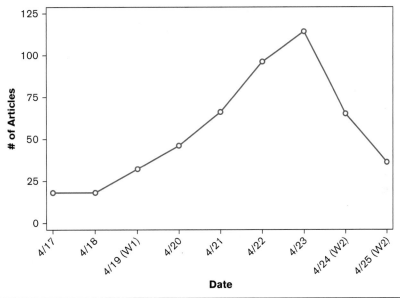

FIGURE 1 ■ Frequency of News Coverage of the March for Science

was high (Wave 2). Figure 1 demonstrates that the selection of these dates was apparently well justified. News coverage of the March for Science was comparatively low when the study began fielding (i.e., N = 30 articles on April 19). The coverage grew rapidly after exiting the field later in the day on April 19, producing about 250 articles between April 22 and April 23, between the two waves.

Of course, the MTurk workers surveyed do not constitute a nationally representative sample (see table S1 for specific details about the sample's demographics). The raw proportions described in the results may not generalize to the American population, which is an important caveat to remember. Still, the movement in attitudes observed across ideological groups over time likely is valid for at least two reasons.

First, it is critical that differences in opinion across waves are not necessarily biased by sample composition. As long as MTurk workers do not process or react differently to the March's increased saliency than the rest of the public, change across waves is less likely to be biased. This appears to

be a reasonable assumption because liberals and conservatives on MTurk were shown to have psychological profiles similar to those surveyed in representative samples, making the site a valid outlet for research on political ideology (Clifford, Jewell, and Waggoner 2015).

Second, to the extent that MTurk and nationally representative samples differ, cross-sample discrepancies can be dramatically reduced with the inclusion of simple demographic controls in multivariate modeling (Levay, Freese, and Druckman 2016). For example, Levay and colleagues found that 93% of the difference in climate-change attitudes across MTurk and representative sampling can be accounted for with the addition of simple demographic controls (e.g., race, age, gender, and education).

Measures

There are two key groups of outcome variables in this analysis. The first concerns attitudes toward scientists and experts, and it is measured using five

(Continued)

(Continued)

different variables. The first three variables are standard 101-point "feeling thermometers" toward "scientists," "college professors," and "intellectuals." The remaining two variables ask respondents whether they agree or disagree (i.e., using a five-point Likert scale ranging from "Strongly Disagree" to "Strongly Agree") with the following statements:

1. "Scientists care less about solving important problems than their own personal gain."

2. "Most experts are untrustworthy."

The second group contains two variables measuring citizens' attitudes toward scientific research. Respondents again were asked whether they agreed or disagreed with the following two statements:

1. "Most scientific research is politically motivated."

2. "You simply can't trust most scientific research."

The key independent variable in this study is respondents' ideological self-identification. This was measured using a standard seven-point self-placement scale, ranging from "extremely liberal" to "extremely conservative." At times, in the analyses that follow, I recoded this variable into a trichotomous indicator of whether individuals identified as liberals (i.e., all scores below the scale's midpoint), moderates (i.e., the midpoint), or conservatives (i.e., all scores above the midpoint).

I controlled for respondents' age, education, race (i.e., black and Hispanic indicators), income, gender (0 = male, 1 = female), and interest in politics in certain multivariate models. All controls were scaled to range from 0 to 1. Full wording of the questions for these variables is in the supplementary materials.

Results

To test my theoretical expectations, I constructed several multivariate difference-in-difference tests.

I chose this analytical design because it directly calculates growth in pre-to-post March for Science levels of polarization. Also, it can provide a statistical estimate of whether this movement is significantly different from what we would ordinarily expect by chance. Typically, this design is used to compare naturally occurring treatment and control groups (Ashenfelter and Card 1985). However, the quasi-experimental design described previously calls for a test of conditional treatment effects. Consequently, the treatment and control groups are pretreatment indicators of whether respondents self-identified as liberals or conservatives, respectively.

Four additional methodological points warrant mentioning. First, the difference-in-difference analyses were restricted to individuals completing both waves of the survey, with moderates excluded ([(]the potential for polarization among moderates is discussed shortly). Second, due to the well-known tradeoffs of including covariates in quasi-experiments (Mutz 2011), I estimated difference-in-difference effects both with and without the covariates listed in the previous section. The results, discussed shortly, are quite similar across specification strategies. Third, I clustered standard errors at the respondent level in both sets of models, as often is recommended (Imbens and Wooldridge 2007). Fourth, in addition to presenting item-specific difference-in-difference tests, I guarded against the possibility of random measurement error by averaging each group of items into corresponding indices (Ansolabehere, Rodden, and Snyder 2008).

The results, presented in table 1, are consistent with the Affective Polarization Hypothesis. In rows 1–7, which pertain to affect toward scientists and experts, I found significant increases in change between liberals and conservatives before and after the March for Science in six of seven models. Without controls, five produced estimates that were significant at the $p<0.05$ level (two-tailed); one approached conventional levels at the $p<0.10$ level. These results were similar when adding controls, except that the "experts are untrustworthy" item dipped below the $p=0.10$ threshold. In addition to being statistically significant, these effects were

TABLE 1 ■ Summary of Difference-in-Difference Tests								
	Wave	One	Wave	Two	Without Covariates		With Covariates	
	Liberals	Conservatives	Liberals	Conservatives	/D-I-D/	p	/D-I-D/	p
Scientist Feeling Thermometer	0.83	0.70	0.86	0.67	0.05	<0.05	0.05	< 0.05
Intellectual Feeling Thermometer	0.77	0.67	0.80	0.64	0.07	<0.05	0.07	< 0.05
College Professor Feeling Thermometer	0.74	0.56	0.75	0.54	0.03	<n.s.	0.02	< n.s.
Index	0.78	0.64	0.80	0.62	0.05	<0.05	0.05	< 0.05
Scientists Care about Personal Gain	0.25	0.39	0.20	0.45	0.11	<0.05	0.12	< 0.05
Experts Are Untrustworthy	0.26	0.40	0.22	0.42	0.05	<0.10	0.05	n.s.
Index	0.26	0.39	0.21	0.43	0.08	<0.05	0.08	< 0.05
Research Is Politically Motivated	0.28	0.53	0.25	0.53	0.03	n.s.	0.03	n.s.
Can't Trust Scientific Research	0.20	0.39	0.17	0.38	0.01	n.s.	0.01	n.s.
Index	0.24	0.46	0.21	0.46	0.02	n.s.	0.02	n.s.

Notes: Multivariate difference-in-difference tests were calculated using the DIFF package in Stata 13. Models were run first without controls and then re-estimated controlling for respondents' gender, race, age, income, interest in politics, and educational attainment. Rows 1–3 are "feeling thermometers" towards "scientists," "intellectuals," and "college professors," respectively (row 4 index $\alpha = 0.85$). Rows 5–6 ask whether respondents agree or disagree (1 = Strongly Disagree, 5 = Strongly Agree) with the following statements: (1) "Scientists care less about solving important problems than their own personal gain," and (2) "Most experts are untrustworthy" (row 7 index $\alpha = 0.76$). Rows 8–9 ask respondents whether they agree or disagree with the following statements: (1) "Most scientific research is politically motivated," and (2) "You simply can't trust most scientific research" (row 10 index $\alpha = 0.80$). All variables were scaled to range from 0 to 1.

substantively large, ranging from a 4% change across ideological subgroups (i.e., college-professor affect in both specifications) to 11% (i.e., belief that scientists are motivated by personal gains; 12% change in the covariate specification).

Furthermore, the results do not provide any evidence that the March for Science polarized citizens' attitudes toward scientific research—even when the items were averaged together to reduce measurement error. In all cases (rows 8–10) and across both specifications, I found small but statistically insignificant increases in polarization across waves. This is consistent with the idea that the March polarized liberals' and conservatives' attitudes about scientists and experts but not their research.

Finally, although I lacked a clear *a priori* expectation about how moderates might respond to the

(Continued)

(Continued)

March for Science, relative to either liberals or conservatives, follow-up tests suggested that they tended to follow conservative opinion after the March. To do this, I re-ran table 1, swapping self-identified conservatives for self-identified moderates (N = 77, for those taking both waves). The results in table S3 show that moderates, relative to liberals, did in fact become significantly more negative toward scientists following the March for Science.

Addressing Potential Confounds

Before concluding, it is important to address three potential concerns with the results presented so far. First is the possibility of differential attrition. Theoretically, it may be that individuals who opted to take both waves of the study differed in their attitudes about science than those who were lost to attrition. Table S4 in the supplementary materials tested this possibility and revealed no significant differences across these two groups.

Second, a common issue with quasi-experimental designs is the ability to disentangle treatment effects from broader time trends. Although this study was conducted during the course of six days, it (theoretically) could be the case that the passage of time itself—and not the March for Science—increased polarization.

To test whether this was true, I added a non-equivalent dependent variable component to the difference-in-difference tests in table 1, as Shadish, Cook, and Campbell (2002) recommended. This was like a placebo test; in which the goal is to run the same models in the table using outcome variables that also should be polarized across ideological lines but that should not be expected to grow over the six-day span. Failing to observe significant difference-in-difference estimates on the nonequivalent dependent variables would provide added confidence that the March for Science—and not the passage of time more broadly—led to affective polarization.

I did this by swapping respondents' attitudes toward Muslims and immigrants for the variables listed in table 1. The results presented in table S5 in the supplementary materials reveal no significant difference-in-difference estimates between liberals and conservatives across waves. This provided added assurance that the quasi-experimental design was not confounded by the passage of time.

Third, given the high correspondence between partisanship and ideology (Bafumi and Shapiro 2009), I re-ran all difference-in-difference models using indicators of whether respondents self-identified as Democrats or Republicans. The results in table S2 of the supplementary materials show that the effects were similar.

Discussion

These results provide a unique look into the polarizing effects of the March for Science on public opinion. Although liberals and conservatives held differing opinions toward scientists, experts, and scientific research before the March, the aftermath appears to have exacerbated those differences. I observed these effects with respect only to citizens' attitudes toward scientists and experts themselves, not the research they produce, which is consistent with the Affective Polarization Hypothesis.

Of course, these analyses are not without limitations. As discussed previously, I drew these conclusions from a non-representative sample of Americans. Whereas the amount of change observed across ideological groups may not differ in more-representative samples, the raw estimates of where liberals and conservatives stand on each item should be interpreted with caution. Furthermore, I studied polarization in response to only one naturally occurring instance of mobilized science. Studying future instances of mobilized science can provide further validation of these results.

Overall, this study advances our understanding of how mobilized science influences public opinion about scientists on two fronts. First, it offers novel insights into an understudied topic in political science: how scientists' political actions shape public opinion about themselves. Moreover, it identifies an important practical tradeoff for those involved in the mobilization of science. As scientists organize to combat skepticism and interference from the Trump administration, they may indeed win support from those most congenial to their cause. However, they risk losing support among those who are less sympathetic. Whether this tradeoff is worth the cost is a question that should surround future mobilized-science efforts.

Supplementary Material

To view supplementary material for this article, please visit https://doi.org/10.1017/S1049096518000938.

References

Abramowitz, Alan I. 2010. *The Disappearing Center: Engaged Citizens, Polarization, and American Democracy.* New Haven, CT: Yale University Press.

Ansolabehere, Stephen, Jonathan Rodden, and James M. Snyder. 2008. "The Strength of Issues: Using Multiple Measures to Gauge Preference Stability, Ideological Constraint, and Issue Voting." *American Political Science Review* 102 (2): 215–32.

Ashenfelter, Orley, and David Card. 1985. "Using the Longitudinal Structure of Earnings to Estimate the Effect of Training Programs." *The Review of Economics and Statistics* 67 (4): 648–60.

Bafumi, Joseph, and Robert Y. Shapiro. 2009. "A New Partisan Voter." *Journal of Politics* 71 (1): 1–24.

Blank, Joshua M., and Daron Shaw. 2015. "Does Partisanship Shape Attitudes Toward Science and Public Policy? The Case for Ideology and Religion." *ANNALS of the American Academy of Political and Social Science* 658 (1): 18–35.

Bolsen, Toby, and James N. Druckman. 2015. "Counteracting the Politicization of Science." *Journal of Communication* 65 (5): 745–69.

Bolsen, Toby, James N. Druckman, and Fay L. Cook. 2015. "Citizens, Scientists, and Policy Advisors Beliefs about Global Warming." *ANNALS of the American Academy of Political and Social Science* 658 (1): 271–95.

Brulle, Robert J. 2018. "Critical Reflections on the March for Science." *Sociological Forum* 33: 255–8.

Clifford, Scott, Ryan M. Jewell, and Phillip D. Waggoner. 2015. "Are Samples Drawn from Mechanical Turk Valid for Research on Political Ideology?" *Research & Politics* 2 (4): 1–9.

Cofnas, Nathan, Noah Carl, and Michael A. Woodley of Menie. 2017. "Does Activism in Social Science Explain Conservatives' Distrust of Scientists?" *The American Sociologist* 49 (1): 1–14.

Druckman, James N., Erik Peterson, and Rune Slothuus. 2013. "How Elite Partisan Polarization Affects Public Opinion Formation." *American Political Science Review* 107 (1): 57–79.

Gauchat, Gordon W. 2008. "A Test of Three Theories of Anti-Science Attitudes." *Sociological Focus* 41 (4): 337–57.

———. 2012. "Politicization of Science in the Public Sphere: A Study of Public Trust in the United States, 1974 to 2010." *American Sociological Review* 77 (2): 167–87.

Gauchat, Gordon, Timothy O'Brien, and Oriol Mirosa. 2017. "The Legitimacy of Environmental Scientists in the Public Sphere." *Climatic Change* 143 (3): 297–306.

Gibson, Caitlin. 2017. "The March for Science Was a Moment Made for Bill Nye." *Washington Post*, April 23. Available at www.washingtonpost.com/lifestyle/style/the-march-for-science-was-a-moment-made-for-bill-nye/2017/04/23.

Hofstadter, Richard. 1963. *Anti-Intellectualism in American Life.* New York: Vintage.

Imbens, Guido, and Jeffrey Wooldridge. 2007. "Differences-in-Differences Estimation." Unpublished manuscript, last modified Summer 2007. Available at www.nber.org/WNE/lect10diffindiffs.pdf.

Kahan, Dan M., Ellen Peters, Maggie Wittlin, Paul Slovic, Lisa Larrimore Ouellette, Donald Braman, and Gregory Mandel. 2012. "The Polarizing Impact of Science Literacy and Numeracy on Perceived Climate Change Risks." *Nature Climate Change* 2 (10): 732–5.

Levay, Kevin E., Jeremy Freese, and James N. Druckman. 2016. "The Demographic and Political Composition of Mechanical Turk Samples." *Sage Open* 6 (1): 1–17.

Lodge, Milton, and Charles S. Taber. 2013. *The Rationalizing Voter.* Cambridge: Cambridge University Press.

March for Science. 2017. "About Us." Available at www.marchforscience.com/mission.

McCright, Arron M., Katherine Dentzman, Meghan Charters, and Thomas Dietz. 2013. "The Influence of Political Ideology on Trust in Science." *Environmental Research Letters* 8 (4): 1–9.

McCright, Arron M., Reily E. Dunlap, and Chenyang Xiao. 2013. "Perceived Scientific Agreement and Support for Government Action on Climate Change in the USA." *Climatic Change* 119 (2): 511–18.

Motta, Matthew. 2017. "The Dynamics and Political Implications of Anti-Intellectualism in the United States." *American Politics Research* 46 (3): 465–98.

Mullin, Megan. 2017. "Will the March for Science Backfire by Politicizing Science? It Depends on This." *Washington Post*, April 21. Available at www.washingtonpost.com/news/monkey-cage/wp/2017/04/21.

Mutz, Diana C. 2011. *Population-Based Survey Experiments.* Princeton, NJ: Princeton University Press.

Nichols, Thomas. 2017. *The Death of Expertise: The Campaign against Established Knowledge and Why It Matters.* Oxford: Oxford University Press.

Nyhan, Brendan. 2017. "How Marching for Science Risks Politicizing It." *New York Times*, May 2. Available at www.nytimes.com/2017/05/02/upshot/how-marching-for-science-risks-politicizing-it.html.

Shadish, William R., Thomas D. Cook, and Donald Thomas Campbell. 2002. *Experimental and Quasi-Experimental Designs for Generalized Causal Inference.* Boston: Wadsworth Cengage Learning.

Smith, Noah. 2017. "March for Science Was Important, Silly Signs Aside." *Bloomberg Science*, April 27. Available at www.bloomberg.com/view/articles/2017-04-27/march-for-science-was-important-silly-signs-aside.

Sturgis, Patrick, and Nick Allum. 2004. "Science in Society: Reevaluating the Deficit Model of Public Attitudes." *Public Understanding of Science* 13 (2): 55–74.

Tobias, Jimmy. 2017. "A Brief Survey of Trump's Assault on Science." *Pacific Standard*, July 24. Available at psmag.com/environment/a-brief-survey-of-trumps-assault-on-science.

Source: Motta, Matthew. "The Polarizing Effect of the March for Science on Attitudes toward Scientists." PS: Political Science & Politics 51, no. 4 (2018): 782–88. doi:10.1017/S1049096518000938.

Q1.   Does the researcher clearly specify the main research question?

Yes, the research question is clearly specified: "When scientists organize politically, and visibly, do their actions influence public opinion?"

Q2.   Does the researcher state the value and significance of the research questions and indicate how his research findings will contribute to scientific knowledge about his topic?

Why is this an important topic? Trust in the scientific community has been declining. Because scientists have organized on behalf of their interests in response to President Trump's skepticism toward science and interference with scientific research, Motta argues that it is important to understand if and how scientists' political activity shapes citizens' attitudes toward scientists and scientific research. Most previous research has not considered how the political action of scientists themselves might shape public opinion.

Q3.   Has the researcher reviewed the relevant literature? Is his review organized around key themes related to his research question?

Motta cites the literature that focuses on individual-level factors that might help explain why some Americans hold negative attitudes toward scientists. These factors include citizens' knowledge about science, ideological conservatism, religious preferences, perceptions of scientific consensus and understanding, and attitudes toward modernization. Perhaps some of these factors will also influence how citizens react to scientists' political activity. In particular, previous research has shown that "conservatives tend to be more distrusting of scientists *writ large* than liberals." Notice how succinct this summary is.

Q4.   Has the researcher proposed clear explanations for the political phenomena that interest him? Does he discuss any alternative explanations?

Motta's explanation of the public's attitude toward scientists focuses on political ideology. He does not propose alternative explanations. He does take other factors into account (age, education, race, gender, and interest in politics) as it is possible that differences in these factors would lead to differences in reactions to the March for Science. In addition, he considers that simply the passage of time could have caused increased polarization. He investigates this possibility by looking for, but not finding, increased polarization for two other attitudes on which liberals and conservatives differ.

Q5.   What are his hypotheses? Are they empirical, general, and plausible?

Motta expects that liberals and conservatives will react differently to the March for Science. He expects that the March for Science has a polarizing effect—that the opinion gap between liberals and conservatives will get larger. He presents two possibilities: (1) Because media coverage of the March for Science focused on who was marching, the Affective Polarization Hypothesis predicts that polarization will involve people's views toward scientists, but not scientific research; (2) the Generalized Polarization Hypothesis suggests that the March for Science would polarize public opinion not only toward scientists, but also toward attitudes about scientific research. He expects the first to have more traction as media coverage focused on the persons (scientists) involved in the March. Both of these expectations are empirical, plausible, and general.

Q6. Are the independent and dependent variables identified? If so, what are they? Are alternative or control variables considered? If so, what are they?

The independent variable is clearly political ideology. The dependent variables are attitudes toward scientists and attitudes toward scientific research. As mentioned above, Motta controls for age, education, race, and gender.

Q7. Are the concepts in the hypotheses clearly defined? If so, what are they? Are the operational definitions given for the variables valid and reasonable? What is the level of measurement for each of the variables?

Motta clearly explains the operationalization of his key concepts or variables. Attitudes toward scientists and experts are measured using five questions, all of which are related to evaluating scientists and experts. All of the measures have multiple response categories. Three are 100-point feeling thermometer scales, and two are five-point Likert scales. Even though these are technically ordinal-level measures and, thus, categorical measures, Motta treats them as numerical (he calculates mean scores). Two questions are used to measure attitudes toward scientific research, and these two items clearly relate to the concept being measured. The response categories to these items were "agree" and "disagree." Thus, these are dichotomous variables. Having multiple measures improves the validity and reliability of the concepts. Motta measures his independent variable, ideology, using a standard seven-point self-placement scale, which he then recoded to create a variable with three categories: liberal, moderate, and conservative.

Q8. What is the unit of analysis? Has the researcher made empirical observations about the units of analysis specified in the hypothesis?

The unit of analysis is the individual and empirical observations of individuals that were made using survey questions. Motta refers to citizens and respondents, both of which indicate that he is studying characteristics of individuals.

Q9. What method of data collection is used to make the necessary observations? Are the observations valid and the measures reliable?

An online survey is used to collect the data. Individuals participating in Amazon's Mechanical Turk responded to the survey questions. Insofar as the survey questions constituted valid measures of the variables and respondents answered them truthfully, it is safe to conclude that the empirical observations were valid and reliable.

Q10. If a sample is used, what type of sample is it? Does the type of sample used seriously affect the conclusions that can be drawn from the research? Does the researcher discuss this?

Motta used an availability sample to collect data for this project by using Amazon's Mechanical Turk (MTurk) service that provides paid survey participants to answer survey questions (783-4). The 428 individuals who answered questions in both waves of the study were not nationally representative, which may have caused bias in the results because Motta was using a nonrepresentative sample to make conclusions about the national population. He addressed this issue on page 784, stating that he believed the survey participants would change their attitudes in a similar way as the target population because (1) MTurk respondents likely process and react to information similarly to the target population because the MTurk respondents have similar psychological profiles in other published work and (2) other published work has demonstrated that by controlling for demographic factors, MTurk respondents are similar to the target population. Motta includes these demographic factors in online supplemental materials so the reader can judge the quality of the sample.

Q11. What type of research design is used? Does the research design adequately test the hypothesized relationships?

Motta employs a quasi-experimental design with a two-wave panel survey. The design is quasi-experimental because it is neither a classical randomized experiment in which the experimenter controls all of the treatment and environmental factors, nor a natural experiment with naturally occurring treatment and control groups. In this design, Motta made use of a one-group (within-participants) pretest–posttest design in which all respondents had an opportunity for exposure to the treatment (learning about the March for Science) and measured the conditional treatment effect across ideological subgroups (conservatives and liberals).

Motta's hypotheses, the Affective Polarization Hypothesis and the Generalized Polarization Hypothesis, are adequately tested in this design. Self-identified liberals and conservatives answered questions about their views on scientists and science in the pretest and posttest. The difference in the conservatives' and liberals' answers across the pre- and posttest tested the claims in the hypotheses. He also compared liberals to moderates.

Q12. Are the statistics used appropriate for the level of measurement of the variables?

Motta's variables were ordinal-, interval-, and ratio-level measures. The statistics reported in Table 1 were means of proportions and p values used to evaluate t tests in the difference-in-difference tests and were appropriate for the levels of measurement.

Q13. Are the research findings presented and discussed clearly? Is the basis for deciding whether a hypothesis is supported or refuted clearly specified?

The research findings are presented and discussed clearly. Motta discussed the two hypotheses earlier in the article and established that in order to find support for each hypothesis, we should see a statistically significant difference between responses of liberals and conservatives. Table 1 reports the measures for which there were statistically significant differences across the liberal and conservative subgroups (Scientist Thermometer, Intellectual Thermometer, and the associated Index; Scientists Care about Personal Gain, Experts Are Untrustworthy, and the associated index), and those for which there were not (Research Is Politically Motivated, Can't Trust Scientific Research, and the associated Index). Motta explains how the reader can interpret the *p* values in Table 1. There was support for the notion that the March for Science polarized liberals' and conservatives' views of scientists and experts, but not of their research.

APPENDIXES

Appendix A

Normal Curve Tail Probabilities. Standard Normal Probability in Right-Hand Tail (for negative values of z, probabilities are found by symmetry)

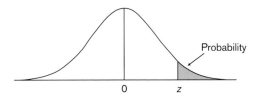

Probability

z					Second Decimal Place of z					
	.00	.01	.02	.03	.04	.05	.06	.07	.08	.09
0.0	.5000	.4960	.4920	.4880	.4840	.4801	.4761	.4721	.4681	.4641
0.1	.4602	.4562	.4522	.4483	.4443	.4404	.4364	.4325	.4286	.4247
0.2	.4207	.4168	.4129	.4090	.4052	.4013	.3974	.3936	.3897	.3859
0.3	.3821	.3783	.3745	.3707	.3669	.3632	.3594	.3557	.3520	.3483
0.4	.3446	.3409	.3372	.3336	.3300	.3264	.3228	.3192	.3156	.3121
0.5	.3085	.3050	.3015	.2981	.2946	.2912	.2877	.2843	.2810	.2776
0.6	.2743	.2709	.2676	.2643	.2611	.2578	.2546	.2514	.2483	.2451
0.7	.2420	.2389	.2358	.2327	.2296	.2266	.2236	.2206	.2177	.2148
0.8	.2119	.2090	.2061	.2033	.2005	.1977	.1949	.1922	.1894	.1867
0.9	.1841	.1814	.1788	.1762	.1736	.1711	.1685	.1660	.1635	.1611
1.0	.1587	.1562	.1539	.1515	.1492	.1469	.1446	.1423	.1401	.1379
1.1	.1357	.1335	.1314	.1292	.1271	.1251	.1230	.1210	.1190	.1170
1.2	.1151	.1131	.1112	.1093	.1075	.1056	.1038	.1020	.1003	.0985
1.3	.0968	.0951	.0934	.0918	.0901	.0885	.0869	.0853	.0838	.0823
1.4	.0808	.0793	.0778	.0764	.0749	.0735	.0722	.0708	.0694	.0681
1.5	.0668	.0655	.0643	.0630	.0618	.0606	.0594	.0582	.0571	.0559
1.6	.0548	.0537	.0526	.0516	.0505	.0495	.0485	.0475	.0465	.0455
1.7	.0446	.0436	.0427	.0418	.0409	.0401	.0392	.0384	.0375	.0367
1.8	.0359	.0352	.0344	.0336	.0329	.0322	.0314	.0307	.0301	.0294
1.9	.0287	.0281	.0274	.0268	.0262	.0256	.0250	.0244	.0239	.0233
2.0	.0228	.0222	.0217	.0212	.0207	.0202	.0197	.0192	.0188	.0183
2.1	.0179	.0174	.0170	.0166	.0162	.0158	.0154	.0150	.0146	.0143
2.2	.0139	.0136	.0132	.0129	.0125	.0122	.0119	.0116	.0113	.0110
2.3	.0107	.0104	.0102	.0099	.0096	.0094	.0091	.0089	.0087	.0084
2.4	.0082	.0080	.0078	.0075	.0073	.0071	.0069	.0068	.0066	.0064
2.5	.0062	.0060	.0059	.0057	.0055	.0054	.0052	.0051	.0049	.0048
2.6	.0047	.0045	.0044	.0043	.0041	.0040	.0039	.0038	.0037	.0036
2.7	.0035	.0034	.0033	.0032	.0031	.0030	.0029	.0028	.0027	.0026
2.8	.0026	.0025	.0024	.0023	.0023	.0022	.0021	.0021	.0020	.0019
2.9	.0019	.0018	.0017	.0017	.0016	.0016	.0015	.0015	.0014	.0014
3.0	.00135									
3.5	.000233									
4.0	.0000317									
4.5	.00000340									
5.0	.000000287									

Source: R. E. Walpole, *Introduction to Statistics* (New York: Macmillan, 1968). Used with permission.

Appendix B

Critical Values from *t* Distribution

Degree of Freedom (*df*)	Alpha Level for One-Tailed Test						
	.05	.025	.01	.005	.0025	.001	.0005
	Alpha Level for Two-Tailed Test						
	.10	.05	.02	.01	.005	.002	.001
1	6.314	12.706	31.821	63.657	127.32	318.31	636.62
2	2.920	4.303	6.965	9.925	14.089	22.327	31.598
3	2.353	3.182	4.541	5.841	7.453	10.214	12.924
4	2.132	2.776	3.747	4.604	5.598	7.173	8.610
5	2.015	2.571	3.365	4.032	4.773	5.893	6.869
6	1.943	2.447	3.143	3.707	4.317	5.208	5.959
7	1.895	2.365	2.998	3.499	4.029	4.785	5.408
8	1.869	2.306	2.896	3.355	3.833	4.501	5.041
9	1.833	2.262	2.821	3.250	3.690	4.297	4.781
10	1.812	2.228	2.764	3.169	3.581	4.144	4.587
11	1.796	2.201	2.718	3.106	3.497	4.025	4.437
12	1.782	2.179	2.681	3.055	3.428	3.930	4.318
13	1.771	2.160	2.650	3.012	3.372	3.852	4.221
14	1.761	2.145	2.624	2.977	3.326	3.787	4.140
15	1.753	2.131	2.602	2.947	3.286	3.733	4.073
16	1.746	2.120	2.583	2.921	3.252	3.686	4.015
17	1.740	2.110	2.567	2.898	3.222	3.646	3.965
18	1.734	2.101	2.552	2.878	3.197	3.610	3.922
19	1.729	2.093	2.539	2.861	3.174	3.579	3.883
20	1.725	2.086	2.528	2.845	3.153	3.552	3.850
21	1.721	2.080	2.518	2.831	3.135	3.527	3.819
22	1.717	2.074	2.508	2.819	3.119	3.505	3.792
23	1.714	2.069	2.500	2.807	3.104	3.485	3.767
24	1.711	2.064	2.492	2.797	3.091	3.467	3.745
25	1.708	2.060	2.485	2.787	3.078	3.450	3.725
26	1.706	2.056	2.479	2.779	3.067	3.435	3.707
27	1.703	2.052	2.473	2.771	3.057	3.421	3.690
28	1.701	2.048	2.467	2.763	3.047	3.408	3.674
29	1.699	2.045	2.462	2.756	3.038	3.396	3.659
30	1.697	2.042	2.457	2.750	3.030	3.385	3.646
40	1.684	2.021	2.423	2.704	2.971	3.307	3.551
60	1.671	2.000	2.390	2.660	2.915	3.232	3.460
120	1.658	1.980	2.358	2.617	2.860	3.160	3.373
∞	1.645	1.960	2.326	2.576	2.807	3.090	3.291

Source: James V. Couch, *Fundamentals of Statistics for the Behavioral Sciences, Second Edition.* (St. Paul, Minn.: West, 1987), 327. © 1987 Wadsworth, a part of Cengage Learning, Inc. Reproduced by permission. www.cengage.com/permissions

Appendix C

Chi-Squared Distribution Values for Various Right-Tail Probabilities

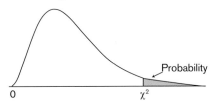

	Right-Tail Probability						
df	0.250	0.100	0.050	0.025	0.010	0.005	0.001
1	1.32	2.71	3.84	5.02	6.63	7.88	10.83
2	2.77	4.61	5.99	7.38	9.21	10.60	13.82
3	4.11	6.25	7.81	9.35	11.34	12.84	16.27
4	5.39	7.78	9.49	11.14	13.28	14.86	18.47
5	6.63	9.24	11.07	12.83	15.09	16.75	20.52
6	7.84	10.64	12.59	14.45	16.81	18.55	22.46
7	9.04	12.02	14.07	16.01	18.48	20.28	24.32
8	10.22	13.36	15.51	17.53	20.09	21.96	26.12
9	11.39	14.68	16.92	19.02	21.67	23.59	27.88
10	12.55	15.99	18.31	20.48	23.21	25.19	29.59
11	13.70	17.28	19.68	21.92	24.72	26.76	31.26
12	14.85	18.55	21.03	23.34	26.22	28.30	32.91
13	15.98	19.81	22.36	24.74	27.69	29.82	34.53
14	17.12	21.06	23.68	26.12	29.14	31.32	36.12
15	18.25	22.31	25.00	27.49	30.58	32.80	37.70
16	19.37	23.54	26.30	28.85	32.00	34.27	39.25
17	20.49	24.77	27.59	30.19	33.41	35.72	40.79
18	21.60	25.99	28.87	31.53	34.81	37.16	42.31
19	22.72	27.20	30.14	32.85	36.19	38.58	43.82
20	23.83	28.41	31.41	34.17	37.57	40.00	45.32
25	29.34	34.38	37.65	40.65	44.31	46.93	52.62
30	34.80	40.26	43.77	46.98	50.89	53.67	59.70
40	45.62	51.80	55.76	59.34	63.69	66.77	73.40
50	56.33	63.17	67.50	71.42	76.15	79.49	86.66
60	66.98	74.40	79.08	83.30	88.38	91.95	99.61
70	77.58	85.53	90.53	95.02	100.4	104.2	112.3
80	88.13	96.58	101.8	106.6	112.3	116.3	124.8
90	98.65	107.6	113.1	118.1	124.1	128.3	137.2
100	109.1	118.5	124.3	129.6	135.8	140.2	149.5

Source: Alan Agresti and Barbara Finlay, *Statistical Methods for the Social Sciences,* 3rd edition (Upper Saddle River, N.J.: Prentice Hall, 1997) p. 670. Used with permission.

Appendix D

F Distribution

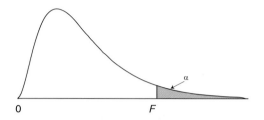

0   *F*

| | | | | | α = .05 | | | | | |
| | | | | | df₁ | | | | | |
df₂	1	2	3	4	5	6	8	12	24	∞
1	161.4	199.5	215.7	224.6	230.2	234.0	238.9	243.9	249.0	254.3
2	18.51	19.00	19.16	19.25	19.30	19.33	19.37	19.41	19.45	19.50
3	10.13	9.55	9.28	9.12	9.01	8.94	8.84	8.74	8.64	8.53
4	7.71	6.94	6.59	6.39	6.26	6.16	6.04	5.91	5.77	5.63
5	6.61	5.79	5.41	5.19	5.05	4.95	4.82	4.68	4.53	4.36
6	5.99	5.14	4.76	4.53	4.39	4.28	4.15	4.00	3.84	3.67
7	5.59	4.74	4.35	4.12	3.97	3.87	3.73	3.57	3.41	3.23
8	5.32	4.46	4.07	3.84	3.69	3.58	3.44	3.28	3.12	2.93
9	5.12	4.26	3.86	3.63	3.48	3.37	3.23	3.07	2.90	2.71
10	4.96	4.10	3.71	3.48	3.33	3.22	3.07	2.91	2.74	2.54
11	4.84	3.98	3.59	3.36	3.20	3.09	2.95	2.79	2.61	2.40
12	4.75	3.88	3.49	3.26	3.11	3.00	2.85	2.69	2.50	2.30
13	4.67	3.80	3.41	3.18	3.02	2.92	2.77	2.60	2.42	2.21
14	4.60	3.74	3.34	3.11	2.96	2.85	2.70	2.53	2.35	2.13
15	4.54	3.68	3.29	3.06	2.90	2.79	2.64	2.48	2.29	2.07
16	4.49	3.63	3.24	3.01	2.85	2.74	2.59	2.42	2.24	2.01
17	4.45	3.59	3.20	2.96	2.81	2.70	2.55	2.38	2.19	1.96
18	4.41	3.55	3.16	2.93	2.77	2.66	2.51	2.34	2.15	1.92
19	4.38	3.52	3.13	2.90	2.74	2.63	2.48	2.31	2.11	1.88
20	4.35	3.49	3.10	2.87	2.71	2.60	2.45	2.28	2.08	1.84
21	4.32	3.47	3.07	2.84	2.68	2.57	2.42	2.25	2.05	1.81
22	4.30	3.44	3.05	2.82	2.66	2.55	2.40	2.23	2.03	1.78
23	4.28	3.42	3.03	2.80	2.64	2.53	2.38	2.20	2.00	1.76
24	4.26	3.40	3.01	2.78	2.62	2.51	2.36	2.18	1.98	1.73
25	4.24	3.38	2.99	2.76	2.60	2.49	2.34	2.16	1.96	1.71
26	4.22	3.37	2.98	2.74	2.59	2.47	2.32	2.15	1.95	1.69
27	4.21	3.35	2.96	2.73	2.57	2.46	2.30	2.13	1.93	1.67
28	4.20	3.34	2.95	2.71	2.56	2.44	2.29	2.12	1.91	1.65
29	4.18	3.33	2.93	2.70	2.54	2.43	2.28	2.10	1.90	1.64
30	4.17	3.32	2.92	2.69	2.53	2.42	2.27	2.09	1.89	1.62
40	4.08	3.23	2.84	2.61	2.45	2.34	2.18	2.00	1.79	1.51
60	4.00	3.15	2.76	2.52	2.37	2.25	2.10	1.92	1.70	1.39
120	3.92	3.07	2.68	2.45	2.29	2.17	2.02	1.83	1.61	1.25
∞	3.84	2.99	2.60	2.37	2.21	2.09	1.94	1.75	1.52	1.00

Source: From Table V of R. A. Fisher and F. Yates, *Statistical Tables for Biological, Agricultural and Medical Research*, published by Longman Group Ltd., London, 1974. Reprinted by permission of Pearson Education Limited.

					$\alpha = .01$					
					df_1					
df_2	1	2	3	4	5	6	8	12	24	∞
1	4052	4999	5403	5625	5764	5859	5981	6106	6234	6366
2	98.49	99.01	99.17	99.25	99.30	99.33	99.36	99.42	99.46	99.50
3	34.12	30.18	29.46	28.71	28.24	27.91	27.49	27.05	26.60	26.12
4	21.20	18.00	16.69	15.98	15.52	15.21	14.80	14.37	13.93	13.46
5	16.26	13.27	12.06	11.39	10.97	10.67	10.27	9.89	9.47	9.02
6	13.74	10.92	9.78	9.15	8.75	8.47	8.10	7.72	7.31	6.88
7	12.25	9.55	8.45	7.85	7.46	7.19	6.84	6.47	6.07	5.65
8	11.26	8.65	7.59	7.01	6.63	6.37	6.03	5.67	5.28	4.86
9	10.56	8.02	6.99	6.42	6.06	5.80	5.47	5.11	4.73	4.31
10	10.04	7.56	6.55	5.99	5.64	5.39	5.06	4.71	4.33	3.91
11	9.65	7.20	6.22	5.67	5.32	5.07	4.74	4.40	4.02	3.60
12	9.33	6.93	5.95	5.41	5.06	4.82	4.50	4.16	3.78	3.36
13	9.07	6.70	5.74	5.20	4.86	4.62	4.30	3.96	3.59	3.16
14	8.86	6.51	5.56	5.03	4.69	4.46	4.14	3.80	3.43	3.00
15	8.68	6.36	5.42	4.89	4.56	4.32	4.00	3.67	3.29	2.87
16	8.53	6.23	5.29	4.77	4.44	4.20	3.89	3.55	3.18	2.75
17	8.40	6.11	5.18	4.67	4.34	4.10	3.79	3.45	3.08	2.65
18	8.28	6.01	5.09	4.58	4.25	4.01	3.71	3.37	3.00	2.57
19	8.18	5.93	5.01	4.50	4.17	3.94	3.63	3.30	2.92	2.49
20	8.10	5.85	4.94	4.43	4.10	3.87	3.56	3.23	2.86	2.42
21	8.02	5.78	4.87	4.37	4.04	3.81	3.51	3.17	2.80	2.36
22	7.94	5.72	4.82	4.31	3.99	3.76	3.45	3.12	2.75	2.31
23	7.88	5.66	4.76	4.26	3.94	3.71	3.41	3.07	2.70	2.26
24	7.82	5.61	4.72	4.22	3.90	3.67	3.36	3.03	2.66	2.21
25	7.77	5.57	4.68	4.18	3.86	3.63	3.32	2.99	2.62	2.17
26	7.72	5.53	4.64	4.14	3.82	3.59	3.29	2.96	2.58	2.13
27	7.68	5.49	4.60	4.11	3.78	3.56	3.26	2.93	2.55	2.10
28	7.64	5.45	4.57	4.07	3.75	3.53	3.23	2.90	2.52	2.06
29	7.60	5.42	4.54	4.04	3.73	3.50	3.20	2.87	2.49	2.03
30	7.56	5.39	4.51	4.02	3.70	3.47	3.17	2.84	2.47	2.01
40	7.31	5.18	4.31	3.83	3.51	3.29	2.99	2.66	2.29	1.80
60	7.08	4.98	4.13	3.65	3.34	3.12	2.82	2.50	2.12	1.60
120	6.85	4.79	3.95	3.48	3.17	2.96	2.66	2.34	1.95	1.38
∞	6.64	4.60	3.78	3.32	3.02	2.80	2.51	2.18	1.79	1.00

					$\alpha = .001$					
					df_1					
df_2	1	2	3	4	5	6	8	12	24	∞
1	405284	500000	540379	562500	576405	585937	598144	610667	623497	636619
2	998.5	999.0	999.2	999.2	999.3	999.3	999.4	999.4	999.5	999.5
3	167.5	148.5	141.1	137.1	134.6	132.8	130.6	128.3	125.9	123.5
4	74.14	61.25	56.18	53.44	51.71	50.53	49.00	47.41	45.77	44.05
5	47.04	36.61	33.20	31.09	29.75	28.84	27.64	26.42	25.14	23.78
6	35.51	27.00	23.70	21.90	20.81	20.03	19.03	17.99	16.89	15.75
7	29.22	21.69	18.77	17.19	16.21	15.52	14.63	13.71	12.73	11.69
8	25.42	18.49	15.83	14.39	13.49	12.86	12.04	11.19	10.30	9.34
9	22.86	16.39	13.90	12.56	11.71	11.13	10.37	9.57	8.72	7.81
10	21.04	14.91	12.55	11.28	10.48	9.92	9.20	8.45	7.64	6.76
11	19.69	13.81	11.56	10.35	9.58	9.05	8.35	7.63	6.85	6.00
12	18.64	12.97	10.80	9.63	8.89	8.38	7.71	7.00	6.25	5.42
13	17.81	12.31	10.21	9.07	8.35	7.86	7.21	6.52	5.78	4.97
14	17.14	11.78	9.73	8.62	7.92	7.43	6.80	6.13	5.41	4.60
15	16.59	11.34	9.34	8.25	7.57	7.09	6.47	5.81	5.10	4.31
16	16.12	10.97	9.00	7.94	7.27	6.81	6.19	5.55	4.85	4.06
17	15.72	10.66	8.73	7.68	7.02	6.56	5.96	5.32	4.63	3.85
18	15.38	10.39	8.49	7.46	6.81	6.35	5.76	5.13	4.45	3.67
19	15.08	10.16	8.28	7.26	6.61	6.18	5.59	4.97	4.29	3.52
20	14.82	9.95	8.10	7.10	6.46	6.02	5.44	4.82	4.15	3.38
21	14.59	9.77	7.94	6.95	6.32	5.88	5.31	4.70	4.03	3.26
22	14.38	9.61	7.80	6.81	6.19	5.76	5.19	4.58	3.92	3.15
23	14.19	9.47	7.67	6.69	6.08	5.65	5.09	4.48	3.82	3.05
24	14.03	9.34	7.55	6.59	5.98	5.55	4.99	4.39	3.74	2.97
25	13.88	9.22	7.45	6.49	5.88	5.46	4.91	4.31	3.66	2.89
26	13.74	9.12	7.36	6.41	5.80	5.38	4.83	4.24	3.59	2.82
27	13.61	9.02	7.27	6.33	5.73	5.31	4.76	4.17	3.52	2.75
28	13.50	8.93	7.19	6.25	5.66	5.24	4.69	4.11	3.46	2.70
29	13.39	8.85	7.12	6.19	5.59	5.18	4.64	4.05	3.41	2.64
30	13.29	8.77	7.05	6.12	5.53	5.12	4.58	4.00	3.36	2.59
40	12.61	8.25	6.60	5.70	5.13	4.73	4.21	3.64	3.01	2.23
60	11.97	7.76	6.17	5.31	4.76	4.37	3.87	3.31	2.69	1.90
120	11.38	7.31	5.79	4.95	4.42	4.04	3.55	3.02	2.40	1.56
∞	10.83	6.91	5.42	4.62	4.10	3.74	3.27	2.74	2.13	1.00

GLOSSARY

Accretion measures. Measures of phenomena through observation of the accumulation of materials.

Actions. Human behavior done for a reason.

Age effects. Effects associated with the process of becoming older.

Alternative-form method. A method of testing measurement reliability. Measures the same concept more than once, but it uses two different measures of the same concept rather than the same measure. These measures are then compared. If they yield similar results, the measures are considered reliable.

Alternative hypothesis. A statement about the value or values of a population parameter. A hypothesis proposed as an alternative to the null hypothesis, represented by H_A.

Analysis of variance (ANOVA). A technique for measuring the relationship between one nominal- or ordinal-level variable and one interval- or ratio-level variable.

Antecedent variable. An independent variable that precedes other independent variables in time.

Applied research. Research designed to produce knowledge useful in altering a real-world condition or situation.

Arrow diagram. A pictorial representation of a researcher's explanatory scheme.

Bar chart. A graphical display of the data in a frequency or percentage distribution.

Branching question. A question that sorts respondents into subgroups and directs these subgroups to different parts of the questionnaire.

Case study design. A comprehensive and in-depth study of a single case or several cases. A nonexperimental design in which the investigator has little control over events.

Categorical measure. A variable measured using categories. A nominal- or ordinal-level measure.

Causally heterogeneous population. A population in which a given cause might have many different effects across different cases or the same cause is linked to the same outcome through different causal mechanisms.

Causally homogeneous population. A population in which a given cause can be expected to have the *same* causal relationship with the outcome across cases in the population.

Causes-of-effects approach. An approach to causal questions that starts with an outcome and works backward to the causes. Emphasis is on identifying causes of outcomes.

Central tendency. The most frequent, middle, or central value in a frequency distribution.

Chi square (χ^2) statistic. A statistic used to test whether a relationship is statistically significant in a cross-tabulation table.

Classical randomized experiment. An experiment with the random assignment of subjects to experimental and control groups with a pretest and posttest for both groups.

Closed-ended question. A question with response alternatives provided.

Cluster sample. A probability sample that is used when no list of elements exists. The sampling frame initially consists of clusters of elements.

Cohort. A group of people who all experience a significant event in roughly the same time frame.

Confidence interval. The range of values into which a population parameter is likely to fall for a given level of confidence.

Confidence level. The degree of belief or probability that an estimated range of values includes or covers the population parameter.

Constant. A concept or variable whose values do not vary.

Construct validity. Validity demonstrated for a measure by showing that it is related to the measure of another concept.

Constructionism. An approach to knowledge that asserts humans actually construct—through their social interactions and cultural and historical practices—many of the facts they take for granted as having an independent, objective, or material reality.

Content analysis. A systematic procedure by which records are transformed into quantitative data.

Content validity. Involves determining the full domain or meaning of a particular concept and then making sure that all components of the meaning are included in the measure.

Control by grouping. A form of statistical control in which observations identical or similar to the control variable are grouped together.

Control group. A group of subjects that does not receive the experimental treatment or test stimulus.

Convenience sample. A nonprobability sample in which the selection of elements is determined by the researcher's convenience.

Convergent construct validity. When a measure of a concept is related to a measure of another concept with which the original concept is thought to be associated.

Correlation. A statement that the values or states of one thing systematically vary with the values or states of another; an association between two variables.

Correlation coefficient. In regression analysis, a measure of the strength and direction of the linear correlation between two quantitative variables; also called product-moment correlation, Pearson's *r*, or *r*.

Counterfactual understanding of causation. The logical argument that support for the claim that A causes B is demonstrated by a case in which A is absent and B does not occur.

Covert observation. Observation in which the observer's presence or purpose is kept secret from those being observed.

Critical theory. The philosophical stance that disciplines such as political science should assess society critically and seek to improve it, not merely study it objectively.

Cross-level analysis. The use of data at one level of aggregation to make inferences at another level of aggregation.

Cross-sectional design. A research design in which measurements of independent and dependent variables are taken at the same time; naturally occurring differences in the independent variable are used to create quasi-experimental and quasi-control groups; and extraneous factors are controlled for by statistical means.

Cross-tabulation or **contingency table.** Also called a cross-classification, this array displays the joint frequencies and relative frequencies of two categorical (nominal or ordinal) variables.

Cumulative. Characteristic of scientific knowledge; new substantive findings and research techniques are built upon those of previous studies.

Cumulative percentage. The total percentage of observations at or below a value in a frequency distribution.

Data matrix. An array of rows and columns that stores the values of a set of variables for all the cases in a data set.

Deduction. The process of reasoning from general theory to making predictions about events or behavior in specific situations.

Demand characteristics. Aspects of the research situation that cause participants to guess the purpose or rationale of the study and adjust their behavior or opinions accordingly.

Dependent variable. The phenomenon thought to be influenced, affected, or caused by some other phenomenon.

Descriptive statistic. A number that, because of its definition and formula, describes certain characteristics or properties of a batch of numbers.

Deviant case. A case that exhibits all of the factors thought to lead to a particular outcome, but in which the outcome does not occur.

Dichotomous variable. A variable with only two categories—these variables are special cases as they can be used at the nominal, ordinal, or even ratio level.

Direct observation. Actual observation of behavior.

Direction of a relationship. An indication of which values of the dependent variable are associated with which values of the independent variable.

Directional hypothesis. A hypothesis that specifies the expected relationship between two or more variables.

Discriminant construct validity. A method of demonstrating measurement validity by comparing two measures that theoretically are expected *not* to be related. If the measures do not correlate with one another, then discriminant construct validity is demonstrated.

Dispersion. The distribution of data values around the most frequent, middle, or central value.

Disproportionate sample. A stratified sample in which elements sharing a characteristic are underrepresented or overrepresented in the sample.

Document analysis. The use of audio, visual, or written materials as a source of data.

Double-barreled question. A question that is really two questions in one.

Ecological fallacy. The fallacy of deducing a false relationship between the attributes or behavior of individuals based on observing that relationship for groups to which the individuals belong.

Ecological inference. The process of inferring a relationship between characteristics of individuals based on group or aggregate data.

Effects-of-causes approach. An approach to causal questions that starts with a potential cause and works forward to measure its impact on the outcome. Emphasis is on measuring the size of the effect that a cause has on an outcome.

Electronic databases. A collection of information (of any type) stored on an electromagnetic medium that can be accessed and examined by certain computer programs.

Element. A particular case or entity about which information is collected; the unit of analysis.

Elite interviewing. Interviewing individuals who possess specialized knowledge about a political phenomenon.

Empirical research. Research based on actual, "objective" observation of phenomena.

Empiricism. Relying on observation to verify propositions.

Episodic records. Materials that are not part of a systematic and ongoing record-keeping effort.

Erosion measures. Measures of phenomena through indirect observation of selective wear of some material.

Estimator. A statistic based on sample observations that is used to estimate the numerical value of an unknown population parameter.

Eta-squared (η^2). A measure of association used with the analysis of variance that indicates what proportion of the variance in the dependent variable is explained by the variance in the independent variable.

Ethnography. A type of field study in which the researcher is deeply immersed in the place and lives of the people being studied.

Expected value. The mean or average value of a sample statistic based on repeated samples from a population.

Experiment. Research using a research design in which the researcher controls exposure to the test factor or independent variable, the assignment of subjects to groups, and the measurement of responses.

Experimental effect. Effect, usually measured numerically, of the experimental variable on the dependent variable.

Experimental group. A group of subjects that receives the experimental treatment or test stimulus.

Experimental mortality. A differential loss of subjects from experimental and control groups that affects the equivalency of groups; threat to internal validity.

Explanatory. Characteristic of scientific knowledge; signifying that a conclusion can be derived from a set of general propositions and specific initial considerations; providing a systematic,

empirically verified understanding of why a phenomenon occurs as it does.

External validity. The ability to generalize from one set of research findings to other situations.

Face validity. When a measure appears to accurately measure the concept it is supposed to measure. Face validity may only be asserted, rather than empirically demonstrated, because face validity is essentially a matter of judgment.

Falsifiability. A property of a statement or hypothesis such that it can (in principle, at least) be rejected in the face of contravening evidence.

Field experiment. Experimental designs applied in a natural setting.

Field studies. Open-ended and wide-ranging (rather than structured) observation in a natural setting.

Filter question. A question used to screen respondents so that subsequent questions will be asked only of certain respondents for whom the questions are appropriate.

Firsthand observation. Method of data collection in which the researcher personally observes political behavior or some physical trace of it.

Frequency distribution (f). The number of observations per value or category of a variable.

General. A characteristic of scientific knowledge is that it be applicable to many rather than just a few cases.

Goodman and Kruskal's gamma (γ). A measure of association between ordinal-level variables.

Goodman and Kruskal's lambda (λ). A measure of association between one nominal- or ordinal-level variable and one nominal-level variable.

Histogram. A type of bar graph in which the height and area of the bars are proportional to the frequencies in each category of a categorical variable or intervals of a continuous variable.

Hypothesis. A tentative or provisional or unconfirmed statement that can (in principle) be verified.

Hypothesis-generating case study. A type of case study that attempts to develop from one or more cases some general theoretical propositions that can be tested in future research.

Hypothesis-testing case study. A type of case study that attempts to test hypothesized empirical relationships.

Idiographic case study. A type of case study that attempts to describe, explain, or interpret a singular historical episode with no intention of generalizing beyond the case.

Independent variable. The phenomenon thought to influence, affect, or cause some other phenomenon.

Indirect observation. Observation of physical traces of behavior.

Induction. The process of reasoning from specific observations to theories about behaviors or events in general.

Informed consent. Procedures that inform potential research subjects about the proposed research in which they are being asked to participate; the principle that researchers must obtain the freely given consent of human subjects before they participate in a research project.

Institutional review board. Panel to which researchers must submit descriptions of proposed research involving human subjects for the purpose of ethics review.

Interaction. The strength and direction of a relationship depend on an additional variable or variables.

Internal validity. The ability to show that manipulation or variation of the independent variable actually causes the dependent variable to change.

Interpretation. Philosophical approach to the study of human behavior that claims that one must understand the way individuals see their world in order to truly understand their behavior or actions; philosophical objection to the empirical approach to political science.

Interquartile range (IQR). The difference between the third and first quartiles.

Interval-level measure. Includes the properties of the nominal level (characteristics are different) and the ordinal level (characteristics can be put in a meaningful order). But unlike nominal and ordinal measures, the intervals between the categories or values assigned to the observations *do* have meaning.

Intervening variable. A variable coming between an independent variable and a dependent variable in an explanatory scheme.

Intervention analysis. A nonexperimental time-series design in which measurements of a dependent variable are taken both before and after the "introduction" of an independent variable.

Interview data. Data that are collected from responses to questions posed by the researcher to a respondent.

Interviewer bias. The interviewer's influence on the respondent's answers; an example of reactivity.

Interviewing. Interviewing respondents in a nonstandardized, individualized manner.

Kendall's tau-*b*. A measure of association between ordinal-level variables.

Kendall's tau-*c*. A measure of association between ordinal-level variables.

Large *N* studies. Quantitative research designs in which the research examines many cases of a phenomenon.

Leading question. A question that encourages the respondent to choose a particular response.

Least likely case. A case in which it is expected that a theory is least likely to apply.

Level of measurement. Refers to the type of information that we think our measurements contain and the mathematical properties they possess. Determines the type of comparisons that can be made across a number of observations on the same variable.

Literature review. A systematic examination and interpretation of the literature for the purpose of informing further work on a topic.

Logistic regression. A nonlinear regression model that relates a set of explanatory variables to a dichotomous dependent variable.

Logistic regression coefficient. A multiple regression coefficient based on the logistic model.

Maximum likelihood estimation. A class of estimators that chooses a set of parameters that provides the highest probability of observing a particular outcome.

Mean. The sum of the values of a variable divided by the number of values.

Measurement bias. A type of measurement error that results in systematically over- or undermeasuring the value of a concept.

Measures of association. Statistics that summarize the relationship between two variables.

Mechanistic understanding of causation. An approach to demonstrating or understanding causation by focusing on the mechanism by which a cause leads to an outcome.

Median. The category or value above and below which one-half of the observations lie.

Method of agreement. A comparative strategy wherein the researcher selects cases that share the same outcome and identifies those conditions or causal factors that the cases also have in common.

Method of difference. A comparative strategy wherein the researcher selects cases in which the outcomes differ, compares the cases looking for the single factor that the cases do not have in common, and concludes that this factor is causal.

Mode. The category with the greatest frequency of observations.

Most likely case. A case in which theory predicts an outcome is most likely to occur.

Multiple-group design. Experimental design with more than one control and experimental group.

Multivariate analysis. Data analysis techniques designed to test hypotheses involving more than two variables.

Multivariate cross-tabulation. A procedure by which cross-tabulation is used to control for a third variable.

Multivariate regression analysis. A technique for measuring the mathematical relationships between more than one independent variable and a dependent variable while controlling for all other independent variables in the equation.

Multivariate regression coefficient. A number that tells how much Y will change for a one-unit change in a particular independent variable, if all of the other variables in the model have been held constant.

Natural experiment. A study in which there is random assignment or "as-if" random assignment of units to experimental and control groups but the researcher does not control the randomization process or the manipulation of the treatment factor.

Necessary cause. A condition that must be present in order for the outcome to occur.

Negative relationship. A relationship in which high values of one variable are associated with low values of another variable or in which low values of one variable are associated with high values of another variable.

Negatively skewed. A distribution of values in which fewer observations lie to the left of the middle value and those observations are fairly distant from the mean.

Nominal-level measure. Indicates that the values assigned to a variable represent only different categories or classifications for that variable.

Nonnormative knowledge. Knowledge concerned not with evaluation or prescription but with factual or objective determinations.

Nonparticipant observation. Observation of activities, behaviors, or events in which the researcher does not participate.

Nonprobability sample. A sample for which each element in the total population has an unknown probability of being selected.

Normal distribution. A distribution defined by a mathematical formula and the graph of which has a symmetrical bell shape in which the mean, the mode, and the median coincide, and in which a fixed proportion of observations lies between the mean and any distance from the mean measured in terms of the standard deviation.

Normative knowledge. Knowledge that is evaluative, value-laden, and concerned with prescribing what ought to be.

Null hypothesis. A statement that a population parameter equals a single or specific value; the hypothesis that there is no relationship between two variables in the target population. Often, a statement that the difference between two populations is zero.

Observational study. A nonexperimental research design in which the researcher simply observes differences in the dependent variable for naturally occurring treatment and control groups.

Open-ended question. A question with no response alternatives provided for the respondent.

Operational definition. The rules by which a concept is measured and scores assigned.

Operationalization. The process of assigning numerals or scores to a variable to represent the values of a concept.

Ordinal-level measure. Indicates that the values assigned to a variable can be compared in terms of having more or less of a particular attribute.

Outlier. A value that is far greater or smaller than other values in a recorded variable.

Overt observation. Observation in which those being observed are informed of the observer's presence and purpose.

Parsimony. The principle that among explanations or theories with equal degrees of confirmation, the simplest—the one based on the fewest assumptions and explanatory factors—is to be preferred; sometimes known as Ockham's razor.

Participant observation. Observation in which the observer becomes a regular participant in the activities of those being observed.

Period effect. An indicator or measure of history effect on a dependent variable during a specified time.

Phi (φ). An association measure that adjusts an observed chi-square statistic by the sample size.

Plausibility probes. A case study that is not expected to provide a definitive test of the connection between a cause and an outcome, but is expected to contribute to conducting such a test in the future.

Population. All the cases or observations covered by a hypothesis; all the units of analysis to which a hypothesis applies.

Population parameter. A characteristic or an attribute in a population (not a sample) that can be quantified.

Positive relationship. A relationship in which the values of one variable increase (or decrease) as the values of another variable increase (or decrease).

Positively skewed. A distribution of values in which fewer observations lie to the right of the middle value and those observations are fairly distant from the mean.

Posttest design. A research design in which the dependent variable is measured after, but not before, manipulation of the independent variable.

Precision. The extent to which measurements are complete and informative.

Pretest. Measurement of variables prior to the administration of the experimental treatment or manipulation of the independent variable.

Primary data. Data recorded and used by the researcher who is making the observations.

Probability sample. A sample for which each element in the total population has a known probability of being selected.

Process tracing. A case study in which a causal mechanism is traced from causal condition to final outcome.

Proportional-reduction-in-error (PRE) measure. A measure of association that indicates how much knowledge of the value of the independent variable of a case improves prediction of the dependent variable compared to the prediction of the dependent variable based on no knowledge of the case's value on the independent variable. Examples are Goodman and Kruskal's lambda, Goodman and Kruskal's gamma, eta-squared, and R-squared.

Proportionate sample. A probability sample that draws elements from a stratified population at a rate proportional to the size of the samples.

Pure, theoretical, or recreational research. Research designed to satisfy one's intellectual curiosity about some phenomenon.

Purposive sample. A nonprobability sample in which a researcher uses discretion in selecting elements for observation.

Quantitative measure. An interval- or ratio-level measure. A measure with numerical properties.

Quasi-experimental design. A research design that includes treatment and control groups to which individuals are not assigned randomly.

Question-order effect. The effect on responses of question placement within a questionnaire.

Questionnaire design. The physical layout and packaging of a questionnaire.

Quota sample. A nonprobability sample in which elements are sampled in proportion to their representation in the population.

Random measurement error. An error in measurement that has no systematic direction or cause.

Randomization. The random assignment of subjects to experimental and control groups.

Range. The distance between the highest and lowest values or the range of categories into which observations fall.

Ratio-level measure. This type of measurement involves the full mathematical properties of numbers and contains the most possible information about a measured concept.

Reactivity. Effect of data collection or measurement on the phenomenon being measured.

Regression analysis. A technique for measuring the relationship between two interval- or ratio-level variables.

Regression coefficient. A statistic that tells how much the dependent variable changes per unit change in the independent variable.

Regression constant. Value of the dependent variable when all of the values of the independent variables in the equation equal zero.

Relationship. The association, dependence, or covariance of the values of one variable with the values of another variable.

Relative frequencies. Percentages or proportions of total numbers of observations in a frequency distribution that have a particular value.

Reliability. The consistency of results from a procedure or measure in repeated tests or trials.

Repeated-measurement design. A plan that calls for making more than one measure or observation on a dependent variable at different times over the course of the study.

Research design. A plan specifying how the researcher intends to fulfill the goals of the study; a logical plan for testing hypotheses.

Research hypothesis. A statement about the value or values of a population parameter. A hypothesis proposed as an alternative to the null hypothesis, represented by H_A.

Resistant measure. A measure of central tendency that is not sensitive to one or a few extreme values in a distribution.

Response rate. The proportion of respondents selected for participation in a survey who actually participate.

Response set. The pattern of responding to a series of questions in a similar fashion without careful reading of each question.

R-squared (R^2). The proportion of the total variance in a dependent variable explained by an independent variable.

Running record. Materials or data that are collected across time.

Sample. A subset of observations or cases drawn from a specified population.

Sample bias. The bias that occurs whenever some elements of a population are systematically excluded from a sample. It is usually due to an incomplete sampling frame or a nonprobability method of selecting elements.

Sample–population congruence. The degree to which sample subjects represent the population from which they are drawn.

Sample statistic. The estimator of a population characteristic or attribute that is calculated from sample data.

Sampling distribution. A theoretical (nonobserved) distribution of sample statistics calculated on samples of size N that, if known, permits the calculation of confidence intervals and the test of statistical hypotheses.

Sampling error. The difference between a sample estimate and a corresponding population parameter that arises because only a portion of a population is observed.

Sampling fraction. The proportion of the population included in a sample.

Sampling frame. The population from which a sample is drawn. Ideally, it is the same as the total population of interest to a study.

Sampling interval. The number of elements in a sampling frame divided by the desired sample size.

Sampling unit. The entity listed in a sampling frame. It may be the same as an element, or it may be a group or cluster of elements.

Scatterplot. A graph that plots joint values of an independent variable along one axis (usually the x-axis) and a dependent variable along the other axis (usually the y-axis).

Search engine. A computer program that visits web pages on the internet and looks for those containing particular directories or words.

Search term. A word or phrase entered into a computer program (a search engine) that looks through web pages on the internet for those that contain the word or phrase.

Secondary data. Data used by a researcher that were not personally collected by that researcher.

Selection bias. Bias due to the assignment of subjects to experimental and control groups according to some criterion and not randomly; threat to internal validity.

Simple random sample. A probability sample in which each element has an equal chance of being selected.

Single-sided question. A question in which the respondent is asked to agree or disagree with a single substantive statement.

Small *N* studies. Research designs in which the research examines one or a few cases of a phenomenon in considerable detail.

Snowball sample. A nonprobability sample in which potential respondents are identified by respondents already participating in the sample.

Social facts. Values and institutions that have a subjective existence in the minds of people living in a particular culture.

Somers' *D*. A measure of association between ordinal-level variables.

Split-halves method. A method of testing reliability by applying two measures of the same concept at the same time. The results of the two measures are then compared.

Standard deviation. A measure of dispersion of data points about the mean for interval- and ratio-level data.

Statistical hypotheses. Two types of hypotheses essential to hypothesis testing: null hypotheses and research or alternative hypotheses.

Statistical inference. The mathematical theory and techniques for making conjectures about the unknown characteristics (parameters) of populations based on samples.

Statistical significance. The probability of making a type I error.

Stimulus or test factor. The independent variable introduced and controlled by an investigator in order to assess its effects on a response or dependent variable.

Stratified sample. A probability sample in which elements sharing one or more characteristics are grouped and elements are selected from each group in proportion to the group's representation in the total population.

Stratum. A subgroup of a population that shares one or more characteristics.

Structured observation. Systematic observation and recording of the incidence of specific behaviors.

Sufficient cause. A condition with which the outcome is always found.

Systematic sample. A probability sample in which elements are selected from a list at predetermined intervals.

Tautology. A hypothesis in which the independent and dependent variables are identical, making it impossible to disconfirm.

Test of statistical significance. A convention for testing hypotheses that focuses on the probability of making a type I error.

Test–retest method. Involves applying the same measure to the same observations at two periods in time, then comparing the results to test for measurement reliability.

Theory. A statement or series of related statements that organize, explain, and predict phenomena.

Time-series design. A research design (sometimes called a longitudinal design) featuring multiple measurements of the dependent variable before and after experimental treatment.

Total variance. A numerical measure of the variation in a variable, determined by summing the squared deviation of each observation from the mean.

Transmissible. Characteristic of scientific knowledge; indicates that the methods used in making scientific discoveries are made explicit so that others can analyze and replicate findings.

Trend analysis. A research design that measures a dependent variable at different times and attempts to determine whether the level of the variable is changing—and, if it is, why.

Two-sided question. A question with two substantive alternatives provided for the respondent.

Type I error. Error made by rejecting a null hypothesis when it is true.

Type II error. Error made by failing to reject a null hypothesis when it is not true.

Unit of analysis. The type of actor (individual, group, institution, nation) specified in a researcher's hypothesis.

Unstructured observation. Observation in which all behavior and activities are recorded.

Validity. Refers to the degree of correspondence between the measure and the concept it is thought to measure.

Variance. A measure of dispersion of data points about the mean for interval- and ratio-level data.

Verification. The process of confirming or establishing a statement with evidence.

Written record. Documents, reports, statistics, manuscripts, photographs, audio recordings, and other recorded materials available and useful for empirical research.

z score. The number of standard deviations by which a score deviates from the mean score.

INDEX